PREHISTORIC LAND DIVISIONS ON SALISBURY PLAIN

The work of the Wessex Linear Ditches Project

Richard Bradley, Roy Entwistle, and Frances Raymond

with contributions by
Wendy Carruthers, Rowena Gale, Dai Morgan Evans, and Ross Whitehead
Foreword by Major General A J G Pollard

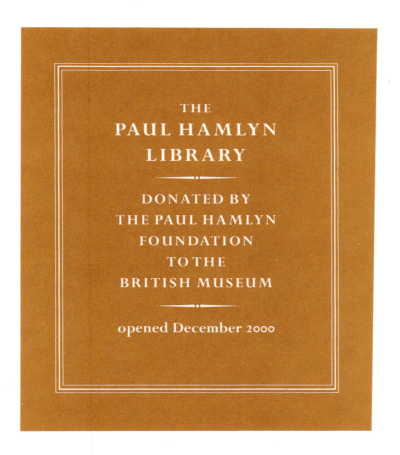

ENGLISH HERITAGE
1994
ARCHAEOLOGICAL REPORT 2

Copyright © English Heritage

First published 1994 by
English Heritage, 23 Savile Row,
London, W1X 1AB

Printed by Hobbs the Printers of Southampton

ISBN 1 85074 647 X
A catalogue record for this book is available from the
British Library

Text edited and brought to press by
Robin J Taylor and David M Jones,
Publications Branch, English Heritage
Layout and cover design by Karen Guffogg,
Design and Interpretation Branch, English Heritage

Contents

Illustrations iv
List of tables v
Acknowledgements vi
Abbreviations vi

Foreword *by Major General A J G Pollard* vii

Summary viii
Résumé ix
Zusammenfassung x

Preface *by Dai Morgan Evans* 1

PART I   AN INTRODUCTION TO THE PROJECT

1   The background to the enquiry *by Richard Bradley*
Introduction: the archaeological setting 3
Investigating the linear ditches systems of the British Isles 6
Some implications of prehistoric land boundaries . 15

2   The selection of a study area *by Richard Bradley*
Introduction 17
Criteria for choosing a study area 17
The location and character of the Study Area . . . 18
The Upper Study Area and the survival of archaeological evidence 21

3   The development and application of the field methodology *by Roy Entwistle*
Introduction 26
Surface collection 27
Miscellaneous artefact collections 33
Aerial photographic information 34
Geophysical survey and augering 34
The excavation programme 39
The excavation sites 41
The dating evidence and ditch morphology 58

PART II   THE SPECIALIST STUDIES

4   The pottery *by Frances Raymond*
Introduction 69
The early background: ceramics in the Upper Study Area before linear ditches 71
Shared and exclusive traditions: Late Bronze Age ceramics and linear ditches 77
The manipulation of style: contrasts in the articulation of common themes 80
The organisation of production: the relationship between technology and style 85
Contrasts in the articulation of shared technologies: further evidence for distinctions within and outside Late Bronze Age territories 86
Focusing on the boundaries: Plain Ware ceramics in linear ditches 87
Fragmentation: the introduction of All Cannings Cross prototypes and the demise of Plain Ware settlement 88

Re-formation: developed All Cannings Cross ceramics and the foundation of new settlements 89
Restructuring: linear ditches and Iron Age ceramics 90

5   The analysis of five flint assemblages from the Upper Study Area *by Ross Whitehead*
Introduction 91
Methodology 92
Chronological assessment 92
Functional assessment 97
Discussion 98

6   The environmental setting of the linear ditches system *by Roy Entwistle*
Introduction: a review of the environmental background to the prehistoric settlement of the southern chalklands 101
The environmental study of the linear ditches system 101
The molluscan sequences 103
Charcoal identification *by Rowena Gale* 119
Carbonised cereal remains *by Wendy Carruthers* . . 119
Discussion 120

7   Settlements, territories, and 'Celtic' fields: the changing role of boundary earthworks *by Roy Entwistle*
Introduction: bounded landscapes 122
The Southern Core Territory 123
The Northern Core Territory 126
Dunch Hill and the Nine Mile River 128
Sidbury Hill and the surrounding area 132
Quarley Hill and the Bourne Valley 134
Final developments 135

PART III   THE EVOLUTION OF THE LINEAR DITCHES SYSTEM IN THE UPPER STUDY AREA AND ITS WIDER IMPLICATIONS

8   Discussion and conclusions *by Richard Bradley, Roy Entwistle, and Frances Raymond*
Introduction 137
The development of the linear ditches system: the Middle to Late Bronze Age 138
The later history of the linear ditches system: the Late Bronze Age to Iron Age 142
Final uses of the boundary system 147
Concluding summary 149
Postscript: last reflections on the linear ditches system 151

Appendices
1   Gazetteer of project sites 153
2   Pottery methodology and data 154
3   Flint data 157
4   Sub-fossil mollusca from excavation sites . . . 163

Bibliography 170

Index 174

Illustrations

1 Map of Britain, showing the principal areas with concentrations of linear ditches
2 Linear ditches and territories of the Yorkshire Wolds
3 Quarley Hillfort, looking north-east, showing the arrangement of linear ditches recorded by Hawkes
4 Plans of Easton Lane and Fengate, showing patterns of enclosure
5 Linear ditches and territories of the Tabular Hills
6 Distribution of linear ditches on the Berkshire Downs
7 Location of the Study Area
8 Distribution map of the Study Area, showing the principal linear features, hillforts, and the locations of earlier excavations
9 Location map, showing the extent of the Military Estate of Salisbury Plain East
10 Map of the Upper Study Area, showing all available aerial photographic information and the location of Thomas's enclosures A and B on Snail Down, just to the north of Sidbury Hill
11 A view eastwards across the Tracked Vehicle Training Area south of Sidbury Hill
12 A view of Sidbury Hillfort from the east, showing the extent of military damage and the locations of linear ditches
13 Plan of surface collection site LDP 093, illustrating the layout of a typical fieldwalking grid
14 The Upper Study Area, showing the location of all project surface collection and excavation sites over linear features
15 Map of the Dunch Hill and Brigmerston Down area, showing the location of surface collection sites LDP 080, 081, 102, 104, 105, 106, and 111
16 The drift geology of the Upper Study Area, showing the location of flint procurement sites LDP 008, 012, 104, and those near Shipton Plantation and on Sidbury Hill
17 Comparative distributions of Middle to Late Bronze Age pottery and burnt flint from surface collection sites LDP 080 and 102
18 Histogram showing proportions of burnt flint recovered from Dunch Hill and Brigmerston Down sites
19 Plan of Milston Down, giving the location of surface collection site LDP 112
20 Plan of Milston Down surface collection site LDP 112, showing the arrangement of collection units
21 Plan of Brigmerston Down, showing the relative density and distribution of Middle to Late Bronze Age pottery
22 'Celtic' fields and linear features on Earl's Farm Down
23 Topography of the Upper Study Area, showing the position of linear ditches confirmed by auger survey and excavation
24 Part of Earl's Farm Down, showing the linear ditch SMR 746, a trackway, and adjoining 'Celtic' fields
25 Sidbury Hillfort looking towards the south-west, showing the principal linear ditches
26 The course of linear ditches on Sidbury Hill and the location of excavation sites LDP 020, 100, and 101
27 The section of the Sidbury Double Linear Ditch exposed at the foot of Sidbury Hill (LDP 020)
28 Schematic section of the Sidbury Double Linear Ditch at LDP 020
29 Section of the eastern ditch and central bank of the Sidbury Double Linear Ditch at LDP 027
30 Section of the terminal of the Sidbury Double Linear Ditch on Sidbury Hill, LDP 100
31 Section of the western ditch of the Sidbury Double Linear Ditch at LDP 101
32 Ditch sections VI and XIV on Snail Down excavated in 1953–5
33 Location of ditch sections on Snail Down and the position of enclosures A and B
34 Ditch sections at LDP 052, 090, and 096, illustrating the 'V'-shaped profiles and recut forms characteristic of later boundary ditches
35 Selected ditch stratigraphies, showing the position of a placed deposit at LDP 091 and a bisequential buried soil in the tertiary silts at LDP 097
36 Worked antler from LDP 097
37 Section and plan of the 'V'-shaped ditch SPTA 2238 at LDP 083
38 East-facing section of the Iron Age ditch at LDP 083
39 Section of the Iron Age ditch excavated by Thomas on Snail Down at site VI
40 Plan of site LDP 084, showing ard marks and a hollow-way
41 Section of an ard mark at LDP 084
42 Plan and sections of the Haxton Down pit alignment at LDP 085
43 The Haxton Down pit alignment (LDP 085)
44 Plan and sections of the Haxton Down pit alignment at the intersection with the Sidbury West Linear Ditch (SPTA 2242) at LDP 099
45 Plan and section of the field ditch and Late Bronze Age midden on Dunch Hill at LDP 081A
46 Location of Dunch Hill sites, showing the relative density and distribution of Middle to Late Bronze Age pottery
47 Plan and section of the double-banked linear ditch SPTA 1971 at LDP 092
48 Contour plan and section of SPTA 1971 on Dunch Hill at LDP 098
49 Schematic section and context descriptions for the excavation of SPTA 2061 on Beacon Hill at LDP 095
50 A view westwards from LDP 082 on Coombe Down
51 The relative proportions of Deverel-Rimbury pottery and Late Bronze Age Plain Ware from settlements with Middle Bronze Age origins
52 Deverel-Rimbury pottery from LDP 112, LDP 109, LDP 092, LDP 102, LDP 080, LDP 098, and LDP 103
53 Decorated sherds of Late Bronze Age Plain Ware from LDP 112, together with a few examples from the same site which may be derived from a slightly earlier phase
54 Late Bronze Age Plain Ware from LDP 112
55 Late Bronze Age Plain Ware from LDP 112, LDP 109, LDP 092, LDP 102, LDP 098, LDP 111, and LDP 103

56 Late Bronze Age Plain Ware from LDP 103, LDP 087, LDP 081, and LDP 081A
57 Late Bronze Age Plain Ware from LDP 081A
58 Early All Cannings Cross pottery from LDP 112, LDP 080, and LDP 081A
59 Examples of a 'bashed lump' and a platform core from surface collection site LDP 104
60 Examples of blade cores recovered from surface collection sites LDP 102 and LDP 080
61 The range of scrapers from surface collection sites LDP 081, 102, 104, and from the excavated midden LDP 081A
62 A range of retouched forms from surface collection site LDP 102 and a hammerstone from the procurement site LDP 104
63 Molluscan diagram for LDP 101 – percentage frequencies
64 Molluscan diagram for LDP 027 – percentage frequencies
65 Molluscan diagram for LDP 083, based on percentage frequencies
66 Molluscan diagram for LDP 083, based on absolute shell numbers
67 Molluscan diagram for LDP 097 – percentage frequencies
68 Molluscan diagram for LDP 092 – percentage frequencies

69 Molluscan diagrams for LDP 091 and 052 – percentage frequencies
70 Part of the Upper Study Area, showing the location of sites with environmental data and summaries of the principal ecological episodes relating to changes in the pattern of landuse
71 Map of the Study Area, showing the distribution of Middle and Late Bronze Age settlement sites in relation to the linear ditches system
72 The area to the east of Beacon Hill, showing the distribution of 'Celtic' fields in relation to the principal linear ditches of the Southern Core Territory
73 A view eastwards across LDP 081, showing the hollow-way and a dark patch marking the position of the Late Bronze Age midden, LDP 081A
74 Section at site LDP 056, showing two parallel trackways separated by a field ditch, running along the edge of a lynchet
75 Section through a lynchet at LDP 082, showing the postholes of a fence line
76 A view of Brigmerston Down
77 A view of the incomplete ditch circuit at Ladle Hillfort, showing traces of an earlier ditch preserved in one of the causeways
78 A view of Yarnbury Hillfort and the area enclosed by linear ditches with 'Celtic' fields abutting from the exterior

List of tables

1 The quantity and date of pottery recovered from surface collection sites outside the Military Training Area
2 The quantity and date of pottery recovered from surface collection sites within the Military Training Area
3 The distribution of burnt and worked flint from Dunch Hill and Brigmerston Down surface collection sites
4 The number of sherds and the date range of pottery recovered from surface collection site LDP 112
5 The quantity and date of pottery recovered during excavation
6 Animal bones from LDP 027
7 Pottery recovered from LDP 100
8 Animal bones from LDP 100
9 Animal bones from LDP 101
10 Pottery recovered from LDP 097
11 Animal bones from LDP 097
12 Animal bones from LDP 083
13 Animal bones from LDP 085
14 Animal bones from LDP 099
15 Pottery recovered from LDP 081A
16 Animal species represented at LDP 081A
17 Pottery recovered from LDP 092
18 Animal bones from LDP 092
19 Pottery recovered from LDP 098
20 Animal bones from LDP 098
21 Animal bones from LDP 095
22 The radiocarbon dates on samples recovered from excavations in the Upper Study Area
23 The distribution of Beaker and Deverel-Rimbury fabrics within the Study Area

24 The relative proportions of Late Bronze Age fabric groups on individual sites within each settlement area
25 Snail species from LDP 020A
26 Carbonised cereal remains from LDP 092B, the western buried soil
27 Surface collection sites
28 Excavation sites
29 The type, quantity, and size range of inclusions, used as criteria to define Beaker and Deverel-Rimbury fabrics
30 The type, quantity, and size range of inclusions, used as criteria to define individual Late Bronze Age fabrics
31 The type, quantity, and size range of inclusions, used as criteria to define individual Iron Age and indeterminate prehistoric fabrics
32 The distribution of Iron Age fabrics within the Study Area
33 The distribution of indeterminate fabrics within the Study Area, arranged according to the most likely date for their production and use
34 The minimum numbers of prehistoric vessels from excavated and surface collection sites
35 Distribution of percussion angles by assemblage
36 Percentages of percussion angles <60° and >65° by assemblage
37 Distribution of breadth/length ratios by assemblage
38 Percentages of breadth/length ratios <3:5 and >5:5 by assemblage
39 Distribution of flake lengths by assemblage
40 Distribution of scraper characteristics

41 Patination characteristics of all struck flint by assemblage
42 Distribution of flake categories by assemblage
43 Amount of cortex on flakes by assemblage
44 Distribution of distal termination types by assemblage
45 Distribution of distal termination types by flake type and assemblage
46 Composition of flint assemblages
47 Core data
48 Distribution of retouched flakes by assemblage

49 Species list for LDP 101
50 Species list for LDP 027A
51 Species list for LDP 027B
52 Species list for LDP 083
53 Species list for LDP 097
54 Species list for LDP 092A
55 Species list for LDP 092B
56 Species list for LDP 092C
57 Species list for LDP 052
58 Species list for LDP 091

Acknowledgements

The Linear Ditches Project spanned a period of three years, from October 1988 to October 1991. It was commissioned and funded by English Heritage, with additional resources and facilities provided by the University of Reading Archaeology Department.

The programme of excavation and surface collection in the Military Estate of Salisbury Plain East was made possible by the cooperation of the Commandant and staff of Salisbury Plain Training Area Headquarters. We also received assistance and encouragement from the staff of the Public Services Agency, Durrington. A singular debt of gratitude is owed to John Loch, Defence Land Agent, for his support and enthusiasm, and to Land Wardens Bill Batner and Bob Lock for their interest and cooperation during the day-to-day running of the fieldwork. Throughout the project, but especially during our work on Salisbury Plain East, we benefited from the invaluable support provided by Roy Canham, the Wiltshire County Archaeologist, and others of his staff, particularly Julian Heath. Although only a minor part of our research took place in Hampshire, a similar debt is owed to Mike Hughes, the County Archaeologist, and to Hampshire County Council for their support.

The successful outcome of the fieldwork is in no small part a reflection of the assistance given by students and graduates of the Department of Archaeology, Reading University. We owe a special debt of gratitude to Peter Hinge, Ian Sanderson, and Martin Tingle for their practical contribution towards the excavations.

Our knowledge of the archaeology of the Training Area has been enhanced by the work of the Archaeological Sub-Group, whose members have been involved in watching briefs and fieldwalking over a number of years, and who willingly made their pottery collection available to us. In particular, we wish to thank Major L C Bond, Chairman of the Salisbury Plain Conservation Group, Bruce Eagles, Chairman of the Archaeological Sub-Group, Nel Duffie, Audrey Goodrich, Nora Morris, Kay Nichol, Eileen Rollo, Leah Scott, and Marjorie Williams.

A number of people have contributed to the post-excavation work. In particular, our thanks must go to Mike Fulford for the identification of the considerable quantity of Romano-British pottery recovered during the project and to Wayne Bonner for undertaking the identification of the animal bones.

The interpretation of our results has been aided greatly by discussions with Nicholas Thomas, whose work on Snail Down has a direct bearing on our own. We must also acknowledge our colleagues at the Trust for Wessex Archaeology, who have made a great deal of unpublished information available. For their interest and cooperation, we wish to thank Andy Lawson, Mike Allen, Sue Davies, Phil Harding, Sue Lobb, Caron Newman, Mick Rawlings, and Julian Richards.

Finally, we take this opportunity to record our thanks to John Barrett for his enthusiastic comments on the pottery study in Chapter 4 and to Martin Bell for his constructive advice on the environmental report in Chapter 6.

Translations of the summary were provided by Annie Pritchard (French) and Katrin Aberg (German).

Abbreviations

Throughout this report two systems are used to identify previously recorded archaeological features and findspots. SMR references are to the County Sites and Monuments Record. However, since the project covered parts of Wiltshire and Hampshire, the prefix 'H' has been used to distinguish references to the Hampshire SMR. Most of the fieldwork was concentrated in the Military Estate of Salisbury Plain East and consequently the system of notation used during a recent survey of that area has been adopted. This consists of the letters SPTA (Salisbury Plain Training Area) followed by a number that identifies the specific site or feature.

Sites investigated or newly identified by this project are prefixed by the letters LDP (Linear Ditches Project), followed by a number which refers to the order in which the site was selected during the initial survey. No distinction is made between surface collection and excavation sites; those in both categories are numbered consecutively.

Foreword

by Major General A J G Pollard CBE

This latest research into prehistoric land divisions once again demonstrates the importance of Wessex to the prehistoric archaeology of lowland Britain. Little is known by the general public about the Wessex linear ditches and, as a subject, they seem unlikely to enjoy the romantic prominence of Stonehenge or Avebury. In many respects, they are among the most enigmatic monuments of late prehistory, but the sheer scale of the earthworks alone is a clear indication of their important role in the organisation of the chalkland landscape during the millennium preceding the Roman period.

Work on this particular project started in the arable farmland, which dominates the landscape of Wiltshire, but where most of the boundary earthworks are now destroyed. Subsequently, the emphasis shifted to the Military Estate of Salisbury Plain East, as it became apparent that the excellent state of preservation in that area offered a unique opportunity to fulfil the research aims. The Military Estate remains primarily a training area, and it is this fact that has led to the survival of so much archaeological heritage there. This contrast between two major landuse zones not only highlights the archaeological richness of the Military Training Area, but also touches on the issue of management and emphasises the challenge faced by archaeologists to define what is genuinely important to them.

The paradox of Salisbury Plain as both a training area and an unrivalled archaeological resource has recently been discussed by Dai Morgan Evans of English Heritage in his excellent article in *Sanctuary* (**20**, Summer 1991), called 'The paradox of Salisbury Plain'. The difficulties, however, are more often perceived than real, and I would recommend this article to anyone interested in the heritage that the Salisbury Plain Training Area offers, since the new management plans to protect sites of special interest are an example of what can be achieved given a spirit of cooperation and a little toleration.

The authors of this research report set themselves a difficult task by seeking to interpret the role played by the Wessex linear ditches system in the landscape history of Wiltshire and its place in the wider context of British prehistory. Those of us with the 'enthusiastic approach' to archaeology hope that this work has gone some way towards elucidating the complex relationship that existed between boundary earthworks and other more prominent, and better known, prehistoric monuments. Whatever our personal approach, however, all those studying the prehistory of Britain, professionally or otherwise, should be aware that the findings of this project will have implications for other research into late prehistoric landuse and settlement, in Wessex and further afield.

Summary

The first part of this report begins with a review of the archaeological record for the chalklands of southern England. It emphasises the special character of the chalk uplands, both in terms of prehistoric settlement and the unusual preservation that has traditionally attracted the attention of archaeologists. The place of linear ditches in this landscape has long been the subject of speculation and, at various times, the focus of more systematic study. However, our understanding of the chronology and function of these prominent, but enigmatic features has advanced little in recent years. It is partly in response to this unsatisfactory state of affairs, and partly because of the continuing threat to surviving earthworks, that a fresh attempt to study linear ditches was set in motion. The historical background to this present study is summarised in Chapter 1. This leads on to the choice of the Study Area, which was influenced by the work of earlier archaeologists, while offering unparalleled opportunities for new research. The concluding chapter of Part I explains the development of the field methodology and evaluates the results from a range of techniques used to complement the excavation programme. The final section contains a digest of the stratigraphies and artefact associations of those sites that form the core of the study, along with the dating evidence.

Part II of this report contains the specialist studies. In each case, the data have been regarded not just as independent subjects for study, but as distinct, yet integrated aspects of the material culture associated with the development of the linear ditches system. This applies equally to the artefacts and to the environment. The latter is considered to be culturally structured in the same sense that raw materials are transformed by social intention into man-made objects. In each study, a number of spatial and chronological themes are identified. These are pursued in the context of the development and organisation of Late Bronze Age settlement within the bounded landscape defined by linear ditches. The final chapter of this part is concerned primarily with the evidence from the excavations. It builds upon the descriptive framework established in Chapter 3, while at the same time drawing on the specialist studies in order to combine changes in the treatment of boundaries with other aspects of settlement.

In the concluding part, some of the issues raised by previous studies of linear ditches are reviewed in the light of this latest research. Certain observations, such as topographic setting, the relationship of linear ditches to 'Celtic' fields, and the morphology of ditches, which have contributed to the idea of Late Bronze Age 'cattle ranches', are of concern here. The reader was shown that the linear ditches system evolved through different stages and that at different times its function varied. It is important to consider from a more theoretical perspective the implications of formal boundaries in the light of this functional variation. In particular, some thought must be given to the related concepts of domestication and intensification. In the evolution of the linear ditches system, it is the character and perception of the landscape that changes with regard to demography, settlement, and cultural interaction. This in turn is linked to subsistence productivity, land ownership, and the scale of domestic production. Shifts in the balance of these ingredients are at the root of the changes that have been recognised in our study of boundaries.

Résumé

La première partie de ce compte-rendu commence par une revue des données archéologiques concernant les terrains calcaires du sud de l'Angleterre. Elle attire l'attention sur les caractéristiques spécifiques des hautes terres calcaires, aussi bien en ce qui concerne leur occupation préhistorique que la qualité exceptionnelle de leur conservation, ce qui a de tout temps suscité l'intérêt des archéologues. Le rôle joué par les longs fossés limitrophes dans ce type de site a depuis longtemps donné lieu à des spéculations et, à différentes époques, il a été l'objet d'études plus systématiques. Toutefois, nous avons peu progressé au cours de ces dernières années dans notre compréhension de la chronologie et de la fonction de ces éléments, proéminents mais énigmatiques. C'est en partie en réaction contre cette situation peu satisfaisante, et en partie à cause des menaces continuelles qui pèsent sur les ouvrages qui subsistent, qu'on a lancé une nouvelle campagne d'études des fossés limitrophes. L'arrière-plan historique qui a précédé les recherches actuelles se trouve résumé dans le premier chapitre. Ce qui nous amène au choix du domaine de recherches. Il a été influencé par les travaux des archéologues qui nous ont précédé tout en offrant des occasions sans précédent pour des études d'un type nouveau. La première partie se termine par un chapitre qui explique l'évolution de la méthodologie sur le terrain et évalue les résultats obtenus grâce aux techniques diverses qui ont été utilisées en complément du programme de fouilles. La partie finale comprend un sommaire des stratigraphies et des collections d'objets façonnés provenant des sites qui constituent l'essentiel des recherches. Il est accompagné de preuves de datation.

La deuxième partie de ce rapport est consacrée aux recherches spécialisées. Dans chaque cas les données ont été considérées non seulement comme un sujet d'étude indépendant mais également comme un aspect distinct et pourtant faisant partie intégrante du répertoire culturel matériel associé au développement du système de fossés limitrophes. Cette règle s'applique aussi bien aux objets façonnés qu'à l'environnement. On a considéré que ce dernier possédait une structure culturelle au même titre que les matières premières qui sont transformées en objets façonnés par un dessein social. Pour chaque étude on a identifié un certain nombre de thèmes spatiaux et chronologiques. Ceux-ci sont développés dans le contexte de l'évolution et de l'organisation de l'occupation de la fin de l'Age du Bronze, à l'intérieur des frontières du territoire délimité par les fossés limitrophes. Le dernier chapitre de cette partie est essentiellement consacré aux témoignages provenant des fouilles. Il consolide et enrichit le cadre descriptif établi au chapitre 3, tout en tirant en même temps des conclusions des études spécialisées de manière à faire ressortir les liens entre le traitement des frontières et d'autres aspects de l'occupation.

Dans la partie 3, qui sert de conclusion, on réexamine certaines des questions soulevées par des recherches antérieures consacrées aux fossés limitrophes à la lumière de cette dernière étude. Certaines observations ont retenu notre intérêt, par exemple la situation topographique, la relation entre ces fossés limitrophes et les champs «celtiques», ainsi que la morphologie des tranchées qui a contribué au concept de «ranch de bétail» de la fin de l'Age du Bronze. On a montré au lecteur que le système de fossés limitrophes avait traversé différentes étapes et qu'à différentes époques il avait assumé des rôles divers. Il est important d'examiner d'un point de vue plus théorique, à la lumière de ces changements de fonction, les implications de ces limites précises. On doit accorder une attention toute particulière aux liens entre les concepts de domestication et d'intensification. Au cours de l'évolution du système de fossés limitrophes, ce sont le caractère et la perception du paysage qui ont changé en fonction de la démographie, de l'occupation et des échanges culturels. Ceci est à son tour lié à la productivité de subsistance, à la propriété des terres et au niveau de la production domestique. Des changements dans l'équilibre de ces éléments sont à l'origine des modifications que nous avons constatées au cours de notre étude des limites.

Zusammenfassung

Der erste Teil dieses Berichtes beginnt mit einer Übersicht des archäologischen Befundes auf den Kreidelandschaften Südenglands. Er betont den Sondercharakter dieser Kreidehochflächen in Bezug auf die vorgeschichtliche Besiedlung und deren außergewöhnlichen Erhaltungszustand, die beide seit geraumer Zeit das besondere Interesse der Archäologen gefunden haben. Die Stellung, die die gradlinigen Grabenführungen in dieser Landschaft einnehmen, ist schon seit langem der Gegenstand von Spekulation und zu verschiedenen Zeiten der Gegenstand systematischer Untersuchungen gewesen. Unser Verständnis der Chronologie und der Funktion dieser auffälligen, doch rätselhaften Anlagen hat jedoch in den letzten Jahren nur geringe Fortschritte gemacht. Teilweise als eine Reaktion auf diesen unbefriedigenden Stand der Dinge und im Hinblick auf die andauernde Bedrohung der noch erhaltenen Erdwerke wurde eine erneute Umtersuchung diesen gradlinigen Grabenführungen angeregt. Der geschichtliche Hintergrund zu diesem gegenwärtigen Studienprojekt wird im ersten Kapital zusammengefaßt. Daraus folgend wird die Wahl des Untersuchungsgebietes besprochen, die durch die Arbeiten früherer Archäologen beeinflußt wurde. Gleichzeitig bot es einmalige Forschungsmöglichkeiten für neue Untersuchungen. Im abschließenden Kapitel von Teil I wird die Entwicklung der Feldforschungsmethododik erklärt. Weiterhin werden die Ergebnisse aus einer Reihe von Techniken bewertet, die zur Ergänzung des Ausgrabungsprogrammes benutzt wurden. Der letzte Abschnitt enthält zusammen mit dem Datierungsbefund eine Auswahl der Schnitte und Artefaktvergesellschaft-ungen aus jenen Fundstätten, die den Kern dieser Studie bilden.

Teil II dieses Berichtes befaßt sich mit den einzelnen Sonderstudien. Für jedes dieser Forschungsprojekte sind die gewonnenen Daten nicht nur als eigenständige Forschungsobjekte betrachtet worden, sondern auch als gesonderte, jedoch integrale Aspekte des Befundes, der mit der Entwicklung des Systems der gradlinigen Grabenführungen in Verbindung steht. Dies gilt in gleicher Weise die Artefakte und die Umwelt für. Für die letztere wird angenommen, daß sie genau so kulturell geformt wurde wie Rohmaterialien, die durch soziale Absicht in Kulturgegenstände umgewandelt wurden. Jede Studie identifiziert eine Reihe von räumlichen und chronologischen Themen. Diese werden im Rahmen von Entwicklung und Organisation der spätbronzezeitlichen Besiedlung innerhalb dieser eingegrenzten Landschaft, die durch die gradlinigen Grabenführungen umrissen wird, verfolgt. Das abschließende Kapital dieses Teiles befaßt sich in erster Linie mit den Ausgrabungsbefunden. Es baut auf der deskriptiven Grundlage auf, die im dritten Kapital zusammengestellt worden ist, während es gleichzeitig die Sonderstudien einbezieht, um Wandlungen der Grenzziehungen mit anderen Siedlungsaspekten zu verbinden.

Im abschließenden Teil III werden die Fragen, die durch frühere Untersuchungen der gradlinigen Grabenführungen aufgeworfen worden sind, im Licht der neuesten Forschung überprüft. Gewisse Beobachtungen, wie etwa topographische Lage, das Verhältnis der gradlinigen Gräben zu "Celtic fields" Äckern und die Morphologie der Gräben, die zu der Vorstellung von einer spätbronzezeitlichen „Weidewirtschaft" geführt haben, sind hierbei von Bedeutung. Dem Leser wird dargelegt, daß das System der gradlinigen Grabenführungen sich durch verschiedene Stadien hindurch entwickelt hat und daß seine Funktion zu verschiedenen Zeiten unterschiedlich gewesen ist. Es ist daher wichtig, daß man die Bedeutung von formalen Grenzziehungen im Hinblick auf diesen Funktionswandel aus einer mehr theoretischen Perspektive betrachtet. Im besonderen sollte man die miteinander verflochtenen Konzepte von Domestikation und Intensivierung in Betracht ziehen. Bei der Entwicklung des Systems der gradlinigen Grabenführungen sind es der Charakter und die Wahrnehmung der Landschaft, die sich in Bezug auf Demographie, Besiedlung und Kulturbeziehungen wandeln. Dies wiederum ist gebunden an die Produktion für den Eigenbedarf, die Form des Grundbesitzes und das Ausmaß der häuslichen Produktion. Verschiebungen im Gleichgewicht dieser Bestandteile sind die Grundlagen für die Wandlungen, die wir bei unserer Untersuchung der Grenzziehungen festgestellt haben.

Preface: Conservation issues in the archaeology of Salisbury Plain

by Dai Morgan Evans

When the idea of National Parks was first discussed, among those with recommendations to make was the archaeologist O G S Crawford. With the benefit of hindsight his advice makes interesting reading. He advocated a National Park on the Marlborough Downs, where the remains of ancient earthworks were, at the time, especially well preserved. He contrasted their preservation with the situation on Salisbury Plain, where, he argued, in the course of military training the archaeological remains had been damaged too severely to warrant preservation.

That contrast is certainly not true today. The Marlborough Downs never became a National Park, and the archaeological sites that still survive there do so as small islands of grassland in the midst of cultivated land. Many of the others have been damaged or destroyed by ploughing. The situation is well illustrated in Gingell's recent monograph on the prehistoric landscape in that area (Gingell 1992).

Paradoxically, it is on Salisbury Plain that much of the archaeology is still intact. Despite the pressures that Crawford described, the region represents an almost unique resource. The present circumstances prevail because so much of the land was acquired by the military authorities before the expansion of cultivation that has obliterated the sites on the Marlborough Downs. The army first purchased land on Salisbury Plain in 1897 and has continued to expand its estate to the present day. As a result, the Military Training Area now covers 93,000 acres – a tract of land as large as the Isle of Wight. This amounts to 9% of the modern county of Wiltshire and contains approximately 2000 recorded sites. Ironically, it seems as if Crawford's very negative position influenced many of his contemporaries, with the result that this area played little part in archaeological research after the early years of the century.

Modern concern with conservation issues on Salisbury Plain began with the Defence Lands Review Committee of 1971–3, the Nugent Report (Ministry of Defence 1973). This recognised the difficulties of protecting ancient monuments on military training land, as well as more general conservation issues, and set up a system of voluntary subgroups to identify the areas of interest and to monitor the problem. It also led to the appointment of a Ministry of Defence Conservation Officer. Changes in training methods and weapons technology led to renewed pressures on the archaeology of the Plain. The conservation subgroups reported a number of cases in which particular sites had been damaged, and these were followed up by the Wiltshire County Archaeologist and by the Inspectorate of Ancient Monuments. Some of these cases were also reported in the media. All these factors created a new awareness of the archaeological potential of Salisbury Plain. This came at just the time that extensive field projects, in such areas as Dartmoor, were leading to a conception of landscape archaeology that went far beyond the recording of individual monuments.

These pressures resulted in a new initiative. In 1984 a working party was established to investigate the situation and to put forward a policy for conservation. This had two components. First, it included a rapid survey of the archaeology of Salisbury Plain, overseen by the County Archaeologist, Roy Canham. This was intended to enhance the county Sites and Monuments Record and drew extensively on the evidence of air photography. The second element was a review of the ways in which the surviving monuments might be managed. It soon became apparent that established methods of protecting the archaeology were not incompatible with the requirements of military training. Indeed, they were far easier to implement than on cultivated land. The resulting report was adopted by the Ministry of Defence (Property Services Agency 1986).

This new policy worked effectively for individual monuments and for 'Archaeological Site Groups' such as barrow cemeteries (Morgan Evans 1992), but two areas continued to raise major problems. Field systems, which can cover very large tracts of ground, did not fit comfortably within this management plan. The other anomaly was represented by the linear earthworks on the Plain. When the report was adopted, it became clear that each of these problems would need to be considered in more detail. The field systems are being assessed as part of a project conducted by Roy Entwistle, Michael Fulford and Frances Raymond, and the problems posed by the linear earthworks are considered in this volume.

For the field systems, a large body of literature is available, and this is sufficient to identify many of the key issues. But, as Richard Bradley argues in Chapter 1, such is not the case with the linear earthworks. They pose problems of chronology and interpretation that extend well beyond the archaeology of Salisbury Plain, and their conservation raises particularly difficult issues.

Because so many of these earthworks are still used as boundaries, their ownership can be split, resulting in major differences in the ways in which they are managed. Where they have been adopted as the edge of fields, their limits may be damaged by the plough, or in other cases they may be obscured by vegetation. Quite frequently these areas are also disturbed by burrowing animals. Where, as often happens, boundaries have changed, the earthworks may run across modern fields, and in such cases they have been levelled by the plough.

These problems occur widely. They certainly extend to the islands of cultivated land found within the Salisbury Plain Military Training Area; but the linear earthworks in that region are also subject to special kinds of damage. They form obstacles to the movement of wheeled and tracked vehicles, which can easily become bogged down in the ruts that develop over the filling of the ditches; the extent of the damage increases as other vehicles attempt to go round these areas of disturbance. The ditches and banks also provide sheltered areas where it is easy for troops to dig in. Apart from the direct effects of military training, the earthworks can suffer from tree planting on the Plain.

Before these remains can be managed effectively, we must know when and why they were created. Without that knowledge, it would be difficult to make a case for their preservation. This monograph is the first stage in that process, and it sheds light on a number of features that must now be integrated into our plans for the archaeology of Salisbury Plain. In particular, it becomes apparent how closely the linear earthworks are integrated into the pattern of settlements, burial mounds and hill-forts – monuments that have hitherto been managed in isolation. The conservation problems remain to be resolved, but our options can now be discussed in a more informed manner. This is particularly timely as the very uses to which the Military Training Area is put may be affected by the new policies emerging after the Cold War. The future of Salisbury Plain remains as uncertain as its past, but at least we have a clearer idea of the range of archaeological sites on the Plain. We must continue to make its use for training a positive force for conservation.

PART I   AN INTRODUCTION TO THE PROJECT

The first part of this report begins with a review of the archaeological record for the chalklands of southern England. It emphasises the special character of the chalk uplands, both in terms of prehistoric settlement and the unusual preservation that has traditionally attracted the attention of archaeologists. The place of linear ditches in this landscape has long been the subject of speculation and, at various times, the focus of more systematic study. However, our understanding of the chronology and function of these prominent, but enigmatic features has advanced little in recent years. It is partly in response to this unsatisfactory state of affairs, and partly because of the continuing threat to surviving earthworks, that a fresh attempt to study linear ditches was set in motion. The historical background to this present study is summarised in Chapter 1. This leads on to the choice of the Study Area, which was influenced by the work of earlier archaeologists, while offering unparalleled opportunities for new research. The concluding chapter of Part I explains the development of the field methodology and evaluates the results from a range of techniques used to complement the excavation programme. The final section contains a digest of the stratigraphies and artefact associations of those sites that form the core of our study, along with the dating evidence.

> Once above all, a Traveller at that time
> Upon the Plain of Sarum was I raised;
> There on the pastoral Downs without a track
> To guide me, or along the bare white roads
> Lengthening in solitude their dreary line,
> Whilst through those vestiges of ancient times
> I ranged, and by the solitude overcome,
> I had a reverie and saw the past........
> ....'Twas my chance
> To have before me on the downy Plain
> Lines, circles, mounts, a mystery of shapes
> Such as in many quarters yet survive,
> With intricate profusion figuring o'er
> The untill'd ground.
>
> William Wordsworth, *The Prelude* (1805 text), Book XII

1   The background to the enquiry

by Richard Bradley

Introduction: the archaeological setting

European prehistory takes different forms at different scales of resolution, but in many areas one basic division can be found. Outside certain quite exceptional environments – the loess, the Alpine lakes, the uplands of Central Europe – early prehistory provides only limited evidence of settlement and landuse, while later developments emphasise the growing importance of mixed farming, food storage, and enclosure. That change lies behind the distinction between an earlier and a later Bronze Age (Coles and Harding 1979, 135).

On a smaller geographical scale important contrasts can be seen. While settlements and agriculture become more obvious in the archaeological record, this process is imperfectly observed before the Iron Age. There is one important exception to this scheme, for the reorganisation of the settled landscape seems to have been under way at an earlier date, and perhaps on a more extensive scale, in the British Isles than on the Continent (Bradley 1978a). This development has been studied in many parts of the country, but at present it is best understood in the uplands of south-west England, where large areas of the Bronze Age landscape have been protected from later disturbance (Fleming 1988).

In other parts of Britain, the sequence is more fragmented, but may also be more characteristic of the pattern of development as a whole, for here the evolution of the landscape continues into the Iron Age and later periods. Although detailed study can reveal local changes in the density of human occupation, whole landscapes only rarely seem to have been abandoned. Three regions have been especially informative in recent years: the river gravels, especially those of the Thames and Kennet; the Fen edge; and the chalk of central-southern England. Nevertheless, there are striking contrasts to be observed. In lowland areas, as a result of more recent landuse, all too little of the settlement pattern survives intact; and, in this case, excavation has provided windows into landscapes whose surviving elements are most effectively mapped by air photography. Even here, experience has shown that the Bronze Age field systems, which form such an important feature of British prehistory, are masked by later elements or are indistinguishable from the components of the Roman landscape (cf Pryor 1980).

Work on the southern English chalk has proved to have advantages and disadvantages. The advantages are obvious. As a result of soil creep, many field divisions are represented by lynchets rather than shallow ditches, and those survive as soil marks long after their destruction by the plough. Such destruction can be quite a recent development, with the result that some of these features were surveyed or photographed before that process began. Moreover, such areas attracted the attention of field archaeologists long before air photography revealed the potential importance of the lowlands. As a result, a significant proportion of the sites that no longer survive above ground were excavated on a limited scale. The pioneering surveys of Sir Richard Colt Hoare, O G S Crawford, Herbert Toms, J P Williams-Freeman and the Curwens were supplemented by important excavations undertaken by General Pitt Rivers, the Cunningtons, the Piggotts, Christopher Hawkes, and J F S Stone.

It has taken some time to appreciate the disadvantages of this emphasis on chalkland archaeology. Much of the evidence survived as a result of later landscape history, for the downland was generally used as pasture. It was rather marginal land, and the main density of human activity was in the river valleys, in the Hampshire Basin, or on the coastal plain of Sussex (Barrett *et al* 1991, chap 2 and 4; Ellison 1978). All are areas in which the archaeological record is fragmentary and little known. The archaeology of the higher downland may not be entirely typical, and, in certain periods, for example the earlier Neolithic, it seems doubtful whether this area played any central role in the pattern of settlement. In the same way, there are indications that the main density of earlier Bronze Age activity was in the fertile lowlands, some distance away from the well-known barrow cemeteries of the period. It may be that the reorganisation of settlement and landuse, that becomes such a prominent feature of chalkland archaeology, started in low-lying areas where much of the archaeological evidence has been hidden or destroyed (Barrett *et al* 1991, chap 5).

Since we could be observing a pattern of landuse that was first established in the lowlands, the contrasts between earlier and later prehistory may seem unusually sharp. A landscape dominated by mortuary monuments, and by the ceremonial centres of earlier generations, was enclosed on an increasing scale. Settlements achieved a degree of archaeological visibility rarely shown by their predecessors, and funerary monuments became less prominent features of the landscape, before they disappeared almost completely. The earthworks that dominated the landscape of the Neolithic and earlier Bronze Age periods were increasingly surrounded by a distribution of field systems and boundary ditches. Some were incorporated into these new land divisions, while others were apparently ploughed out (Bradley 1981).

There are two major problems with this portrayal, however. The changes look so striking because the chalkland was colonised from the lowlands. The mortuary monuments of the existing landscape may have been located some distance away from the main areas of year-round settlement, and changes effected in the latter areas must have taken some time to extend to the higher ground. The earlier stages of that process may be largely lost, but they need not have been characterised by such abrupt contrasts. The second problem is rather more subtle, and is often overlooked in general accounts of these developments. In fact, the reorganisation of landuse on the chalk was a relatively local phenomenon and did not happen throughout the chalkland until the Early Iron Age. Before that time, Middle Bronze Age activity was concentrated in certain quite limited areas, such as Cranborne Chase (Barrett *et al* 1991, chap 5), the Marlborough Downs (Gingell 1992), the Itchen Valley around Winchester (Fasham *et al* 1989), and the South Downs close to Worthing (Ellison 1978). There are other areas, such as the Berkshire Downs (S Ford pers comm), in which the first lasting settlements are of Late Bronze Age origin. Thus, some areas were reorganised earlier than others, and in a few cases that reorganisation may have been relatively short-lived.

Apart from the settlement sites themselves, the clearest evidence for such changes is provided by 'Celtic' fields, and by the network of linear earthworks that have sometimes been described as 'ranch boundaries'. Neither term is satisfactory, but both are rather revealing. The term 'Celtic field' was adopted in order to distinguish earthworks of this kind from the field systems of the invading 'English' (Bowen 1961, chap 1). The name 'ranch boundary' perpetuates an interpretation of certain earthworks, which has never been tested systematically (Bowen 1978). The confusion extends to the relationship between these separate phenomena, on the chalk and across the British Isles as a whole. There are two key problems here, and they lie at the heart of our own investigation. First, the distribution of linear ditches is by no means the same as that of 'Celtic' field systems. At the regional scale, the main distribution of linear ditch systems is on the chalk of Wiltshire, Hampshire, and Berkshire, with only shorter lengths of earthwork in neighbouring counties: the so-called cross-ridge dykes and spur dykes of Sussex and Dorset (Bradley 1971, fig 1). This distribution excludes some of the main areas with early field systems, notably the downland north of Dorchester, Dorset, and most of Cranborne Chase. At a national level, extensive systems of linear ditches have been studied on the Yorkshire Wolds and the Tabular Hills (Fig 1), but in neither area have field systems survived on any scale.

This means that there are only limited areas in which it may be possible to investigate the relationship between these two phenomena. Here, opinion is sharply divided, some authorities interpreting these features as the component parts of a well-organised agricultural landscape; in this scheme, the ditches and the fields go together to form an integrated system of pastoral and arable landuse (Appelbaum 1954). This argument depends largely on the dating evidence for both these elements, and, as we shall see, this leaves much to be desired. The alternative view is that the linear ditches do not conform to the layout of the fields in the way that this interpretation demands. Although some of the ditches do bound blocks of 'Celtic' fields, others seem to cut across them, meaning that both elements could not have been used at

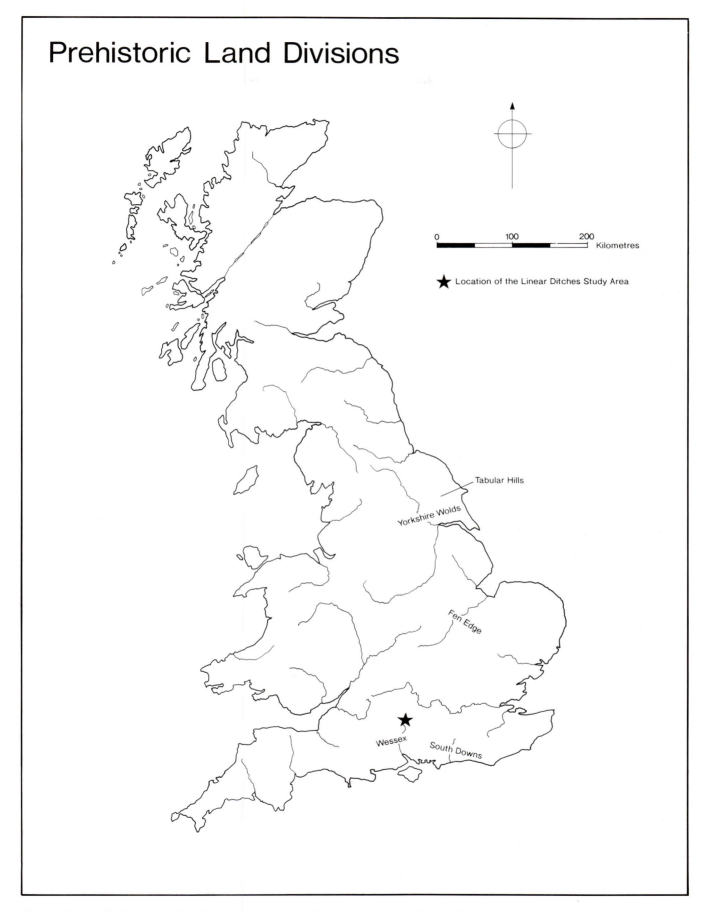

Prehistoric Land Divisions

0   100   200
Kilometres

★ Location of the Linear Ditches Study Area

Tabular Hills

Yorkshire Wolds

Fen Edge

Wessex   South Downs

Fig 1   Map of Britain, showing the principal areas with concentrations of linear ditches

the same time. In certain cases, a clear sequence has been observed on the ground, suggesting that these features represent successive stages in the evolution of the landscape (Bowen 1975 and 1978).

Some of these questions have been addressed in recent work, but others remain intractable. In Wessex, the shifting margin of downland settlement was investigated by the Cranborne Chase Project, which compared the sequence of occupation on the chalk with the evidence from the Hampshire Basin 20km to the south (Barrett *et al* 1991). Similar questions have been asked by pollen analysts working in Wessex and Sussex (Thorley 1981; Waton 1982), and, on a smaller scale, archaeologists in the latter area have considered the relationship between settlement on the South Downs and the occupation of the coastal plain (Bedwin 1983). This research has shed considerable light on the pattern of Middle Bronze Age settlement, including the history of a number of occupation sites, together with their cemeteries and fields. Excavation and survey have certainly increased our understanding of one component of the later prehistoric reorganisation of the landscape, but the picture remains frustratingly incomplete. These are areas in which linear ditches play little, if any, role, and their history of settlement rarely extends into the Late Bronze Age. The changing use of the chalk may be better understood, but the sequence is too short. There is very little to close the gap between Middle Bronze Age activity and the settlement pattern of the Early Iron Age. The point is made explicitly in the publication of fieldwork in Cranborne Chase (Barrett *et al* 1991, chap 6).

In some ways, the present investigation is the successor of that project, for it takes as its main focus the linear ditches system that is largely absent in Cranborne Chase. But it does so against a very different background. Like the Cranborne Chase Project, it took place in a landscape with a long history of archaeological investigation and an unusually high proportion of standing monuments. There the comparison ends, for the prehistoric landscape discussed on this occasion lies partly in a military training area, where the balance between management and destruction is a difficult one to resolve, and where part of that difficulty is created by gaps in our understanding of the archaeological remains. Fieldwork in other parts of Wessex has been concerned with investigating the character and chronology of particular Bronze Age settlements and landscapes before their destruction by agriculture or other agencies. Such work has been conducted with specific questions in mind, and the results have often been illuminating. As its name suggests, the Wessex Linear Ditches Project is viewed as a further contribution to that programme of research, but it has another equally important brief. Its conclusions will be of lasting value only if they provide an informed assessment of features whose continued survival depends on careful planning. That may seem a limited objective, but, as we shall see, the linear ditches system is so extensive that it offers our best prospect of linking together the separate elements in the archaeological landscape. Like work on the Dartmoor reaves, this investigation provides an opportunity, unusual in public archaeology, of investigating the Bronze Age and Iron Age settlement pattern at a large geographical scale.

Investigating the linear ditches systems of the British Isles

Almost every account of linear earthworks stresses the difficulties of studying them. That is as true of great frontier works as it is of the much slighter features found on the chalk of southern England. In the latter case, even the terminology betrays this confusion. Early writers talked of 'traveling' or 'wandering' ditches (Colt Hoare 1812), and it was not until the early years of this century that these terms were replaced by the more neutral name 'linear ditch'. Even then, this proved too neutral for some, who preferred the alternative 'ranch boundary'.

Although General Pitt Rivers interpreted the linear earthworks of the Yorkshire chalk as the successive land holdings of a force of invaders (Pitt Rivers 1882), most authorities have agreed that the relatively insubstantial earthworks found in upland areas probably played an essential role in the everyday life of settled communities. The main source of disagreement between early students of the earthworks was whether these should be regarded as land boundaries or roads. As it happens, that disagreement is revealing, for our own fieldwork in Wessex has shown how difficult it is to distinguish between the two on the basis of surface evidence.

Pitt Rivers had favoured a 'military' interpretation of these earthworks, consistent with his parallel studies of Sussex hillforts (Lane Fox 1868), but more progress was made by two other pioneers of field archaeology. Sir Richard Colt Hoare (1812) mapped quite substantial tracts of the linear ditches system in Wiltshire, including the area around Sidbury hillfort, which was to form the main focus of our research. Although he tended to interpret these earthworks as roads rather than boundaries, he was aware of the close connection between the linear ditches and the local topography. He also noticed the integration between these features and the settlement sites on Salisbury Plain. J R Mortimer, working on the Yorkshire Wolds, likewise stressed the relationship between the course taken by the ditches and the details of the local relief, publishing a remarkable map, which reconstructed a number of ditched 'territories' in detail (1905, 365–80; map redrawn in Fig 2). He also carried out a crucially important investigation on the dyke system at Fimber, where he found that a pit containing Late Bronze Age weapon moulds had been dug into the tail of an existing bank (ibid, 188–9). This was the first convincing dating evidence from that system, and, until the recent work of Manby at Thwing and the programme of air photograph interpretation conducted by RCHME (C Stoertz pers comm), there was all too little to add to Mortimer's analysis.

It was in the south that greater attention was paid to the linear ditches system. Again, General Pitt Rivers's contribution is important here. Although he had little conception of landscape archaeology and was actually a rather poor observer of earthworks, he did undertake one of the largest excavations on a feature of this type. In 1893, he excavated no less than 90m of one of these ditches, not far from the Deverel-Rimbury enclosure at Martin Down (Pitt Rivers 1898, 185–215). Although this feature contained pottery of the same kind as the

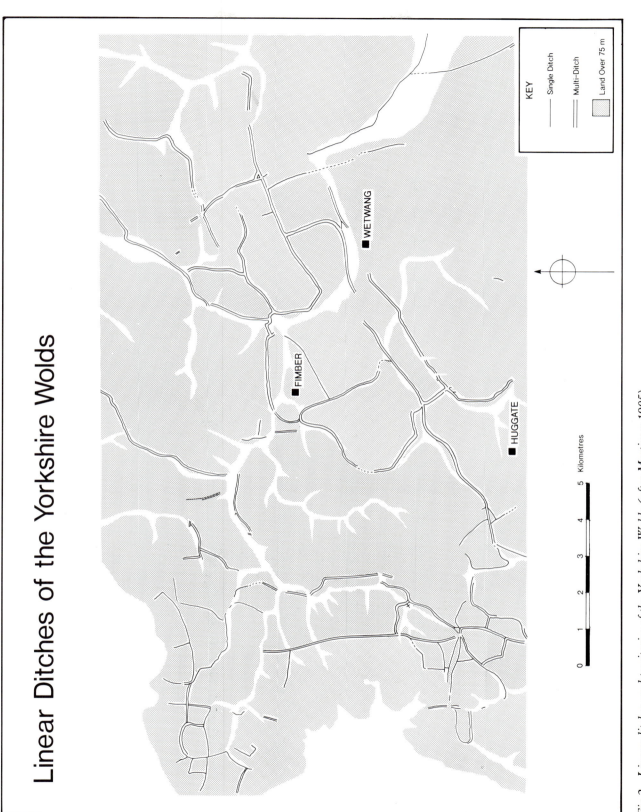

Linear Ditches of the Yorkshire Wolds

KEY

—— Single Ditch

═══ Multi-Ditch

Land Over 75 m

WETWANG

FIMBER

HUGGATE

Kilometres

0 1 2 3 4 5

Fig 2   Linear ditches and territories of the Yorkshire Wolds (after Mortimer 1905)

Martin Down settlement, it is characteristic of his approach to archaeology that he did not observe that the ditch had been cut through older fields, or that the enclosure itself overlay part of the same system.

Such observations were first made by O G S Crawford, working with air photographs that showed linear earthworks before their destruction by cultivation. In combination with ground survey, he mapped an extensive series of fields and linear earthworks on Salisbury Plain for a publication by the Ordnance Survey that was never issued, although some of this material was reworked in a general account of linear earthworks that appeared in his book *Archaeology in the field* (Crawford 1953, chap 10). This also described similar observations on the linear earthworks of the Berkshire Downs.

The same period saw the development of analytical field survey in Sussex, stimulated by the appointment of Pitt Rivers's former assistant, Herbert Toms, to a post at Brighton Museum. He was already familiar with the earthworks of Cranborne Chase, and his surveys of sites on the South Downs (eg Toms 1917) laid the foundations for a series of more ambitious projects undertaken by the Curwens. Two of these are particularly relevant here: their study of 'Celtic' field systems on the Sussex Downs (Curwen and Curwen 1923) and a series of careful surveys of the earthworks that they described as 'covered ways' (1917).

The term 'covered way' is actually borrowed from field fortification, but in this case it was applied to the distinctive linear earthworks running across the open ridges of the South Downs ('cross-ridge dykes'), or, alternatively, crossing the spurs between adjacent coombes ('spur dykes'). Such earthworks could also be found in parts of Dorset. The Curwens's interpretation of these features echoed Colt Hoare's thoughts on the linear ditches of Salisbury Plain: they were essentially roads, crossing exposed ground and linking more sheltered areas in which there was evidence of settlements and fields. In this case, the interpretation was augmented by excavation, which showed that they were not hollow-ways, but carefully excavated ditches, often with a bank of spoil on one or both sides. An example on Glatting Down in West Sussex contained a Globular Urn (Curwen and Curwen 1917, 57–8). The faces of these chalk-cut ditches seemed rather unusual, as if they had been worn smooth by the passage of animals. By the 1920s, similar observations were being made in Wiltshire, where Clay sectioned a number of linear ditches, again putting forward the suggestion that they had been used to facilitate the movement of livestock (1927).

By this stage, more extensive field survey was already undermining the idea of 'covered ways'. Sites were discovered in Hampshire, Sussex, and Wiltshire where small enclosures were joined directly to these earthworks, using the linear ditch as one side of the enclosed area. In other cases, linear ditches seemed to be joined directly to the defensive circuit of hillforts. In neither case could an interpretation as protected droveways be sustained. A particularly useful example of this relationship was recorded at Boscombe Down East, where it appeared that an enclosure associated with Deverel-Rimbury pottery had been joined to an existing linear earthwork (Stone 1936).

Such observations provided the background for the first sustained analysis of the linear ditches system in Wessex: Hawkes's famous excavation at Quarley Hill near Andover (Hawkes 1939; Fig 3). During the 1930s, a number of scholars, including Crawford and Stone, had mapped the linear earthworks extending from the edge of Salisbury Plain eastwards into the Hampshire chalkland. These earthworks seemed to define a whole series of land blocks on either side of the Bourne valley, as well as others along the River Avon, but there was one site (Quarley Hill) where they could be brought into relation with a class of monument whose chronology and character were already well known. Throughout the 1930s, Christopher Hawkes had been investigating the hillforts of Hampshire, a concerted programme of research that began with an excavation at St Catherine's Hill that firmly established the Iron Age credentials of these monuments (Hawkes 1931).

Like the arrangement first noted by Colt Hoare at Sidbury, Quarley Hillfort lay at the apex of an extensive system of linear ditches (Fig 8). Excavation was to prove that the hillfort, and the slighter enclosure that preceded it, overlay the meeting point of these earthworks, while a further ditch was dug in order to link one of the major components of this system to the new fort defences. Excavation behind the rampart at Quarley Hill provided evidence of a substantial midden, completely sealing the filling of two of the ditches. This midden contained decorated pottery which would now be dated to the sixth century BC. This was a particularly elegant exercise and was carried out in combination with the mapping of the linear ditches system in the surrounding countryside. This combination of small-scale excavation and more extensive survey was enough to establish the credentials of the linear ditches as a major system of boundaries. Hawkes concluded his report with the observation that these must be the oldest land divisions in Western Europe.

It seems paradoxical that, after such a promising beginning, studies of this kind largely lapsed. To some extent, this is because the progress of research was changed by the Second World War, but it may also be because this project seemed to be so definitive. The chronological evidence from Quarley Hill could be combined with other observations in the area to provide a consistent interpretation of the linear ditches system. Crawford had argued that linear ditches on the edge of Salisbury Plain could cut through existing field systems (1953, 107–11); Stone's work at Boscombe Down East showed how a distinctive rectangular enclosure, with parallels elsewhere in this region, could be integrated with one of the earthwork boundaries; now Hawkes's paper documented the full extent of the system and its influence over the positioning of hillforts. Enclosures such as Boscombe Down East had been extensively excavated by General Pitt Rivers in the last decade of the nineteenth century, among them the earthwork at Martin Down mentioned earlier (Pitt Rivers 1898). The fact that these sites appeared to be free of domestic buildings seemed to indicate a specialised role in the Bronze Age economy (Piggott 1942). Viewed in combination with the great tracts of upland defined by the linear ditches, it seemed only natural to connect them with the large-scale enclosure of livestock. The accepted terminology altered subtly: the linear ditches became known as 'ranch

Fig 3 Quarley Hillfort, looking north-east, showing the arrangement of linear ditches recorded by Hawkes; ditch 1 is the Quarley High Linear (reproduced by courtesy of the RCHME)

boundaries', and earthworks such as those at Martin Down or Boscombe Down East were described as 'pastoral enclosures'.

A similar development took place in other parts of the chalkland. Fieldwork in south Wiltshire suggested that cross-ridge dykes and spur dykes might also have acted as territorial boundaries (Fowler 1964). Although E C Curwen held to his view that similar features in Sussex should be interpreted as covered ways (1951), it soon became apparent that, like the linear ditches of Wessex, these earthworks could be closely integrated with small earthwork enclosures and perhaps hillforts (Bradley 1971). Around the Hampshire–Sussex border, the complementary distribution of boundary ditches and field systems even suggested that they had been used to

enclose areas of upland pasture (ibid).

Given such apparent unanimity, why is it necessary to think again now? In fact, this interpretation rested on weak foundations, and very little of this framework has remained intact during the resurgence of Bronze Age studies of the last 15 years.

The first difficulty concerns the evidence of 'pastoral enclosures'. As early as 1973, Stuart Piggott suggested that the absence of timber buildings on these sites might be more apparent than real (1973, 397). Given the pioneering nature of General Pitt Rivers's excavations, could postholes have gone unnoticed? This was to be confirmed by the re-excavation of the General's famous site at South Lodge Camp between 1977 and 1981, which showed that the supposedly empty interior of the site contained the postholes of at least two timber buildings as well as platforms, pits, and a burnt mound. Equally important, it became clear that the enclosure owed its distinctive shape and size to the fact that it had been inserted into an already existing field system (Barrett *et al* 1991, 144–83). In the light of that experience, it was possible to reconsider the evidence from the General's other sites at Martin Down and Angle Ditch, and to suggest a similar sequence there (ibid, 219–22). Far from being a distinctive type of enclosure, associated with stock management, these sites were very much part of an arable economy.

Other problems arose from a better understanding of ceramic chronology. All the work summarised so far was undertaken in the belief that Deverel-Rimbury pottery was of Late Bronze Age date and had been replaced directly by Early Iron Age ceramics. During the 1950s, this view became untenable (Butler and Smith 1956; Smith 1959). Deverel-Rimbury material was backdated to the Middle Bronze Age and may even have originated in an earlier phase (Barrett 1976); this is confirmed by radiocarbon dates obtained in the recent campaign of fieldwork in Cranborne Chase (Barrett *et al* 1991, chap 5). As a result, it appears that most of the Bronze Age enclosures associated with Celtic fields had a limited lifespan. By contrast, work at Quarley Hill had suggested that the linear ditches system was still in use when the hillfort was created early in the Iron Age. As a result of these modifications, Late Bronze Age settlements no longer seem so common, and, in place of a clear-cut sequence, there is something of a chronological vacuum.

It only remains to add that even the existing evidence for the date of the linear ditches system was not all it seemed to be. Finds of isolated sherds are largely unhelpful and, until recently, there were only two major groups of material from linear ditches in Wessex: the pottery from the linear earthwork at Martin Down and the finds from Boscombe Down East. Neither can bear the weight normally assigned to it. The ditch at Martin Down is not linked to the enclosure and in fact cuts through its field system. Although Deverel-Rimbury pottery was certainly found in this ditch, it could well be residual (Pitt Rivers 1898, 214–15). The evidence from the enclosure on Boscombe Down East is even less reliable, for its relationship to the boundary ditch is by no means free of problems. A recent survey of the earthworks at this site suggests that the linear ditch actually cut across the Middle Bronze Age enclosure (D McOmish pers comm). That ditch may not have formed the fourth side of the enclosure, which may always have been incomplete, like several of the excavated sites in Cranborne Chase (Barrett *et al* 1991, figs S 27 and S 47). If so, the pottery merely provides a *terminus ante quem* for the linear ditch.

The results of a recent excavation at Easton Lane, Winchester, may also be relevant here (Fasham *et al* 1989; Fig 4). Large-scale stripping in advance of road construction revealed a number of ditches associated with pottery extending from the Middle Bronze Age to the Early Iron Age. These earthworks are too close together to be compared with the land divisions described so far and seem to include a number of droveways. Their basic layout finds a close parallel among the contemporary land divisions on the Fen

Edge, where they define a series of large fields used for seasonal grazing (Pryor 1980; Fig 4). On the other hand, the sequence at Easton Lane can shed some light on changes in territorial organisation. In the Middle Bronze Age, the excavated area was divided into units as little as 80 to 100m across, some of which contained a number of houses. In the Late Bronze Age, only two of these ditches remained in use. Now they ran parallel to another, 220m apart, and were contemporary with an isolated group of timber buildings. Only one of these ditches was retained in the Early Iron Age, and this divided a rectilinear enclosure from a large area that contained virtually no contemporary features. Even if some of these earthworks were used to define fields or settlement areas, it seems as if the landscape was being divided into progressively larger units.

There is only one other area with much excavated dating evidence. This is the Yorkshire Wolds, where the investigation of linear ditches again goes back to the nineteenth century. This region still lacks a project comparable to Hawkes's work at Quarley Hill, but Manby's recent excavations at Thwing have drawn attention to a major Late Bronze Age fortified site, which is again situated at the apex of a series of boundary earthworks. The little dating evidence that is available from components of the Yorkshire system suggests an origin in the Late Bronze Age (Manby 1980, 327–8). The currency of these earthworks extends well into the Iron Age, however, and some of the Wolds dykes actually provide the boundaries for the square barrow cemeteries in this area; others are closely integrated into the pattern of settlement around Garton and Wetwang Slack (Dent 1982, 447–56). There is broadly comparable dating evidence from the northern limit of the Wolds at West Heslerton, where ditches and pit alignments of Late Bronze Age/Early Iron Age date have been excavated towards the edge of the Vale of Pickering (Powelsland 1986, 127–60). Their excavator has suggested that some of these boundaries define coherent territories based on the defended settlements at Devil's Hill and Staple Howe (Powelsland 1988). This suggestion is attractive, but it would be unwise to extrapolate from his case study to the character of the system as a whole. For our purposes, it is more important to note the overall currency of these earthworks, for this bears some resemblance to the evidence from southern England.

So far, we have considered the detailed evidence from a number of separate projects. Nearly all of them share the same problems. First, there are difficulties in deciding what weight to place on the results of individual excavations. This is because the ditches have been dated by quite small amounts of pottery, whose origin is sometimes in doubt. Could these finds consist of residual material, especially where the ditches had been dug through older features? That is a problem that cannot be addressed until more observations are available. Isolated records cannot count for much; what is needed is a body of consistent observations, preferably from a limited area. At the same time, that is unlikely to be obtained, unless excavation priorities are assessed explicitly. Very little has been learnt from the recording of threatened sections of earthwork, because so few of them contain many artefacts. Targets for sample excavation need to be carefully selected.

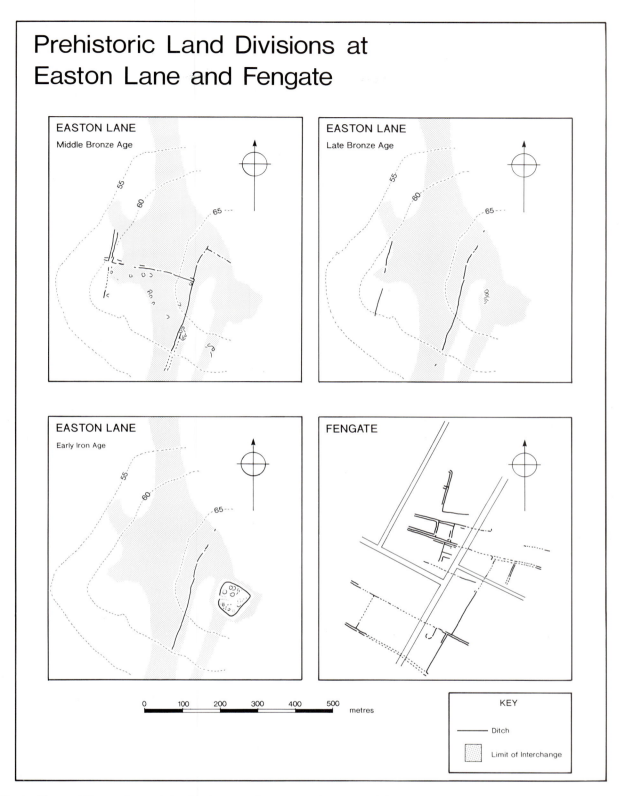

Prehistoric Land Divisions at Easton Lane and Fengate

EASTON LANE
Middle Bronze Age

EASTON LANE
Late Bronze Age

EASTON LANE
Early Iron Age

FENGATE

0   100   200   300   400   500
metres

KEY

— Ditch

Limit of Interchange

Fig 4 Plans of Easton Lane (after Fasham et al *1989) and Fengate (after Pryor 1980), showing patterns of enclosure*

Second, there are dangers in extrapolating the history of the linear ditches system from the excavation of major settlement sites. Excavation at Quarley Hill was valuable because it fixed certain points in the history of these boundaries, but it would be wrong to suppose that they represent the entire sequence. That is because boundary earthworks are likely to have been regularly maintained in the vicinity of settlements, with the result that the earliest ditches might have been removed by later recutting. This point can be demonstrated from the excavation of the hillfort at Danebury, which is surrounded by earthworks of this type. For over a decade, these ditches were assigned to one of the later structural phases on the site. Now it appears that they may predate the hillfort altogether, but this was only discovered because one short length of earthwork had escaped subsequent refurbishment (Cunliffe 1990, 323–6).

The third problem is much more serious. The most obvious deficiency of the Quarley Hill excavation is that it added very little to what could have been worked out from surface observation. The relationships between individual ditches and the fort defences could be established by field survey, and, in this sense, Hawkes's results simply confirm what had been published by Williams-Freeman over 20 years before (1915, 121–4 and 396–7). Excavation was of value in establishing the date and sequence of the successive enclosures, but it could not supply much more than that. Hawkes's results were far more important, because he linked his excavations to a wider programme of survey. It is to that subject that we turn our attention next.

In fact, it is through field survey, rather than through excavation, that most progress has been made, both in Wessex and in other parts of the country. While linear ditches rarely feature in excavation reports, they play a major role in more general accounts of the prehistoric landscape, including Spratt's analysis of the earthworks of the Tabular Hills (Spratt 1989), Bowen's discussion of the monuments around Bokerley Dyke (Bowen 1990), the surveys of the Stonehenge Environs undertaken by RCHME (1979) and Richards (1990), and Palmer's interpretation of the air photographic evidence from the area around Danebury (1984).

These studies extend the kind of detailed observations made by Hawkes at Quarley Hill over a much wider area, combining the evidence of soil marks, cropmarks, and surface survey. This has clarified many of the relationships between specific earthworks and datable features of the landscape. All of these studies share a common point of departure: the linear earthworks seem to post-date the long barrows and round barrows in their respective study areas, and, in many cases, they appear to have been laid out between already existing burial mounds. In certain instances, they were probably aligned on these earthworks. A small number of the barrows were incorporated directly into the new system, while in at least one case a ditch containing a sherd of Globular Urn cut through the edge of a Beaker-associated round barrow (Smith 1991, 18 and 31). Although there are a very few cases in which such barrows overlie 'Celtic' fields, there is one instance in which a mound overlies a linear earthwork: the North Kite, on Wilsford Down near to Stonehenge. Since its bank seals fresh sherds of Beaker pottery, it is likely to have been an abnormally early example (RCHME 1979, 26 and 28; Richards 1990, 184–92). With that exception, the evidence from Wessex is consistent with observations made on the dyke systems of eastern Yorkshire.

At the same time, linear ditches show a less consistent relationship with 'Celtic' fields. Two arrangements are commonly noted in the literature on Wessex; similar field systems do not seem to survive on the Yorkshire Wolds. The ditches may bound individual groups of fields, or they may cut across them. In the latter case, the two could not have been in use at the same time. Some of the field systems that were put out of use by linear ditches had been laid out on a series of parallel axes (Bowen 1975 and 1978).

Such evidence must be used with caution, yet caution is what has been lacking in its interpretation. On undamaged sites, it is not difficult to establish the chronological relationship between ditches and fields, but it can be over-simplified. Where a ditch cuts across a series of well-preserved lynchets, the sequence is not in doubt, but, where it bounds a group of fields, it may require excavation to establish their chronological relationship. Were the two features established at the same time? Did the ditch bound an already existing field system? Or did the fields grow up against an older earthwork? These questions can rarely be answered by surface observation, and on ploughed sites they cannot be resolved. The same problem can arise when ditches show as cropmarks or soil marks cutting across field systems. It has been customary to suggest that the fields were the earlier feature, but, as we shall see, there are cases in which traces of an older land boundary may show through the soil marks of a later field system.

We must stress the true complexity of the evidence. There has always been a temptation to look for regularities in the evolution of the landscape and to extrapolate from well-preserved surface evidence to the more exiguous traces visible from the air – this writer has been guilty on both counts. For this reason, the number of instances in which linear ditches cut older fields may well have been exaggerated. At the same time, there has also been a danger of drawing inappropriate analogies. The discovery of well-preserved Bronze Age landscapes on Dartmoor has influenced our perception of other areas. The long land boundaries on Dartmoor have been equated with the Wessex linear ditches, and the coaxial field systems on the moor have been compared with the 'Celtic' field systems of the chalk (Fowler 1983, 104–7). For a while, the parallel reaves were treated as if they represented a cultural 'type fossil', so that their interpretation and chronology could be extended directly to other areas. We now know that very few of the coaxial field systems in Britain originated at such an early date; in fact, they seem to have been built in many different periods (Fleming 1987). Thus, there is no reason to assign them chronological priority over other features of the agrarian landscape.

This is where field survey has its limitations. There are certainly well-documented cases in which linear earthworks do cut across older 'Celtic' fields. Some of the most convincing cases were observed by O G S Crawford and Collin Bowen before large tracts of the downland came under the plough (Crawford 1953, chap 10; Bowen 1975 and 1978). There are also cases in which their relationship is much more ambiguous, or must obviously be the other way round. The problem is that so little of the evidence can really be assessed on the basis of surface observation, especially in cultivated areas. One effect of small-scale excavation has been to show that the situation is far more complicated than it seems from the literature.

If it is often difficult to establish the relationship between the development of linear ditches and the history of 'Celtic' field systems, it is rather easier to appreciate their relationship to hillforts and enclosures. The precise details may be hard to elucidate by limited excavation, but, on a broader geographical scale, it has often been observed that linear ditches run up to these sites and that some of the major hillforts in Wessex were located at the meeting point of several of these earthworks (Cunliffe 1990). In other cases, it seems likely that individual enclosures were butted on to linear ditches, or that particular boundary earthworks skirted existing sites. Similar observations are occasionally made in northern England. If the defended ringwork at Thwing is at the meeting point of several of the Wolds dykes (Manby 1980), the hillfort at Boltby seems to be contemporary with the Cleave Dyke (Spratt 1982a).

Although such evidence is complicated, a few broad relationships can be observed on sites in Wessex. Very few of the smaller enclosures have been dated, but this does not apply to the evidence of the hillforts, which has recently been discussed by Cunliffe (1990). There are two basic relationships to consider here. There are cases in which hillfort defences clearly overlie linear ditches. This was first observed by Hawkes at Quarley Hill (1939), but exactly the same point was documented in Stuart Piggott's study of the unfinished fort on Ladle Hill (1931). The same sequence could be represented at Damerham Knoll (Bowen 1990, fig 32). There are also cases in which linear ditches abut existing hillfort ramparts. This was documented for one of the ditches on Quarley Hill, but the same relationship had already been observed by the Cunningtons in their excavation of the much smaller site of Lidbury on Salisbury Plain (1917). The same is true of the cross-ridge dyke abutting the hillfort of Chiselbury in south Wiltshire (Crawford and Keiller 1928, 74–7).

There are rather more instances in which the layout of the linear ditches system appears to have influenced the choice of location for a hillfort. In this case, no physical link may survive between the ditch and the fort defences, although this could be the result of later damage. This relationship is found in two types of location. There are examples in which a hillfort develops at the end of a long boundary represented by a single linear ditch. This is the case at Ladle Hill where the hillfort defences, and the earthwork of an older enclosure, respect an existing boundary ditch (Piggott 1931), and the same pattern is found on several sites where the precise chronological sequence is no longer apparent. These include Uffington Castle (S Palmer pers comm), Liddington Castle (P Rahtz pers comm), Woolbury (Cunliffe 1990, 328–9), Damerham Knoll (Bowen 1990, fig 32), and perhaps Danebury (Cunliffe 1990, 323–6). Alternatively, a hillfort may be sited at the meeting point of a number of different ditches. In most cases, it is uncertain whether the hilltop or its defensive circuit was the focal point of the boundary system. Examples of this relationship are recorded at Quarley Hill (Hawkes 1939), Sidbury Hill (Bowen 1975, fig 6), Suddern Farm (Palmer 1984, fig 16), and Whitsbury (Bowen 1990, 75). At Quarley Hill, the boundary system was in place before the creation of the hillfort, but some of its elements remained in use after the defences were built.

Such evidence of relative chronology can be linked only rarely to any absolute dates. We have seen already how two of the ditches truncated by the defences at Quarley Hill have a *terminus ante quem* in the sixth century BC. This would be broadly consistent with the dating of the first hillforts at Woolbury and Danebury (Cunliffe 1990), while a rather earlier origin seems likely

for those at Lidbury (Cunnington and Cunnington 1917), Liddington Castle (P Rahtz pers comm), and Uffington (S Palmer pers comm). On the other hand, the defences at Whitsbury may have been built in either the Early or the Middle Iron Age (Ellison and Rahtz 1987).

Lastly, it is worth adding that certain of the linear ditches close to Whitsbury and Bokerley Dyke provide evidence of a very much later date. These include the earthworks known as the Grims Ditch complex (Evans and Vaughan 1985) and a series of cross-ridge dykes excavated by Rahtz (1990). Although Pitt Rivers's site on Martin Down is located within the same area, these seem to be a specialised and probably separate phenomenon, contemporary with the rich Late Iron Age site on Gussage Cow Down (Barrett *et al* 1991, 323–6). In this case, their main association is with banjo enclosures rather than hillforts. They provide another warning, if warning is needed, of the dangers of placing too much weight on surface evidence alone.

To some extent that problem can be addressed by a second level of field survey, concerned less with dating individual ditches than with studying their relationship to the topography. This is another approach that can be traced back to the pioneering work of Hawkes (1939) and Crawford (1953, chap 10).

Both these writers emphasised the distinctive configuration of the linear ditches in between Quarley Hill and Salisbury Plain. These earthworks tend to follow the contours, running down the sides of valleys to meet the main rivers at right-angles. On the high ground, a number of them terminate against the watershed, which is sometimes marked by a similar earthwork. The effect was to create a whole network of narrow land blocks, defined by roughly parallel ditches, approximately a kilometre apart. These 'strip' territories were not unlike the historical parishes in the same area, or the smaller estates that seem to have preceded them in other parts of Wessex (Taylor 1970, 49–72). One important feature of this layout is the way in which the ditches extend from the higher parts of the chalkland into the major river valleys, for this provides some answer to the argument that the archaeology of the Wessex Downs is biased towards the uplands. Despite the problems created by the later use of the valleys, these land units cut right across the grain of the country. In Christopher Taylor's terms, they are represented equally in the 'zone of survival' and the 'zone of destruction' (1972).

This layout resembles the arrangement of strip parishes, and both could have allowed an equitable division of resources (cf Ellison and Harriss 1972, 941–59). A further implication has been overlooked until recently. Since settlement sites survived best outside the areas of medieval landuse, there was a tendency to think of these boundaries in terms of the exploitation of the uplands, when they are better described as forming separate valley-based territories. This mistake is understandable, but it was especially unfortunate considering that J R Mortimer had already defined rather the same pattern on the Yorkshire Wolds (1905, 365–80). Again, the major linear ditches conform very closely to the local topography, following the edges of the valleys and dividing them from the higher ground (Fig 2). Some of the principal boundaries had developed on a monumental scale. Exactly the same arrangement has now been identified by Don Spratt

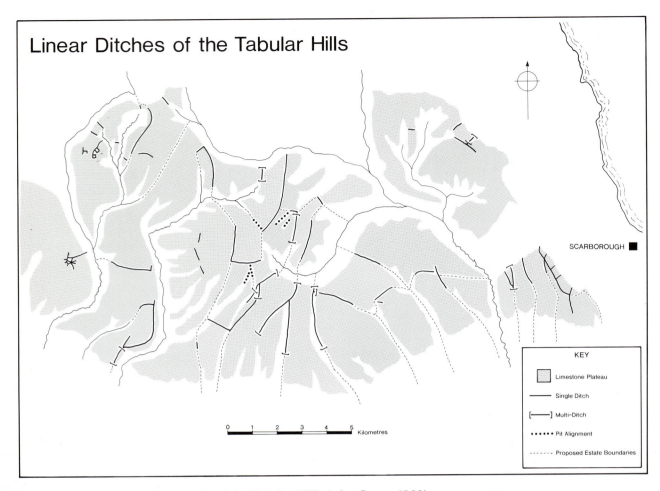

Fig 5   Linear ditches and territories of the Tabular Hills (after Spratt 1989)

in his study of the dyke systems on the opposite side of the Vale of Pickering. Here, a series of earthworks define long narrow territories running down into the lowlands (Fig 5), and once again this has a precise counterpart in the medieval pattern of land division (Spratt 1989). A rather more distant parallel may also be provided by the watershed reaves of Dartmoor (Fleming 1988).

Such studies reveal the essential coherence of early boundary systems, which are too often broken down into a series of separate field monuments, divided from one another by areas of later destruction. Spratt's work, which combines air survey and ground observation, is a model of what could be achieved elsewhere in northern England. By emphasising the logic that lies behind the placing of the dykes, he has moved the discussion on from an account of boundary earthworks *per se* to the study of complete territories. It is only at this level that there can be much prospect of relating such material to the broader pattern of settlement.

Even so, there is something of a disparity between detailed studies of the surface evidence and the results of excavation. On the Yorkshire Wolds, where at least an outline chronology is available for the dyke system, the overall configuration of these earthworks has not been analysed on a large enough scale, and Mortimer's ideas have yet to be followed up by systematic fieldwork. The same applies to the programme of air photograph analysis undertaken by the Royal Commission (C Stoertz pers

comm). By contrast, on the Tabular Hills, Spratt has provided an attractive model of prehistoric territorial organisation, which does justice to the complexities of the surface evidence, but, in this case, the dykes themselves are virtually undated. His scheme still needs to be followed by a programme of excavation. Without that source of evidence, Spratt is forced to date his earthworks by analogy with those in Wessex (1989, 12).

At present, there has been only one project to achieve a satisfactory balance between these two approaches to the archaeology of linear earthworks. This is the work of Ford on the Berkshire Downs (1982a and 1982b), an area where these features had been largely neglected after the pioneering observations of O G S Crawford. Working on a small scale, Ford was able to follow the course of the linear earthworks on the ground. Once again, he identified a series of valley territories, defined by linear ditches running along or just below the watershed (Fig 6). One of these earthworks ran up to an Early Iron Age hillfort, Uffington Castle. At the same time, Ford recorded the distribution of all the surface artefacts along the course of the earthworks, and also in a narrow zone to either side of them. This allowed him to select a number of targets for more detailed examination in the field. In some places, it seemed as if these earthworks bounded scatters of occupation debris, while in others there were sufficient artefacts in the modern ploughsoil to suggest suitable locations for small-scale excavations.

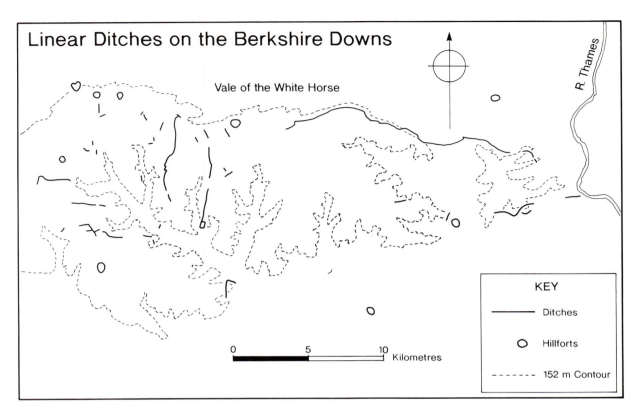

Fig 6   Distribution of linear ditches on the Berkshire Downs (after Ford 1982a)

In each case, the strategy was the same: to relate the use of the earthworks to a range of datable artefacts and environmental evidence. Taken in combination, these methods allowed him to reconstruct the basic configuration of a series of valley-based land units and to suggest that they had developed during the Late Bronze Age. A subsequent study of the coaxial field systems in this area showed them to originate in the Roman period (Ford *et al* 1988). This overturned an earlier claim by this writer that they were cut by a linear ditch (Bradley and Ellison 1975, 185).

Some implications of prehistoric land boundaries

It seems ironic that, when Ford's work was published, it appeared to be a special case. The valley territories did not immediately recall the evidence from other parts of Wessex, and the absence of Middle Bronze Age pottery was completely unexpected. So too was the inversion of the anticipated sequence, with coaxial field systems and evidence of ploughwash both postdating the establishment of the boundary system. This was particularly surprising, since his work concluded that 'Celtic' field systems had overridden the earlier land boundaries. At the time, it seemed possible that these findings were exceptional, as the Berkshire Downs were towards the edge of the distribution of linear ditches. Perhaps the system had been adopted later than in other areas and had never achieved its full development.

With the benefit of hindsight, Ford's conclusion may have had a more general application than he claimed. Deverel-Rimbury pottery is very rare on the Berkshire

Downs, and the development of these earthworks in the Late Bronze Age would be consistent with the wider sequence of settlement. In the same way, the argument that a major coaxial field system was cut by one of the linear ditches depended to some extent on the evidence of air photography, but much more on analogy with the 'accepted' sequence in areas further to the south.

It is precisely because such orthodoxies are so hard to uphold that the emergence of land boundary systems has been difficult to accommodate in wider interpretations of British prehistory. This chapter began with the assertion that the later Bronze Age witnessed a gradual transformation of the landscape, combined with new developments in settlement and landuse. But every attempt to interpret the building of land boundaries in terms of this general framework rapidly runs into difficulties, for none of the basic questions can be answered.

Some of the problems concern chronology. When did the linear ditch system first emerge? The evidence is extremely slight, and what exists is rather ambiguous. Apart from the unusual results from the North Kite, close to Stonehenge (Richards 1990) – on any account, an exceptional part of the landscape – the earliest finds are of Deverel-Rimbury pottery, but their precise status is in doubt. Are the artefacts from the Martin Down linear ditch contemporary with its use, or could they be residual? Is the linear ditch on Boscombe Down East contemporary with the Deverel-Rimbury enclosure, or is it a later feature? Should any of the ditches at Easton Lane, Winchester, be considered as part of this system, and, if so, which of them? It is necessary to retreat from the rather specific chronology suggested in the literature, and to place more weight on the terminal dates indicated by excavation and survey at early hillforts. Even then, the problems are not resolved. If Hawkes's excavation at Quarley Hill suggested that some of the ditches were built before the hillfort, the boundary system obviously continued in use after its construction, as a further ditch was excavated to link the new defences to an existing earthwork nearby. In the light of such observations, it becomes more uncertain than ever how long such land divisions remained in use. In short, a critical review of the dating evidence for linear ditches in Wessex does nothing to contradict the results of Ford's survey, but nor does it demand the same chronology. It is uncertain when the system was established and how long it continued to be important.

Precisely the same is true of the earthworks in other areas. The earliest of those in Sussex is associated with a Globular Urn (Curwen and Curwen 1917, 57–8), but other examples seem to be of the same general date as early hillforts (Bradley 1971). Similarly, in Yorkshire there are sherds of Late Bronze Age pottery from a very small number of earthworks, but they seem to have maintained their role in the landscape at least as late as the middle years of the Iron Age (Manby 1980; Dent 1982, 447–56). We have already seen how Spratt dates the dyke system on the Tabular Hills by analogy with the evidence in Wessex; it may be equally injudicious to compare the evidence from these two areas of the chalk. The process is no more acceptable than the enthusiastic espousal of territorial models developed on Dartmoor by those working in quite different areas. Chronological connections must be demonstrated and not assumed.

Such questions remain fundamental to an understanding of later prehistory, but there are many gaps in our information. Was the adoption of linear ditches part of the same reorganisation as the widespread adoption of 'Celtic' fields, or do these represent two different phases of landscape history? Here, there is scope for fundamental differences of opinion, but very little evidence to deploy. Recent work has certainly shed light on the origins and operation of Deverel-Rimbury settlements and field systems, but this work has taken place in regions where linear earthworks are uncommon. Moreover, the developments traced in that research often came to an end during the Middle Bronze Age (Barrett et al 1991, 228). Those who favour the idea that linear ditches evolved during the same period as the early 'Celtic' field systems emphasise the finds of Deverel-Rimbury pottery from some of these earthworks, and those instances in which the ditches seem to bound areas of arable land (Bradley 1978b, 46–8). In other cases, they stress the complementary distribution of fields and enclosed areas of unploughed ground (Appelbaum 1954). The basic suggestion is the same: that 'Celtic' fields and linear ditches were adopted together as part of a wider intensification of mixed farming. The ditches were not necessarily 'ranch boundaries', but they can still be taken as evidence of large areas of enclosed grazing land. This system of land allotment forms the basis for a period of sustained agricultural growth, epitomised by the gradual development of fortified food stores (Gent 1983).

This argument is tempting, but its opponents contend that it overlooks real evidence of discontinuity. The field systems, they argue, may be partly a Middle Bronze Age development, but there is little to show that linear ditches were widely distributed during this period, and in the best studied areas with concentrations of Deverel-Rimbury field systems and settlements, such earthworks are rare or absent (Barrett et al 1991, chaps 5 and 6). At the same time, local landuse had slackened or ceased well before the Iron Age. They also emphasise those cases in which linear ditches can be seen to cross older field systems, putting them out of use (Bowen 1975 and 1978). The number of instances of this relationship can be exaggerated, but its existence cannot be denied. It has two serious implications: that linear ditches may have been established after 'Celtic' fields and that the two were not necessarily used in combination. Instead of stable mixed farming, they postulate drastic change.

If these suggestions are right, there may be little continuity between the Middle Bronze Age impact on the landscape and the adoption of boundary systems, but a much closer link between the division of that landscape and the development of hillforts. Again the argument can extend in several directions. Does the abandonment of certain areas of 'Celtic' fields indicate an increased emphasis on livestock, as the very term 'ranch boundary' suggests? If so, how closely were the earliest hillforts implicated in the large-scale management of animals? While it might be tempting to see the accumulation of livestock as one of the factors favouring the growth of elites (Cunliffe 1990), it is easy to forget that hillforts are virtually absent on the Yorkshire Wolds where a similar boundary system developed.

An alternative reading of the same evidence would stress the distinctive layout of the linear ditches system in Yorkshire as well as Wessex, comparing the valley-based territories in both areas with the land units of the post-Roman period. These were not connected with large-scale stock raising, but seem to have allowed communities to secure an equal share of different agricultural resources, from damp meadowland on the lowest ground, through areas of well-drained arable, to tracts of upland pasture. If this analogy is correct, the development of the prehistoric boundary system is more consistent with the existence of stable mixed farming, and perhaps with growing pressure on land. Again, this view has been suggested in the literature (Appelbaum 1954). It would be easy to link this argument with the evidence for protected food stores in some of the earliest hillforts (Gent 1983). The case is quite attractive, but it fails for lack of evidence.

Each of these competing arguments is important. If the British landscape really was organised earlier and more thoroughly than comparable parts of the Continent, these components of the archaeological record are a valuable resource and should be investigated further. Hawkes may well have been right to suggest that the Wessex linear ditches were among the oldest land boundaries in Europe, but, half a century after his words were written, we seem no nearer to understanding the significance of these earthworks. Yet, while we have been prepared to agree on their exceptional history, research has lost its momentum and much of our raw material has been destroyed. That is why a new approach was necessary. It was essential to improve our understanding of prehistoric land boundaries and to use that understanding to secure the proper management of what still survives.

2 The selection of a study area

by Richard Bradley

Introduction

In Chapter 1, we emphasised how the work of the Cranborne Chase Project had depended to a considerable extent on the evidence of surviving earthworks. This made it possible to reinterpret Pitt Rivers's 'pastoral enclosures' and to see them as part of a landscape that included areas of 'Celtic' fields. We also saw how our studies of linear ditches systems would be most productive where selective excavation could be linked to a programme of survey and topographical analysis.

On the other hand, there is a major contrast in the circumstances under which the two projects took place. In Cranborne Chase, elements of the Bronze Age landscape survived because they had been incorporated in medieval hunting forest and had escaped later agricultural damage. In other parts of Wessex, however, extensive traces of prehistoric land divisions remain intact only in those areas of Salisbury Plain used for military training. Although these earthworks lasted into recent centuries through their siting in upland pasture, the current landuse regime has had two quite separate effects: it has ensured the survival of earthworks that might otherwise have been ploughed out, but it has also exposed them to a threat that is rarely experienced by archaeological sites. The agencies involved include damage by tracked vehicles, building operations, large-scale earthmoving, and the disturbance of numerous infantry trenches. The extent of the problem has been reviewed already in a recent report (Canham and Chippindale 1988).

Our study of territorial divisions in prehistoric Wessex took place for two distinct reasons. First, their interpretation posed a whole series of problems that would need to be addressed if we were to understand the reorganisation of landuse during later prehistory. At the same time, our inability to account for these earthworks set limits on our prospects of ensuring their continued survival. It is a paradox that is not uncommon in modern archaeology. Archaeological features may be managed so effectively that they are secured from damage, but in some cases they are also secured from understanding. Unless they can be explained, however tentatively, their protection is difficult to justify to those who own them. Small-scale disturbance by archaeologists themselves may be essential, if these monuments are to be interpreted at all. The threat to archaeological monuments in a military training area raises this problem in acute form. As large areas are controlled by a single authority, it may be possible to arrange for their careful management, but conservation issues are necessarily subordinate to military considerations. Only when we can present a reasoned case for the national or international importance of particular parts of the landscape can a productive dialogue take place.

There is a further issue to consider. It is clear that much of the Wessex linear ditches system has been destroyed by agriculture since the pioneering work of Christopher Hawkes. Part of the area that he studied in such detail has changed its character entirely, and some of the earthworks that could once be followed on the ground must now be mapped from the air (Palmer 1984). If features of this kind were to be carefully managed, it would be necessary to include the evidence in cultivated areas, as well as those earthworks that still survive above ground. This is particularly important as small areas of military training land are ploughed every few years.

Thus, the project had two requirements to fulfil: to provide an academic assessment of the character and importance of the Wessex linear ditches and to investigate their present condition, so that plans could be made for their selective management in the future.

Criteria for choosing a study area

The choice of an appropriate study area required a delicate balance between these different elements. It seemed essential to select a region in which the cultivated land ran right up to a zone where earthworks still survived, thus allowing the nature of agricultural destruction to be assessed. At the same time, it was equally important to select a study area with a reasonably varied topography. Earlier research, both in Berkshire and in parts of Yorkshire, had shown how closely the layout of prehistoric territories exploited the lie of the land, resulting in the creation of narrow land units, incorporating contrasting topographies. We could lose a vital clue to the logic behind these systems if we worked in an area that lacked significant topographical contrasts. Indeed, that may be why Hawkes had defined such a coherent series of land divisions in the Bourne and Avon valleys, when all semblance of order was lost on the chalk plateau further to the east, where natural features imposed fewer constraints on how the land was organised (cf Hawkes 1939, fig 1 and Bowen 1978, fig 2).

There seemed every reason to build on the results of the most rewarding work of our predecessors. This was important for two reasons. They had been able to carry out their research in a landscape where far more of the evidence survived above ground. For that reason, it was likely that a greater proportion of the prehistoric layout could be studied than in areas in which we would be working from the evidence of air photography. Earlier generations had been able to record the original character and setting of the ditches, as well as their relationship to features that no longer survive above ground. At the same time, they had already carried out small-scale excavations. Often the results were limited or even ambiguous, but their records could be combined with those of fresh fieldwork, and, in some cases, the structure of earthworks that had lacked any finds of artefacts might still be drawn into a more general interpretation. The same applied to recent work recording threatened

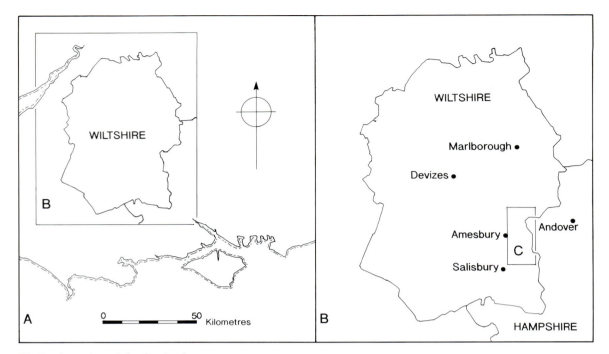

Fig 7   Location of the Study Area

sections of earthwork. In most cases, dating evidence was lacking, but environmental data were available (for instance, Bellamy 1992 and Arnold 1972). In order to use this framework, we wished to select an area with suitable deposits for molluscan analysis.

It was also important to choose a study area in which the main kinds of settlement were already known, for it was outside the brief of this project to indulge in large-scale excavation. Given our uncertainty about the chronology of the linear ditches, that evidence had to be both of Bronze Age and Iron Age date. While a large number of Iron Age settlements had been excavated on the Wessex chalk, Bronze Age settlement excavations tended to concentrate in a few small areas. The decision to select a region with a long history of fieldwork was important for another reason, for we did not wish to construct an artefact chronology of our own. It was essential to locate the study area in a region where that was established already. For the Bronze Age, it posed a quite significant problem, although there were a series of radiocarbon dates for the large urnfield at Kimpton (Dacre and Ellison 1981). The fullest pottery sequence for an Iron Age site in Wessex came from the hillfort at Danebury (Cunliffe 1984b), and it was necessary to remain within the distribution of the main ceramic styles represented at that site, while avoiding any overlap with the work of the Danebury Environs Project.

In Chapter 1, we emphasised how the study of boundary systems depended as much on the relationships between different earthworks in the field, as it did on the dating of finds from excavation. For this reason, it was very important to work in a region where such relationships were widely available. The main ones to consider were those between linear ditches and barrows, field systems, enclosures, and hillforts. Naturally, those would be most apparent in the grassland of the Military Training Area, but it would be unrealistic to suppose that a representative sample would survive. In view of this,

we also needed to consider an area with good quality air cover.

In some ways, that last criterion was decisive, for in the region that had already been studied by Christopher Hawkes a unique combination of sources was available. Some of the surface earthworks had been mapped by Crawford, Stone, or Hawkes, while others had been surveyed in greater detail by the Salisbury office of the Royal Commission on the Historical Monuments of England. Indeed, their brief had extended recently to selective surveys in the Salisbury Plain Military Training Area. At the same time, a study of the archaeology of that area had been completed, which included the plotting of all the available air cover (Wilkinson 1986). In turn, that could be complemented by Palmer's analysis of air photographs over a wide region extending westwards from the River Test as far as the edges of Salisbury Plain (1984). Consequently, when the Wessex Linear Ditches Project began its work, we already had an overview of the archaeological record in the very area in which linear ditches had received most attention from our predecessors. At the same time, there was the prospect of linking our own fieldwork to analytical survey of selected earthworks by the Royal Commission.

The location and character of the Study Area

The area that fulfilled all of our requirements was defined by a transect of approximately 21 by 11km (Fig 7), stretching from just north of Salisbury and terminating at the SU 54 northing. This encompassed a tract of land of about 231 sq km, bounded by Quarley and Sidbury hillforts. It also incorporated the valleys of two major rivers, the Bourne and the Avon, as well as the upper reaches of the Nine Mile River (Fig 8). The watersheds

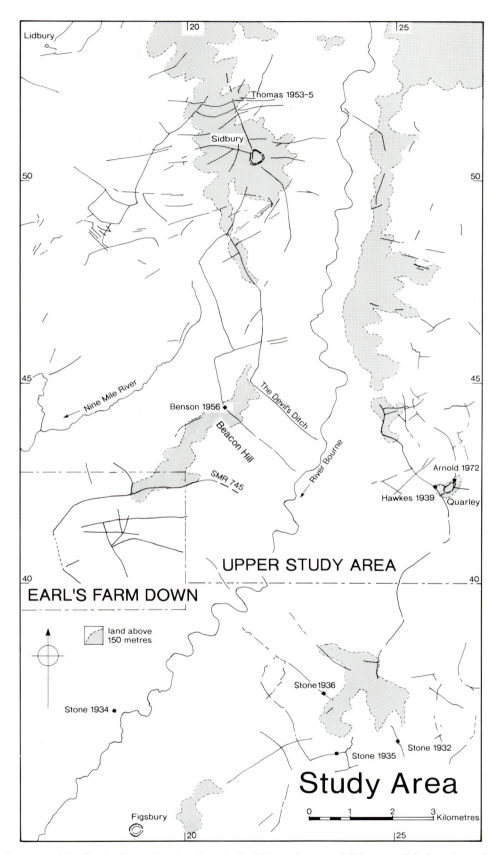

Fig 8   Distribution map of the Study Area, showing the principal linear features, hillforts, and the locations of earlier excavations; the dashed lines mark the boundaries of the Upper Study Area and Earl's Farm Down (for details of Benson's excavation of SPTA 2061, see N Thomas 1956)

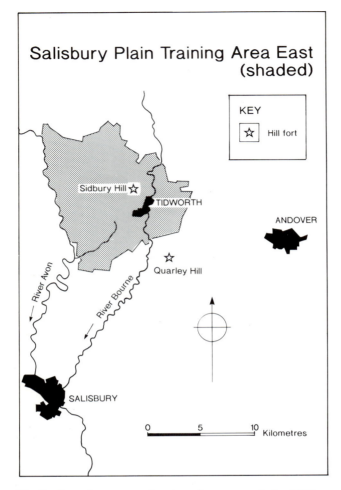

Fig 9   Location map, showing the extent of the Military Estate of Salisbury Plain East which also corresponds to the area of ancient, unploughed grassland mentioned in the text

in between them follow a north-west alignment, with a series of spurs running down towards the floodplains. The main ridges are generally between 150 and 200m above sea level, while the valley floors are at heights of less than 100m. The solid geology is Upper Chalk, capped over limited areas by Clay-with-Flints and Plateau Gravels. In areas of long established farmland, many of the dry valleys contain variable depths of colluvial soil over mixed deposits of periglacial drift material. In the river valleys, alluvial deposits are generally of limited extent, especially to the north of Amesbury where the floodplains are confined by steep-sided valley ridges.

The Study Area sampled both the modern ploughland and tracts of ancient grassland which still survive in the Military Estate of Salisbury Plain East (Fig 9). In a number of instances, boundary earthworks could be traced across both these zones, and their surviving remains could be compared directly. At the same time, the Study Area incorporated the main region previously examined by Hawkes (1939). It contained a number of his valley-based territories and included two of the nodal points in the system that had been occupied by hillforts: Quarley Hill and Sidbury Hill. As we shall see, that meant that the Study Area crossed a region of varied topography, extending from the high chalk down into the river valleys. The precise placing of the transect was

based on the distribution of field monuments, as it seemed important to maximise the number of potential relationships with hillforts. For that reason, the Study Area was initially selected to take in the following sites: Quarley Hill, Sidbury Hill, Lidbury, and Figsbury Rings. The first three of these were known to be linked directly to the linear ditches system, and, in the event, they were studied in preference to Figsbury Rings. Both Lidbury and Sidbury Hillfort were surveyed by the Royal Commission during the period of the project.

An important consideration that had influenced our choice of study area was the existence of a rich and varied archaeological record. Not all the earlier discoveries can be given the same weight, or are likely to have an impact on our understanding of linear ditches. What follows is therefore a selective account of what is known.

Earlier Neolithic developments are of limited relevance to this project. There are a considerable number of long barrows in the region, but none have been investigated in modern times. The nearest long barrow to be excavated to an adequate standard is at Fussell's Lodge, just to the south of the Study Area (Ashbee 1966). There are also two groups of flint mines, at Easton Down and Martin's Clump. The Easton Down mines have been fully published, but provide only one radiocarbon date (Stone 1931), while work at Martin's Clump was published only in summary form (Ride and James 1989). As we shall see, our own work provided evidence for the extraction of flint nodules from superficial deposits at a number of other locations. Again, axes were being made there, but the dating evidence is inadequate.

The evidence for later Neolithic activity is hardly more extensive. Two sites – Easton Down and Winterbourne Dauntsey – are associated with finds of Peterborough Ware, while there may be two henge monuments at opposite ends of the Study Area. One such site, at Everleigh (SU 20635260: SPTA No 2252), is largely ploughed out (Harding and Lee 1987, 292), while the identification of a similar earthwork below the later hillfort at Figsbury Rings depends on reinterpreting an unsatisfactory excavation report (Guido and Smith 1982). In the absence of recent fieldwork, neither can be treated with complete confidence. Some additional evidence of later Neolithic activity is attested at Snail Down by the discovery of Grooved Ware sherds from a phase of pre-barrow occupation (Thomas and Thomas 1956).

In fact, it is only with the appearance of Beaker pottery that the archaeology of the Study Area takes on a distinctive character. Most unusually, two sites produced evidence of Beaker domestic structures. Again, those at Easton Down have been fully published. They consist of a number of chalk-cut hollows, surrounded by rings of stakeholes; a rectangular trench-built structure, originally dated to the Neolithic, probably belongs to the same phase (Stone 1933a and 1935). The other domestic site was on Snail Down, where large numbers of stakeholes, associated with Beaker pottery, were sealed below later round barrows. These have yet to be published, but they do not seem to have formed any obvious pattern (N Thomas pers comm). The other clue to the character of domestic activity is provided by possible ploughmarks recognised below round barrows on Earl's Farm Down, but these are not closely dated (Christie 1964, 33 and 1967, 347).

Like those in other parts of Wessex, the round barrows of the Study Area have been extensively excavated, but only rarely is it possible to relate the obvious signs of disturbance to any published account or specific grave-goods. This limits our chances of dating individual mounds. On the other hand, parts of two large barrow cemeteries have been excavated in modern times, and both exhibit a complex sequence of activity extending from the Beaker period throughout the Early Bronze Age. Excavations on Earl's Farm Down are published in full (Christie 1964 and 1967), while the results of more extensive work at Snail Down have yet to appear in final form (Thomas and Thomas 1956). Older work is less informative. A number of the barrows on Bulford, Brigmerston, and Figheldean Downs were excavated by Colonel Hawley at the beginning of the century (Hawley 1910), and others belonging to the Silk Hill group have also been investigated, although the results of that work are not known in any detail (Grinsell 1957, 183–4). The only flat cemetery of Early Bronze Age date was again on Easton Down (Stone 1933b).

The Middle Bronze Age is represented by two enclosures and a major urnfield. The enclosure at Thorny Down was completely excavated (Stone 1941) and has been reanalysed recently by Ellison, using unpublished records showing the distribution of artefacts around the site (1987). Although it lacks a substantial earthwork, it can probably be compared with the enclosure on Boscombe Down East, which is also associated with Deverel-Rimbury pottery (Stone 1936). As we saw in Chapter 1, this enclosure may well have been cut by a linear ditch. The burial record has also benefited from the publication of the cremation cemetery at Kimpton, one of the largest of its kind in Britain. Dacre and Ellison (1981) recognised a complex sequence of deposits on this site and linked this to a series of radiocarbon dates. Secondary burials of the same general period were found in the barrows explored by Colonel Hawley, in particular those on Brigmerston and Figheldean Downs (Hawley 1910).

As so often in Wessex, the Late Bronze Age presents something of a lacuna (Piggott 1973). There is a small quantity of bronzework from the Study Area, notably the important hoard from Figheldean Down (Coombs 1979) and a complete sword from the hillfort of Figsbury Rings (Cunnington 1925, 50), but the only evidence of domestic activity comes from sites of the Late Bronze Age/Early Iron Age transition. The best known of these is Lidbury hillfort (Cunnington and Cunnington 1917).

On the other hand, Iron Age activity is represented very widely. Iron Age pottery has often been recovered in settlement excavations (Palmer 1984, 15–18), and a high proportion of the cropmark enclosures are likely to be of this date (ibid, 22–6). Major rescue excavations have been undertaken in the Study Area close to Amesbury and Quarley (A Lawson pers comm), and, just outside its limits, a whole series of enclosed settlements were recorded during the expansion of Andover (Dacre pers comm). One of these, at Old Down Farm, has now been published (Davies 1981). Open settlements are much more elusive, but they are represented by the wartime excavation at Boscombe Down West, which involved observation and recording over an area of more than 50ha (Richardson 1951). Among the features observed on the site was a double-ditched enclosure comparable to a small hillfort. Two lesser known enclosed sites are those of Chisenbury Trendle and the concentrically ditched enclosure on Coombe Down. Chisenbury Trendle was levelled in 1931 by the RAF, and the only dating evidence we have is the Early Iron Age pottery from beneath its bank (Cunnington 1932). Recent excavation has shown that the Coombe Down enclosure began life during the Middle Iron Age. Other hillforts have been examined on a limited scale at Quarley Hill (Hawkes 1939), Figsbury Rings (Cunnington 1925), and Lidbury (Cunnington and Cunnington 1917). While Boscombe Down West was occupied late in the Iron Age (Richardson 1951), these other sites seem to have been built at a much earlier date.

The Upper Study Area and the survival of archaeological evidence

Within the broadly defined landscape of the Study Area, our work focused mainly on a sample area with its southern boundary running between Quarley Hill and Amesbury, taking in the Bourne Valley and the eastern margin of the Avon Valley. The northern limit of the transect was positioned so as to incorporate the Lidbury enclosure and the full northern extent of the Sidbury ditch system, including Snail Down where some investigation of linear ditches had already taken place (Thomas and Thomas 1956). This region, which has been designated the Upper Study Area (Fig 10), also embraced two of the main watersheds, the lesser known basin of the Nine Mile River, and several of the spurs that Hawkes had taken to define his valley-based territories. These characteristics influenced the decision to concentrate our attention on the Upper Study Area, but perhaps the single most important factor was that this area exhibited the most coherent pattern of linear ditch territories. This can be seen most clearly in the area between the Bourne Valley and Dunch Hill, where two adjoining blocks of land are delineated by a well-preserved layout of ditches. Partly because of their uniquely cohesive appearance, and for other reasons that are discussed in Chapter 7, these two areas are referred to as the Northern and Southern Core Territories (Fig 10).

Certain additional features came to influence the planning of the project, and all supported the decision to concentrate on this particular part of the Study Area. These elements included both excavated and surface evidence. The body of excavated material had been augmented recently by the work of the Trust for Wessex Archaeology during the widening of the A303 trunk road between Andover and Amesbury (Bellamy 1992). This crossed the full extent of the Upper Study Area, on roughly the same line as the major land boundaries extending between Quarley Hill and the Avon Valley. Although this work included mostly settlement excavation, a further contribution was made by molluscan analysis where the road cut through elements of the linear ditches system (Allen 1992). At a more general level, we would also be in a position to make direct comparisons with the major landscape study of the Stonehenge Environs, only a short distance to the west

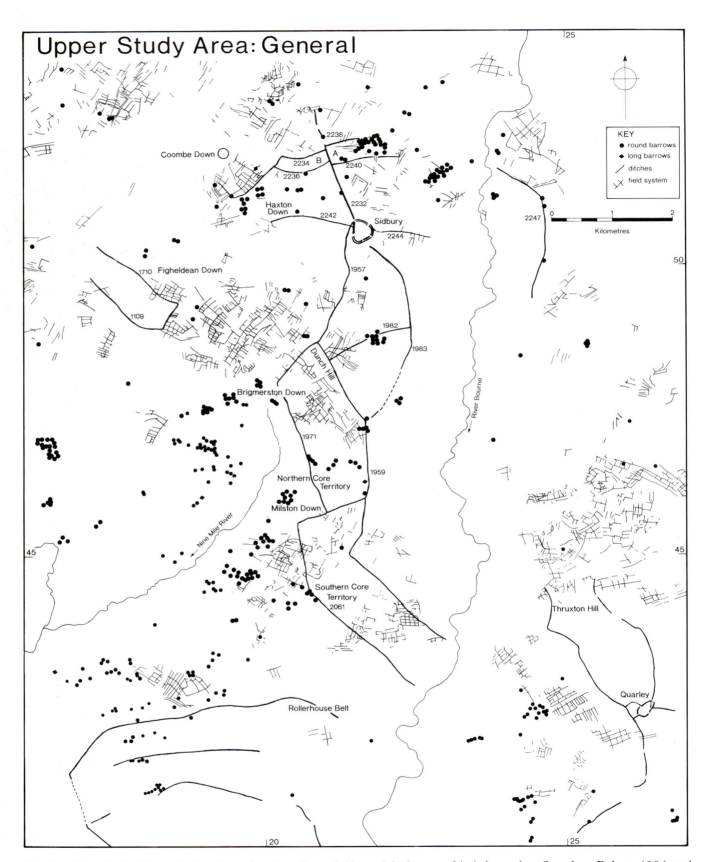

Fig 10   Map of the Upper Study Area, showing all available aerial photographic information (based on Palmer 1984 and Trowbridge overlay) and the location of Thomas's enclosures A and B on Snail Down, just to the north of Sidbury Hill (N Thomas forthcoming)

Fig 11   A view eastwards across the Tracked Vehicle Training Area south of Sidbury Hill; this shows the most extreme example of the type of damage caused by concentrated vehicle activity

of our own Study Area (Richards 1990). In the Military Estate itself (Fig 9), areas of arable land had been examined already by members of the Salisbury Plain Conservation Group, with the result that some knowledge of artefact distributions was available to us. Examination of their discoveries, together with field-walking undertaken as part of this project, revealed an unexpectedly high proportion of prehistoric pottery. In contrast to the material recovered outside the Military Training Area, these ploughsoil assemblages were the product of very few episodes of cultivation, and even the more friable prehistoric fabrics survived. This has implications that are discussed in Chapter 3.

The region combines two areas with radically different patterns of landuse – the Training Area to the north-west with extensive tracts of ancient downland and, to the south and east, areas that have been under cultivation for many centuries. In view of the enhanced preservation in the Military Estate, this area was the focus for much of the excavation programme, while the majority of surface collection sites were concentrated in the surrounding farmland. This juxtaposition of contrasting landuse patterns had an important influence on the formulation of our field methodology and, as we shall see in the following chapter, it also had important implications for the interpretation of our results.

The archaeology of this area may be remarkably rich, but, at the same time, it is subject to the unusual pressures posed by military training. Set against this, there are substantial parts of the Training Area where earth-

works survive on a more extensive scale than anywhere else in Wessex. Only in limited areas was the destruction on such a scale as to rule out the possibility of fieldwork. The most serious damage has been caused by tracked vehicle exercises, and in places this has resulted in the complete destruction of linear earthworks, barrows, and especially the more vulnerable features such as field systems (Fig 11). Barrows in particular seem to have presented an irresistible challenge for tank crews on exercise, and as a result they have suffered severe damage. Some mounds have been truncated or levelled, while others have been cut about by the movement of tracked vehicles. An extreme example of this kind can be witnessed between Weather Hill and Haxton Down, where the mound of SPTA 2191 has been bisected in two directions by vehicle damage over many years. Several of the barrows on Snail Down have been severely disfigured in the past and, even though this important barrow cemetery is now protected, erosion still occurs from time to time. In the past, Sidbury Hillfort has experienced similar damage (Fig 12), although gravel and clay extraction has also contributed to its mutilated condition. Military use of the site has simply continued the process of destruction. The northern flank of the hill has been disturbed by the excavation of seating terraces, built in order to provide a viewpoint for the Everleigh Dropping Zone, and modern afforestation has increased the damage to the slighter earthworks associated with the hillfort.

Fig 12   A view of Sidbury Hillfort from the east, showing the extent of military damage and the locations of the double linear (A) and the Sidbury West Linear Ditch (B–B) (reproduced by courtesy of the RCHME)

More widely across the Training Area, numerous trackways have cut deeply into field systems and other features, and, where these intersect, large areas of topsoil and chalk have been churned up. However, perhaps the most common form of damage is caused by infantry trenches. Although these are usually quite small, they are particularly destructive, because the most favoured locations are often the slight hollows or embankments of standing earthworks.

While the scale of this damage is alarming, it needs to be seen in perspective. Large numbers of standing monuments still survive, even if they have suffered sporadic disfigurement. The effects of this are devastating for the smaller monuments, such as barrows or enclosures. For the more extensive features, such as linear ditches and field systems, it is less of a problem, for the scale of them ensures that significant parts of the original pattern will survive.

Unfortunately, we cannot be so sanguine about the condition of archaeological sites in other parts of the Study Area, where arable cultivation has had a more uniformly destructive effect. Within the Training Area, this has been less of a problem, and there are large tracts of ancient downland that have so far escaped long-term or intensive ploughing. The situation is not as stable as it might appear, however, and over the last few decades there has been a steady encroachment from farmland on the edges of the area. This seems to have affected the Eastern Training Area most, but for the time being little of the interior is ploughed and, apart from a few isolated examples, arable fields are mostly confined to the margins of the main river valleys.

With the exception of a few small pennings, the grassland that once characterised the area is now mostly ungrazed, allowing thorn scrub to flourish quite widely. Along with the scrub regeneration and the persistence of some old woodland, afforestation has reduced further the amount of open ground. This aspect of the Training Area has had important implications, for it means that air survey has not been able to establish the full extent of surface features because of the patchwork of woodland or scrub. Even in open grassland, the lack of grazing pressure means that for most of the year slight features, such as ditches and lynchets, are hidden by dense vegetation. In the following chapter, we will return to these issues, to illustrate how ground survey, combined with augering and geophysical work, has filled in many of the gaps in the linear ditches system and revealed further relationships with other standing earthworks. Obviously, conditions in the Training Area are varied, and they have affected the survival and visibility of archaeological features in different ways. Nevertheless, this unique landscape offers opportunities for enhancing the archaeological record that have few parallels in any other part of Wessex.

On the other hand, archaeological research in the Training Area is no easy matter. The timing and location of fieldwork were often dictated as much by the military training schedule, as they were by the project timetable. Consequently, certain areas have been studied in less detail than others. One such is that around the spring line of the Nine Mile River, which lies within the danger area behind the Bulford Rifle Ranges. Access to this part of the Training Area is extremely limited and extended fieldwork was almost impossible. Nonetheless, in the short time available to us, we were able to establish that this part of the landscape had been a major focus of Bronze Age activity. This was an important discovery in itself, but it sheds very little light on an area that deserves to be studied more thoroughly than was possible during the course of our fieldwork. Such restrictions necessitated a flexible approach to the fieldwork, and inevitably this was not always in accordance with our research design. Yet, despite these constraints, much has been accomplished, and it would not be an exaggeration to say that the research in the Training Area has proved to be the key to our understanding of the linear ditches system.

Outside the Military Training Area, the major limitations on fieldwork were those more familiar to archaeologists: the annual cycle of cultivation, planting, and harvesting; the existence of areas masked by colluvial or alluvial deposits; and, just occasionally, difficulties in obtaining access to agricultural land. If these limitations were of the more familiar kinds, so too was the condition of the archaeology. Legal provisions for the protection of earthworks in modern farmland have largely failed to achieve their objective, and very few now survive above

ground. Over large areas, most linear ditches can be recognised only as soilmarks, though in exceptional circumstances a few stretches are preserved as standing earthworks. The most notable example is the Devil's Ditch, which survives above ground because it forms a part of the Hampshire–Wiltshire county boundary (Fig 8). Other ditches, such as SMR 745 (Fig 8), are preserved where they have been protected by old woodland, and, in this particular instance, that chance survival provided the only incontrovertible evidence for the double banks, which have been destroyed elsewhere. It was mostly in these areas that fieldwalking was employed to identify artefact concentrations, which could be used to target stretches of ditch for subsequent excavation. However, in some areas this strategy was defeated by the recent introduction of agricultural 'set aside'. During the period of our fieldwork, this had not drastically reduced the amount of land available for surface collection, but it did affect certain areas of particular importance to the study quite by chance. It was especially unfortunate that extensive areas of farmland between Beacon Hill and the Bourne Valley had been taken out of cultivation, since this denied us the opportunity to examine the interior of the Southern Core Territory (Fig 10).

As we have seen, there are important contrasts between the landuse history of the two parts of the Upper Study Area. This has profound implications for the nature of the evidence from each zone, and, although this introduced difficulties from the point of view of comparison, it did have certain advantages. In fact, the two parts of the Upper Study Area complemented each other rather well. In the areas of intensively cultivated farmland, it was possible to gain an overview of prehistoric land divisions, by using a surface collection strategy that had a limited application in the old grassland of the Training Area. However, in that area we were able to trace the full extent of some of the linear ditch territories on the ground and to investigate relationships between standing earthworks by excavation. Although the relative distribution of excavation and surface collection sites was a function of this pattern of modern landuse, sufficient fields were walked in the Training Area to provide a comparable sample. This has demonstrated that the area preserves not only standing earthworks, but also a remarkably intact prehistoric pottery distribution, which no longer survives elsewhere. Although the information recovered from sites in areas of modern farmland is important, it is the sheer quality of the evidence from the Training Area that makes it so exceptional, and, for that reason, it became the principal focus of our study. The development of that study is described in the following chapter.

3 The development and application of the field methodology

by Roy Entwistle

Introduction

The general design of the field methodology developed for the Linear Ditches Project was centred on a programme of selective fieldwalking and small-scale sample excavation. Within the Study Area, there exists a broad topographic division between areas of long-standing arable land to the south and east, and extensive tracts of ancient pasture mostly confined to the Military Estate of Salisbury Plain East (Fig 9). This contrasting landuse pattern determined the relative distribution of surface collection and excavation sites. In some instances, restricted access or unconducive land-use did prevent the implementation of the basic field strategy, and consequently a greater reliance was placed on geophysical and auger surveys. Additionally, it was envisaged that these ancillary techniques would provide a rapid and efficient method for determining the character of linear features when time constraints prevented more detailed investigation.

A number of the surface collection sites were devoid of artefacts relevant to the period of this study and are consequently mentioned only briefly in the main text. Likewise, many of the excavated sites failed to produce datable artefacts and are chiefly of interest insofar as they preserved evidence for recutting and variation in ditch morphology. In order to present the fieldwork results with greater clarity, we have restricted our discussion to a selected number of sites, where the stratigraphic, chronological, or spatial information is of particular relevance to the development of major themes. Table 27 (Appendix 1) contains a complete list of all the surface collection sites along with the grid references and SPTA or SMR notations. Corresponding details for the excavation sites are listed in Table 28 (Appendix 1). Context records, plans, and section drawings for all of the sites excavated during the Linear Ditches Project are included in the archive, which will be lodged at Devizes Museum.

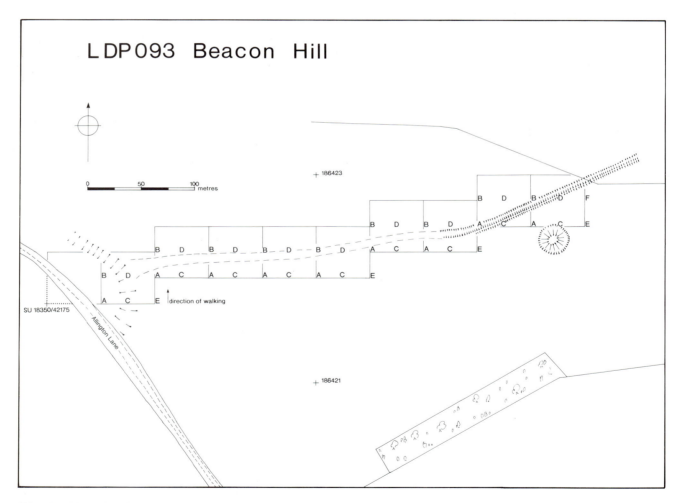

Fig 13   Plan of surface collection site LDP 093, illustrating the layout of a typical fieldwalking grid

Surface collection

The methodology employed for surface collection was based on the system devised for the Stonehenge Environs Project (Richards 1984; 1990), but it differed in one important respect. The fieldwalking undertaken during the Linear Ditches Project was not intended to provide an extensive landscape cover. Instead, it was employed to locate surface artefact concentrations adjacent to linear features and thus provide a means of 'targeting' potential excavation sites. The value of this approach had been demonstrated by research on the Berkshire linear ditches (Ford 1982a), and accordingly it was adopted as a preliminary survey technique.

Since this involved covering comparatively limited areas, it was decided to substitute a 50m grid for the more usual hectare unit. Each square was subdivided into 25m collection units, and the entire grid was set out along the axis of the linear earthwork (Fig 13). The arrangement of squares was aligned on the National Grid using 1:2500 scale Ordnance Survey maps. The direction of walking was always across the axis of the soil mark, either from south to north or west to east. Recording of finds was by 25m collection unit except for sherds of pottery, which were plotted individually on the standard field forms. This provided a more refined level of spatial control for the most chronologically sensitive artefact class.

Most of the surface collection sites were concentrated in a region of the Study Area that has been cultivated more or less continuously since the medieval period, and this is reflected in the composition of the pottery assemblages. Predictably, the destructive effects of ploughing over many centuries has had a considerable influence on sherd size and on the survival rate for different fabrics. Some of the more friable prehistoric pottery will have been broken down by mechanical impact and frost exposure, leaving a survival pattern that may owe as much to taphonomy as to deposition.

Generally, the amount of Romano-British pottery is proportionally greater in surface collection assemblages from outside the Training Area, and some fields, notably LDP 019 on Earl's Farm Down (Fig 14), have produced substantial quantities (Table 1). Although the survival potential of these harder fabrics is in part responsible for their widespread occurrence, it is perhaps an oversimplification to attribute the relative distribution of prehistoric and later pottery to taphonomic variables alone. Nonetheless, we must conclude that the pottery distribution revealed by surface collection outside the Training Area is considerably biased in favour of the harder and later fabrics. Yet, despite the attrition of prehistoric pottery in areas of long-term intensive cultivation, a residual pattern does remain, which, in conjunction with other artefact distributions, still has considerable potential for interpretation.

Within the boundaries of the Military Training Area, arable cultivation is limited, but, where it does occur, it is relatively recent and has been less intensive than in other parts of the Study Area. This has resulted in an exceptionally high preservation rate for prehistoric pottery, and, consequently, there is a much greater scope

Table 1 The quantity and date of pottery recovered from surface collection sites outside the Military Training Area (percentages represent proportions of the total weight of sherds from each site)

LDP code	no sherds	wt sherds (grams)	date range
001	9	54	IA (37%); RB (63%)
002	7	48	IA (33%); RB (67%)
003	47	299	RB (6%); AS/Early Med (94%)
004	1	23	RB
008	26	174	LBA (2%); IP (3%); RB (95%)
009	3	22	IP (82%); RB (18%)
010	2	26	Late RB
011	2	13	RB
012	2	6	LBA (50%); RB (50%)
015	1	3	RB
016	5	19	RB
017	22	140	EBA (13%); DR (31%); LBA (42%); IP (14%)
018	6	25	LBA (4%); IA (24%); RB (72%)
019	193	1374	EBA (1%); DR (1%); LBA (1%); IA (4%); IP (4%); RB (89%)

Key: EBA = Early Bronze Age; DR = Deverel-Rimbury; LBA = Late Bronze Age Plain Ware; IA = Iron Age; IP = indeterminate prehistoric; RB = Romano-British; AS/Early Med = Anglo-Saxon to Early Medieval

Table 2 The quantity and date of pottery recovered from surface collection sites within the Military Training Area (percentages represent proportions of the total weight of sherds from each site)

LDP code	no sherds	wt sherds (grams)	date range
075	25	215	EBA (7%); IA (18%); RB (75%)
080	79	529	DR (4%); LBA + ACC (90%); IP (6%)
081	147	725	LBA (99%); IP (1%)
102	73	423	EBA (1%); DR (18%); LBA (79%); IP (2%)
103	156	792	EBA (1%); DR (5%); LBA (84%); IP (10%)
104	1	8	LBA
108	7	48	DR (46%); LBA (52%); IP (2%)
109	59	473	EBA (4%); DR (46%); LBA (42%); IP (8%)
111	14	75	EBA (5%); LBA (94%); IP (1%)
112	507	3547	EBA (1%); DR (6%); LBA + ACC (88%); IA (1%); IP (3%); RB (1%)

Key: EBA = Early Bronze Age; DR = Deverel-Rimbury; LBA = Late Bronze Age Plain Ware; LBA + ACC = Late Bronze Age Plain Ware, including Early All Cannings Cross as a minor component; IA = Iron Age; IP = indeterminate prehistoric; RB = Romano-British

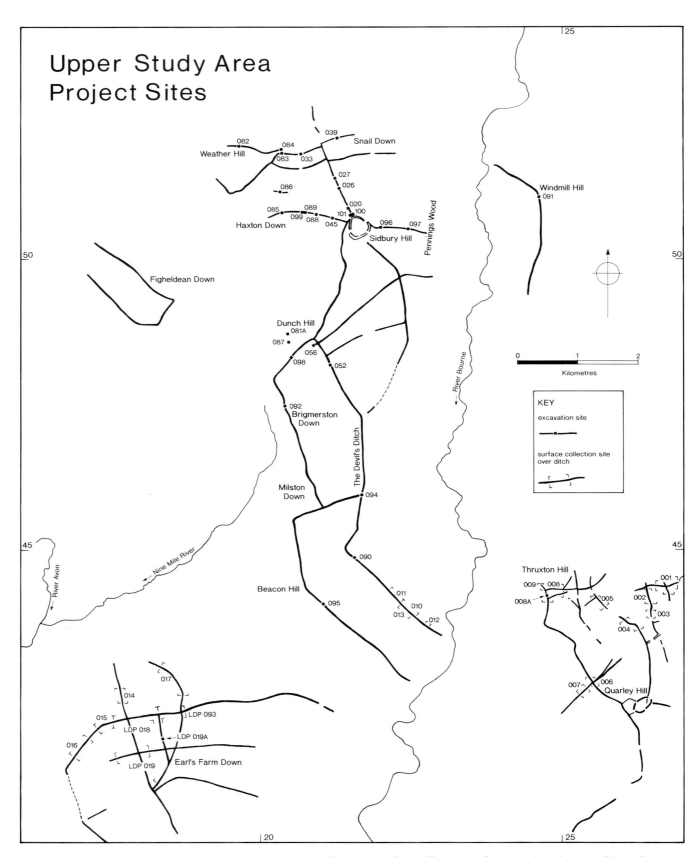

Fig 14   The Upper Study Area, showing the location of all project surface collection and excavation sites over linear features

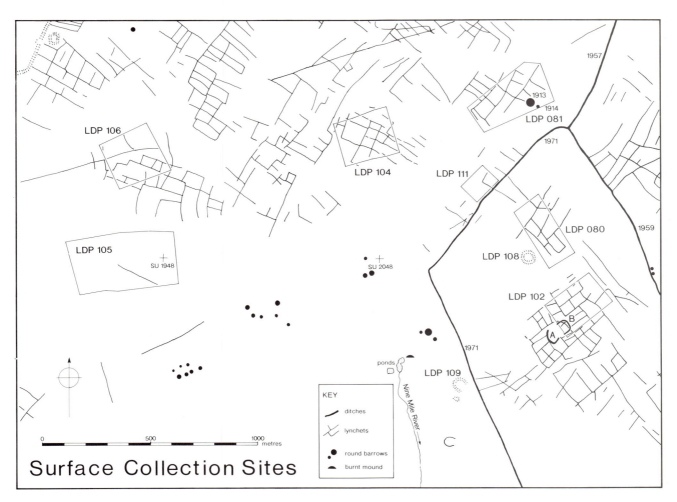

Fig 15   Map of the Dunch Hill and Brigmerston Down area, showing the location of surface collection sites LDP 080, 081, 102, 104, 105, 106, and 111, including associated enclosures, 'Celtic' fields, and soil mark sites A and B (numbers without the prefix LDP refer to the SPTA records)

for recovering settlement patterns. The recognition of this remarkable potential led to an extension of the surface collection strategy to include the interior of the Northern Core Territory (Fig 10) and a number of other fields outside (Fig 15). The pottery assemblages recovered from these areas are consistently Late Bronze Age, with Early Bronze Age, Deverel-Rimbury, Iron Age, and Romano-British sherds forming only a minor component (Table 2).

There can be little doubt that the distribution of pottery in the Military Training Area represents a uniquely coherent picture of the relative density of settlement and landuse throughout the prehistoric and Romano-British periods. This is abundantly clear even from the limited investigations conducted by the Linear Ditches Project. Yet, so far this enormous potential for landscape archaeology has not been evaluated. In almost all respects, we can only guess at the full extent of this important resource and hope that any future agricultural encroachment or change in training practice will be closely monitored.

In areas where the predominant pattern of landuse has involved long-term or intensive cultivation, it is often the distribution of more durable material, such as worked and burnt flint, which is the most ubiquitous source of evidence for prehistoric activity. However, since most of

the flint assemblages from these areas have a limited application to the study of linear ditches, it was not envisaged that detailed analysis would form part of the post-excavation programme. This material has been deposited with the site archive, along with field recording forms and annotated copies of the 1:2500 Ordnance Survey maps.

Even so, certain general observations can be made. Against a background of more subtle variation, two surface collection sites were distinguished both by the quantity of struck flint recovered and by a preponderance of cortical flakes, cores, and 'tested nodules'. Of these two unusually prolific sites, one is located within a relict Clay-with-Flints deposit on Thruxton Hill (LDP 008), and the other (LDP 012) is on the gravel terrace of the River Bourne near Cholderton (Fig 16). Both are located on relatively accessible sources of flint, and the composition of the assemblages indicates a long period of exploitation. On the basis of this admittedly superficial appraisal, the Thruxton Hill and Cholderton sites conform to the criteria set out in the Stonehenge Environs Project to define procurement/reduction sites (Richards 1990).

Thruxton Hill is one of a number of procurement sites spreading in a discontinuous pattern along the eastern margin of the Bourne Valley (Fig 16). One such example

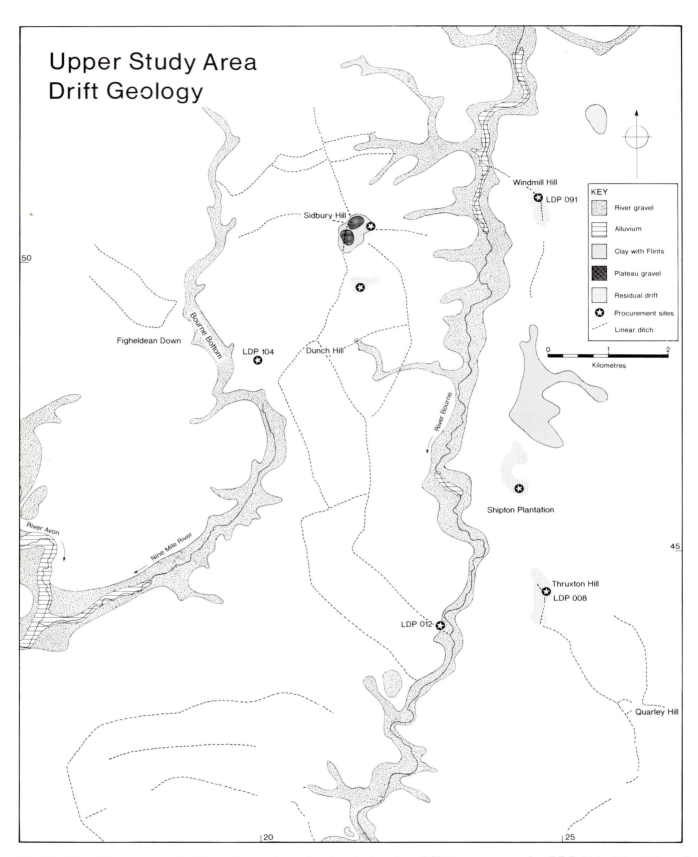

Upper Study Area
Drift Geology

KEY

River gravel

Alluvium

Clay with Flints

Plateau gravel

Residual drift

Procurement sites

Linear ditch

Windmill Hill

LDP 091

Sidbury Hill

Figheldean Down

Bourne Bottom

LDP 104

Dunch Hill

River Bourne

Shipton Plantation

River Avon

Nine Mile River

Thruxton Hill

LDP 008

LDP 012

Quarley Hill

0   1   2

Kilometres

Fig 16   The drift geology of the Upper Study Area, showing the location of flint procurement sites LDP 008, 012, 104, and those near Shipton Plantation and on Sidbury Hill

Table 3   The distribution of burnt and worked flint from the Dunch Hill and Brigmerston Down surface collection sites (values are for numbers of pieces, expressed as percentages of the total assemblage)

category	LDP 104		LDP 102		LDP 080		LDP 081		LDP 081A	
	no	%	no	%	no	%	no	%	no	%
burnt	36	12	219	48	37	34	32	51	60	26
unburnt	266	88	241	52	71	66	31	49	171	74
totals	302	–	460	–	108	–	63	–	231	–

is the extensive flint scatter near Shipton Plantation, at SU 243461, which revealed a similar range of material to the Thruxton Hill and Cholderton sites. These sites are known only from limited observations made at intervals along the ridge as far north as Tidworth, but all are situated on eroded Clay-with-Flints. The excavation at LDP 091 on the northern edge of this distribution, at SU 24645104, produced quite large quantities of struck flint from the buried soil and the ditch. The only diagnostic elements of the assemblage were a flaked axe fragment from the buried soil and a complete example from a shallow feature cut into the secondary ditch silts.

This pattern of exploitation has its counterpart to the west of the Bourne Valley, on Sidbury Hill. The summit of the hill is crowned with a superficial deposit of Tertiary gravels and Clay-with-Flints and, at several points close to the hillfort, clay and gravel extraction has exposed large quantities of struck flint; from one of these disturbances, at SU 21835053, a broken, flaked axe and several discarded rough-outs were recovered. In 1957, a section through the inner hillfort rampart close to the south-east entrance produced a small flint assemblage, including a large, flaked axe and two rough-outs (SMR No SU25SW101; Megaw 1967). Further to the south, at SU 217495, another extensive area of flint working was discovered during the current project, but it was not investigated because it lies within the Tracked Vehicle Training Area (Fig 11). Even allowing for the cursory nature of this evidence, there seems little reason to doubt that Sidbury Hill and other locations along the margins of the Bourne Valley were important sources of flint for local communities over a long period. We can be certain that they were exploited from at least as early as the Neolithic, and, in all probability, their use continued into later prehistory.

In other parts of the Military Training Area, concentrations of burnt and worked flint were recovered in association with unusual amounts of Late Bronze Age Plain Ware pottery. This offered the opportunity to examine flint assemblages which were unambiguously linked to a well-defined period of settlement. Four of the surface collection sites, representing three settlements (LDP 080, 081, and 102), and a procurement site in the vicinity of a settlement (LDP 104), together with one excavation site (LDP 081A) were chosen for closer study. The analysis of this material (discussed in Chap 5) sets out to answer a number of specific questions relating to the chronology of the sites, and the identification of technological characteristics which might serve to distinguish between domestic and procurement activity.

In broad landscape terms, other surface collection studies have shown that concentrations of burnt flint might be a useful guide to the location of prehistoric and Romano-British activity (S Lobb pers comm; Richards 1990). With this in mind, the material was gathered, weighed, and counted as part of the standard collection procedure. At the level of the individual site, the value of this exercise is demonstrated by the correlation between burnt flint and Late Bronze Age pottery concentrations at Dunch Hill and on Brigmerston Down (Table 3 and Fig 17). In the Stonehenge area, a similar correspondence was noted in the ploughsoil assemblages from the Middle to Late Bronze Age settlement adjacent to Fargo Wood (Richards 1990, 196).

This relationship is a strong indication that settlement sites are represented and that the patterns recovered are not merely the product of manuring practices or random sampling biases. The point is made graphically in Figure 18, which shows the disparity between the amount of burnt flint recovered from the procurement site (LDP 104) and the three settlement sites. The difference is less pronounced in the case of LDP 081A, but this might be explained by taphonomic factors. LDP 081A was a partly intact domestic midden. Consequently, it represents a more discrete sequence of deposition than the surface collection assemblage from the surrounding area (LDP 081), where the superficial patterning has become blurred. However, despite the caveats that necessarily predicate comparisons of this kind, there remains a marked distinction between domestic and procurement sites in terms of the ratio of burnt to worked flint.

Referring to Figure 17, we can see that a spatial correlation also exists between the concentrations of burnt flint and pottery at two of the settlements. It is unlikely that all of the burnt flint recovered from these sites belongs to the same periods as the pottery, but the marked correspondence between the patterns strongly suggests that the bulk of the material is contemporaneous.

There are of course many objections to the general application of such observations. Rarely can we assign concentrations of burnt flint to a single period, and there are activities not connected directly with settlement that can generate large quantities of burnt flint – 'burnt mounds' provide the most obvious evidence of this. However, from the point of view of the present study it is the correlation between the burnt flint and pottery distributions that is most significant. We are able to use this as a means of distinguishing between in situ settlement debris and other practices that may have given rise to pottery accumulations, such as the use of domestic refuse to manure fields.

Manuring has been cited as the chief origin for much of the prehistoric pottery recovered in association with 'Celtic' field systems (Fowler 1983). This view overlooks the possibility, however, that some, if not all of this

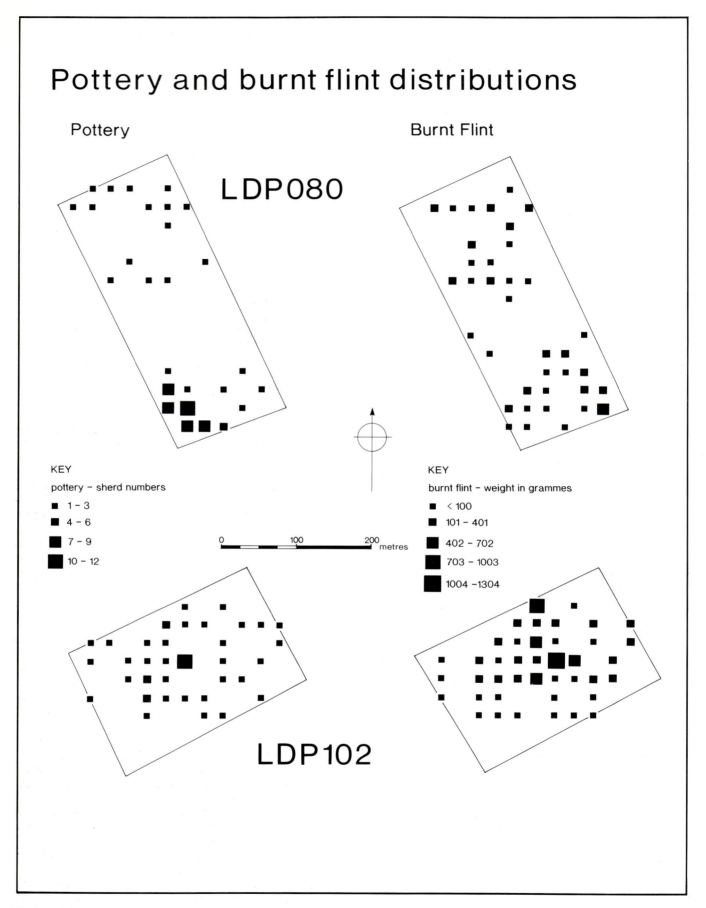

Fig 17   Comparative distributions by number of Middle to Late Bronze Age pottery and burnt flint from surface collection sites LDP 080 and 102

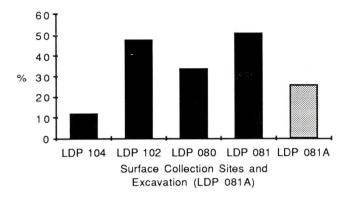

Fig 18 Histogram showing proportions by number of burnt flint recovered from Dunch Hill and Brigmerston Down sites

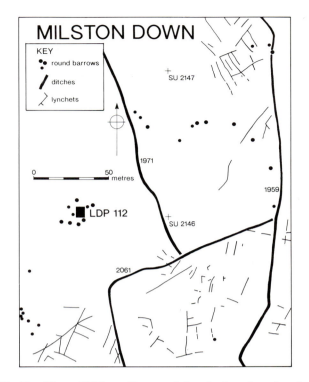

Fig 19 Plan of Milston Down, giving the location of surface collection site LDP 112

material may be residual, being incorporated into the ploughsoil of later fields by the ploughing of earlier settlement sites. The presence sometimes of considerable quantities of burnt flint along with pottery appears incongruous, if this debris resulted from manuring alone. It seems unlikely that, in an area where soils are often naturally flinty, farmers would choose to add even more flint to their fields. Far from being evidence of the innovative character of late prehistoric farming (Fowler 1983), the concentrations of burnt flint and pottery associated with field systems preserved in the Upper Study Area are almost without exception from ploughed-out settlement sites.

Viewed retrospectively, a greater emphasis on surface collection might have contributed significantly to our understanding of the late prehistoric settlement pattern. Unfortunately, logistical constraints were imposed by the small labour force and the recognition that many questions could only be answered satisfactorily by an extended programme of excavation. Nonetheless, despite its limitations, the evidence from fieldwalking has provided a valuable insight into the changing patterns of landuse and settlement associated with the development of the linear ditches system.

Miscellaneous artefact collections

Numerous casual finds were discovered and recorded during the course of the fieldwork and, when relevant, these are discussed in the appropriate part of the text. A detailed catalogue of casual finds has been included in the SMR enhancement document, which summarises all the results from the Linear Ditches Project.

The resurfacing of the Old Marlborough Coach Road in 1989, which runs across Weather Hill and Haxton Down (Fig 14), and a military trackway just north of Sidbury Hill in 1990 provided an opportunity to examine areas which had previously been unavailable for study. Aside from the potential for artefact recovery, the topsoil stripping also enabled the investigation of several linear features exposed during the course of the work. For the most part, these were shown to be hollow-ways, and consequently they can be usefully eliminated from the overall layout of the linear ditches system.

Further exposures have been created by tracked vehicle exercises, which, although limited, enabled us to

make some assessment of the extent of known artefact scatters, such as the Late Bronze Age settlement on Dunch Hill. Finally, during the winter of 1989/90, gale-force winds uprooted many trees in the Training Area and, in effect, created an extemporary series of test-pits. The survey of fallen tree hollows was particularly informative in the Dunch Hill area, where substantial quantities of pottery were recovered (LDP 103). Another survey to the east of Sidbury Hill, in Pennings Wood (Fig 14), gave some indication of the extent of Late Bronze Age activity around LDP 097. Very few sherds were recovered from this survey, but they were sufficient to establish the northern and eastern limits, if not the intensity, of this activity.

Fieldwalking undertaken by members of the Salisbury Plain Conservation Group since the early 1970s has generated a considerable quantity of pottery. It is mostly Romano-British, but the collection does include a sizeable assemblage of Middle and Late Bronze Age sherds from Milston Down (LDP 112: Fig 19). Although this material was recovered by systematic collection, the technique used is not compatible with the strategy employed by the Linear Ditches Project. In consequence, the results have been presented in tabular form, according to period (Table 4), instead of by the more usual distribution plan. The positions of the collection units on which the table is based are shown in Figure 20. Members of the Conservation Group also recovered pottery from the enclosure on Brigmerston Down (LDP 109). Subsequently, during the project fieldwork, a small collection of pottery was recovered from the surface of a second enclosure near Brigmerston Plantation (LDP 108). Although small, these assemblages are particularly important, since they represent the only dating evidence from these two sites (Fig 21).

Table 4   The number of sherds and the date range of pottery recovered from surface collection site LDP 112 (indeterminate fabrics are not included)

				run				
	A	B	C	D	E	F	G	unprov
period								
EBA	–	–	–	–	–	–	–	5
DR	–	7	3	2	–	2	1	11
LBA	22	57	124	28	8	1	3	191
IA	–	–	–	–	–	1	–	2
RB	1	–	2	–	–	–	–	–
Totals	23	64	129	30	8	4	4	209

Key: EBA = Early Bronze Age; DR = Deverel-Rimbury; LBA = Late Bronze Age Plain Ware; IA = Iron Age; RB = Romano-British

Aerial photographic information

A study of the various photographic collections was not undertaken as a part of this project. There were two reasons for this. First, the existing information transcribed on the 1:10,000 scale SMR maps provided a comprehensive and up-to-date record of linear features within the Study Area. Gaps in the existing transcription were created mostly by woodland, extensive military disturbance, or by modern trackways, and in these instances surface survey was the only practicable means of recovering the 'missing' elements. Second, in certain areas a complex palimpsest of Iron Age and Romano-British fields lies over the ditch system, with the result that the original layout is obscured by a confusing pattern of lynchets and trackways. Such complexity is decipherable only at ground level, and indeed the application of elementary survey techniques was found to be a very effective method for clarifying these relationships.

Geophysical survey and augering

In the face of this complexity, we relied extensively upon surface survey techniques to eliminate spurious ditches and, by this means, we were able to refine the pattern of territorial boundaries. As a result of this work, a number of linear features are now known to be hollow-ways. Their removal from the overall distribution has allowed a very much simpler pattern to emerge, which now shows a closer correlation with the local topography. But, in addition to eliminating spurious ditches, we were also able to fill in gaps in the distribution. This was achieved by tracing the course of ditches that had been obscured by the palimpsest of Iron Age and Romano-British fields mentioned previously.

A fluxgate gradiometer was available to the project, but the effectiveness of magnetic survey was reduced by interference from considerable metallic contamination of the soil within the Training Area. For that reason, all of the geophysical evaluations undertaken were based upon resistivity measurement. Initially, these surveys

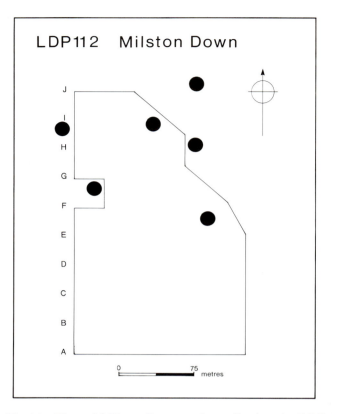

Fig 20   Plan of Milston Down surface collection site LDP 112, showing the arrangement of collection units (based on information provided by the Salisbury Plain Conservation Group); the round symbols represent round barrows

were employed in an attempt to compile a series of comparative resistance profiles, which could be used to distinguish between hollow-ways and ditches. For a number of reasons, this proved to be less helpful in practice than in theory. Although the solid geology throughout the Study Area is chalk, there is wide variation in the extent and composition of superficial drift deposits. In some instances, this made the interpretation of individual surveys quite difficult, and it also added considerably to the problems of making comparative evaluations. These difficulties were often exacerbated by the formation of positive lynchets in association with many linear features, which in a number of cases resulted in a considerable accumulation of flinty colluvium. Consequently, with the exception of certain specific resistivity evaluations, the majority of surveys were backed up with auger traverses, which invariably produced more conclusive results.

Although augering was used primarily to supplement the programmes of fieldwalking and excavation, it was employed independently to investigate stretches of the linear ditches system that were not targeted for excavation. This technique proved invaluable in the Military Training Area, where excavation was limited mainly to the reopening of military trenches. Largely because of this restriction, none of the linear features in the extensive network on Figheldean Down could be sectioned, and consequently they were characterised entirely by augering (Fig 10, SPTA Nos 1100, 1109, 1126, and 1710). The results of this survey showed that the northern extension of SPTA 1710 and 1126 are in fact

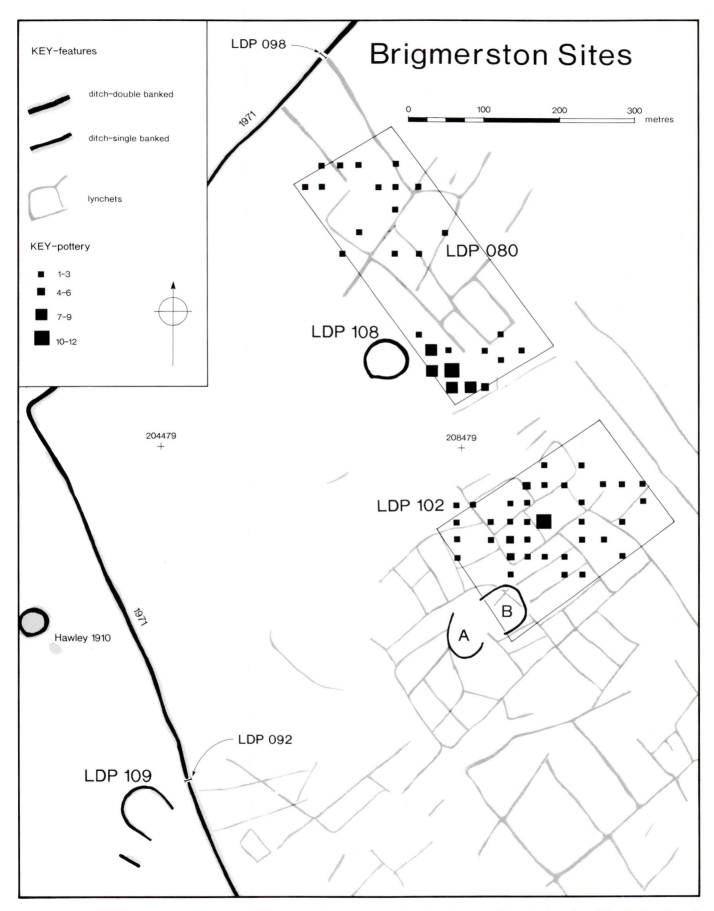

Fig 21   Plan of Brigmerston Down with the position of enclosures LDP 108 and 109, soil mark sites A and B, the location of the excavations LDP 092, 098, and surface collection sites LDP 080 and 102, showing the relative density and distribution of Middle to Late Bronze Age pottery; the ploughed-out enclosures A and B are shown in Fig 76

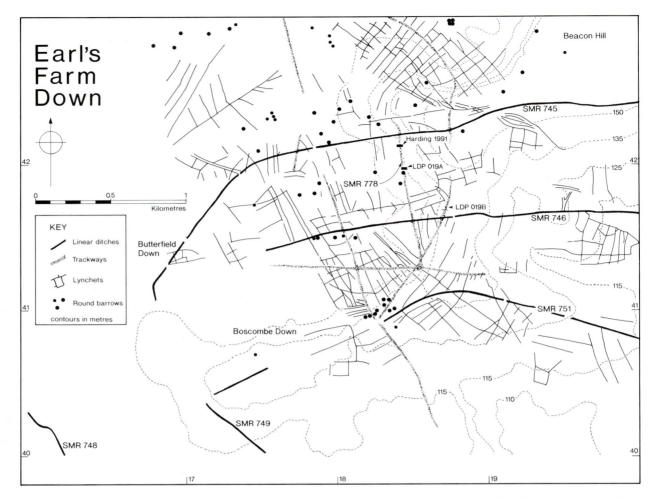

Fig 22   'Celtic' fields and linear features on Earl's Farm Down, with the location of the Trust for Wessex Archaeology site (Harding 1991) and LDP sites 019A and 019B

trackways and that the only ditches in the network are SPTA 1100, 1109, and 1710. These form the boundaries of an enclosed area stretching between Bourne Bottom and Figheldean Down (Fig 16).

Resistivity and auger surveys were used successfully to unravel the confusing arrangements of linear features on Earl's Farm Down (Fig 22), where excavation (LDP 019A) had demonstrated that at least one of the major soilmarks in the network was a trackway (SMR 778). A subsequent excavation of this feature by the Trust for Wessex Archaeology revealed a shallow ditch 0.78m deep and 1.3m wide, which did not appear in the section at LDP 019A (Harding 1991). The most likely explanation for this discrepancy is that SMR 778 was a boundary ditch associated with the field system and that for only part of its course was it paralleled by the trackway. Although linear ditches tended to show a stronger correlation with aspects of local topography, this was not a sufficiently reliable basis for distinguishing between these features and hollow-ways. Moreover, surface appearances are often very misleading, especially in cultivated areas, where ploughing soon erodes the sharper ditch profiles and fills hollow-ways with colluvium. To add to these difficulties, further confusion can occur when trackways have developed along the course of an earlier ditch, as for example to the north of Sidbury Hill, where the trackway SPTA 2131 (Thomas and

Thomas 1956, site IX) runs into ditch SPTA 2234. This creates an entirely misleading impression from the air and on the ground. The excavations at Lain's Farm, just to the north-east of Quarley Hill, illustrate the point particularly well. Here, a linear feature appeared on aerial photographs, and on the ground, to be more like a substantial hollow-way, but, on excavation, it proved to be a small 'V'-shaped ditch only 0.55m wide and 0.35m deep (Bellamy 1992).

However, by using a combination of augering and geophysical survey on Earl's Farm Down, it was possible to isolate the network of trackways, leaving a residual pattern of linear ditches which closely resembles the layout between Dunch Hill and the River Bourne (Fig 23). The trackways appear to be related to a concentration of Iron Age and Romano-British settlements, including the excavated site at Boscombe Down West (Richardson 1951), and an extensive 'Celtic' field system (Fig 24). Like many similar field systems in the Study Area, it is later than the linear ditches and presumably belongs, at least in its most developed form, with the accumulating evidence for widespread Romano-British cultivation in and around the Training Area.

From a methodological point of view, the survey on Earl's Farm Down highlights the potential for misinterpreting superficial patterns, especially in areas where these exist only as soilmarks. Yet, the difficulties of

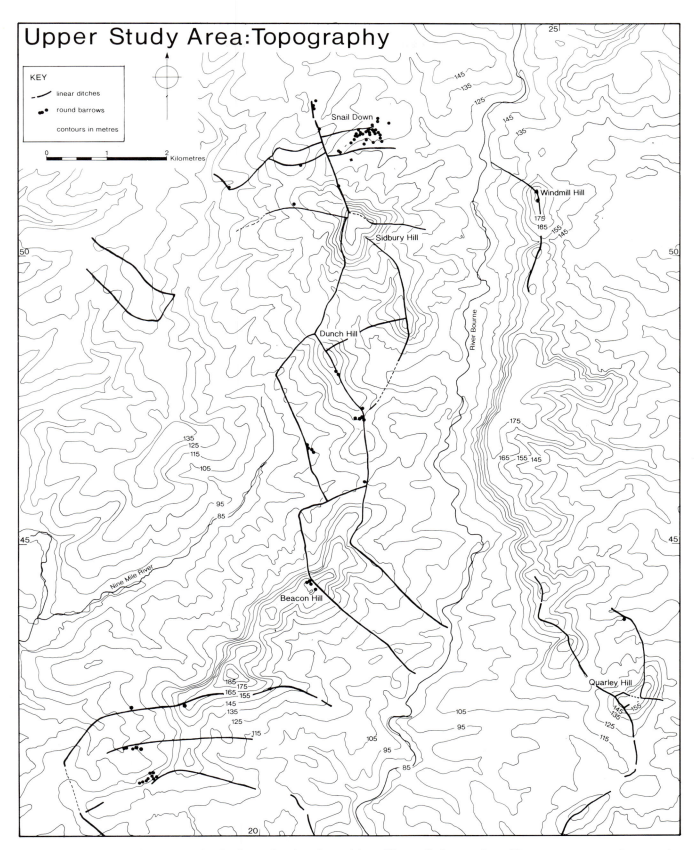

Fig 23   Topography of the Upper Study Area, showing the position of linear ditches confirmed by auger survey and excavation; the round barrows shown in this figure are those directly associated with the boundary ditches

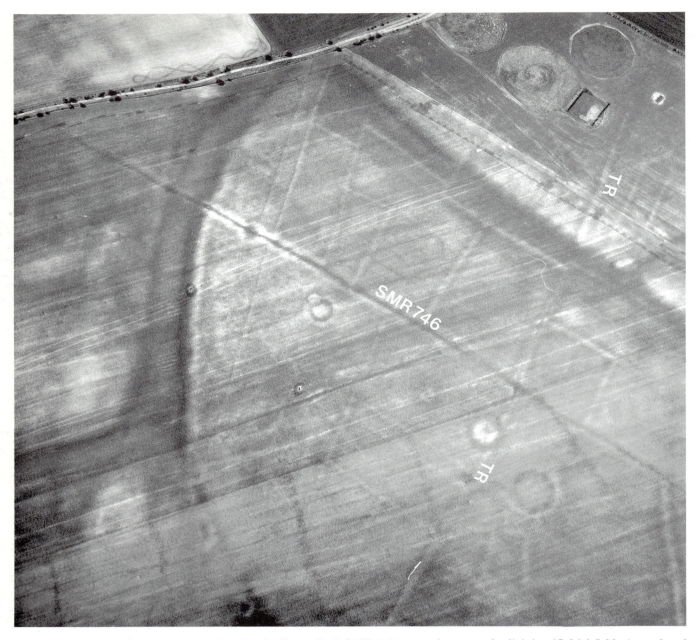

Fig 24   Part of Earl's Farm Down, showing the linear ditch SMR 746, a trackway, and adjoining 'Celtic' fields (reproduced by courtesy of the RCHME)

distinguishing between ditches and hollow-ways are often just as formidable, where both survive as extant earthworks. Even the presence of a bank, or banks, accompanying a linear feature may prove to be an unreliable guide to the nature of the earthwork. Hollow-ways sometimes appear to be flanked by single or double banks, possibly created during periodic resurfacing of the rutted trackway, and, in some instances, the prior existence of a ditch and bank along the same course introduces further complications.

The relationship of ditch SPTA 1957 to Sidbury hillfort was another important question which could not be answered adequately by excavation. No military damage was recorded along the course of the earthwork north of Dunch Hill, and, on the southern flank of Sidbury Hill, it was obscured in places by the lynchets of a field system. An aerial photograph taken in 1968, before the

flanks of the hill were planted with conifers, showed traces of a ditch running from the south along the western scarp of the hill (Fig 25). Several auger traverses were made across the projected alignment, and the course of the ditch was established as far as the western outworks of the hillfort (Fig 26). Having demonstrated that SPTA 1957 reaches the hillfort, we can argue with some confidence that it is in fact the same ditch that represents the penultimate phase of the sequence revealed at LDP 101 (Cut 2A: Fig 31). This is important from the point of view of the overall development of the territorial layout, for it establishes a physical link between the Sidbury–Snail Down system and the Northern Core Territory. Originally, SPTA 1957 may have been joined by the Sidbury West Linear Ditch (SPTA 2242), close to SU 21475067, but the junction is no longer visible.

The Sidbury East Ditch (SPTA 2244) was traced by

*Fig 25   Sidbury Hillfort looking towards the southwest, showing the Sidbury Double Linear SPTA 2232 (A) and linear ditches
SPTA 2242 (B) and 1957 (C) (reproduced by courtesy of the RCHME)*

similar means to the edge of the track bounding the northern ramparts of the hillfort, but at this point it is obscured by the trackway and probably by the hillfort ramparts. These observations confirm and strengthen the case for Sidbury Hillfort, like Quarley to the south-east (Hawkes 1939), being superimposed on a major intersection of several long-established territories.

The excavation programme

The greater part of the excavation programme was concentrated in the eastern part of the Salisbury Plain Military Training Area (Fig 9). Here, the ditches and banks survive as a series of extant earthworks, and overall the system displays a higher degree of cohesion than elsewhere. Although the general preservation of linear

ditches in the Training Area is exceptional, there are frequent examples of military damage ranging from small-scale infantry trenches to large machine disturbances. Regrettable as this damage is, it did offer a solution to one of the more intractable problems of planning excavations on an expansive ditch system – namely, the severe limitations placed on the interpolation of evidence when only a few widely spaced sites are involved.

This problem was overcome with an economy of effort by reopening the numerous military cuttings and recording the stratigraphy. In a number of instances, the upcast from military trenches and disturbances contained sherds of pottery, and this provided a useful source of information for 'targeting' the most likely sites for re-excavation. Many of these revealed undisturbed contexts containing bone, pottery, and worked flint, and

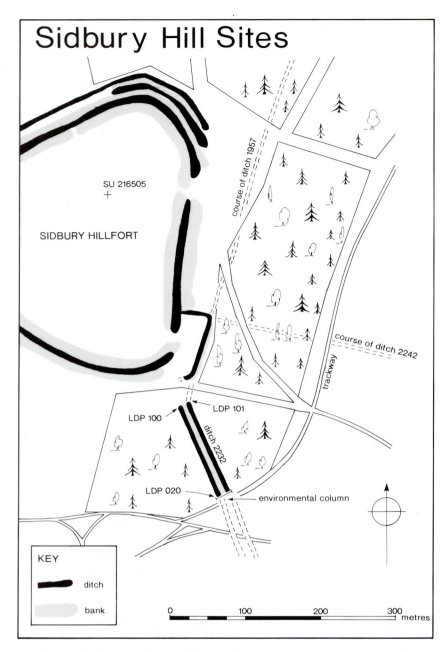

Fig 26   The course of linear ditches on Sidbury Hill and the location of excavation sites LDP 020, 100, and 101

provided the basis for a comprehensive environmental sampling programme based on land snail analysis. This series of excavations was augmented by others in undisturbed areas, where key relationships with field lynchets or dense artefact scatters were identified. Altogether a total of 30 excavations were undertaken (Fig 14), but of these only a minority produced satisfactory dating evidence. Nonetheless, this large sample has enabled us to identify certain structural characteristics which are related clearly to chronology and function. The pottery from all excavations is recorded in Table 5.

In most sections where banks were preserved, these proved to be much slighter than the surface contours had indicated. Although it is difficult to extrapolate from the limited evidence, all banks seem to have been of simple 'dump' construction, which must have rendered them particularly susceptible to slumping and erosion. Since

we lack any clear understanding of the structure or function of the banks and because several ditch profiles show evidence of remodelling, no attempt has been made to estimate their original size from the volume of the ditches. The process of bank degradation may have been quite rapid, and initially it seems to have been caused by natural erosion. But, in several instances, there is direct evidence to show that later prehistoric and Romano-British ploughing completed the process and gave rise to the colluvial sediments common in excavated sections. As this is a widespread phenomenon, but particularly well attested in the Training Area, we must assume that the linear ditches system was considerably degraded during the Romano-British period by the expansion of arable farming.

The information from individual excavations is discussed at two levels. The following section contains a

Table 5 The quantity and date of pottery recovered during excavation (percentages represent proportions of the total weight of sherds from each site)

LDP code	no sherds	wt sherds (grams)	date range
008A	13	87	IA (27%); IP (22%); Early RB (51%)
019A	4	51	IP (25%); RB (75%)
027A	2	2	RB
081A	297	1523	DR (1%); LBA + ACC (98%); IP (1%)
082	256	1152	EBA (1%); LBA (1%); IA (16%); IP (1%); RB (81%)
083	2	4	IA (50%); RB (50%)
084	1	4	RB
087	41	173	EBA (2%); LBA (98%)
087A	4	7	LBA
090	5	131	RB
092	33	168	DR (22%); LBA (72%); IP (6%)
095	3	33	Early RB (18%); Post Med (82%)
097	17	56	EBA (2%); DR (13%); LBA (82%); IP (3%)
098	27	138	DR (28%); LBA (39%); IA (4%); IP (29%)
099	2	11	Late RB
100	16	35	LBA (11%); ACC (75%); IA (11%); IP (3%)
101	3	9	IP (33%); Early RB (67%)

Key: EBA = Early Bronze Age; DR = Deverel-Rimbury; LBA = Late Bronze Age Plain Ware; LBA + ACC = Late Bronze Age Plain Ware, including Early All Cannings Cross as a minor component; ACC = All Cannings Cross of uncertain phasing; IA = Iron Age; IP = indeterminate prehistoric; RB = Romano-British; Post Med = post-medieval

silting. The timescale and taphonomic implications of the distinctive processes involved have recently been reexamined by Bell (1990). Bell's conclusions are particularly relevant to this present study, for our chronology mostly depends upon the status of artefacts and faunal assemblages stratified at various levels in ditch silts. In summary, primary, or basal, silts are characterised by coarse material rapidly formed by erosion of the ditch sides. The rate is variable and depends upon factors such as the size and shape of the ditch, its aspect, and the physical nature of the bedrock (ibid). But, generally speaking, for the size of ditches encountered during this project, the formation of the primary silts probably took no more than a few decades. The secondary silts are much finer and accumulate more slowly once the ditch environment has stabilised – several centuries may have been involved for the formation of the secondary silts described in this report. Tertiary silts are the product of cultivation directly encroaching on the ditch and, in the instances reported here, these may have formed rapidly over a few years.

Certain conventional abbreviations have been used to identify pedological horizons in ditch silts or beneath banks; these are:

Ah identifies an uncultivated mull humus horizon; however, such horizons are frequently truncated in buried soils formed in ditches

Ap identifies a cultivated upper soil horizon

SH refers to the sorted horizon, or stone accumulation, at the base of a soil; these are typical of the calcareous Rendzinas which form the dominant soil type in the Study Area

A/C weathering zone; transition between the chalk bedrock and the lower soil horizon.

The excavation sites

LDP 020: The Sidbury Double Linear Ditch (SPTA no 2232)

This excavation was located at the edge of a trackway skirting the foot of Sidbury Hill. It was undertaken in order to record a complete section of both ditches and the central bank. The excavated area was 14 × 0.5m along the verge of the track, where considerable erosion had exposed the upper stratigraphy of both ditches (Fig 27). No trace of the central bank survived. The eastern ditch was 3m wide and 0.95m deep. Its western counterpart was 3m wide and 1m deep, and both ditches were flat bottomed (Fig 28).

No bone or artefacts were recovered from the narrow section. On the opposite side of the trackway, a remnant of the central bank did survive along with a thin buried soil. This was sampled for land snails (LDP 020A: Fig 28), and the results are recorded in Table 25, Chapter 6.

LDP 026: The Sidbury Double Linear Ditch (SPTA no 2232)

A backfilled military trench approximately 2m long and 1m wide cut into the central bank of the earthwork. This was reopened in order to record a section of the bank and buried soil. The bank itself was very slight, varying in depth between 30 and 110mm. The buried soil was a typical rendzina, overlying an A/C horizon formed over weathered Coombe Rock. No artefacts were recovered from this excavation.

digest of the stratigraphies and diagnostic pottery from those sites referred to in subsequent chapters. With the exception of LDP 081A, the animal bone assemblages are too small and fragmentary to warrant separate discussion. For that reason, the full bone report by Wayne Bonner has been reserved for the archive, but tables summarising bone numbers are included under each site heading. Bone samples submitted for radiocarbon assay are mentioned by site, along with the relevant contextual details.

The second level involves a more comprehensive interpretation from a wider perspective, which in turn builds upon the specialist studies contained in Part II. In their own right, these studies represent an important step forward in our understanding of the evolution of Late Bronze Age settlement in Wessex. The routine order of discussion has been inverted, so that the foundation, use, and decline of the linear ditch system can be seen against this background more clearly than might otherwise have been the case. This somewhat unusual approach has been adopted, because the specialist studies draw on information that permits the development of major chronological and spatial themes above and beyond the level of the individual site.

Throughout this report, the sedimentation of ditches is discussed in terms of primary, secondary, and tertiary

Fig 27   The section of the Sidbury Double Linear Ditch exposed at the foot of Sidbury Hill, showing the section cleaned up prior to excavation (LDP 020)

LDP 027: The Sidbury Double Linear Ditch (SPTA no 2232)

This excavation was also located in a disturbed area, stretching across the central bank and eastern ditch. A military trench of approximately 6.3 × 1.5m was reopened, revealing a relatively undisturbed ditch stratigraphy (Fig 29). The fully excavated ditch was 2.3m wide and 1m deep with a broad, rounded base. Unlike the ditch stratigraphy revealed at LDP 020, the section at LDP 027 showed little evidence of primary silt formation. The particle size graph in Figure 64 indicates some accumulation of chalk rubble at the base, but this was barely visible during excavation. Although this is unusual for a chalk-cut ditch, it is by no means unique. One of the ditches excavated by Thomas on Snail Down contained a similarly fine silt, which the excavator contrasted with the typical rubble fill of the round barrow ditches nearby (Thomas forthcoming). The ditch sequence at the North Kite earthwork, to the south of Stonehenge, was similarly devoid of rapidly formed basal silts, and this was taken to indicate that the original ditch fill had been scoured out (Richards 1990). Scouring is the most likely explanation for the silting pattern at LDP 027 and, in conjunction with similar evidence from other ditch sections, it has important implications for the later landscape history of the ditch system (see Chap 7).

Two sherds of Romano-British pottery were found in the tertiary silts (context 4). Environmental samples were taken from the bank section and the ditch. The analytical results are discussed in Chapter 6.

LDP 100: The Sidbury Double Linear Ditch (SPTA no 2232)

Two excavations were undertaken at the termination of the Sidbury Double Linear Ditch just outside the western ramparts of Sidbury Hillfort. Site LDP 100 was a 3 × 3m trench positioned over the terminal of the eastern ditch. The fully excavated section revealed that the ditch was 2.7m wide and 0.95m deep (Fig 30). The primary silts (context 10) contained numerous flecks of charcoal and occasional larger aggregations. Above the primary silts, a band of clay with chalk pieces, derived by erosion from superficial geological deposits, had accumulated. This was cut through by a shallow scoop (cut 7) which contained a human skull and a few other bone fragments. Incorporated in the fill of this feature, there were also numerous pieces of worked flint, as well as some burnt flint and comminuted charcoal. A soil (context 5) had developed above cut 7, and, over the top of this, a lynchet had formed (context 6). This caused some disturbance to the buried soil and the feature below (cut 7), which may account for the presence in context 5 of a human mandible and a single phalange. Above the lynchet, a second buried soil (context 4) represented a major break in cultivation. This was followed by a further period of ploughing during which the ditch became completely silted up.

Pottery was recovered from the secondary and tertiary silts of the ditch. The distribution by context is shown in Table 7. The human skull from context 8 (the fill of cut 7) was submitted for radiocarbon assay.

Table 6   Animal bones from LDP 027

context	bone
3	1 sheep/goat humerus
3	1 unidentified fragment
5	1 unidentified fragment
6	6 unidentified fragments

Table 7   Pottery recovered from LDP 100

context	description
4	2 Iron Age sherds
5	2 haematite-coated sherds
5	3 All Cannings Cross sherds
5	1 Late Bronze Age Plain Ware sherd
6	3 haematite-coated sherds
9	2 haematite-coated sherds
13	1 haematite-coated sherd

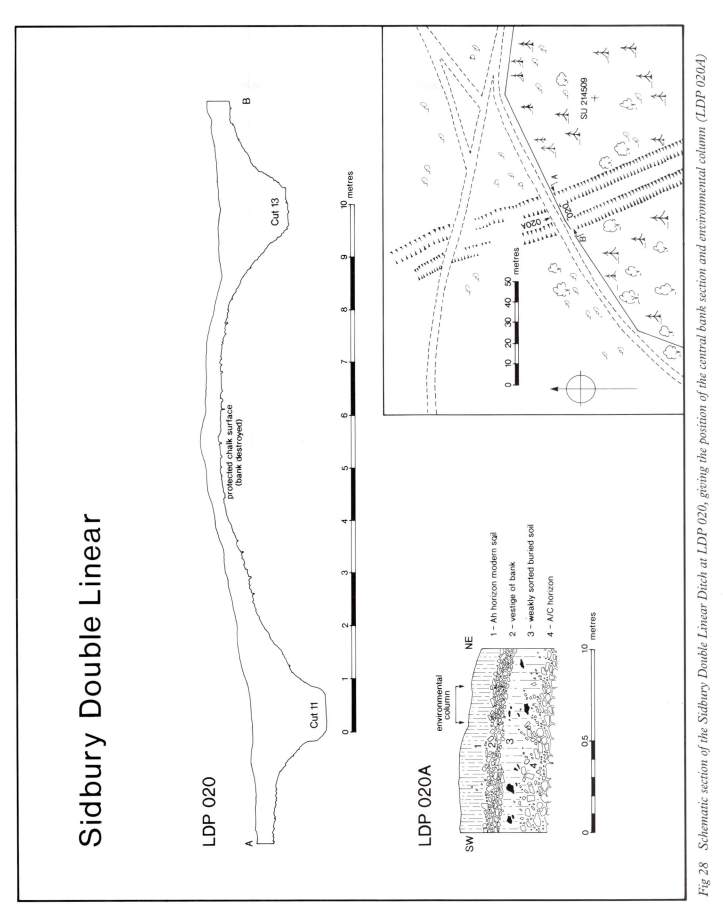

Fig 28   Schematic section of the Sidbury Double Linear Ditch at LDP 020, giving the position of the central bank section and environmental column (LDP 020A)

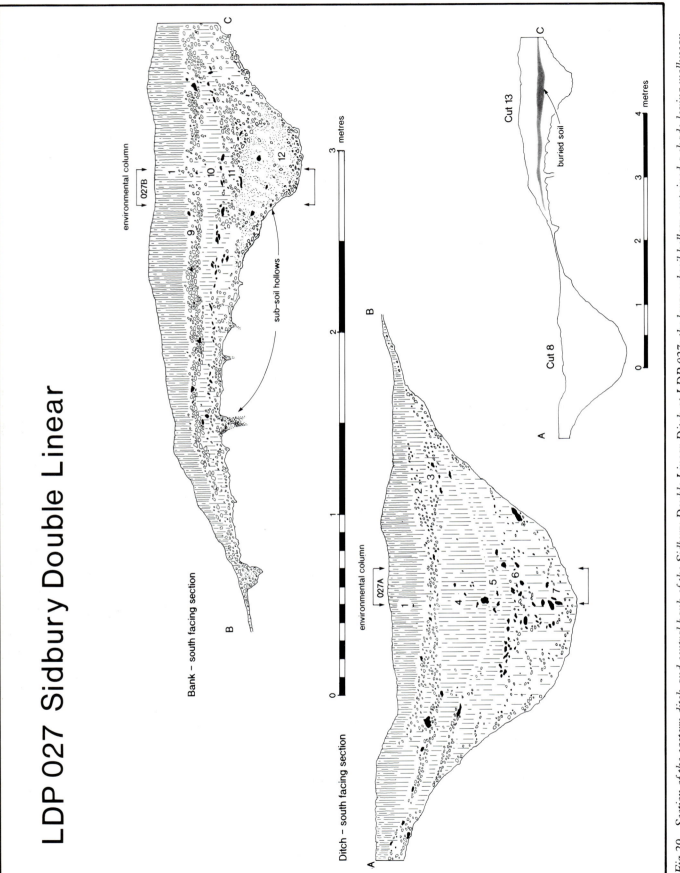

LDP 027 Sidbury Double Linear

Fig 29   Section of the eastern ditch and central bank of the Sidbury Double Linear Ditch at LDP 027; the large subsoil hollow contained a shade-loving molluscan fauna and has been interpreted as a fossil tree cast

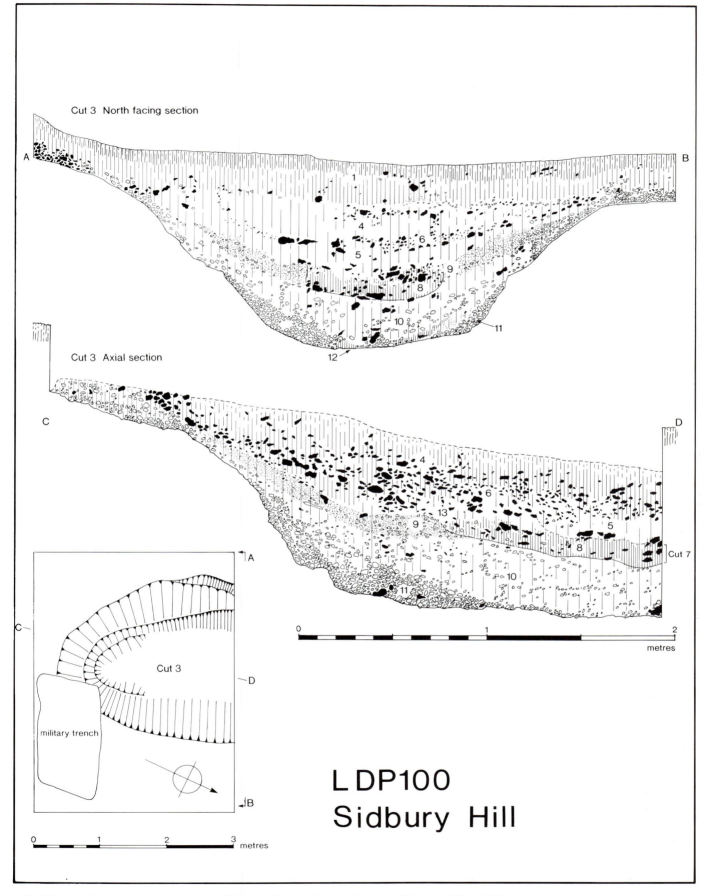

Cut 3 North facing section

Cut 3 Axial section

Cut 7

military trench

Cut 3

LDP100
Sidbury Hill

Fig 30   Section of the terminal of the Sidbury Double Linear Ditch on Sidbury Hill, LDP 100

Table 8   Animal bones from LDP 100

context	bone
4	1 sheep/goat molar
4	1 pig humerus
4	1 horse astragalus
4	2 sheep/goat pre-molars
4	3 sheep/goat ribs
4	3 unidentified fragments
10	1 cattle radius
10	2 unidentified fragments
20	1 unidentified fragment

LDP 101: The Sidbury Double Linear Ditch (SPTA no 2232)

The second excavation of this earthwork was located on the western terminal adjacent to site LDP 100. Signs of a slight hollow, leading from this point towards the outer ramparts of the hillfort, hinted at the possibility of the ditch continuing beyond the presumed terminal to take up a southerly course along the scarp of the hill. Traces of a possible ditch following this alignment are visible on a 1968 aerial photograph (Fig 25), but, because of the recent conifer plantations and the confusion created by several lynchets in the area, this could not be confirmed by surface observation. Moreover, geophysical survey would have been of little value, because a wide, metalled trackway intervened at a critical point between the end of the double linear ditch and the hillfort.

A 4 × 4m area was excavated in order to resolve the question. As expected, this revealed that a deep lynchet had formed over the ditch, with the result that much of the original upper stratigraphy had been destroyed. However, it was apparent that the western ditch of the earthwork did not terminate at this point and that it indeed turned towards the hillfort. In the northern trench section, the ditch (cut 2) was 2.2m wide and 1.25m deep with a flat bottom (Fig 31). The subsequent cutting of an environmental column in this section revealed the edge of what appeared to be a recut through the floor of the ditch (cut 33), but, because of the circumstances of its discovery, there was some uncertainty over the exact phasing. The ditch recorded in the south-western section (cut 2A) was 2.2m wide and 0.95m deep with a clearly defined recut in the base.

For reasons that will become apparent, cut 2 and cut 2A have been interpreted as separate ditch phases. Both shared the same stratigraphic sequence down to the secondary silts (context 5). Below this horizon, the primary silts were distinguished by the frequent occurrence of charcoal in context 27 (cut 2) and the virtual absence of charcoal in contexts 15 and 25 (cut 2A). Although it was difficult to separate these two contexts in plan, a junction was indicated by a shallow scoop in the floor of the ditch which corresponded to a change in the composition of the primary silts. The significance of this was reinforced by the position of a causeway between the two recuts (cuts 22 and 33), which occupied much the same position.

In terms of the stratigraphy, the interpretation of cut 2 and 2A as separate phases of ditch is tenuous, but there is other evidence to support the idea. The silting sequence of the two recuts (cuts 22 and 33) differs markedly, and yet they occupy the same relative position in both ditch cuts. This suggests that the process of erosion was different for each, which would be surprising if they were contemporary elements of the same ditch. The insertion of a feature (cut 20) containing a cattle skull in cut 2 is a further indication that this was not a continuous ditch. This occupies an analogous position to the scoop containing human remains found in the terminal section at LDP 100, although the radiocarbon assay has shown this to be a much earlier deposit (see Table 22). Alternative interpretations are not ruled out, but we are inclined to regard cut 2 as the terminal of a later ditch cut through one preceding it on the same alignment.

Both cuts 2 and 2A were preceded by still earlier ditches. One of these (cut 16) entered the trench obliquely from the north-east and terminated just short of the southern section. It had been backfilled with chalk rubble and soil from which a worn antler pick was recovered (not illustrated). The second was represented by cut 30, which origi-

nally may have followed a similar alignment to cut 16. The significance of these earliest elements is unclear, but traces of a similar sequence were detected by Thomas (forthcoming) in the eastern ditch section of the same earthwork (Fig 32) further north on Snail Down (Fig 33).

Only three sherds of pottery were recovered from LDP 101, all from context 3 – a buried soil in the upper tertiary ditch fill. One of these was a rim sherd from a Romano-British vessel, the other two were unidentifiable, but are probably prehistoric. Environmental samples were taken from the northern trench section. These have been analysed and the results are recorded in Chapter 6. Animal bones from the excavation are listed in Table 9; the cattle skull from context 21 (the fill of cut 20) was submitted for radiocarbon assay.

Table 9   Animal bones from LDP 101

context	bone
3	1 cattle incisor
3	6 unidentified fragments
4	3 sheep/goat cranial fragments
4	1 cattle molar
4	1 cattle mandible
4	2 cattle ribs
4	6 unidentified fragments
5	1 sheep/goat first phalange
5	1 sheep/goat rib
5	3 unidentified fragments
7	1 red deer antler (pick)
10	1 cattle metapodial
10	1 cattle cranial fragment
10	9 unidentified fragments
21	1 cattle skull
23	1 cattle molar

LDP 096: The Sidbury East Linear Ditch (SPTA no 2244)

This was the first of two excavations carried out on a linear ditch running between Sidbury Hill and the Bourne Valley. It was a 6 × 1m trench in open woodland, close to the summit of the hill. The fully excavated ditch was 2.6m wide and 1.03m deep (Fig 34). Originally, it had been flat bottomed, but was subsequently recut to form a stepped 'V'-shaped profile. No dating evidence was recovered from this site.

LDP 097: The Sidbury East Linear Ditch (SPTA no 2244)

The second excavation on this ditch was more informative. A 5 × 2m trench revealed that the ditch at this location was flat bottomed, 2.6m wide, and 1.1m deep (Fig 35). Sherds of pottery were present throughout the stratigraphy and, although a wide date range is represented, they are mostly from Late Bronze Age Plain Ware vessels. The upper fill of the ditch was complicated by the presence of two successive buried soils, the lower of which (context 4) contained sherds of Late Bronze Age Plain Ware and an abraded antler object, possibly an unfinished harness cheek piece (Fig 36). The dating of the few British antler cheek pieces is based typologically on Continental examples with Late Urnfield associations (Britnell 1976). This would suggest a date range between the eighth and seventh centuries BC, which corresponds to the period during which Early All Cannings Cross pottery was in use (Cunliffe 1978; 1984c).

The environmental samples taken from the ditch have been analysed and the results are discussed in Chapter 6. A small quantity of bone from the primary silts (context 9) was considered for radiocarbon assay, but, in view of the inclusion of both Middle and Late Bronze Age pottery at this level, it was thought that the bone might be residual.

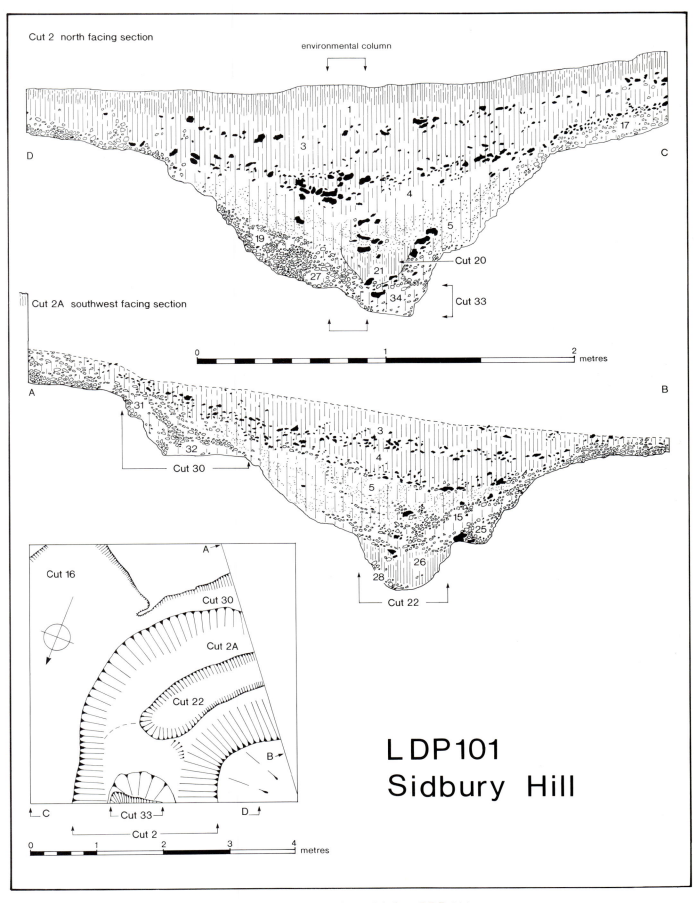

Fig 31   Section of the western ditch of the Sidbury Double Linear Ditch at LDP 101

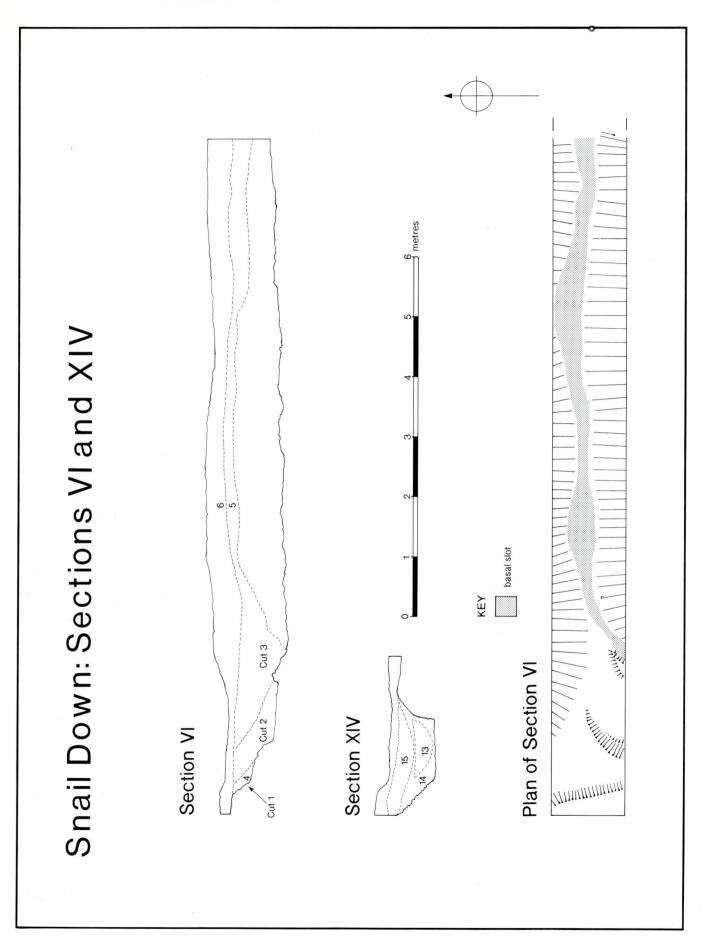

Snail Down: Sections VI and XIV

Section VI

Cut 1
Cut 2
Cut 3

6
5
4

Section XIV

15
14
13

KEY

basal slot

Plan of Section VI

0   1   2   3   4   5   6 metres

Table 10   Pottery recovered from LDP 097

context	description
3	4 Plain Ware sherds
4	4 Plain Ware sherds
5	1 Beaker sherd
6	1 Plain Ware sherd
8	3 Plain Ware sherds
9	1 Deverel-Rimbury sherd
9	1 Plain Ware sherd

Table 11   Animal bones from LDP 097

context	bone
2	1 unidentified fragment
4	1 antler tine (horse harness cheek piece)
8	2 unidentified fragments
9	3 unidentified fragments

LDP 083: The Weather Hill Linear Ditch (SPTA no 2234)

The excavation of this site was carried out after the topsoil had been stripped by contractors, in preparation for the upgrading of the Old Marlborough Coach Road. Unfortunately, the work involved the removal of 0.2–0.3m of the chalk subsoil. This may account for the absence of the bank, which can be seen in the grassland on either side of the stripped area flanking the southern side of the ditch. Fully excavated, the ditch was symmetrically 'V'-shaped, 4m wide, and 1.4m deep with a steep-sided slot at the base (Figs 37 and 38). The size and shape of the ditch profile closely resembles that excavated by Thomas on Snail Down (Thomas and Thomas 1956; Figs 38 and 39). In fact, the ditch excavated at LDP 083 (SPTA 2238) forms one boundary of Thomas's enclosure B, which abuts the Sidbury Double Linear close to Snail Down (Fig 33).

Only two sherds of pottery were recovered. An Iron Age sherd came from context 3, which overlies a chalk rubble horizon (context 4) derived from erosion of the bank. The second sherd is Romano-British and it was discovered in the base of the modern topsoil (context 1). Environmental samples were taken from the oblique ditch section at the edge of the stripped area; the analytical results are discussed in Chapter 6. The bone from context 5, the lower secondary silts, was submitted for radiocarbon assay.

Table 12   Animal bones from LDP 083

context	bone
3	19 unidentified fragments
5	2 unidentified fragments

LDP 084: Weather Hill (SPTA no 2310)

This site was adjacent to LDP 083 on the Old Marlborough Coach Road, and it too was excavated during the upgrading of the route. A linear feature could be seen in grassland on either side of the trackway. Before stripping, its course across the track was marked by deep wheel ruts, which suggested that it might be a ditch. However, when the stripped area was cleaned it was clear that the feature was a hollow-way (Fig 40). Fortunately, less of the chalk subsoil had been removed in this area and, because of this, it was possible to identify a network of ard marks (Fig 40 and Fig 41), presumably associated with the field system on the northern flank of Weather Hill (Fig 10). The stratigraphic evidence for the relationship between the hollow-way and the ard marks was slight, but it appeared that the hollow-way was the later element. Curiously, a series of four truncated postholes were discovered, running between the wheel ruts of the hollow-way. These probably formed part of an early field boundary which had fallen into disuse long before the hollow-way developed. The only dating evidence from this site is an unstratified sherd of Romano-British pottery found during cleaning of the chalk surface.

LDP 085: Haxton Down Pit Alignment (SPTA no 2242)

The final site excavated along the course of the Old Marlborough Coach Road again involved a linear feature thought to be a ditch. After the stripped area had been cleaned, it was obvious that the slight hollow in the grassland either side of the Coach Road was produced by a series of closely spaced pits (Figs 42 and 43). Three of these were exposed in the stripped area, as well as several other smaller features. One of these was excavated, but it proved to be of natural origin – probably a tree hollow. Two of the pits were excavated fully. They were between 0.4 to 0.5m deep and oval in plan, varying between 2 × 1.4m and 1.7 × 1.1m at the chalk surface. One of the pits (cut 1) had supported a central post, but there was no sign of a corresponding posthole in the second pit. Aside from a few worked flints, no other artefacts were recovered from the excavation.

Table 13   Animal bones from LDP 085

cut	context	bone
1	2	1 cattle femur
1	2	9 unidentified fragments
1	11	1 unidentified fragment
5	6	5 unidentified fragments
7	8	2 unidentified fragments

LDP 099: The Haxton Down Linear Ditch/Pit Alignment (SPTA no 2242)

The objective of this excavation was to investigate the relationship between the pit alignment at LDP 085 and the Sidbury West Linear Ditch. Three military disturbances on this ditch had been reopened previously (Fig 14). At one of these (LDP 089), the narrow section revealed an irregularity in the base of the ditch, which was thought to be the edge of a truncated pit. In order to follow this up, a 3.5 × 3m trench was excavated 0.5m to the west of LDP 089. The ditch here was 2.5m wide and 0.85m deep, and it had been cut through by an oval pit approximately 2.1m in length and 1.5m wide (Fig 44). The recutting of the ditch was not apparent in section above the level of the primary silts, because the upper stratigraphy had been destroyed by a negative lynchet. As a result, it was very difficult to define the edges of the pit (cut 4) in the loose chalk rubble, and this was compounded by the presence of postholes at either end of the recut. However, it was quite clear that the Sidbury West Linear Ditch had been remodelled to form a pit alignment and, since there was no trace of a ditch at LDP 085 (Fig 42), this must have involved the extension of the boundary beyond its original westerly limit.

The only pottery from this site were two sherds of late Romano-British New Forest Ware. One of these came from an accumulation of ploughsoil (context 3) in the top of the ditch, while the other was recovered from a rabbit burrow in context 17 – the upper primary ditch silts. The fragmentary remains of a sheep/goat cranium from context 14 (the primary silts of the pit: cut 4) were submitted for radiocarbon assay.

LDP 081A: The Dunch Hill Midden

This was the only site excavated during the Linear Ditches Project that produced structural features, relating directly to a Late Bronze Age settlement. The excavated area was a 9 × 2m trench (Fig 45) located in a small arable field (LDP 081), where surface collection had identi-

Fig 32 (opposite)   Ditch sections VI and XIV on Snail Down excavated in 1953–5 (after N Thomas forthcoming)

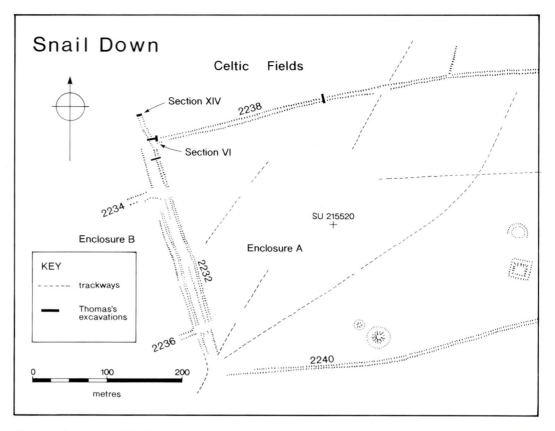

Fig 33   Location of ditch sections on Snail Down and the position of enclosures A and B (after N Thomas forthcoming); note that the linear features within the enclosure are all known to be trackways

fied a concentration of pottery, and burnt and worked flint (Fig 46). Stratigraphically, the earliest feature on the site was a shallow ditch 1m wide and 0.6m deep. This was paralleled by a hollow-way, with clearly defined wheel ruts containing pulverised flint and compacted silt. At a later date, a midden deposit had accumulated in the hollow-way and had spread over the silted-up ditch. It is assumed that the midden contained domestic waste from a nearby habitation and, indeed, close

tradition. The relationship of the site to the field system, and its place in the broader context of Late Bronze Age settlement on Dunch Hill and Brigmerston Down, are discussed at some length in Chapter 7.

The midden deposit contained a considerable amount of burnt and worked flint and the largest excavated assemblage of animal bone. A discrete cluster of animal bone securely stratified within context 3 was submitted for radiocarbon assay.

Table 14   Animal bones from LDP 099

context	bone
3	1 cattle zygomatic arch
3	1 sheep/goat metatarsal
3	5 unidentified fragments
5	1 sheep/goat humerus
5	2 sheep/goat first phalanges
5	1 sheep/goat second phalange
5	1 unidentified fragment
7	1 sheep/goat tibia
7	1 unidentified fragment
14	2 sheep/goat horn core fragments
14	27 sheep/goat cranial fragments

Table 15   Pottery recovered from LDP 081A

context	description
1	115 Plain Ware sherds
3	3 All Cannings Cross sherds
3	167 Plain Ware sherds
5	2 Plain Ware sherds
9	7 Plain Ware sherds

Table 16   Animal species represented at LDP 081A

	context			
species	1	3	9	10
cattle	+	+	+	+
sheep/goat	+	+	+	−
pig	+	+	+	−
horse	+	−	−	−
hare	+	−	−	−
fragments	44	167	6	4
ribs	12	23	1	1

+ = present

to the site two or three slight platforms may represent the house sites.

In all probability, the ditch and hollow-way were associated with the field system which is clearly visible in the surrounding area. A series of ard marks were preserved in the surface of the chalk at the eastern end of the trench. There were also three distinctive grooves, and one set at right-angles, cut into the chalk and running parallel with the ard marks. These have been interpreted as plough stripes. They could be connected with the subsequent expansion of the field system during the Romano-British period, but we cannot rule out the possibility that they are modern. The pottery from this site is predominantly Late Bronze Age Plain Ware, but with elements of an Early All Cannings Cross

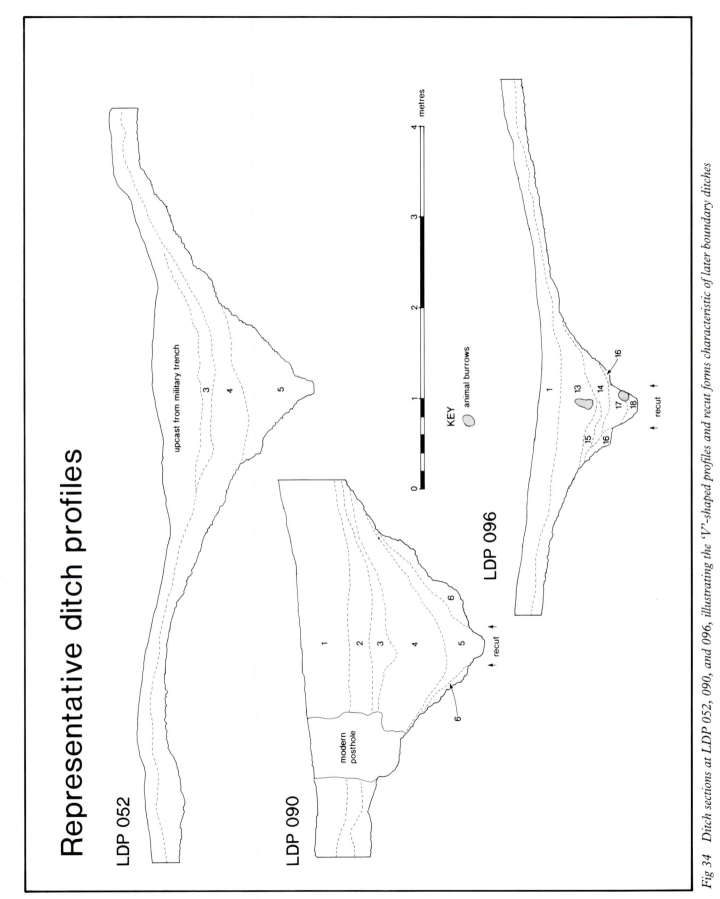

Fig 34 Ditch sections at LDP 052, 090, and 096, illustrating the 'V'-shaped profiles and recut forms characteristic of later boundary ditches

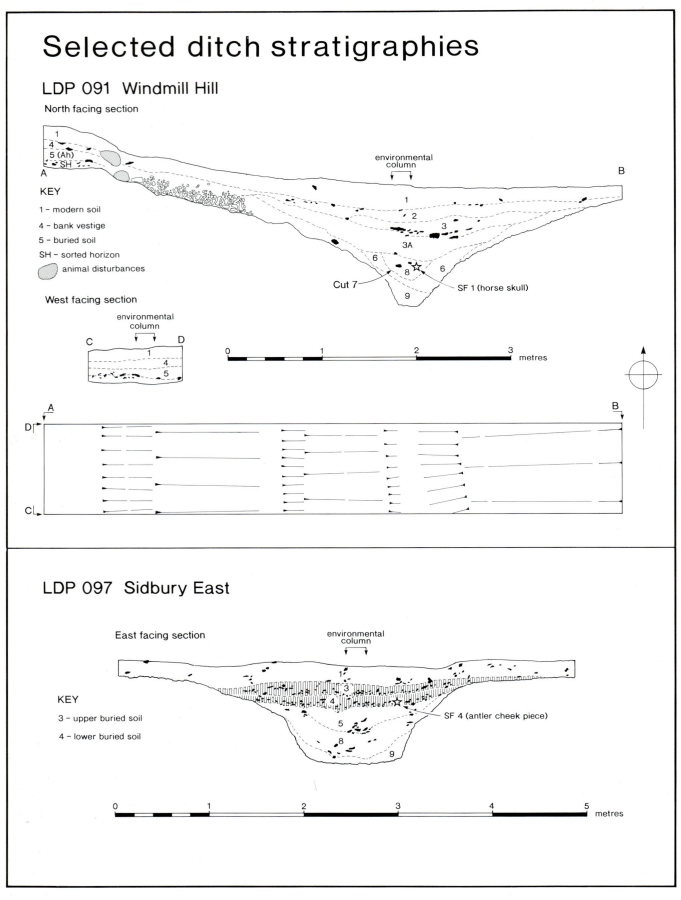

Selected ditch stratigraphies

LDP 091 Windmill Hill

North facing section

KEY

1 – modern soil
4 – bank vestige
5 – buried soil
SH – sorted horizon
animal disturbances

environmental column

SF 1 (horse skull)
Cut 7

West facing section

environmental column

0   1   2   3   metres

LDP 097 Sidbury East

East facing section

environmental column

KEY

3 – upper buried soil
4 – lower buried soil

SF 4 (antler cheek piece)

0   1   2   3   4   5   metres

Fig 35   Selected ditch stratigraphies, showing the position of a placed deposit at LDP 091 and a bisequential buried soil in the tertiary silts at LDP 097

LDP 097

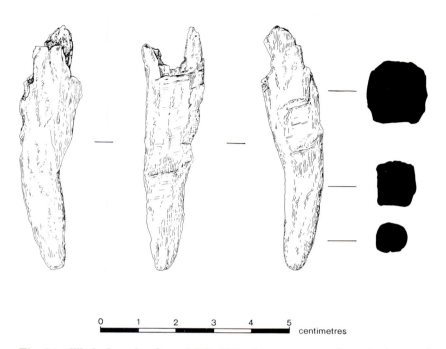

0 1 2 3 4 5

centimetres

Fig 36   Worked antler from LDP 097; this appears to be a broken and unfinished example of a cheek piece from a horse's harness

LDP 087: Dunch Hill Burnt Feature

This feature was discovered at the edge of a military trackway close to Dunch Hill Plantation (Fig 46). It was within the extensive area of Late Bronze Age settlement defined by surface collection sites LDP 081 and 103 and the excavation LDP 081A. In section, it appeared as a shallow hollow filled with burnt flint and charcoal-rich soil. Close by, along the edge of the same trackway, two other small irregular features were recorded (LDP 087A and B). These resembled shallow postholes, but because of the vehicle damage it was not possible to investigate further. However, four sherds of Late Bronze Age Plain Ware were recovered from LDP 087B. A narrow strip approximately 0.3m wide was excavated along the exposed section of LDP 087. This produced 41 sherds of pottery, mostly of Late Bronze Age Plain Ware, but including a single sherd of Beaker pottery. Only a few fragments of bone were discovered, but, except for a horse molar and a sheep molar, these were unidentifiable.

LDP 052: The Devil's Ditch (SPTA no 1959)

The site was located in a beech belt at the edge of a backfilled military trench cut into the ditch. The excavation of a 10.5 × 1m section revealed a 'V'-shaped profile approximately 4.9m wide and 1.75m deep, terminating in a steep-sided basal slot (Fig 34). The stratigraphy at this site was relatively undifferentiated. Beneath the upcast from the military trench, a recent leaf litter horizon (context 3) lay above a buried soil (context 4). The remaining fill of the ditch (context 5) was made up of a uniformly fine sediment with a minor coarse component 15% small sub-angular chalk. Although there is no direct evidence to indicate recutting, the character of the silts, and also the 'V'-shaped profile suggest that the ditch may have been remodelled by scouring out the original silts (cf LDP 027). Lynchets of an extensive field system abut this part of the Devil's Ditch, which appears to be an integral feature of the layout. Though the ditch has double banks along part of its course (SPTA records), no trace of these survived at LDP 052.

With the exception of worked flint, no artefacts were recovered from this excavation. Since most of the upper stratigraphy was disturbed by tree roots, samples for environmental analysis were taken from the basal silts only. The results of the analysis are presented in Chapter 6.

LDP 090: The Devil's Ditch (SPTA no 1959)

The ditch excavated at this site was 3.7m wide and 1.3m deep. Originally, it was flat bottomed, but had been substantially recut to create a 'V'-shaped profile (Fig 34). A fully articulated cattle skull, but lacking the lower jaw, was lying just above the base of the recut. Of the two banks noted elsewhere along the Devil's Ditch, only the eastern one appeared in section. However, the failure to locate the western bank may have resulted from the limited size of the excavated area which was only 4.2m long and 1m wide. A substantial lynchet had accumulated over the silted-up ditch, which appears to have formed the boundary of an extensive, but fragmentary field system (Figs 10 and 14).

Five sherds of Romano-British pottery were recovered; four of these were from the lynchet filling the top of the ditch (context 2) and the fifth from the upper secondary silts (context 4). The cattle skull from the primary silts (context 5) of the recut ditch was submitted for radiocarbon assay.

LDP 092: The Brigmerston Down Linear Ditch (SPTA no 1971)

This site was a 10 × 1m section of the double-banked linear ditch forming the western boundary of the Northern Core Territory (Fig 47). The ditch was flat bottomed, approximately 3m wide and 1.4m deep. Buried soils were preserved beneath both banks. At the base of each, a single posthole was discovered, but, since these were on the eroded edges of the ditch, their stratigraphic phasing was uncertain. In an attempt to clarify this, and to determine if they formed part of an alignment, the trench was subsequently extended to take in a larger area of the western bank. No further postholes were detected, and for that reason it seems unlikely that the bank had been surmounted by a post alignment, unless it was very widely spaced. There is a more detailed discussion of the postholes and the buried soil profiles in Chapter 7. The ditch had silted up naturally. Towards the top of the secondary silts, a stone accumulation (context 6) suggested a period of stability and soil formation, superseded by a phase of colluviation and the development of the modern soil profile.

Worked flint was present throughout the ditch silts, but bone and pottery were not found below context 6 – this horizon produced one

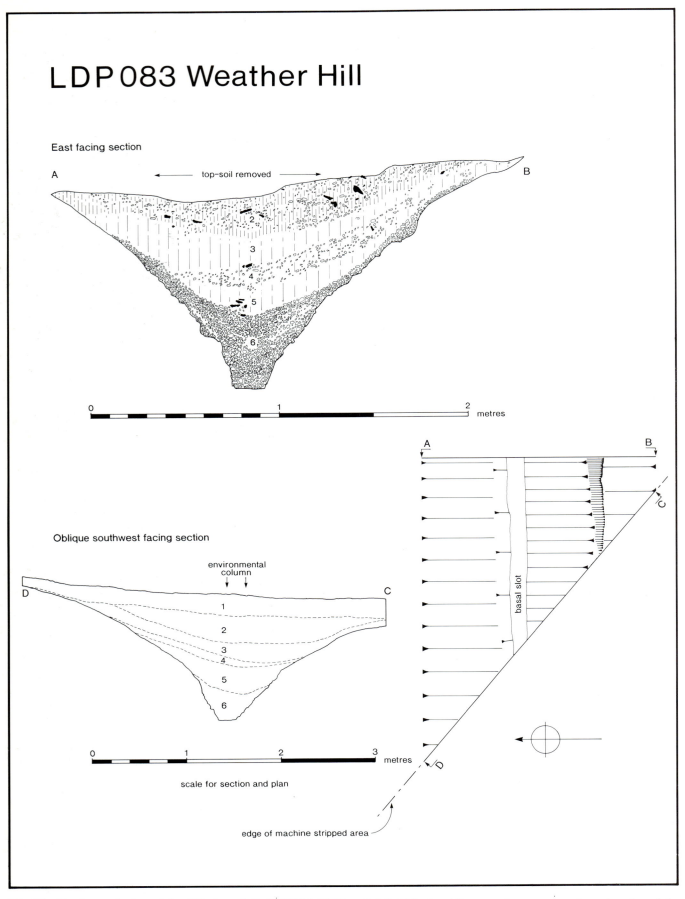

LDP 083 Weather Hill

East facing section

A

← top-soil removed →

B

2

3

4

5

6

0 ———————— 1 ———————— 2
metres

Oblique southwest facing section

environmental
column

D

C

1

2

3

4

5

6

0 —— 1 —— 2 —— 3
metres

scale for section and plan

A   B

C

basal slot

D

edge of machine stripped area

Fig 37   Section and plan of the 'V'-shaped ditch SPTA 2238 at LDP 083; the oblique section corresponds to the edge of the trackway which had been stripped of topsoil during upgrading

Fig 38   East-facing section of the Iron Age ditch at LDP 083, showing the characteristic 'V'-shaped profile and the so-called cleaning slot; this ditch forms the northern boundary of Thomas's enclosure B (scale in metres)

sherd of Deverel-Rimbury pottery and two Plain Ware sherds. With the exception of these, all of the pottery was recovered from the adjoining buried soils. The sherd numbers by context are recorded in Table 17, which shows that the assemblage was composed predominantly of Deverel-Rimbury pottery and Late Bronze Age Plain Ware.

Environmental samples were taken from the ditch silts and both of the buried soils. The results from the analysis of these samples are discussed in Chapter 6. Fragments of bone were recovered from contexts 5 and 6, but, since these sediments appeared to have been derived from late cultivation, any included material might well have been of mixed origin. The bone sample chosen for radiocarbon assay came from the base of the buried soil beneath the eastern bank. This was far from an ideal choice, because this soil had been subjected to cultivation, and the incorporation of residual material could not therefore be ruled out. However, since cultivation preceded the construction of the ditch, and the bone and associated pottery appeared to be part of a spread of occupation debris, this was thought to be a more reliable sample than bone from the upper ditch stratigraphy.

Table 17   Pottery recovered from LDP 092

context	description
3	1 Deverel-Rimbury sherd
3	5 Plain Ware sherds
3 (sorted horizon)	2 Deverel-Rimbury sherds
3 (sorted horizon)	7 Plain Ware sherds
3A	1 Deverel-Rimbury sherd
3A	1 Plain Ware sherd
4	1 Plain Ware sherd
6	1 Deverel-Rimbury sherd
6	2 Plain Ware sherds

LDP 098: The Dunch Hill Linear Ditch (SPTA no 1971)

The ditch had been excavated previously at LDP 092. This second excavation was undertaken in order to investigate the intersection of the earthwork and a prominent lynchet. The site consisted of a 10 × 1m trench. Fully excavated, the ditch was 3m wide and 1.65m deep with a rounded base (Fig 48). The infilling of the ditch was unusual: following the formation of a small amount of primary chalk rubble, a mixed deposit of soil and chalk had accumulated (contexts 11 and 12). For reasons discussed in Chapter 7, this was interpreted as evidence for deliberate backfilling. Subsequently, during a period of natural weathering, a soil had developed in the ditch (context 10). This horizon was rather disturbed and characterised by irregular patches of burning indicating an episode of clearance, presumably in preparation for cultivation. The upper ditch stratigraphy (context 8) was a colluvial deposit derived from this earliest phase of tillage. Subsequently, a more intensive phase of cultivation began, and this gave rise to the lynchet (context 3) which seems to have built up more or less continuously. A single sherd of Late Bronze Age Plain Ware came from context 10, but most of the pottery was recovered from the lynchet. The lack of stratification in this deposit is reflected in the mixed pottery assemblage which contains Deverel-Rimbury, Late Bronze Age Plain Ware, and Iron Age sherds.

Table 18   Animal bones from LDP 092

context	bone
1	1 cattle ulna
3A	2 unidentified fragments
4	27 unidentified fragments
5	1 horse astragalus

Fig 39   Section of the Iron Age ditch excavated by Thomas on Snail Down at site VI, again showing the typical 'V'-shaped profile of these later ditches (scale in feet; reproduced by kind permission of N Thomas)

Table 19   Pottery recovered from LDP 098

context	description
2	5 Plain Ware sherds
3	2 Deverel-Rimbury sherds
3	9 Plain Ware sherds
3	1 Iron Age sherd
9	1 Plain Ware sherd
12	1 Plain Ware sherd

Table 20   Animal bones from LDP 098

context	bone
3	6 unidentified fragments
10	6 unidentified fragments
11	1 cattle molar
11	1 sheep/goat mandible
11	1 rabbit mandible
11	1 unidentified fragment
12	2 cattle molars
12	1 cattle second phalange
12	1 rabbit skeleton
12	1 unidentified fragment
13	1 unidentified fragment

LDP 095: The Beacon Hill Linear Ditch (SPTA no 2160)

The location for this excavation was on the eastern flank of Beacon Hill, close to the edge of an extensive field system. The excavation consisted of a 10 × 1m trench. No trace of the double banks survived, although these were clearly visible just to the west, where the earthwork entered the Military Training Area. The fully excavated ditch was 5m wide and 1.3m deep, terminating in a pronounced 'V'-shaped base (Fig 49). There is no primary dating evidence for this ditch. Only three sherds of pottery were recovered, all from the upper stratigraphy: a rim from a Romano-British vessel dated to the first/second century AD (from the topsoil) and two post-medieval sherds from context 2.

LDP 091: The Windmill Hill Linear Ditch (SPTA no 2247)

The final site was on the linear ditch running northwards along the eastern ridge of the Bourne Valley opposite Sidbury Hill. A 6 × 1m section revealed a 'V'-shaped ditch 3.4m wide and 1.4m deep, with a bank and buried soil surviving on the eastern side (Fig 35). A considerable quantity of worked flint was recovered from the buried soil and the ditch silts. The site was on the edge of an eroded deposit of Clay-with-Flints, and it was from the exploitation of this that the knapping debris was derived. The only flint implements recovered from the excavation were a flaked axe fragment from the buried soil and a complete flaked axe from context 8.

The ditch had silted up naturally to a depth of approximately 0.5m, but at this level a shallow feature (cut 7) had been cut into the secondary

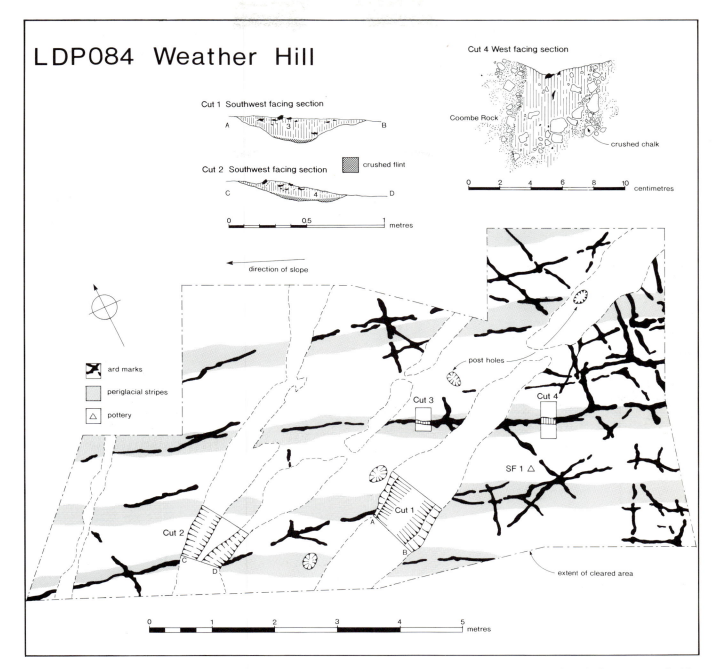

Fig 40 Plan of site LDP 084, showing ard marks and a hollow-way; the postholes along the line of the hollow-way probably marked a field boundary which was superseded by the track

silts. This contained a fragmentary horse skull and the flaked axe mentioned above. The overlying 0.75m of tertiary silt was formed during an episode of cultivation. This appears to have encroached from the western side, reducing the bank and creating a negative lynchet in the eastern edge of the ditch.

No pottery was recovered from this site, but the 354g of bone from cut 7 were submitted for radiocarbon assay. The buried soil and ditch silts were sampled for environmental data, but only those from the buried soil and the lowest two samples from the ditch were analysed; the results are discussed in Chapter 6.

Table 21   Animal bones from LDP 095

context	bone
2	1 rib
4	1 sheep/goat molar
5	5 unidentified fragments
7	10 unidentified fragments

Fig 41   Section of an ard mark at LDP 084; note the crushed chalk on the convex face resulting from pressure during the use of the implement (scale in centimetres)

The dating evidence and ditch morphology

Pottery chronology

Only a few sites produced pottery from contexts that we considered reliable enough for dating purposes. The single most important example is LDP 092, where a stratified sequence containing Middle and Late Bronze Age ceramics was preserved beneath the western bank. Although Plain Ware sherds were present throughout the profile, many in fresh condition were found lying on the buried soil surface. In contrast, all of the Middle Bronze Age pottery was in an abraded state and confined to the sorted horizon. Two additional sherds of Plain Ware were recovered from a buried soil formed *in situ* at the top of the secondary ditch silts. The pottery evidence from LDP 092 is examined more closely in Chapter 4. Here, we are concerned only with the chronological implications, which confirm that the ditch was constructed some time after the adoption of Plain Ware and that this style was still in use when the ditch was mostly silted up.

Two other sites (LDP 097 and 098) produced small collections of Plain Ware, but in both instances the contextual integrity of the assemblages is questionable. However, despite the range of pottery recovered from the excavations (Table 5), none of the ditches forming the Southern and Northern Core Territories, or the territories centred on Sidbury Hill, have produced earlier or later ceramics from reliable primary contexts. The quality of the pottery evidence from the excavations is variable, but it must be considered in conjunction with the more substantial assemblages recovered from Late Bronze Age settlements in the Study Area. Viewed together, these two sources of evidence are seen to be complementary, and there can be no doubt that the system of ditched boundaries originated as an integral component of Late Bronze Age settlement.

Radiocarbon chronology

The samples submitted for radiocarbon assay were recovered from secure contexts at sites free from any sign of military disturbance and each was chosen with a particular objective in mind. However, from the outset, we were conscious that fluctuations and plateaux on the calibration curve were likely to negate attempts to refine the dating of many of the episodes identified by excavation. Since no satisfactory body of dating evidence existed for the linear ditches system, however, even a low-resolution chronology makes a valuable contribution to our understanding of these prehistoric boundaries. No statistical evaluation of the probability distribution within the calibrated bandwidths has been attempted and, consequently, no direct comparison between highest probability dates can be made. Therefore, where date ranges overlap, it is the replication of common types of activity (for instance, the placing of skulls in ditches) which is taken to suggest a broad contemporaneity. The radiocarbon date list is presented in Table 22; what follows is a summary of the objectives underlying the choice of particular samples.

Table 22   The radiocarbon dates on samples recovered from excavations in the Upper Study Area

lab no	site code	material	date range
OxA-2987	LDP 100	charcoal	2480±80 BP; *c* 795–410 cal BC (2σ)
OxA-2988	LDP 101	charcoal	2490±80 BP; *c* 795–410 cal BC (2σ)
OxA-3042	LDP 099	bone	2310±70 BP; *c* 760–190 cal BC (2σ)
OxA-3043	LDP 100	bone	2090±75 BP; *c* 365 cal BC–AD 60 (2σ)
OxA-3044	LDP 101	bone	2460±90 BP; *c* 795–400 cal BC (2σ)
OxA-3045	LDP 092	bone	4770±75 BP; *c* 3700–3370 cal BC (2σ)
OxA-3046	LDP 090	bone	2170±70 BP; *c* 395–50 cal BC (2σ)
OxA-3047	LDP 091	bone	2130±80 BP; *c* 385 cal BC–AD5 (2σ)
OxA-3048	LDP 081A	bone	2420±70 BP; *c* 770–395 cal BC (2σ)
OxA-3130	LDP 083	bone	2810±80 BP; *c* 1255–815 cal BC (2σ)

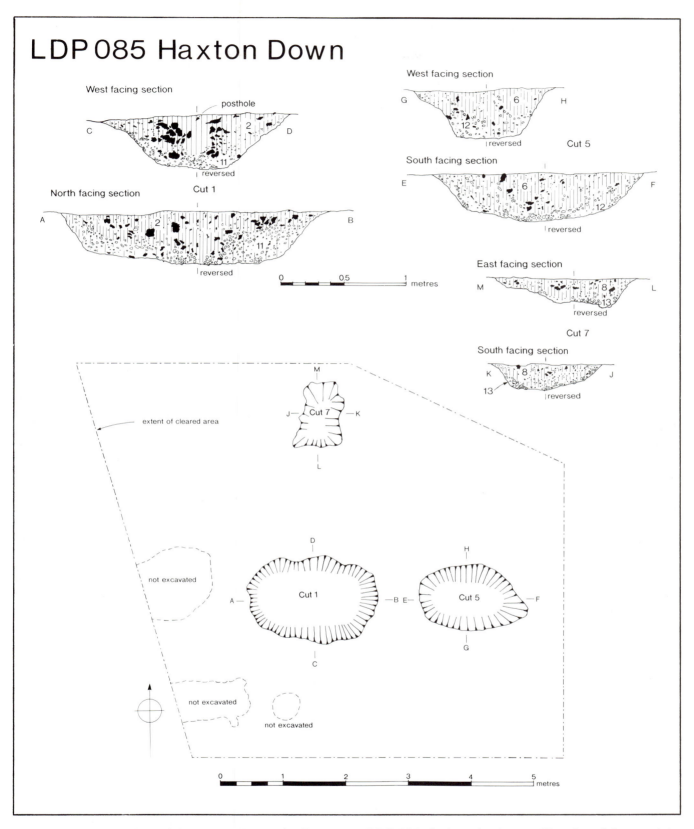

LDP 085 Haxton Down

Fig 42   Plan and sections of the Haxton Down pit alignment at LDP 085; the irregular feature (Cut 7) and the remaining unexcavated features are probably fossil tree casts; only one pit appears to have held a post (cf Fig 44)

Fig 43   The Haxton Down pit alignment (LDP 085) in the machine-stripped area adjacent to the Old Marlborough Coach Road (scales in metres)

The two charcoal samples from LDP 100 and LDP 101 were recovered from lenses within the primary silts of the Sidbury Double Linear Ditch in each of the terminal sections. These were selected in order to provide dates for the final construction phase of this prominent boundary earthwork. Samples OxA-3043 (human skull) and OxA-3044 (cattle skull) are from placed deposits at the same sites. They were submitted for assay in order to date events which were repeated elsewhere in the ditch system and which appeared to represent a discrete cultural horizon. The single sample (OxA-3042) came from the primary silts of a pit cut into the Sidbury West Linear Ditch at LDP 099. This was one of the series of pits forming an alignment across Haxton Down. Since no datable material was recovered from the ditch, OxA-3042 was intended to provide a *terminus ante quem* for this feature as well as a date for the pit alignment. OxA-3045 came from the buried soil beneath the eastern bank of the linear ditch at LDP 092. The sample was selected to provide a *terminus post quem* for the construction of the earthwork. The cattle and horse skulls (OxA-3046 and 3047) came from secondary contexts in linear ditches at LDP 090 and LDP 091 respectively and were intended to provide dates for a phase of activity connected with the reuse of the Late Bronze Age boundary system, which was thought to be contemporary with OxA-3043 and 3044 at the Sidbury

Double Linear Ditch. Sample OxA-3048 was stratified within a midden containing a uniformly Late Bronze Age pottery assemblage (LDP 081A). It was submitted in order to date what appeared to be a discrete phase of activity, occurring late in the history of the associated settlement. The final sample (OxA-3130) came from the secondary silts of a 'V'-shaped boundary ditch at LDP 083. This was one of the ditches delineating Thomas's enclosure B (forthcoming). It was considered to be part of a late stage in the evolution of the boundary system, connected with an altogether different kind of landscape organisation. The date ranges quoted in Table 22 are at the 95% level of confidence (2σ), and it is this level that is used throughout the remainder of the report in referring to specific dates.

In broad terms, the radiocarbon dates support the chronological scheme based on the pottery evidence. There are, however, a number of discrepancies which require explanation. The unexpectedly early date on bone from LDP 083 (OxA-3130) can only mean that this material was residual and, for that reason, we must rely on the other evidence, discussed below, for the dating of this ditch. The date on the cattle skull from the Sidbury Double Linear (LDP 101, OxA-3044) is also somewhat earlier than expected. The stratigraphic position of the sample suggested that the skull had been deposited after the formation of the ditch primary silts, but before any

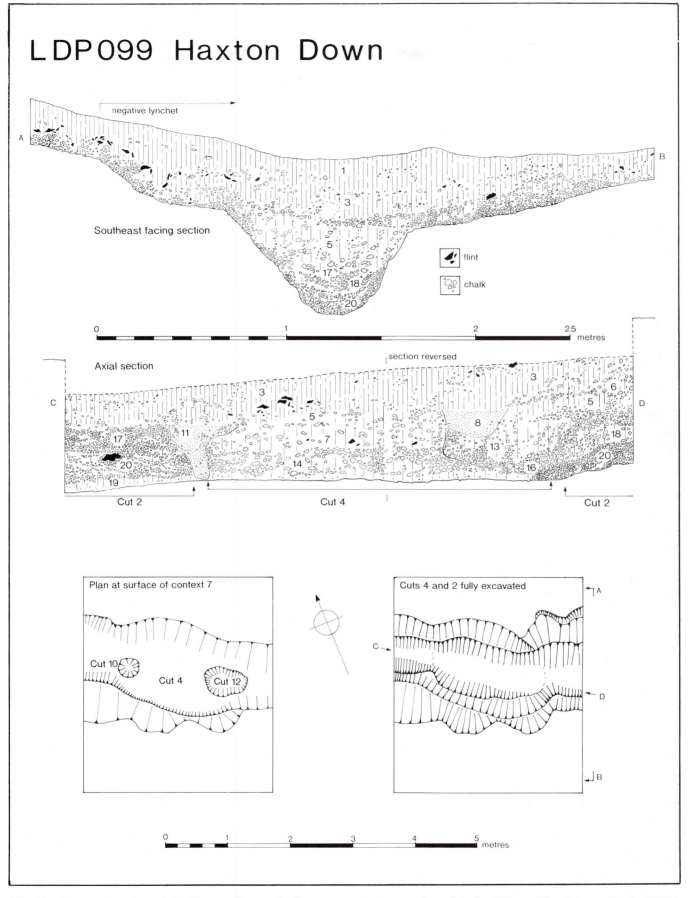

LDP099 Haxton Down

negative lynchet

Southeast facing section

flint

chalk

0   1   2   2.5 metres

Axial section

section reversed

Cut 2   Cut 4   Cut 2

Plan at surface of context 7

Cut 10   Cut 4   Cut 12

Cuts 4 and 2 fully excavated

0   1   2   3   4   5 metres

Fig 44   Plan and sections of the Haxton Down pit alignment at the intersection with the Sidbury West Linear Ditch (SPTA 2242) at LDP 099; Cuts 10 and 12 are postholes at either end of the pit

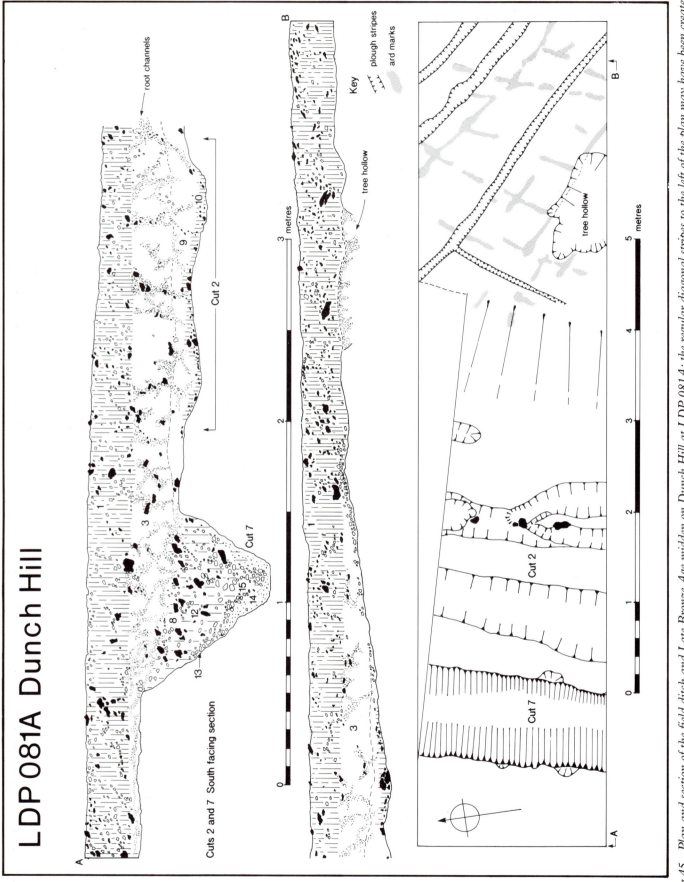

LDP 081A Dunch Hill

root channels

Cut 2

3

13

8

12

15

14

Cuts 2 and 7 South facing section

B

tree hollow

3 metres

Key

plough stripes

ard marks

0 1 2 3 metres

Cut 2

Cut 7

tree hollow

0 1 2 3 4 5 metres

A

B

Fig 45   Plan and section of the field ditch and Late Bronze Age midden on Dunch Hill at LDP 081A; the regular diagonal stripes to the left of the plan may have been created by ploughing, alternatively they could have been caused by the laying of practice antitank bar mines

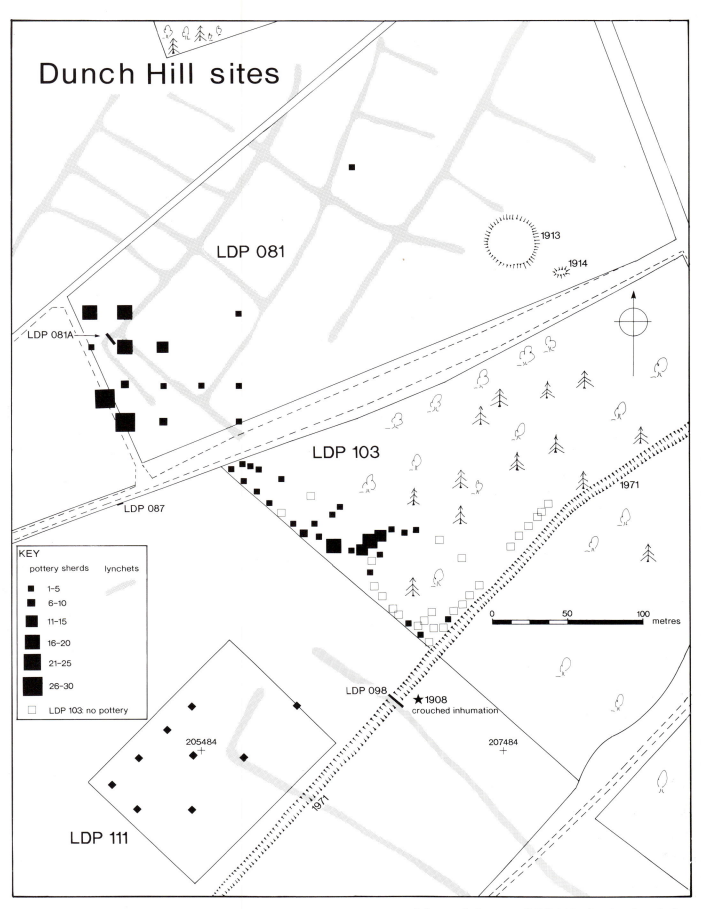

Dunch Hill sites

LDP 081

LDP 081A

LDP 087

LDP 103

1913

1914

1971

KEY

pottery sherds   lynchets

■ 1–5
■ 6–10
■ 11–15
■ 16–20
■ 21–25
■ 26–30
□ LDP 103: no pottery

0   50   100 metres

LDP 098   ★ 1908
crouched inhumation

205484

207484

1971

LDP 111

Fig 46   *Location of Dunch Hill sites LDP 081, 081A, 087, 098, 111, and the tree-hole survey LDP 103, showing the relative density and distribution of Middle to Late Bronze Age pottery*

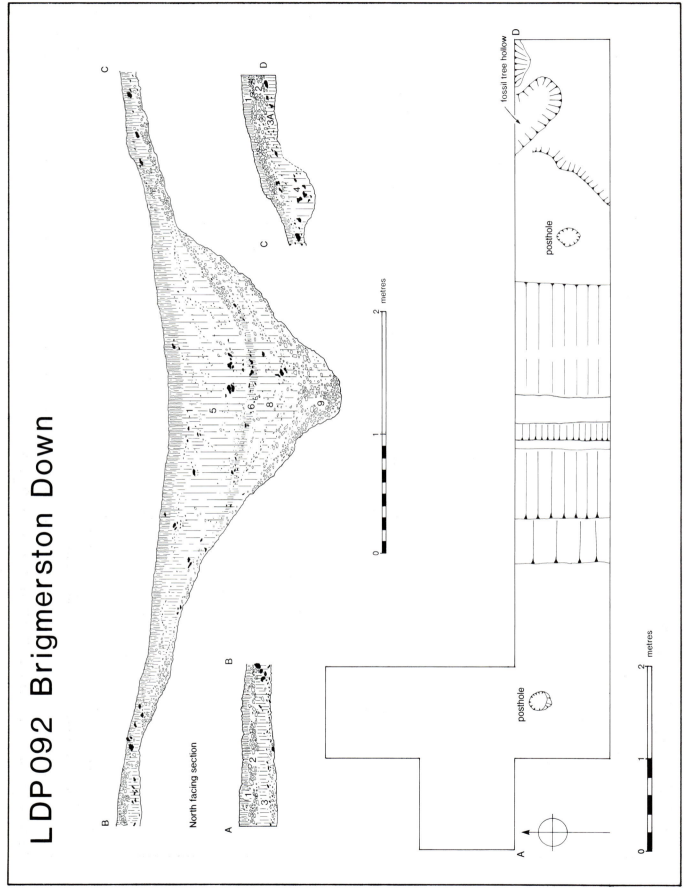

LDP092 Brigmerston Down

North facing section

Fig 47   Plan and section of the double-banked linear ditch SPTA 1971 at LDP 092

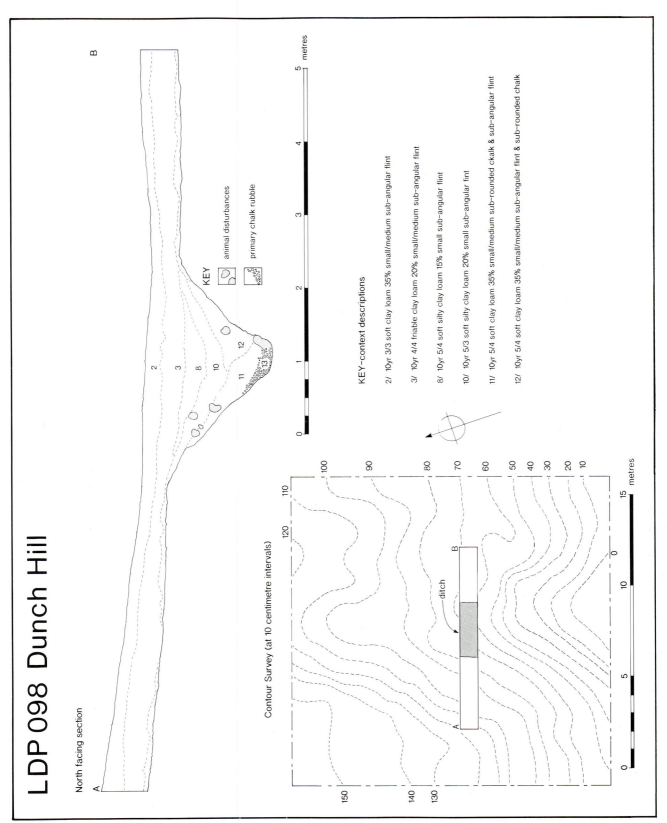

LDP 098 Dunch Hill

North facing section

KEY

animal disturbances

primary chalk rubble

KEY-context descriptions

2/ 10yr 3/3 soft clay loam 35% small/medium sub–angular flint

3/ 10yr 4/4 friable clay loam 20% small/medium sub–angular flint

8/ 10yr 5/4 soft silty clay loam 15% small sub–angular flint

10/ 10yr 5/3 soft silty clay loam 20% small sub–angular flint

11/ 10yr 5/4 soft clay loam 35% small/medium sub–rounded ckalk & sub–angular flint

12/ 10yr 5/4 soft clay loam 35% small/medium sub–angular flint & sub–rounded chalk

Contour Survey (at 10 centimetre intervals)

ditch

Fig 48   *Contour plan and section of SPTA 1971 on Dunch Hill at LDP 098*

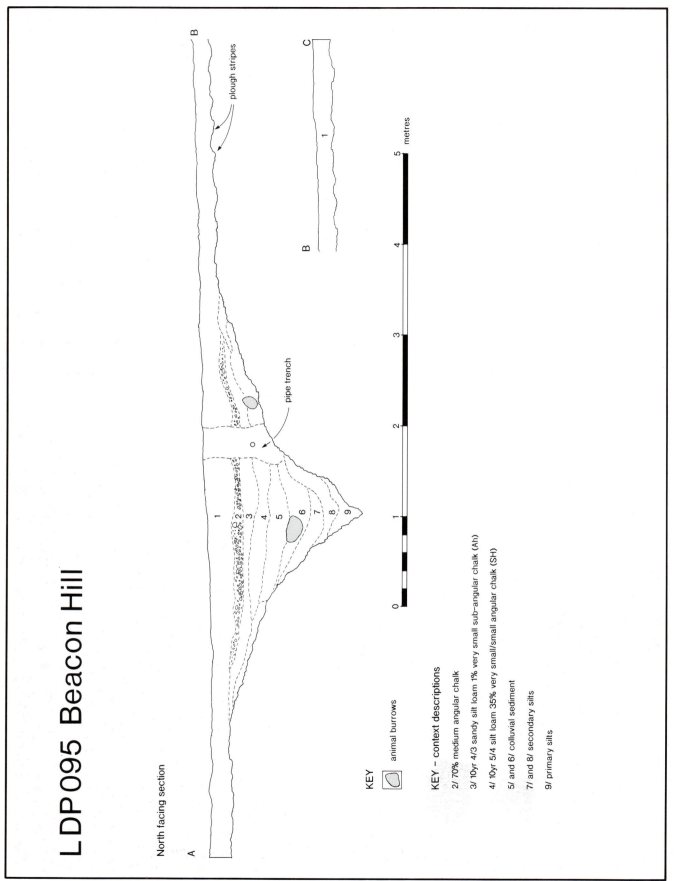

LDP095 Beacon Hill

North facing section

A

B

plough stripes

pipe trench

C

B

1

KEY

animal burrows

KEY – context descriptions

2/ 70% medium angular chalk

3/ 10yr 4/3 sandy silt loam 1% very small sub–angular chalk (Ah)

4/ 10yr 5/4 silt loam 35% very small/small angular chalk (SH)

5/ and 6/ colluvial sediment

7/ and 8/ secondary silts

9/ primary silts

0   1   2   3   4   5
metres

Fig 49   Schematic section and context descriptions for the excavation of SPTA 2061 on Beacon Hill at LDP 095

great depth of secondary silt had accumulated (Fig 31). Although these circumstances are not identical to those connected with the deposition of the human skull in the parallel ditch at LDP 100 (Fig 30), there were similarities which suggested that the two deposits might be related. This now seems untenable and we must conclude that the two deposits are widely separated in time, which implies a continuing regard for the special significance of the ditch terminals over many centuries.

The remaining date that is difficult to incorporate into the chronological scheme is on bone from LDP 092 (OxA-3045). Earlier in this chapter, the reasons for selecting material from the eastern buried soil, rather than from the ditch, were discussed. In view of the anomalously early date on the bone from the ditch at LDP 083 (OxA-3130), those reasons now seem vindicated, for it is clear that dates on small pieces of bone from ditch silts are inherently unreliable. Unfortunately, the same must be said of material from buried soils. However, in this instance the Early Neolithic date (OxA-3045) is of interest, since it can be tentatively linked to the environmental sequence preserved in the pre-bank soil (see Chap 6).

Ditch morphology

Modifications and additions to the original ditch system appear to have continued through into the Iron Age, but these later ditches can be distinguished by their unusu-ally symmetrical profiles. Thomas, in his report on the excavation of a linear ditch on Snail Down (SPTA no 2238), remarks on the regular 'V'-shaped form of the ditch and presence of a vertically sided basal slot (Thomas forthcoming; Fig 39). The ditch, which defines the northern boundary of enclosure A (ibid; Fig 10), has been dated to the Middle Iron Age by sherds recovered from the base of the secondary silts. Another 'V'-shaped ditch which was excavated nearby on Weather Hill (LDP 083: Figs 37 and 38) forms part of a second enclosure (Thomas forthcoming, enclosure B) and, like its counterpart to the east, it also abuts the Sidbury Double Linear Ditch (Fig 33). A single sherd of Iron Age pottery was recovered from the lower secondary silts (context 3), suggesting that this boundary and those to the east were part of a contemporary layout. Unfortunately, the argument is undermined by the anomalously early radiocarbon date of c 1255–815 cal BC (OxA-3130) that was obtained from bone stratified lower down, in context 5. However, the weathered condition of the sample strongly suggests that it was residual. In view of this, Thomas's pottery evidence and the relationship of the ditches forming enclosures A and B to the Sidbury Double Linear (dated to the eighth century BC at the earliest) seem a more reliable guide to the dating of the ditch at LDP 083.

The significance of the change in ditch morphology during the Iron Age is emphasised by the recutting of Late

Fig 50   A view westwards from LDP 082, towards the site of the Coombe Down enclosure; the earthworks on the hillside are of Roman and post-Roman date

Bronze Age ditches to create 'V'-shaped profiles. Examples of this were recorded at LDP 090, LDP 096, and possibly LDP 052 (Fig 34). This refurbishment of parts of the boundary system is dated to c 395–50 cal BC by radiocarbon assay on the ox skull from LDP 090 (Table 22, OxA-3046). At other sites, we can recognise similarly dated events, such as the burial of a horse skull at LDP 091, c 385 cal BC–cal AD 5 (Table 22, OxA-3047), and the burial of a human skull at LDP 100, c 365 cal BC–cal AD 60 (Table 22, OxA-3043), both of which seem to be connected with a reuse of the boundary system.

The frequent occurrence of Romano-British pottery in the upper stratigraphy of many ditches has been mentioned previously, in connection with the emergence of a more extensively cultivated landscape. On the basis of the existing evidence from ditch sections, it is not possible to comment in greater detail, although at a few sites variations in the duration and intensity of cultivation have been recognised. However, some indication of the time scale that might be involved was provided by the excavation of a lynchet (LDP 082), 2km to the north-west of Sidbury Hill (at SU 19625197). This was one element of a cohesive field system opposite the settlement on Coombe Down (Fig 50). Despite the inherent lack of fine detail, a chronological trend was preserved. The lower part of the lynchet contained Iron Age pottery and early, locally produced Romano-British wares, giving way higher up to pottery of the second century AD. A major break in the stratigraphy separates this earlier sequence from a subsequent period of lynchet formation, containing pottery mainly of the mid third to early fifth centuries AD. Although this is an isolated example, the bipartite structure is reminiscent of the sequences recorded in the tertiary silts at LDP 097 and LDP 101, which might indicate that it reflects a wider trend, perhaps signifying some relaxation in the intensity of cultivation.

There is no comparable pottery evidence from the ditch excavations. In almost all cases, the inadequate dating prevents further elaboration and, for the most part, the later history of the linear ditches system rests upon the interpretation of the environmental data. That forms the subject of Chapter 6, but, before moving on to discuss the environment, we must examine the artefacts, which provide the crucial link between linear ditches, the territories that they defined, and the material culture of the settlements.

PART II   THE SPECIALIST STUDIES

The second part of this report contains the specialist studies. In each case, the data have been regarded not just as independent subjects for study, but as distinct, yet integrated aspects of the material culture repertoire associated with the development of the linear ditches system. This applies equally to the artefacts and to the environment. The latter is considered to be culturally structured in the same sense that raw materials are transformed by social intention into man-made objects. In each study, a number of spatial and chronological themes are identified. These are pursued in the context of the development and organisation of Late Bronze Age settlement within the bounded landscape defined by linear ditches. The final chapter of this part is concerned primarily with the evidence from the excavations. It builds upon the descriptive framework established in Chapter 3, while at the same time drawing on the specialist studies in order to combine changes in the treatment of boundaries with other aspects of settlement.

4   The pottery

by Frances Raymond

Introduction

Although the ceramics recovered from the Upper Study Area were produced and used during many different prehistoric and historic periods (see Chap 3: Tables 1, 2, and 5), the linear ditches system in its earliest and most coherent form was constructed by groups who had been making and, indeed, breaking Late Bronze Age Plain Ware for a number of years. The pottery from each of the three extensive open settlements in the area belongs predominantly and, in some cases, almost exclusively to this style. While its occurrence within the buried soil beneath the banks at LDP 092 (Fig 14) indicates that the ditches of the Northern Core Territory (Fig 10) at least were dug after Plain Ware had become an established part of the local material culture repertoire. That it continued to occupy this position, during the time when such boundaries remained as open and significant features within the landscape, is attested by sherds recovered from the ditch silts at LDP 097 and LDP 092 (Tables 10 and 17).

There has been, in the past, a certain amount of speculation concerning the precise chronology of Plain Ware in Wessex (Barrett 1980a; Barrett and Bradley 1980; Gingell 1980; Raymond 1990). This has arisen partly out of the absence of securely stratified assemblages, associated with material suitable for radiocarbon assay. The Wessex chronology has relied, therefore, on the extrapolation of absolute dates, clustering between *c* 1200 and *c* 850 BC, available for groups of Plain Ware from sites in the Thames Valley. One of the problems with this form of dating is that it assumes an identical ceramic sequence within two very different regions. The apparent scarcity of Plain Ware assemblages in Wessex challenged the validity of this assumption and led to the development of alternative hypotheses. Gingell, for instance, suggested that Middle Bronze Age pottery may have survived much later in the region (1980), although the majority of radiocarbon dates available to him at the time failed to fill a 200-year hiatus prior to the emergence of All Cannings Cross ceramics (Barrett 1980a). Using only unstratified material from the Marlborough Downs, Gingell proposed that Plain Ware and Deverel-Rimbury forms may have been separate components within entirely contemporary assemblages (1980). Subsequent fieldwork failed to substantiate this argument, which, in view of its spurious nature, should perhaps have been a predictable result. Plain Ware ceramics were either unstratified and in close association with Deverel-Rimbury pottery, or were produced using fabrics and technologies established largely during the Middle Bronze Age (Raymond 1990).

This background of uncertainty, surrounding the chronology and material culture associations of Plain Ware in Wessex, serves to highlight the importance of the assemblages recovered from the Upper Study Area. In the first place, they are anything but scarce and, in the second, none of the Plain Ware collections is associated with substantial quantities of earlier material, except in contexts where this seems most likely to represent successive occupations, as for example at the horseshoe-shaped enclosure (LDP 109, Fig 21), which was probably of Middle Bronze Age origin and which seems to have been superseded by an extensive Late Bronze Age open settlement. The impression supplied by a consideration of the contexts and characteristics of Plain Ware assemblages within the Upper Study Area is of a group of material that belongs to a discrete chronological horizon. It may owe its origins to the Middle Bronze Age, but it is not a contemporary part of the Deverel-Rimbury repertoire and should be assigned more substantially to the Late Bronze Age.

Whatever the situation in the rest of Wessex, and there is no reason to suppose that uniformity was the norm throughout the region, the sequence of ceramic stylistic development within the Upper Study Area mirrors that of the Thames Valley. This is particularly fortunate as far as any attempt to assess the longevity of the linear ditches system is concerned. It allows for a refinement of the chronology, which may not have been possible if Plain Ware vessels and Deverel-Rimbury forms had been in contemporary use. In the Upper Study Area, at least, the origins of linear ditches have been transferred from the Middle to the Late Bronze Age, thereby reducing substantially our conception of the length of time during which they were constructed and maintained as boundaries within the landscape.

The adoption of a new ceramic style, characterised by a series of traits that are similar over relatively large regional areas, among others, raises the question of the extent to which transformations in material culture are linked inextricably to changes in the perception and organisation of social relations. Research into the stimuli that provoked the abandonment of traditional ceramic forms in favour of new styles, and indeed technologies, is beyond the scope of this chapter. It is envisaged that such processes were the result of complex internal dynamics, involving changing relationships between people and their perception of the world in both cultural and natural terms and, concurrently, a transformation in the meaning and ideology expressed by at least one portion of material culture. It is surely of significance that this change should have occurred immediately after the emergence of open settlements and before the first use of physical boundaries to define cohesive areas of the landscape.

The phenomenon of enclosure may provide us with fairly firm evidence for the emergence of a concept of territory, but it leaves us wondering how this notion was perceived during the Late Bronze Age. The exploration of this theme formed the major stimulus for the detailed analysis of the ceramics. The results are presented in order to demonstrate the ways in which distinctive fabrics and styles moved across, or were excluded by, physical boundaries within the landscape. This is not an attempt to impose the kind of naive correlation between dissimilarity and lack of contact, promulgated by the advocates of various forms of social interaction theory. Instead, contrasts are viewed as indicative of the separate ways in which distinctive communities constituted themselves in the world (see pp 80–85 for an expanded discussion of this process). Although they were well acquainted with, and drew upon, a similar range of stylistic motifs and technological processes, the occupants of settlements within each of the discrete territorial units articulated this common repertoire in a very different way. In this manner, the ceramic data support the physical evidence for a highly developed sense of unity at a very local level during the Late Bronze Age.

The expanded discussion of these themes exploits the evidence derived from each of the three foci of extensive open settlement: the first within the Northern Core Territory (LDP 080 and 102), the second on Dunch Hill (LDP 081, 081A, 087, 087A, 103, 104, and 111), located just beyond the upper boundary of the Northern Core Territory, and the third on Milston Down (LDP 112), again outside the area enclosed by linear ditches. It also draws on more disparate data from buried soils (LDP 092), ditch silts (LDP 092, 098, and 097), and surface collections (LDP 017, 018, 019, 108, and 109); see Figures 14 and 21 for the location of these sites.

The ceramic evidence for the periods that precede and succeed the Late Bronze Age Plain Ware horizon is sparse. It does, however, provide a minimum of information concerning the origins of this phase, together with a series of tantalising insights into major transformations in the nature and location of settlement within the Upper Study Area. The following pages include an outline of these data, where they are of relevance to an interpretation of the linear ditches system. Since there is no evidence that this was a functioning entity during the Romano-British period, the pottery derived from this and later phases is omitted from the text. Tables 1, 2, and 5 (Chap 3) list the contexts which produced this material, while more detailed information (including a series of preliminary identifications by Prof M G Fulford) is available in the archive. These results will be published at a future date, as part of an integrated programme of research aimed towards an elucidation of Iron Age and Romano-British settlement and landuse on Salisbury Plain.

Before embarking on more specific phases of the discussion, there are a few conventions applied in the text that require explanation. These concern the coded sequence of letters and numbers used to describe individual fabrics, which follows a similar method devised during the analysis of ceramics recovered from the area around Stonehenge (Richards 1990, 289). In each case, a series of letters arranged in alphabetical order precedes a colon. These are the initials of the inclusions present in individual fabrics. They include: C – chalk; cl – clay pellets; F – flint; fe – iron minerals; G – grog; I – ironstone; M – mica; S – quartz sand; sh – shell; and V – voids. The colon is succeeded by a date or style attribution, which in most cases is obvious, but in the event of uncertainty, the keys to Tables 1, 2, and 5 (Chap 3) offer the full rendering of each abbreviation. The numbers that mark the end of each code are employed simply to distinguish between wares that share the same inclusions, but in contrasting quantities and/or sizes. Apart from their utilisation to identify unique fabrics, these figures have no other significance.

Should it be of interest, the methodology employed during the sorting process is outlined briefly in Appendix 2. Other information relevant to this chapter and recorded in Appendix 2 includes: the fabric descriptions of all prehistoric pottery, presented in tabular form (Tables 29, 30, and 31), the distribution of Iron Age and indeterminate prehistoric wares within the Study Area (Tables 32 and 33), the most likely chronology of undiagnostic fabrics (Table 33), and the minimum numbers of vessels identified within assemblages from surface collections and excavations (Table 34). Finally, the illustrated pottery is arranged primarily in a series of chronological groups. Sherds of the same period are ordered according to site, beginning with assemblages from settlement foci in the south of the Upper Study Area and ending with the most northerly examples. The arrangement of ceramics from each site is based on stylistic criteria, since they are represented in order to support this section of the narrative. Individual sherds are identified by unique numbers, which have the sole merit of increasing the clarity of the cross-referencing employed within the text. These are correlated in the archive with the special find numbers assigned during collection and excavation.

The early background: ceramics in the Upper Study Area before linear ditches

The earliest pottery recovered during fieldwork within the Upper Study Area is of Early Bronze Age date. All sherds that represent this phase are made from fabrics typical of Beaker ceramics (for detailed descriptions, see Table 29, Appendix 2). The few fragments with stylistic attributes, including comb-impressed linear motifs (feGS: BKR/4 from LDP 111; G: BKR/1 and GS: BKR/1 from LDP 112), incised lines (GS: BKR/1 from LDP 112), and rusticated decoration (feGS: BKR/5 from LDP 112), are most likely to be derived from Beakers of Middle or Late Styles (Case 1977).

These sherds are scarce (27 sherds, weighing 106g), and distributed widely across the landscape (see Table 23). With the exception of one very small abraded fragment from the upper tertiary silts (Context 5) at LDP 097, none of the Early Bronze Age pottery was associated with a linear ditch. Both the character and the context of this single example are entirely consistent with its interpretation as a residual artefact. Neither is there much evidence to suggest that any of the Late Bronze Age settlements were founded during this earlier period. Although Early Bronze Age pottery is represented in the Northern Core Territory (LDP 102), on Dunch Hill (LDP 087, 103, and 111, Fig 15 and Tables 2 and 5) and on Milston Down (LDP 112, Fig 19 and Table 4), it is an extremely minor component within predominantly later assemblages. The abraded condition of the Beaker sherds in both the Northern Core Territory and on Dunch Hill contrasts sharply with the freshness of Deverel-Rimbury and Plain Ware ceramics, again contributing towards an impression of residuality. The only exceptions are the unworn fragments collected on Milston Down, which are most likely to have been derived from the nearby barrow cemetery during a recent episode of ploughing.

There is some indication that by the Early Bronze Age fairly close contacts had been established between people occupying different parts of the Upper Study Area. The evidence for this takes the form of identical Beaker fabrics recovered from sites separated by distances of between 5 and 8km (see Table 23). This particular distribution is repeated by three of the eight wares identified (feGS: BKR/3, feGS: BKR/4, and G: BKR/1). The incomplete nature of such evidence precludes a refinement of this interpretation, so that it is not possible to move any closer towards deciding whether this might represent the movement of people, pottery, the exchange of technological knowledge, or a combination of several of these and similar factors. Nor is it feasible to link this information to the evidence for style, so that any contrasts that may have existed in the articulation of form and fabric remain obscure.

The impression that separate communities within the Upper Study Area were sharing details relating to technological processes, before the inception of the Late Bronze Age, is reinforced by the results of the analysis of the Deverel-Rimbury ceramics. In this case, it is the fine wares alone (CFS: DR/2, F: DR/2, and FS: DR/5) that recur on sites separated by distances of up to 8km (see Table 23). In fact, two of these fabrics are particularly common (F: DR/2 and FS: DR/5), being represented on as many as seven or eight individual sites (see Table 23). This situation is reminiscent of the wider distribution of fine Deverel-Rimbury pottery, mostly Globular Urns and less frequently Barrel Urns, noted elsewhere in Wessex (Calkin 1962; Barrett and Bradley 1980; Ellison 1980). It has been argued that this reflects the exchange of such vessels over relatively large areas, or the presence of specialist itinerant potters (Ellison 1980). It could equally be the result of an increase in the interchange of productive techniques, stimulated by the need to develop a higher level of control during the manufacture of fine pottery. As an alternative to this purely functional explanation, the contexts in which fine wares were used might also have had a profound effect on their manu-

Table 23   The distribution of Beaker and Deverel-Rimbury fabrics within the Study Area

fabric	017	019	075	080	081A	082	087	092	097	098	102	103	108	109	111	112
feGS: BKR/1							+									
feGS: BKR/3		+									+			+		
feGS: BKR/4		+				+		+							+	
feGS: BKR/5			+											+		+
feGSsh: BKR/1											+	+				
G: BKR/1	+	+														+
GlS: EBA/1	+	+														
GS: BKR/1											+					+
CFfe: DR/1	+															
CFS: DR/2	+							+			+					+
CFS: DR/3													+			
F: DR/1					+											
F: DR/2	+	+						+	+	+	+			+		+
Ffe: DR/1														+		
FfeS: DR/8														+		+
FS: DR/3								+				+	+	+		
FS: DR/5	+	+		+				+		+	+					+
FS: DR/9														+		+

facture. It may well be that they were deployed in situations that made reference to extended and complex relationships, perhaps with more distant communities (Barrett 1980a). Such associations or meaning could well have been implicit within the series of shared fabrics.

In contrast, the Deverel-Rimbury coarse wares have a very confined distribution. Even though some of the fabrics (FfeS: DR/8, FS: DR/3, and FS: DR/9) were found in up to four different locations, these were only separated by distances of between 0.5 and 1.25km. In effect, this charts the development of a series of highly localised, technological traditions, even though the occupants of these settlements were well acquainted with more efficient productive techniques. Once again, this distribution is reminiscent of a similar pattern recorded in another area of Wessex. In Cranborne Chase, neutron activation analysis of coarse wares from a series of sites indicates that these ceramics were produced using local clay sources (Barrett *et al* 1978). As with the fine wares, it is tempting to suggest that this may have very little connection with utilitarian motives. It could well be related to the production of pottery with purely insular referents.

In addition to having a far more restricted distribution, the coarse wares appear to mark a distinction between sites located within and to the north of the landscape later defined by the linear ditches of the Northern Core Territory and settlements outside this enclosed area, between its western boundary and the Nine Mile River. The evidence is very tenuous, for the sample size is small (31 sherds of coarse ware, weighing 315g, and 49 sherds of fine ware, weighing 434g), but is nevertheless worth outlining, in view of the later developments that it apparently prefigures. Two of the coarse wares (FfeS: DR/8 and FS: DR/9) are represented both at the horseshoe-shaped enclosure (LDP 109) and at the settlement on Milston Down (LDP 112; see Table 23). Neither fabric occurs elsewhere, even though adjacent and apparently contemporary sites (LDP 102, 108, and 103) fall well within the 1.25km limit, marking the maximum distribution for this type of pottery. The counterpart of this situation is reflected by the movement of another coarse ware (FS: DR/3), between settlements located within and to the north of the area defined at a later stage by linear ditches (LDP 102, 108, and 103). In this instance, the fabric is not found on sites beyond the western boundary of the Northern Core Territory (LDP 109 and 112).

Such distributions seem to reflect the presence of two traditions of coarse ware production within the Upper Study Area during the Middle Bronze Age. The geographical confinement of each of these technologies – one to settlements later included within the Northern Core Territory (LDP 102 and 108) and incorporating sites that were destined to lie just outside its upper boundary (LDP 103), and the other to communities that occupied the land to the west of this enclosed area (LDP 109 and 112) – may mark the early foundations of a conceptual north to south division of the landscape. It is remotely possible that the exclusive method of coarse ware manufacture, employed by potters to the east of this notional divide, was just one of a range of shared activities and ideas that eventually led to a unique expression of territorial identity.

However, during the years that elapsed between the emergence of this concept in the Middle Bronze Age and its physical manifestation during the Late Bronze Age, there were a number of changes. The occupation of the settlement that developed in the vicinity of the horseshoe-shaped enclosure (LDP 109) seems to have dwindled or ceased. There also appears to have been a realignment in inter-community relations, which may have involved a closer affiliation between people living on Dunch Hill and Milston Down. The evidence for this is derived from the analysis of the Plain Ware fabrics, indicating that the occupants of the settlement on Dunch Hill were using a ceramic technology that they shared closely with the community on Milston Down. The Plain Ware assemblage in current use on these sites during this phase contrasted more sharply with contemporary pottery produced by people within the Northern Core Territory. It is this situation that appears to have been encapsulated by the original layout of the linear ditches system. Within the Northern Core Territory, the sense of belonging to a particular terrain was formalised, but on Dunch Hill and Milston Down this never happened. It may well be that these communities, involved in a sphere of local contacts that contrasted with those held by the occupants of the area enclosed by linear ditches, had evolved a very different perception of the landscape. This seems to resemble its Middle Bronze Age precursor, to the extent that it was never defined by an act of enclosure. However, such a resemblance could be entirely superficial, for, by the Late Bronze Age, boundaries may not have been appropriate within the terrain surrounding Dunch Hill and Milston Down because this was used for a variety of liminal activities (see Chap 7).

In addition to supplying the earliest evidence, albeit tenuous, for a distinction between two different zones in the Upper Study Area, the ceramics of the Middle Bronze Age mark the foundation of the majority of open Bronze Age settlements in the vicinity of the Northern Core Territory (see Fig 51). Three of these sites are located adjacent to small enclosures, where unfortunately evidence for chronology is either tenuous or missing. LDP 109 did produce a number of Deverel-Rimbury sherds, but it also yielded fragments of Plain Ware. A similar ceramic repertoire came from LDP 108, but here the overall number of sherds recovered from the surface was very low. Pottery was not found in association with either of the two levelled enclosures in the vicinity of LDP 102 (A and B on Fig 76). Even if uncertain, the evidence does point in very broad terms to a degree of overlap in the occupation of enclosed and open settlements. However, it is too crude to contribute towards an understanding of the relationship between these two forms of site.

If the chronology of the enclosures must remain conjectural, there is rather more information concerning the origins and duration of the open settlements. Unlike the Beakers, most of the Deverel-Rimbury sherds from these sites are unabraded, a condition consistent with their having entered the ploughsoil from *in situ* deposits. It seems likely that the history of such occupations began towards the end of the Middle Bronze Age, for pottery of this period is represented in relatively low proportions (Fig 51). The only exception is the open settlement that

Northern Core Territory

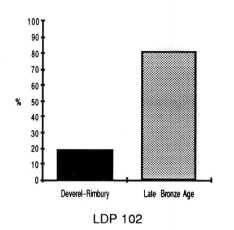

LDP 102

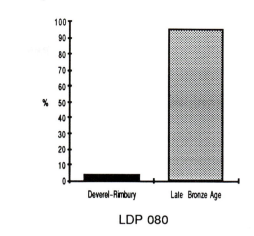

LDP 080

Dunch Hill

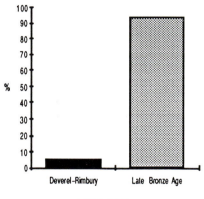

LDP 103

Settlements outside linear ditches system

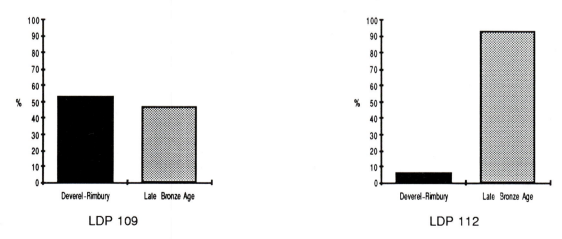

LDP 109

LDP 112

Fig 51   The relative proportions of Deverel-Rimbury pottery and Late Bronze Age Plain Ware from settlements with Middle Bronze Age origins (percentages represent proportions of the total weight of sherds from each site)

developed in the vicinity of the horseshoe-shaped enclosure (LDP 109). Here, the proportions of Deverel-Rimbury sherds and fragments of Late Bronze Age Plain Ware are almost equal (Fig 51). It is possible that this

represents the earlier origin and/or abandonment of this site. The postulated decline of this area of settlement during a relatively early phase of the Late Bronze Age is supported by structural evidence. It is the only Plain

Ware occupation bisected by a linear ditch (SPTA 1971). The construction of the bank alongside this boundary at LDP 092 occurred before sherds deposited on the land surface had weathered, or had been sorted down the soil profile. On all other sites, the relative proportions of Deverel-Rimbury and Late Bronze Age sherds are consistent with occupations continuing for a longer time period, an assertion supported by the appearance of All Cannings Cross forms on settlements within the Northern Core Territory (LDP 080), on Dunch Hill (LDP 081A), and on Milston Down (LDP 112).

In contrast to the ceramic data from the extensive open sites, there is absolutely no evidence for the construction of linear ditches during the Middle Bronze Age. Although Deverel-Rimbury pottery was found in association with three of the excavated sections (LDP 092, 097, and 098), it was in each case residual. At LDP 092, this interpretation is supported by the recovery of Plain Ware sherds, in remarkably fresh condition, from the surface of the buried soil (Context 3) beneath the western bank. This evidence alone suggests that Deverel-Rimbury pottery was no longer in current use when the ditch SPTA 1971 was constructed. The case is strengthened further by a consideration of the stratigraphic position of the four Middle Bronze Age sherds within this buried soil. These were confined to the sorted horizon and all display signs of weathering. The single Deverel-Rimbury sherd recovered from the buried soil below the eastern bank (Context 3a), occupied an analogous position at the base of this layer, where it had sunk into the top of the subsoil hollow (Cut 7). In the light of this sequence, the fragment of Middle Bronze Age pottery found within the stabilisation horizon at the base of the secondary silts within the ditch (Context 6) must also assume a residual character. A similar interpretation applies to the sherd derived from the primary silts of the ditch at LDP 097 (Context 9). This was stratified well below a tiny fragment of Beaker and was so heavily abraded that neither surface survived. At LDP 098, the two Deverel-Rimbury sherds were found within a lynchet overlying the linear ditch, which also yielded fragments of Late Bronze Age and Iron Age pottery.

In addition to negating any suggestion that the linear ditches system was constructed during the Middle Bronze Age, the ceramic evidence implies that this phase of landscape organisation followed in the wake of other important changes. At LDP 092, Plain Ware sherds were present throughout the buried soil profile, suggesting that they had been produced and used in the area for some years before the Northern Core Territory was established. Their adoption involved rather more than the manufacture of a new series of forms, although this in itself, together with the implied abandonment of traditional styles, must have signalled major transformations. The introduction of Plain Ware seems to have been accompanied by, or to have triggered, a substantial shift in technological practice. Within the Upper Study Area, the subtleties of this process of change are at present impossible to follow. Very few of the Deverel-Rimbury sherds from settlements that must have witnessed these events carry diagnostic attributes. The only recognisably classical form is the fragment of Barrel Urn from LDP 109 (Fig 52, P3). The assemblages from all other sites contain the usual selection of decorated and plain

cordons (Fig 52, P6 and P8–9), together with rims from apparently straight-sided vessels (Fig 52, P1–2, P4–5, P7, and P10). These are too fragmentary to determine whether they share certain attributes in common with Plain Ware styles. Neither is it possible to identify a phase during which new forms were produced using traditional methods, as seems to have taken place at the Fargo Wood settlement in the Stonehenge area (Raymond 1990).

While the process of change remains elusive within the Upper Study Area, its outcome in the form of newly established technologies is readily identifiable. This is illustrated by a number of gross contrasts between the fabrics of the Middle and Late Bronze Ages. As with many Deverel-Rimbury wares in Wessex, large quantities of crushed flint (comprising between 20 and 40% of the clay matrix) are the most common kind of tempering (for detailed fabric descriptions, see Table 29, Appendix 2). In the case of the fine fabrics, particular care must have been exercised in the preparation of such inclusions, for they are sorted to sizes of less than 3mm. This is reflected by the surface finishes, which tend to be of a far higher quality than is displayed by the coarse pottery. Although the evidence is tenuous, it indicates that both fine and coarse fabrics were used to produce similar ranges of thin- and thick-walled vessels.

In contrast, by the Late Bronze Age the majority of wares tempered with flint contained only 10% or less of these inclusions. However, the proportion of non-plastics within the clay matrix was raised by the addition of between 15 and 50% quartz sand. This mixture was reversed in the case of a small number of examples (CF: LBA/1, CFfeS: LBA/2, CFfeS: LBA/3, and FfeS: LBA/2), which included between 25 and 40% of flint particles, but only small amounts of quartz sand (for detailed descriptions, see Table 30, Appendix 2). The inverse relationship, between the quantities of flint and sand in Late Bronze Age fabrics, may indicate that the different properties of these materials were being recognised and controlled. This does not appear to have been happening during the Middle Bronze Age. Most of the fabrics made in the Upper Study Area at this time contained little or no sand. There are only two exceptions (FS: DR/5 and FS: DR/9) and these are characterised by equally high proportions of both materials (see Table 29, Appendix 2).

If the Late Bronze Age ceramic data do represent a manipulation of the mechanical properties of contrasting fabrics, then it is intriguing that this should coincide with an increase in the number of forms produced. Barrett has suggested that the widening of the stylistic repertoire at this time might be indicative of the increased use of pottery in connection with a greater variety of daily activities (1980a). A process of this kind may have been accompanied by the development of fabrics suited to new functions. While both flint and quartz sand are siliceous, and therefore share identical expansion and contraction rates under cycles of heating and cooling, the resultant mechanical stresses are reduced in the case of sand because of its smaller particle size (Shepard 1956; Rye 1976; Braun 1983; D Arnold 1985; Bronitsky and Hamer 1986). Vessels made from fabrics tempered with this material tend to be more resilient during firing and are more likely to last longer, if used for functions such

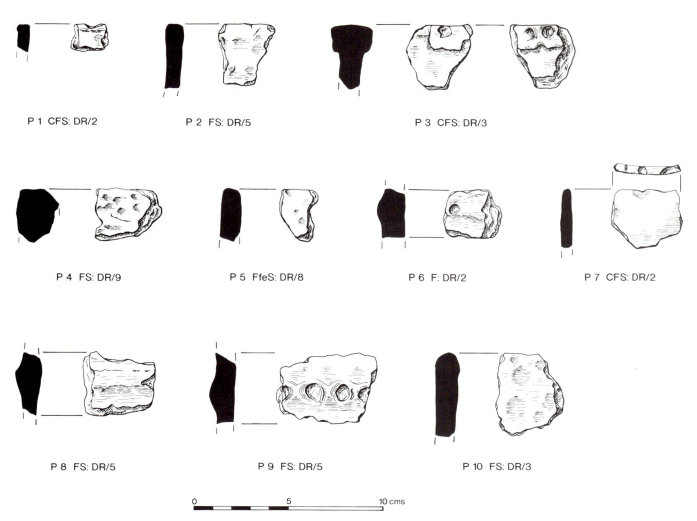

P 1 CFS: DR/2   P 2 FS: DR/5   P 3 CFS: DR/3

P 4 FS: DR/9   P 5 FfeS: DR/8   P 6 F: DR/2   P 7 CFS: DR/2

P 8 FS: DR/5   P 9 FS: DR/5   P 10 FS: DR/3

0   5   10 cms

Fig 52   Deverel-Rimbury pottery from LDP 112 (P1–2), LDP 109 (P3–5), LDP 092 (P6), LDP 102 (P7), LDP 080 (P8), LDP 098 (P9), and LDP 103 (P10)

as cooking. Unfortunately, the pottery from the Upper Study Area is too fragmentary to allow for a detailed exploration of the way in which distinctive wares and separate styles co-vary. It does, however, indicate that the more durable fabrics were used for vessels carrying elaborate stylistic traits, none of which were essential to the fulfilment of a strictly utilitarian role. The most striking examples are the series of bowls made from FS: LBA/1 which, apart from having been fired at a higher temperature than most other Late Bronze Age vessels, are characterised by exceptionally fine surface finishes including burnishing, by an even dark grey or black colouring, and by more regular and controlled decorative motifs. It would seem that the greatest technological effort was being expended in the production of pottery made singular by attributes of a symbolic character.

It may well be, therefore, that we should be equating the new forms and altered technology of the Late Bronze Age with a transformation in meaning rather than in utility. The increased variability within Plain Ware assemblages offers a far greater potential for creating a complex series of material culture categories. These can act as a grid, which may be used within different fields of social practice to establish the significance of the

events taking place (Miller 1985). This point has been pursued by Barrett, who argues that categories provide points of reference within networks of authority and obligation (1991). They are involved in a dynamic process, whereby people compare their understanding of the organisation of society, gained through indoctrination, with their actual experience of that order (ibid). One method of provoking change within, or of fragmenting, an existing system of categorisation is provided by the introduction of new prototypical elements (Barrett 1991).

It seems entirely possible that the changes within the ceramic record mark simply one aspect of an alteration of the ways in which the consensus opinion compelled people to act in the world. Whatever the answer, this archaeologically visible transformation was followed by the construction of linear ditches, which, together with the implied development of new attitudes towards the landscape, appears to represent yet another conceptual shift. At this point, it would seem pertinent to move discussion towards the centre of this period, in order to explore the ways in which contemporary ceramics were articulated within and outside the bounded environment of the Late Bronze Age.

Table 24   The relative proportions of Late Bronze Age fabric groups on individual sites within each settlement area

fabric	Dunch Hill							core territory			sites adjacent to core territory			Milston Down	sites in peripheral locations						
	081	081A	087	087A	103	104	111	080	102	108	098	092	109	112	008	017	018	019	082	097	100
CF: LBA/1	1%	<1%			1%					+											+
CFfeS: LBA/1	13%	10%	24%	+	7%			7%	13%		9%		1%	1%		+				9%	
CFfeS: LBA/2	1%	2%			12%			8%	1%							+	+	+		7%	
CFfeS: LBA/3											8%	21%		1%		+	+	+			
clSsh: LBA/1	<1%	2%												1%							
FfeM: LBA/1		<1%																			
FfeS: LBA/1	48%	50%	27%		38%		26%	10%	11%	+	16%	5%		39%		+			+		
FfeS: LBA/2	18%	5%	9%		8%		4%	36%	13%		26%	2%	4%	9%						26%	
FfeS: LBA/3	6%	15%	9%		3%	+	47%	9%	6%			2%	9%	13%						41%	
FfeS: LBA/4	5%	1%			<1%									<1%		+					
FfeS: LBA/5	<1%	<1%						12%				2%		<1%							
FfeS: LBA/6			7%		5%		7%	5%	8%		8%	8%						+			
FfeS: LBA/9														2%							
Ffesh: LBA/1		<1%			<1%																
FS: LBA/1	1%	12%	2%		13%		16%	13%	43%			10%	3%	8%							
FS: LBA/2	5%	22%	22%		4%							25%	41%	22%						17%	
FS: LBA/4									5%				1%	1%							
FS: LBA/6											33%	25%	27%	2%	+						
FSshV: LBA/1					6%								14%	1%							
feSsh: LBA/1	1%				2%																
sh: LBA/1		1%																			

Note: percentage calculations are based on the total weight of sherds belonging to this period on each site; + = present, but in insufficient numbers for percentages to be meaningful

Shared and exclusive traditions: Late Bronze Age ceramics and linear ditches

With the introduction of Plain Ware during the Late Bronze Age, there appears to have been an increase in the exchange of ideas concerning style and technology. This is indicated by the widespread sharing of certain formal attributes and fabrics within the Upper Study Area. At the same time, there is evidence that the occupants of separate settlements were maintaining a degree of exclusiveness within their ceramic repertoires. Each community seems to have been producing a few vessels, either with unique stylistic traits, or made from unparalleled wares. These differences are reflected and reinforced by further distinctions in the relative proportions of the fabrics that do have a widespread distribution. The ware FfeS: LBA/1, for instance, comprises 50% of the assemblage from LDP 081A and only 11% of the ceramics from LDP 102 (see Table 24). It would seem that, although each settlement was drawing on a common stylistic and technological repertoire, separate communities were choosing to highlight selected aspects of the entire range of available possibilities. This level of distinction is congruent with the territorial unit defined by the linear ditches of the Northern Core Territory. It occurs between assemblages from settlements divided by a physical boundary, but not between the collections of pottery from sites located in the same territory. Here, the contrasts are even more subtle and may reflect shifts in the focus of population through time, or the production of ceramics by different groups within the same community.

The evidence for the range of pottery styles used in the Upper Study Area during the Late Bronze Age is limited to sites in the Northern Core Territory (LDP 080 and 102), on Dunch Hill (LDP 081, 081A, 087, and 103, Fig 46; 111, Fig 15), and on Milston Down (LDP 112, Fig 19). In addition, there are a few sherds with formal attributes from the settlement in the vicinity of the horseshoe-shaped enclosure (LDP 092 and 109), from the section through SPTA 1971 (LDP 098), and from the occupation foci to the north of Snail Down (see Fig 71; Raymond forthcoming). The assemblages from all other sites that yielded Plain Ware (LDP 008, 012, 017, 018, 019, 082, 087A, 097, 100, 104, and 108, Fig 14) consist of wall or body sherds lacking any diagnostic feature other than their fabrics. These are paralleled elsewhere in the Upper Study Area, either by identical wares used only for Late Bronze Age forms, or by analogous examples derived from sealed contexts belonging to this period alone.

The text that follows is confined to inter-site comparisons between the occupation foci in the Northern Core Territory, on Dunch Hill, and on Milston Down. Other settlements in the Upper Study Area (Fig 14), around the horseshoe-shaped enclosure (LDP 092 and 109), on Earl's Farm Down (LDP 017), to the west of Sidbury Hill (LDP 097 and Pennings Wood, see Fig 14), and to the north of Snail Down (Raymond forthcoming; Fig 10) are peripheral to the themes explored during the discussion. Although they appear to have been drawing on similar Plain Ware prototypes, either in terms of fabric or style, the quantity of pottery from each location is too low to allow for an assessment of the way in which these common attributes were articulated. Similar limitations apply to detailed intra-settlement analyses.

None of the sites provided the kind of evidence necessary for the construction of a series of chronological phases within the Plain Ware tradition. The numbers of sherds from successive contexts in ditches are so low that any attempt at seriation would be rendered meaningless. Where assemblages are of sufficient size, they are derived from unstratified locations. The exception is the group of pottery from the midden on Dunch Hill (LDP 081A, Table 15, Chap 3), which appears to have accumulated over a relatively short period towards the end of the currency of Plain Ware. The evidence from this site has a limited application, since it does not refer to earlier phases of development. These shortcomings mean that it is only possible to date the construction of linear ditches to some unknown point within the currency of a fairly long-lived ceramic tradition.

In addition, the lack of chronological refinement places certain qualifications on the evidence for contacts between separate local communities during the Late Bronze Age. Short-term changes, which may or may not have occurred, especially across the threshold marked by the construction of linear ditches, remain undetected. This factor must, to an unknown extent, have distorted or blurred the more general results. In addition, the relative longevity of the Plain Ware tradition means that apparently contemporary sites may not have been occupied at the same time. It is not, for instance, possible to determine with any certainty, whether the settlement on Milston Down continued alongside sites in the Northern Core Territory after the construction of linear ditches, or whether it had dwindled or ceased 10 or even 100 years previously.

In opposition to this rather negative outline, there are a series of broad chronological trends identifiable within the ceramic evidence, which are suggestive of a degree of absolute contemporaneity. As we have seen, Plain Ware settlements within the Northern Core Territory, on Dunch Hill and on Milston Down, appear to have been founded towards the end of the Middle Bronze Age (see Fig 51). Each of these occupations continued into the period when Early All Cannings Cross forms were being introduced to the Upper Study Area. This new ceramic style is represented in minute proportions and appears only in selected occupation foci. Within the Northern Core Territory, for example, it occurs at LDP 080, but not at LDP 102 or LDP 108 (Table 2). Similarly on Dunch Hill, Early All Cannings Cross forms are isolated to the midden at LDP 081A (Tables 5 and 15). This may be indicative of the kind of settlement drift through time, represented by the earlier shift in occupation away from LDP 092 and LDP 109. The identification of this process at a later phase, however, lacks the support of structural evidence and contains two inherent sources of uncertainty.

The first of these is of a material nature and concerns the criteria used in the identification of Early All Cannings Cross vessels. For a number of reasons, discussed at a later stage in the text, these are thought to represent the beginnings of an adoption of a new ceramic style. At this introductory stage, such vessels are made from

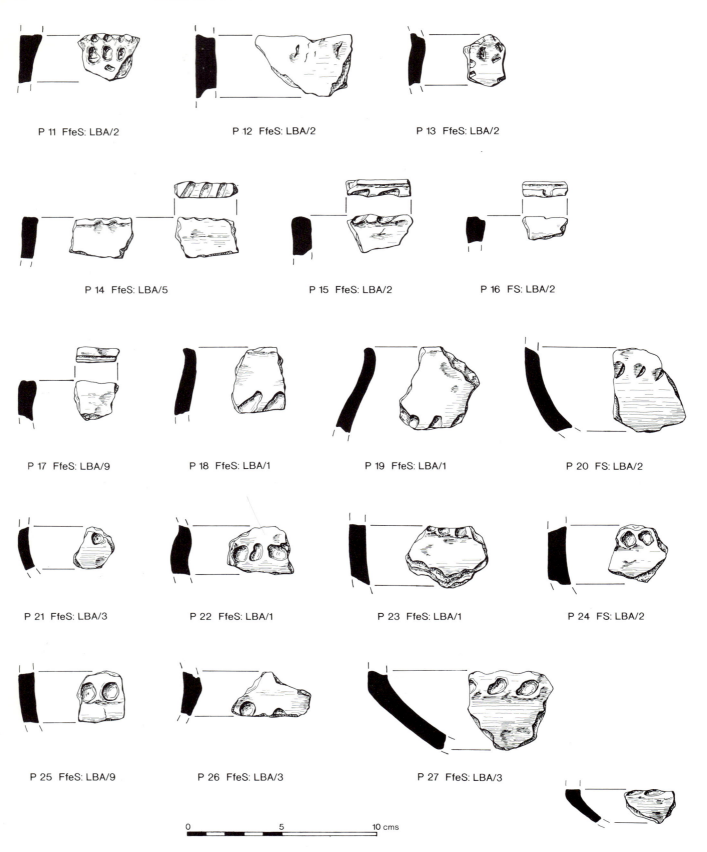

P 11 FfeS: LBA/2   P 12 FfeS: LBA/2   P 13 FfeS: LBA/2

P 14 FfeS: LBA/5   P 15 FfeS: LBA/2   P 16 FS: LBA/2

P 17 FfeS: LBA/9   P 18 FfeS: LBA/1   P 19 FfeS: LBA/1   P 20 FS: LBA/2

P 21 FfeS: LBA/3   P 22 FfeS: LBA/1   P 23 FfeS: LBA/1   P 24 FS: LBA/2

P 25 FfeS: LBA/9   P 26 FfeS: LBA/3   P 27 FfeS: LBA/3

0   5   10 cms

P 28 FS: LBA/2

Fig 53   Decorated sherds of Late Bronze Age Plain Ware from LDP 112 (P14–28), together with a few examples from the same site which may be derived from a slightly earlier phase (P11–13)

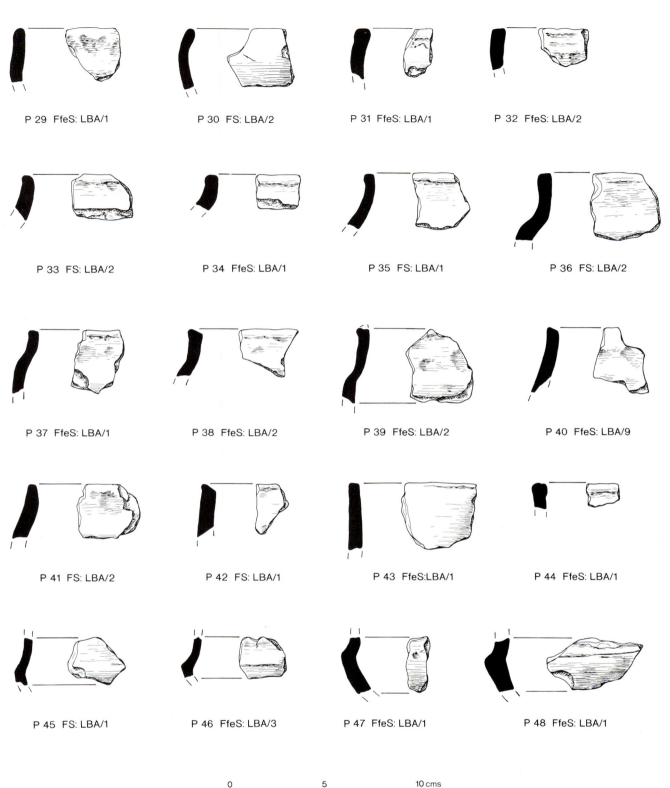

P 29 FfeS: LBA/1   P 30 FS: LBA/2   P 31 FfeS: LBA/1   P 32 FfeS: LBA/2

P 33 FS: LBA/2   P 34 FfeS: LBA/1   P 35 FS: LBA/1   P 36 FS: LBA/2

P 37 FfeS: LBA/1   P 38 FfeS: LBA/2   P 39 FfeS: LBA/2   P 40 FfeS: LBA/9

P 41 FS: LBA/2   P 42 FS: LBA/1   P 43 FfeS:LBA/1   P 44 FfeS: LBA/1

P 45 FS: LBA/1   P 46 FfeS: LBA/3   P 47 FfeS: LBA/1   P 48 FfeS: LBA/1

0   5   10 cms

Fig 54   Late Bronze Age Plain Ware from LDP 112

established Plain Ware fabrics and can therefore only be identified by stylistic criteria. This raises the possibility that undiagnostic wall or base sherds could be derived equally from Plain Ware or Early All Cannings Cross forms. The apparent absence of the second of these two ceramic styles from certain sites could, therefore, be a product of lack of recognition.

The other qualification is theoretical and returns once again to the notion that change is a consequence of internal dynamics, rather than being the result of external stimuli. According to this particular point of view, innovations are adopted deliberately, because they aid the social stratagems being pursued by individuals or groups. These may be concerned with the incorporation of new ideas in order to strengthen an existing system, or with the subversion of established discourse. In the absence of motives of this kind, prototypes developed in outside contexts will have very little impact, for they would be meaningless additions to traditional fields of expression. Innovations will not, therefore, be adopted synchronically, because the conditions necessary for their incorporation will exist only within certain social groups. It is entirely possible that the absence of Early All Cannings Cross forms from some of the sites in the Upper Study Area is not a product of chronology, but a reflection of their deliberate exclusion by particular elements within a larger community.

Although the ceramic evidence for absolute contemporaneity is not especially reliable, it can be used to identify situations in which observed contrasts and similarities are more likely to be the products of cultural, rather than chronological processes. In practice, this involves the utilisation of comparisons between sites that have produced assemblages representing the same range of phases. While this is not necessarily indicative of total synchroneity, it does increase the likelihood of an overlap in the occupation of such sites. This in turn provides a small measure of control against which to assess the reliability of other observations.

The manipulation of style: contrasts in the articulation of common themes

Within the Plain Ware assemblages from the Upper Study Area, there are a number of recurrent stylistic motifs that have a widespread distribution. This extends to sites in locations well outside Wessex. Common characteristics include decoration and vessel shape. As with all Plain Ware assemblages, decorative themes are restricted in both technique and application. Fingertip and fingernail rustication, arranged in horizontal bands, are confined to rims and shoulders. This style of decoration occurs on some of the pottery from Dunch Hill (Fig 55, P66; Fig 56, P74 and P83–6) and Milston Down (Fig 53, P15–16 and P18–28). In any one assemblage, such motifs are limited to less than 3% of the total number of sherds represented. A second, but rarer, form of decoration also has an extensive distribution. This consists of a series of short linear devices, impressed deeply into the clay and set on a diagonal axis. Again these motifs are arranged in horizontal bands, located on the rim tops and shoulders of vessels from Dunch Hill (Fig 55, P65; Fig 56, P82), the Northern Core Territory (Fig 55, P60), and Milston Down (Fig 53, P14).

In addition, these settlement foci share a number of attributes relating to vessel shape. Such stylistic elements include plain rounded rims, together with a second group of examples characterised by flattened mouldings, some of which have a slight internal bevel (plain rims: Fig 53, P15 and P19; Fig 54, P29–30; Fig 55, P62 and P64; Fig 56, P75–9; Fig 57, P90, P92–3, P95–6, and P100; flattened mouldings: Fig 53, P14; Fig 54, P32,

P36, P41, and P43; Fig 55, P60; Fig 57, P99; internal bevel: Fig 54, P37–8, P40, and P42; Fig 56, P71; Fig 57, P88–9 and P97–8). The extensive distribution of these features is paralleled by the geographical spread of the two main base forms. The first of these is simple and unelaborate (Fig 55, P52; Fig 57, P104–6), and the second has a foot ring (Fig 55, P53–4 and P59; Fig 56, P72–3 and P80–81; Fig 57, P103). The list can be extended to incorporate a whole series of analogous features. These comprise a range of convex (Fig 54, P30–32; Fig 55, P62; Fig 56, P67 and P87; Fig 57, P88), short concave (Fig 54, P33–5; Fig 55, P55, P57, and P64; Fig 56, P68 and P75–6; Fig 57, P90–91 and P94–6), and upright necks (Fig 53, P14–17; Fig 54, P36, P42, and P43; Fig 55, P60; Fig 56, P69 and P71; Fig 57, P92), together with shoulders of slack (Fig 54, P29; Fig 57, P101), rounded (Fig 53, P18–22; Fig 54, P36–7 and P45; Fig 55, P56 and P66; Fig 56, P82 and P84–5; Fig 57, P102), and sharply angled forms (Fig 53, P27–8; Fig 54, P46–8; Fig 55, P49–51; Fig 56, P83 and P86; Fig 57, P89 and P95).

At this general level of comparison, the impression is one of uniformity. This is, however, misleading, for it is partly a product of the classificatory method. The fragmentary nature of most prehistoric ceramic assemblages means that the search for parallels is conducted at the level of single stylistic elements. These cannot, however, be equated with a predictable formal outcome. Such a model ignores the potential for the creation of different vessel styles through the contrasts in the combination of shared features. There are hints that distinctions of this nature were being made in the Upper Study Area, although here too the assemblage is fragmentary and therefore hardly suitable for the adequate demonstration of such an hypothesis. In this case, the information is confined to the articulation of rounded rims, shoulders, and decorative motifs. It is only possible to identify this at Dunch Hill and Milston Down, since the evidence pertaining to style within the Northern Core Territory is very limited.

At both Dunch Hill and Milston Down, rounded rims are found on vessels, probably bowls, with open or slightly closed mouths (Fig 54, P29–30; Fig 56, P67). In addition, they characterise a series of forms with upright or concave necks and rounded bodies (Fig 53, P19; Fig 54, P33–5; Fig 55, P55; Fig 56, P68 and P76; Fig 57, P90–96). At Dunch Hill, the shoulders of such vessels tend to be of well-defined curvilinear or angular shape (Fig 57, P92 and P95), in contrast to those from Milston Down, which are less pronounced (Fig 53, P19). This distinction is supported by a slight difference in the shape of the rims on the Milston Down group, which have a faint outer lip. There is also some contrast between the two sites in the articulation of decoration and shoulder shape. Although in each location fingertip impressions are used to emphasise otherwise ill-defined shoulders, at Milston Down they occur on sharply angled varieties (Fig 53, P27–8). This never happens at Dunch Hill, where such motifs are confined to gently rounded or weakly angled shoulders (Fig 55, P66; Fig 56, P83–6), leaving the more noticeably bipartite vessels plain (Fig 57, P89 and P95).

The evidence for the maintenance of distinctions between ceramic assemblages within the Upper Study

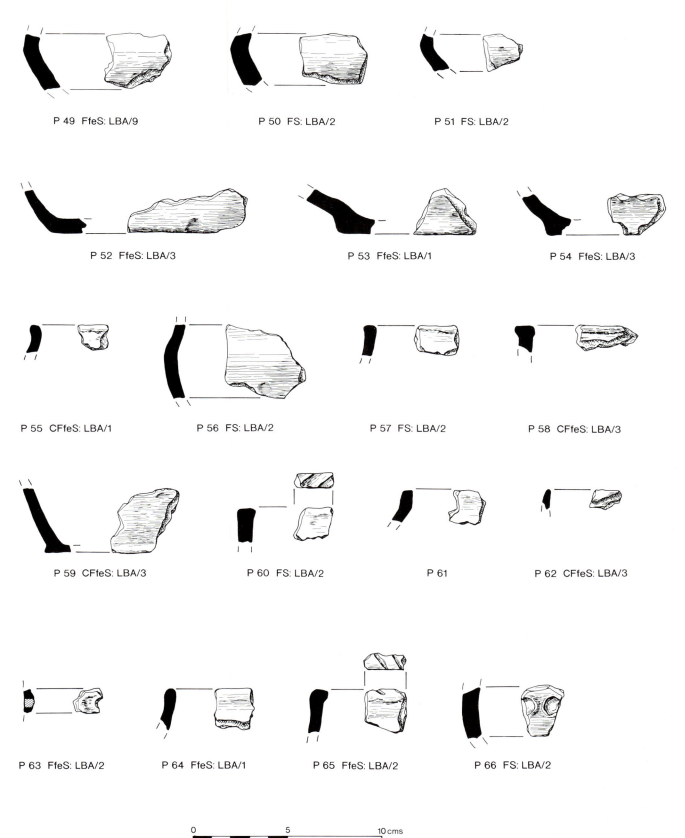

P 49 FfeS: LBA/9   P 50 FS: LBA/2   P 51 FS: LBA/2

P 52 FfeS: LBA/3   P 53 FfeS: LBA/1   P 54 FfeS: LBA/3

P 55 CFfeS: LBA/1   P 56 FS: LBA/2   P 57 FS: LBA/2   P 58 CFfeS: LBA/3

P 59 CFfeS: LBA/3   P 60 FS: LBA/2   P 61   P 62 CFfeS: LBA/3

P 63 FfeS: LBA/2   P 64 FfeS: LBA/1   P 65 FfeS: LBA/2   P 66 FS: LBA/2

0   5   10 cms

Fig 55   Late Bronze Age Plain Ware from LDP 112 (P49–54), LDP 109 (P55–6), LDP 092 (P57–9), LDP 102 (P60), LDP 098 (P61–3), LDP 111 (P64), and LDP 103 (P65–6)

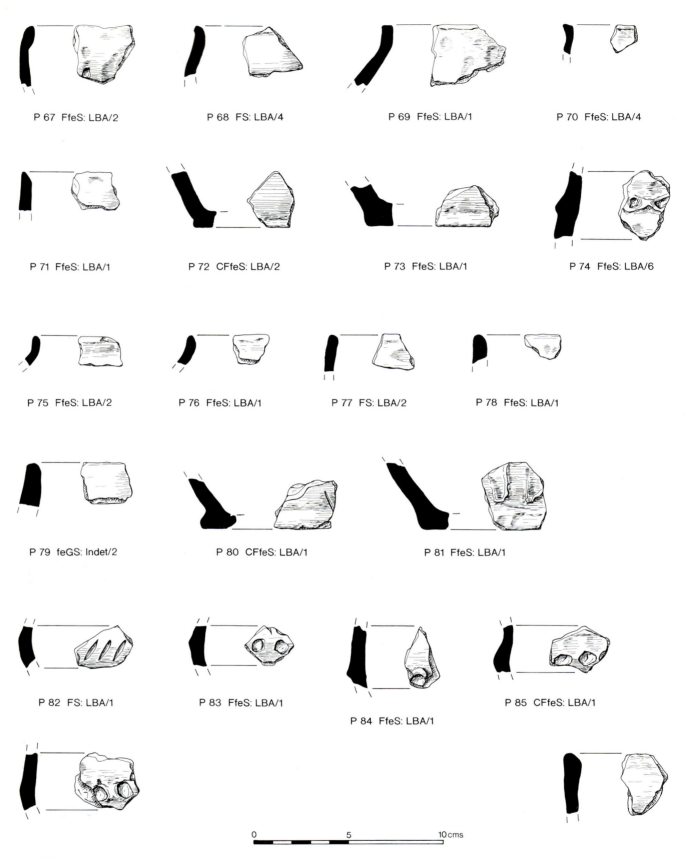

P 67 FfeS: LBA/2   P 68 FS: LBA/4   P 69 FfeS: LBA/1   P 70 FfeS: LBA/4

P 71 FfeS: LBA/1   P 72 CFfeS: LBA/2   P 73 FfeS: LBA/1   P 74 FfeS: LBA/6

P 75 FfeS: LBA/2   P 76 FfeS: LBA/1   P 77 FS: LBA/2   P 78 FfeS: LBA/1

P 79 feGS: Indet/2   P 80 CFfeS: LBA/1   P 81 FfeS: LBA/1

P 82 FS: LBA/1   P 83 FfeS: LBA/1   P 85 CFfeS: LBA/1

P 84 FfeS: LBA/1

0   5   10 cms

P 86 FfeS: LBA/3   P 87 FfeS: LBA/1

Fig 56   Late Bronze Age Plain Ware from LDP 103 (P67–73), LDP 087 (P74), LDP 081 (P75–81), and LDP 081A
(P82–7)

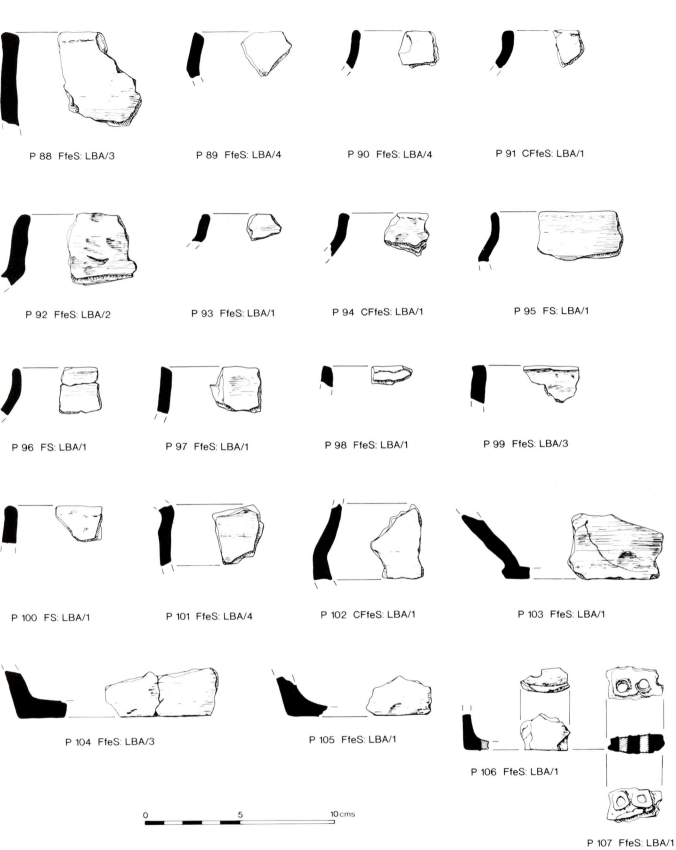

P 88 FfeS: LBA/3   P 89 FfeS: LBA/4   P 90 FfeS: LBA/4   P 91 CFfeS: LBA/1

P 92 FfeS: LBA/2   P 93 FfeS: LBA/1   P 94 CFfeS: LBA/1   P 95 FS: LBA/1

P 96 FS: LBA/1   P 97 FfeS: LBA/1   P 98 FfeS: LBA/1   P 99 FfeS: LBA/3

P 100 FS: LBA/1   P 101 FfeS: LBA/4   P 102 CFfeS: LBA/1   P 103 FfeS: LBA/1

P 104 FfeS: LBA/3   P 105 FfeS: LBA/1

P 106 FfeS: LBA/1

P 107 FfeS: LBA/1

0   5   10cms

Fig 57   Late Bronze Age Plain Ware from LDP 081A

Area is strengthened by a number of unique stylistic features, which exhibit confined distributions. Perhaps the most striking of these is the decorative motif found only on vessels from Milston Down. This comprises a single linear impression running around the circumference of a rim top (Fig 53, P15–17), accompanied occasionally by fingertip devices (Fig 53, P15–16). This too is unique, for fingertip decoration is confined to the shoulders of vessels from all other sites in the Upper Study Area. Conversely, Dunch Hill is the only settlement to produce pottery with deeply cut, diagonal impressions on a shoulder (Fig 56, P82). Elsewhere, such motifs are found on rim tops alone. In addition, Milston Down yielded a few sherds with fingertip and trapezoidal motifs arranged in apparently random patterns on vessel surfaces (Fig 53, P11–13). These have been omitted from the following discussion, because they may be of Deverel-Rimbury origin. Although the fabric from which they are made (FfeS: LBA/2) was used throughout the Plain Ware sequence, it could well have been developed initially in a Middle Bronze Age context.

In parallel with the production of unique motifs, the occupants of some of the settlements appear to have been making and using vessel shapes not exploited by their neighbours. Ceramics with pronounced convex necks and raised shoulders occur only on Milston Down (Fig 54, P47–8), while the expanded shape of the foot-ring base is a feature peculiar to Dunch Hill (Fig 56, P80; Fig 57, P103). In addition, although both sites have a series of rims with internal bevels, at Milston Down they tend to be everted or enlarged externally (Fig 53, P18; Fig 54, P37–8, P40, and P43). Finally, Dunch Hill seems to have been the only settlement where a form of strainer was in current use (Fig 55, P63 and Fig 57, P106–7).

By this stage, it is increasingly clear that the identified patterns are extremely complex, seemingly contradictory, and often nebulous. They are not, however, negative, for it is entirely possible to move towards an interpretation that encompasses these very qualities. At a fundamental level, we need to introduce the idea that culture is neither a concrete nor a static entity, but that it is a dynamic process concerned with the constitution of human society. Here, the term 'culture' is used to mean a series of complex relations organised according to an historically specific perception of the world. The realisation of these relations, which constantly alter and sometimes contradict one another, relies entirely on their expression: on their embodiment as perceptual categories. This field of expression incorporates the humanly constructed environment in which nature, architecture, and a variety of other media, including portable objects, exemplify and help to create relationships, obligations, and a particular authority structure (Bourdieu 1977 and 1979; Tilley 1982; Kus 1982; Hodder 1986; Conkey 1989 and 1990; Barrett 1991; and Thomas 1991).

Essentially, the situation is extremely fluid. The multiple significance of objects, comprising a range of associated ideas inherent in their form, may exist at a purely subliminal level. In certain circumstances, such meaning can remain relatively dormant and extremely ill defined. This might occur, for instance, if a single artefact class occupies a peripheral position in relation to stratagems directed towards the formation, re-formation, and transformation of society.

Under other conditions, the same group of objects may come to fulfil a central role in the realisation of such strategies. This is achieved only through the appropriation of meaning, involving attempts to impose prejudiced interpretations. Processes of this kind have been identified in a number of ethnographic case studies. These demonstrate that material symbols can become essential elements within strategies aimed towards the control and neutralisation of contradictions and ambiguities (Hodder 1981 and 1982; Braithwaite 1982). In addition, they may be used to articulate ideas about the social, natural, or ancestral environment (David, Sterner, and Gavua 1988; Deboer 1990). In other contexts, certain formal attributes or particular objects are read as emblems of institutionalised identities, including ethnicity, age, status and gender groups, and individuality (Hodder 1977 and 1982; Wiessner 1983, 1985, and 1990; Davis 1985; Larich 1985; Deboer 1990).

Whether the appropriation of material symbols is directed towards the resolution of contradictions, the maintenance of relative identities, or a mixture of these and a plethora of alternative aims will depend upon the specific tactics being pursued. Whatever the motive, the attempt to fix meaning, in the sense of arriving at a consensus interpretation, is a difficult process and one unlikely to meet with enduring success. The meanings conveyed by style may be distinct or vague, but they are also innately ambiguous. Their appropriation requires repeated reassertion through the use of objects in confined contexts, and with a specific range of associations, in order to evoke a particular understanding. This will not necessarily meet with a predictable result, for it involves a further act of interpretation on the part of the audience, who, because of their different relative positions, may tend to highlight alternative meanings inherent within the same artefacts. This, in turn, might result in a re-formation of the original statement in order to take account of its reception. The situation becomes even more complex in the case of portable objects. These contain an increased potential for the expression of a variety of ideas, as they are moved from one context to another and articulated within contrasting spheres of interaction.

A useful descriptive framework for these processes is provided by the analogy between material culture and written text (Hodder 1988; Thomas 1991). According to this, multiple authors pursuing different and contrasting aims appropriate and stress the meanings most likely to result in the success of those intentions. Objects are an essential part of such social discourse, which is concerned with imparting prejudiced knowledge about a labyrinthine network of human relations. By increasing the available 'vocabulary', greater stylistic variation within an artefact set enhances its potential as an aid to the expression of richer and more complex ideas. Essentially, all formal variation is significant, whether it is equated with vague subliminal meanings, or is exploited in a deliberate and tactical manner.

This is extremely important because, as suggested at an earlier stage in this chapter, it means that the increased repertoire of styles within Late Bronze Age Plain Ware assemblages represents unequivocally the mobilisation of ceramics within an extended series of discourses. It is not possible to be certain whether these were subliminal or overtly manipulative. Nor can we hope to recover the exact symbolism, or the precise nature of social strategies, from our position in the present, where we have no direct access to the specific historical and cultural world of the Late Bronze Age. However, the equation between variation and multifaceted meaning provides a way of approaching a data set, not with perplexity at the inconsistencies and contradictions, but with an expectation that these should be present as a product of the real complexities and oppositions that characterise social relations and that people are forced to confront as they interact.

Within the Upper Study Area, we are looking at the fragmentary remnants of social discourse. At a certain level, the physical boundaries that divided the landscape were highly permeable, in the sense that they were not reinforced by the limited distribution of individual stylistic elements. It seems likely that these common themes carried with them a notion of the wider community. Their contrasting articulation within separate settlements may have been one method, through which local groups maintained their distinctive identity. However, this is rather over-simplistic and deterministic as an explanation and it seems more likely that common stylistic motifs were being drawn into different spheres of discourse, which referred to the unique set of relations existing between people occupying each of the extensive open occupation sites. Thus, the intra-site stylistic similarities express unity as a by-product of shared significance, rather than being exploited as aggressive emblems of identity.

The organisation of production: the relationship between technology and style

With the exception of FS: LBA/1, used for a distinctive series of bowls (Fig 54, P35 and P45; Fig 56, P82; Fig 57, P95–6), none of the identified wares appears to have been confined to a specific ceramic style. This observation applies to both Dunch Hill (LDP 081A and 103) and Milston Down (LDP 112). The manner in which fabric and style were articulated in the Northern Core Territory is unknown, because of the insufficient number of sherds with formal attributes. The evidence for this apparently haphazard exploitation of different wares is derived from an analysis of six fabrics (CFfeS: LBA/1, FfeS: LBA/1, FfeS: LBA/2, FfeS: LBA/3, FfeS: LBA/4, and FS: LBA/2). These are the only examples where sherds with formal attributes occur in sufficient quantities to render such an exercise valid. Of the remaining 14 fabrics, 6 are represented by featureless wall and base fragments (CF: LBA/1, FfeM: LBA/1, Ffesh: LBA/1, FSshV: LBA/1, feSsh: LBA/1, sh: LBA/1) and 8 are confined to an occasional rim, base angle, or decorated shoulder (CFfeS: LBA/2, CFfeS: LBA/3, clSsh: LBA/1, FfeS: LBA/5, FfeS: LBA/6, FfeS: LBA/9, FS: LBA/4, and FS: LBA/6). It is possible that any one, or all, of these 14 examples were used for a more restricted range of styles, although certainly the majority were exploited for the production of vessels with different wall thicknesses and surface treatments.

A similar variation in size and finish is exhibited by the pottery made from each of the six fabrics, where stylistic information is available (CFfeS: LBA/1, FfeS: LBA/1, FfeS: LBA/2, FfeS: LBA/3, FfeS: LBA/4, and FS: LBA/2). Wall thicknesses can measure anywhere between 4 and 12mm. Some vessels have received no surface treatment; on others, either the inner, the outer, or both faces have been smoothed, so that none of the inclusions protrude; while the tempering of a further group has been covered with a layer of clay, so that it is no longer visible – again this can occur on the inside, on the outside, or on both surfaces. In addition, the bases of certain examples have been encrusted with large quantities of flint grit. This range of finishes is found on pottery of similar shapes and with analogous decorative motifs. There is a lack of correspondence between fine wares or decorated vessels and high-quality surface treatments. In fact, there is a tendency, especially at Dunch Hill, for the sherds with fingertip impressions to have a fairly rough appearance.

The awareness of the mechanical properties of different tempers, which was earlier proposed as one possible explanation for the inverse relationship between quartz sand and flint (see p75), was mobilised and exploited for an extremely limited range of vessels within the entire ceramic repertoire. This is illustrated most clearly by the fabric FS: LBA/1, which is, in addition, the only ware with a demonstrably restricted application. For the most part, it was used to make fairly open vessels with a distinctly bipartite form. These are represented within the assemblages from Dunch Hill (Fig 57, P95 and P96) and Milston Down (Fig 54, P45). The particularly high percentage of sand incorporated in the clay not only increased the resilience of such vessels, but also decreased the likelihood of sagging during manufacture. This allowed for the moulding of a thin-walled uniform shape, which could be fired at much higher temperatures. This level of uniformity and control was extended to the surface finishes, which include burnishing and are generally of a very high quality, and the colour, which is usually black or dark grey. None of the other vessels in the ceramic repertoire display any evidence for burnishing or the manipulation of colour. In fact, it is fairly common for single sherds to exhibit a range of shades, typical of open bonfire firings.

For the most part, the variable physical benefits of contrasting fabrics were not controlled, in the sense that single wares were used for many different ceramic forms. Conversely, the same pottery styles were made from several alternative fabrics. The advantages of such wares were apparently ignored, in terms of increasing the utility of vessels for specific functions. This should come as no surprise, since there is no reason to suppose that Late Bronze Age society was permeated with twentieth-century cost-benefit obsessions.

It is possible that the observed relationship between fabric and style is a consequence of the production of pottery by many different groups within a single settlement. If this was the case, then each set of potters may have favoured a specific fabric or range of wares, which they used in the manufacture of a broad repertoire of forms with diverse surface finishes and sizes. The lack of correspondence between fabric and all other attributes could be a reflection of two distinctive processes: domestic production and the creation of multiple categories of similarity and difference, through the manipulation of stylistic criteria.

To a certain extent, the high degree of diversity may be misleading, for it arises partly out of a perspective that tends to compress successive events into a single synchronous dimension. We do not know how far preferred mixtures of clay and temper changed through time, although some fabrics certainly persisted throughout the period when Plain Wares were produced and used in the Upper Study Area. These comprise five examples represented both at LDP 092 and LDP 081A (FfeS: LBA/1, FfeS: LBA/2, FfeS: LBA/3, FfeS: LBA/5, and FS: LBA/1), which yielded assemblages belonging respectively to the early and final phases of this Late Bronze Age ceramic tradition.

The observation of similar characteristics in the relationship between fabric and style at Dunch Hill and Milston Down may imply that the production of pottery was organised in an analogous manner. In this respect, it is surely of consequence that both sites were peripheral to the bounded landscape of the Northern Core Territory. At a broad level, the resemblance in the productive practice of the two communities echoes their common occupation of an unenclosed terrain. The organisation of space on a more focused plane seems also to have been perpetuated by material culture. As we have seen, the occupants of geographically distinct settlements were producing unique styles and were articulating common traits in a contrasting way. In addition, the significance of the fabrics may not have been the same on Dunch Hill and Milston Down, since identical ceramic traits are likely to have contrasting meanings in different contexts. This applies just as much to fabric as it does to style. As Dietler and Herbich have demonstrated (1989), through their research into the production and use of pottery by the Luo in western Kenya, separate communities exploit the same vessels for different functions. These transformations in meaning are achieved through the changing relationships between style and utility, which are not archaeologically visible. Although such shifts in significance must remain conjectural as far as the prehistoric past is concerned, we can observe the way in which the same fabrics in each of the settlements were used to produce unique vessel shapes and decorative motifs. This provides at least some evidence for the involvement of ceramics in two distinctive fields of local discourse, in spite of the resemblance between their productive bases.

Contrasts in the articulation of shared technologies: further evidence for distinctions within and outside Late Bronze Age territories

The evidence for the exchange of technological knowledge is reinforced by the extensive distribution of many of the fabrics throughout the Study Area (see Table 24). Although this parallels the geographical spread of Beaker and Deverel-Rimbury ceramics, it represents a new development. By the Late Bronze Age, the coarse wares were no longer restricted to specific localities: their distribution mirrored that of the fine wares. This is indicative of the sharing of a much broader spectrum of technical information.

Superficially, the impression is one of homogeneity, but, as with the consideration of style, this depends entirely on the perspective from which the evidence is viewed. Although each of the settlements shares a series of identical fabrics, these are represented in contrasting proportions on separate sites. The occupants of Dunch Hill, Milston Down, and the Northern Core Territory must have had access to information, relating to a common series of different clay and temper mixtures. They were then favouring different fabrics from that central pool, according to criteria that were irrational in the sense that the preferred wares have no utilitarian advantage over the slighted examples.

In any comparison of the percentages from the separate Dunch Hill sites, the results for LDP 087 and LDP 111 should be regarded with caution. The amount of pottery recovered from both locations is low and the percentage distributions are therefore likely to be skewed. In general, the relative proportions of fabrics from the various occupation foci at Dunch Hill are similar, although at LDP 103 there is a decrease in the quantity of FfeS: LBA/1 and an increase in the amount of FS: LBA/2. The higher percentage of CFfeS: LBA/2 at LDP 103 may be a reflection of the earlier beginnings of this site. Although the fabric was used to produce Plain Ware pottery, its characteristics suggest that its origins may lie in the Middle Bronze Age. Similar intra-settlement contrasts occur between the two sites in the Northern Core Territory (Table 24). Again, these may result from chronological factors, but they could also reflect the selection of favoured fabrics, or even the acquisition of ceramics from a preferred potter, by different people belonging to the same community.

At the inter-site level, the percentage distributions of wares from Dunch Hill and Milston Down are remarkably similar, with the exception of FS: LBA/2, which is more common on the second of these two settlement foci. The problem with interpreting these patterns is that we do not know what processes led to the interchange of technological knowledge, nor do we know how closely the assimilation of this information was controlled. Although a high degree of correlation is not necessarily indicative of an increased rate of interaction between the two communities, it could have arisen because they shared very similar ideas: in this case, a series of preconceived notions about technical practice.

These ideas were evidently somewhat different in the Northern Core Territory. Contrasts in the relative proportions of identical fabrics are most marked between the assemblages from occupation foci within this territorial unit and those from the settlements outside its boundaries (Table 24). Whereas FfeS: LBA/1 predominates on Dunch Hill and Milston Down, it is a relatively minor component within the groups of pottery from LDP 080 and LDP 102. The fact that both of these sites exhibit almost identical proportions of this fabric, in spite of the possible differences in their chronologies, suggests that the patterning is the result of cultural, and not temporal, processes. Other contrasts between either LDP 080, or LDP 102 and the Dunch Hill and Milston Down settlements include FfeS: LBA/2 and FfeS: LBA/5, which are more common at LDP 080 than elsewhere, and FS:

LBA/2, which comprises a far higher percentage of the assemblage from LDP 102 than it does on any other site.

The presence of singular attitudes towards the appropriateness of particular fabrics within the Northern Core Territory finds additional empirical support in the exclusion of 11 wares from this area (Table 24). These include all clays tempered with shell (Ffesh: LBA/1, FSshV: LBA/1, feSsh: LBA/1, sh: LBA/1, and clSsh: LBA/1) and incorporating mica (FfeM: LBA/1). Neither is the fabric FS: LBA/1 represented among the assemblages from LDP 080 and LDP 102. In this case, it exemplifies more than the omission of a singular mixture of clay and temper, for specific productive techniques are also absent. These include high firing temperatures, burnishing, and uniform colouring. Again, this proscription is unlikely to have been an effect of chronology. The recurrence of FS: LBA/1, both within the early Plain Ware occupation around LDP 092 and LDP 109 and in the late Plain Ware to Early All Cannings Cross midden at LDP 081A, is indicative of its longevity. Yet, in spite of the correspondence between the currency of this fabric and the period spanned by the settlements at LDP 080 and LDP 102, FS: LBA/1 remains conspicuously absent from the ceramic assemblages of the Northern Core Territory. Such contrasts are reinforced further by the lower diversity of fabrics from this area, when compared with the range of wares within assemblages from Milston Down and Dunch Hill (Table 24).

Drawing together the results of the ceramic analysis, we seem to have a situation in which the spatial organisation of the landscape during the Late Bronze Age was complemented by at least one element of the material culture repertoire. The geographical separation of settlements was reflected in subtle distinctions between the pottery assemblages from each discrete occupation. In the case of Dunch Hill and Milston Down, both groups were exploiting a similar repertoire of fabrics and technical processes, but were using these to produce two contrasting ranges of ceramic styles. The occupants of the Northern Core Territory favoured a different series of wares and techniques. Whether or not these were reinforced by distinctions in their manipulation of stylistic themes must, on present evidence, remain a matter for conjecture. But this is simply one dimension of an extremely complex situation. Once the perspective moves beyond the domain of the settlement into the wider landscape, we can begin to see ways in which material culture encapsulated, and indeed helped to constitute, the organisation and perception of territory. While the contrasts between the ceramics of Dunch Hill and Milston Down may refer to the unique set of relations that existed among the people living in each location, within the context of a distinctive settlement, the similarities were paralleled by the setting of these sites within an unenclosed zone. The distinctive quality of the pottery used by the occupants of the Northern Core Territory was reinforced by, and reinforced, the bounded landscape that surrounded their settlements. The topographical location of the linear ditches was such that they emphasised visibility from within the territories (see Chap 8), and this finds additional analogues within the ceramic assemblage. This inward focus of space was paralleled by the singular articulation of common attributes. At the same time, the impression that the boundaries were not

designed as barriers is strengthened by the way in which ideas about technology and style moved freely across their limits. The theme was not one of exclusion, but was concerned with incorporation and transformation.

Focusing on the boundaries: Plain Ware ceramics in linear ditches

None of the sections through linear ditches provided evidence for the deliberate placement of pottery in territorial boundaries. The few Plain Ware sherds from LDP 092, LDP 097, and LDP 098 are small, in variable condition, tend to be featureless wall or base fragments, appear to have been derived from different vessels, and are scattered within the ditch silts. The single Late Bronze Age sherd from the terminal of the double linear ditch (LDP 100) is residual. It occurred in the same context (Context 4) as fragments of haematite-coated ware. Its presence on this site, however, is significant, since it may mean that Sidbury Hill was the focus of settlement for a long period preceding the construction of the hillfort.

Although pottery was derived from the sorted horizon of the buried soil at LDP 092, it was not incorporated in the primary silts of the ditch. However, two sherds in relatively fresh condition were recovered from the stabilisation horizon at the base of the secondary silts (Context 6), providing a *terminus post quem* for their formation. The only other sherd which came from the ditch was located within the tertiary silts. The higher degree of abrasion which characterised this fragment may have resulted from its incorporation after the end of the Late Bronze Age (see Chap 6).

Plain Wares were represented throughout the primary, secondary, and tertiary silts of LDP 097. In general, they exhibit a high degree of abrasion, in keeping with the condition of the antler cheek piece (Fig 36). Sherds from the primary silts are abraded just as heavily as those from the upper stratigraphic contexts. The extent of the time lapse between their deposition and incorporation within the ditch must remain a matter for conjecture. However, they do indicate that SPTA 2244 cut through, or came close to, yet another Late Bronze Age settlement located to the north of this territorial boundary.

At LDP 098, there is a marked contrast between the mixed period assemblage from the lynchet (Context 3) and the group of pottery located within the ditch silts. Here, it was confined to the lower contexts (Context 9, 10, and 12) and appeared to be of Late Bronze Age date alone. Of the six sherds from this location, four were attributed to an indeterminate phase within the prehistoric sequence, but all display characteristics whose closest analogies are within the Late Bronze Age (see Appendix 2, Table 33). Although the pottery from Contexts 9 and 10 was heavily abraded, fragments from Context 12 were in good condition. This, together with the confinement of the assemblage to a single phase within the Late Bronze Age, may indicate that SPTA 1971 was backfilled during, or soon after the currency of Plain Wares (see Chap 7 for an expanded discussion of this episode). Since it is entirely possible, however, that older deposits were thrown back into the ditch during

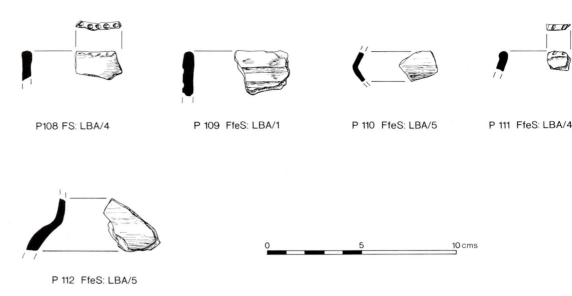

P108 FS: LBA/4   P 109 FfeS: LBA/1   P 110 FfeS: LBA/5   P 111 FfeS: LBA/4

P 112 FfeS: LBA/5

Fig 58   Early All Cannings Cross pottery from LDP 112, LDP 080, and LDP 081A

this process, the proposed chronology should be regarded as extremely tentative.

Fragmentation: the introduction of All Cannings Cross prototypes and the demise of Plain Ware settlement

If the ceramics fail to provide definitive answers to questions concerning the precise chronology of a specific alteration in the boundary between two territories, they do reflect a transformation on a much larger scale in the organisation of the landscape. The settlements within and outside the areas defined by linear ditches survived just long enough to witness the introduction of Early All Cannings Cross pottery styles. They then ceased before these new prototypes came to dominate the ceramic repertoire, and before alterations in technical practice were made and adopted. The radiocarbon date from the midden on Dunch Hill (LDP 081A) suggests that this occurred sometime between *c* 770 and *c* 395 cal BC (Chap 3, Table 22: OxA-3048), although the presence of Plain Ware throughout this deposit, and the absence of Iron Age ceramics, would favour a date at the beginning of this rather broad range. Once again, changes in material culture prefigure major transformations: this time a dislocation in settlement. This disruption affected all Late Bronze Age occupation foci, with the possible exception of the example to the north of Enclosure A on Snail Down (see Raymond forthcoming). This must have changed the significance of the territories defined by linear ditches, as they no longer marked the landscapes occupied and used by separate local communities. We may well be seeing a progression away from a sense of unity focused inwards on individual settlements, towards the closer integration of a much larger group. Indeed, the emergence of a ceramic style zone centred on Wessex during the eighth century BC (Cunliffe 1978) has been equated with the development of a sense of regional identity (Barrett 1980a and 1980b). Although we cannot be sure that pottery was used as an

aggressive symbol of ethnicity at this time, it may well have signalled a greater cohesion over a much wider area.

Early All Cannings Cross forms occur within the ceramic assemblages from three Plain Ware occupation foci (LDP 080, 081A, and 112). On each site, they are extremely scarce. Although not found at the very base of the midden on Dunch Hill (081A), sherds from vessels with attributes derived from this new ceramic style were represented throughout the rest of the deposit (Context 3). This may indicate that their adoption was a fairly protracted process, although the midden was not particularly thick and we do not know how rapidly it accumulated. The single Deverel-Rimbury sherd from LDP 081A was derived from a much earlier field ditch (Context 12) and probably relates to a phase when the trackway was still in use. It cannot, therefore, be appropriated as evidence for the longevity of the midden.

There is very little information concerning the overall form of the All Cannings Cross vessels, so that it is entirely possible that they exhibited close affinities with the Plain Ware assemblages. In fact, elsewhere in southern England the basic repertoire of vessel types is similar for both style groups. Within the Upper Study Area, the identification of Early All Cannings Cross pottery relies on single attributes, either decorative motifs, shoulder shape, or surface treatment. The only All Cannings Cross sherd from the settlement on Milston Down is characterised by a series of deeply impressed circles (Fig 58, P108). Although the decorative motif is new, the shape of the vessel to which it was applied and its location along the top of the rim are well-established stylistic attributes, found within the Plain Ware assemblage from the same site. This fragment is paralleled by an analogous example from the Dunch Hill midden (Fig 58, P111), which also produced a haematite-coated sherd and a shoulder from a vessel with a typically All Cannings Cross profile (Fig 58, P112). Within the Northern Core Territory, at LDP 080, the only two featured sherds display similar affinities. These include the strongly developed bipartite shape of the shoulder fragment (Fig 58, P110) and the shallow furrows used to decorate the neck of the other example (Fig 58, P109).

The fabric analysis supports the impression, derived from a consideration of stylistic criteria, that the new prototypes were being introduced rather tentatively into a pre-existing framework. All of the vessels with All Cannings Cross attributes were being constructed from traditional fabrics (FfeS: LBA/1, FfeS: LBA/4, FfeS: LBA/5, and FS: LBA/4). The only exception is the haematite-coated sherd from Dunch Hill, made from a ware not represented among the Plain Ware assemblages (FfeM: LBA/1). The micaceous clay used in the production of this vessel either denotes the exploitation of a new raw material source, or the importation of pottery from outside the immediate locality. Whatever the answer, the processes involved were unusual, for they are represented by a single sherd alone.

Re-formation: developed All Cannings Cross ceramics and the foundation of new settlements

By the time developed All Cannings Cross assemblages were being used in the Study Area, the focus of settlement had shifted. The presence of haematite-coated sherds within derived contexts in the terminal of the double linear (LDP 100) indicates a settlement of unknown scale or form on Sidbury Hill, which perhaps preceded the construction of the ramparts. Apart from their surface treatment, these fragments are entirely undiagnostic and could belong equally to All Cannings Cross assemblages of either Late Bronze Age or Early Iron Age date. The fabric (S: indet/3) is not particularly helpful in this respect, for it is paralleled by wares used to produce vessels representing both of these ceramic phases in the north-western corner of the Study Area. These comprise Early All Cannings Cross forms from Upavon Aerodrome and later styles from the old land surface beneath the bank at Chisenbury Trendle (Cunnington 1932). In fact, S: indet/3 may have been produced throughout the Iron Age, since it occurred in the lynchet at LDP 082, which began to accumulate towards the end of this period.

With the exception of Sidbury Hill, the ceramic evidence for All Cannings Cross settlement is derived from Chisenbury Trendle (Cunnington 1932), Lidbury (Cunnington and Cunnington 1917), and Upavon Aerodrome (Grinsell 1957). It was collected and excavated during the early years of this century and, unfortunately, the contextual information is extremely limited. It does, however, demonstrate that these occupations were new: they did not originate during the earlier period. There is absolutely no resemblance between the ceramic styles and fabrics from these north-western sites and any of the Plain Ware assemblages from the Upper Study Area.

The evidence for a pre-rampart phase of occupation on Sidbury Hill is reinforced by a similar phenomenon at Chisenbury Trendle (Cunnington 1932). In this case, the pottery occupied a secure stratigraphic position below the bank of the hillfort on the old land surface (ibid). Its closest parallels lie within All Cannings Cross-Meon Hill assemblages, which were in current use during the sixth and fifth centuries BC (Cunliffe 1978 and 1984c). As is typical of this style, the fine pottery from Chisen-

bury Trendle is dominated by haematite-coated cordoned bowls. In addition, a small percentage of vessels are decorated with geometric motifs, scratched into the surface of the clay after firing.

The occupation of Lidbury was to a certain extent contemporary with this settlement. A sherd from a scratched-cordoned bowl of All Cannings Cross-Meon Hill type was recovered from Pit 1. However, there is also a Late Bronze Age phase at Lidbury, for Pit 7 produced a fine black-burnished bipartite bowl with a profile typical of this period, while the main ditch section yielded two residual haematite-coated sherds from vessels with gently rounded shoulders, together with a single fragment from a lugged bowl.

The early foundation of Lidbury is paralleled by the nearby settlement at Upavon Aerodrome, which was occupied during the eighth and/or seventh centuries BC (this lies just outside the Upper Study Area at SU 1554). Although the provenance of the pottery attributed to this site is not entirely secure (Grinsell 1957), it is certainly of Early All Cannings Cross date. The fine wares are almost exclusively furrowed bowls (a minimum of ten vessels), some with haematite coating, others with black-burnished surfaces, and one with white inlay.

Unfortunately, it is not possible to place the first enclosure at Lidbury, represented by the outer or 'supernumerary' ditch, to such a precise position within the All Cannings Cross sequence. This is partly because the stratigraphic evidence has been lost, because, although the ceramics were archived according to the specific features from which they were excavated, there are no records providing information concerning the relative vertical location of any of the sherds. In addition, the sample of pottery from the outer ditch is small and most of the haematite-coated fragments lack diagnostic features, so that they could equally be of Late Bronze Age or Early Iron Age origin. These limitations apply to similar sherds derived from an unknown context within the main ditch section and from two of the pits inside the enclosure (Pits 3 and 4). The only identifiable form within the assemblage from the outer ditch comprises a sherd from a single furrowed bowl with white inlay. However, since this lacks a rim, it is not possible to assign it to a particular phase within the All Cannings Cross sequence.

The later Iron Age development of Lidbury must remain the subject of future research, for it is the early phase alone which is relevant to the present discussion. Although the second enclosure could have been constructed at any time during the period beginning with the eighth and finishing with the fifth century BC, unlike the main ditch it does not incorporate later ceramics. The Linear Boundary, which abuts the outer ditch, must have been constructed at some time during the period, when this earliest enclosure was still a functioning entity.

While a detailed analysis of the ceramics from Lidbury and the Upavon area was beyond the scope of the work encompassed by the project, there are a few general observations which contribute to ideas extending beyond the establishment of a chronological framework. Quite simply, these support the earlier suggestion that the ceramics of this period reflect a greater regional cohesion between local communities (see p 88). Not only do the styles appear to emphasise wider referents, but some of the pottery seems to have been imported from outside, carrying with it implications of a relationship with more distant populations. This includes the scratched cordoned bowl, with a suggested origin somewhere in the vicinity of Salisbury (Cunliffe 1984c), and a number of oolitic wares (including one haematite-coated vessel) deposited in the outer ditch and Pit 3, which must have been derived from somewhere along the Jurassic Ridge. At the very least, this represents the transferral of certain themes concerning external referents to a new medium of expression.

Restructuring: linear ditches and Iron Age ceramics

There was very little Iron Age pottery recovered during the project and even less in direct association with linear ditches. Most of the sherds representing this period are undiagnostic wall and base fragments of uncertain phasing. Exceptions include a Late Iron Age bead-rim jar from LDP 001 and a Late Iron Age or early Romano-British rim from LDP 019.

Even though infrequent, two of the associations between Iron Age sherds and linear ditches are particularly important. The first of these relates to a section excavated through SPTA 2238 by Thomas, where three sherds, including a Middle Iron Age rim, were found at the base of the secondary silts. These were stratified above two further fragments of pottery made from a similar fabric (see Raymond forthcoming). This reinforces the evidence recovered during the excavation of SPTA 2234 at LDP 083. In this case, a single Iron Age sherd of uncertain phasing was located in an analogous stratigraphic position, in the lower secondary silts (Context 3). Both of these ditches display a marked V-profile, and both form part of relatively small enclosures, which may have been utilised for the containment of stock (see Chap 7). Although Iron Age pottery was recovered from the sections through ditches defining the larger territories that form part of the Late Bronze Age layout (LDP 008A and 098), it was confined to lynchets overlying or spilling into the very top of these features. It would seem that the new boundaries, concerned with the management of a largely arable landscape, were contemporary at least in part with the hillfort on Sidbury Hill.

Besides providing brief glimpses into the chronology of this form of organisation, the quality of the ceramic evidence precludes a more detailed interpretation of this period in the Study Area. The elucidation of the relationships between settlements and people within and outside this vicinity during the Iron Age must remain the subject of future research. To this extent, the ceramics converge with the original intentions of the project, since the evidence becomes increasingly sparse as the focus of attention moves away from linear ditches.

5 The analysis of five flint assemblages from the Upper Study Area

by Ross Whitehead

Introduction

The decision to take a selective approach to the treatment of the bulk flint from surface collection and excavation sites was discussed in Chapter 3. A number of observations were made in connection with several sites, where the composition of the flint assemblages suggested raw material procurement (Fig 16). LDP 104 was one of these, but in this instance more detailed analysis was undertaken, because the potential existed to relate procurement to domestic activity at settlements associated with the Northern Core Territory (Fig 15). The surface collection material from these latter sites included large quantities of Late Bronze Age Plain Ware pottery (Figs 21 and 46), and consequently they offered an ideal opportunity to relate lithic technology to an independently devised chronology.

The lithic assemblages from these sites are of further value, insofar as they provide an additional source of evidence for the character and spatial organisation of a range of activities, contemporary with the construction and use of the linear ditches system. The groups of material selected for analysis were collected from the two settlements on Brigmerston Down (LDP 102 and 080), from parts of another settlement on Dunch Hill (LDP 081 and LDP 081A), and from an extensive surface scatter between Bourne Bottom and Dunch Hill (LDP 104; see Fig 16).

This detailed study aims to compare and contrast the chronological and functional characteristics of the flint assemblages from each of the selected sites. The first of these themes draws on the background provided by the ceramic evidence, which indicates certain temporal distinctions between the different settlements (Chap 4). Of the sites under discussion, those in the Northern Core Territory (LDP 102 and 080) apparently have the earliest beginnings, towards the end of the Middle Bronze Age. Both continued throughout the Plain Ware horizon, but LDP 102 may have ceased before LDP 080, which lasted until the beginning of the eighth century BC. The few Beaker sherds from LDP 102 seem to represent a separate episode of a rather different character: while they may provide evidence of the repeated use of the landscape from an early period, there is nothing to suggest continuous settlement. The occupation of the area of Dunch Hill represented by LDP 081 and 081A began and ended during the Late Bronze Age, although here too there are differences in the time-depth represented by the two assemblages. The midden (LDP 081A) appears to have accumulated during a relatively restricted phase leading up to the early years of the eighth century BC, whereas the more general scatter of material in the same area (LDP 081) refers to a longer time period.

The ubiquity and high survival properties of worked flint make it particularly amenable to analysis encompassing both chronological and functional traits. Chronological attributes may reside in specific tool types, in certain morphological characteristics, or in the relative condition of the flintwork arising from post-depositional alterations, such as the degree of patination. Our ability to recognise functional patterning depends on an understanding of a number of important processes: procurement, manufacture, use, and discard (Burton 1980; Richards 1990, 18–19). Each of these stages is associated with the particular attributes of the flakes, cores, and tools that make up a lithic assemblage. However, such processes can only be recognised with any confidence, if they took place in different areas, and this must be investigated, not assumed.

The main characteristic of later prehistoric lithic technology is a gradual decline in precision and control over flaking (Ford *et al* 1984; Ford 1987). This is reflected both by a reduction in percussion angle during the course of the Early and Middle Bronze Ages and by changes in the breadth to length ratio of the flakes. The blade production that forms such a prominent characteristic of earlier assemblages necessitates a considerable degree of control. The evidence for this lies in the relatively high percussion angle that is a feature of Neolithic technology. In the majority of cases, this falls between 70° and 90° and can be contrasted, for example, with a range of 65° to 74° for Late Bronze Age flintwork from the South Dorset Ridgeway (Harding 1990, 219). The decline in percussion angle ought to be paralleled by an increase in the breadth to length ratios, as a relatively high percussion angle is needed in order to strike long flakes. Such a change should result in an increasing proportion of flakes that are either shorter or broader than those produced in earlier periods. These transformations are reflected in both cores and implements. Specialised blade cores become rarer and, during the Late Bronze Age, tools appear to have been produced by increasingly expedient and unsystematic working.

Finally, the degree of patination on a piece of worked flint may provide some indication of its relative age. Although patination rates vary with differing depositional conditions and rates of groundwater percolation, there ought to be some relationship between the duration of deposition at any one location and the extent to which artefacts are patinated. This can have the virtue of providing an index of age that is independent of technological attributes.

If the processes of procurement, manufacture, use, and discard took place in different areas, we might expect this to be reflected in the contrasting attributes of the cores, flakes, and 'tools' from separate locations. Following Richards (1990, 18–19), assemblages resulting from procurement activities are characterised by a high proportion of primary reduction material, by hammerstones, and by cores, including flawed cores and 'tested nodules' (cf Burton 1980; Ford 1987). Assemblages of this kind may be typified by fairly unsystematic working, as the primary aim is to prepare cores for subsequent reduction and not to produce flakes suitable for retouch. Where procurement involved shallow extraction or surface collection, there will be a clear correlation between the pattern of primary working sites and the distribution of superficial flint sources, such as river or plateau gravels.

By contrast, manufacture is directed primarily towards the production of flakes suitable for making tools. For that reason, it will often be concentrated on domestic sites, which are not necessarily located close to flint sources. It may also involve the more systematic working of the raw material, and the resulting debitage ought to represent later stages in the reduction sequence and include higher proportions of retouched and utilised flakes. Cores are likely to be extensively worked down, exhausted, or failed and should be more systematically flaked than those associated with procurement (Burton 1980).

Based on these general propositions, the study adopts two basic approaches, each focused on a different objective. The first is concerned with the quantification of those technological traits that could be used to shed light on the relative chronology of the sites. The second involves a functional analysis that is aimed primarily at refining certain observations regarding the flintwork from LDP 104. At a superficial level, the assemblage appeared to be substantially different from the collections recovered from the settlement sites. It contains elements that suggested an emphasis on the stages of reduction associated with raw material procurement, but, before we could confirm or reject this impression, a more detailed study was required.

Methodology

Since one aim of this analysis was to investigate the spatial organisation of activity, the recording system was based on the position of different groups of debitage in the reduction sequence. In addition, more conventional morphological categories were used to describe the tools. In broad outline, the system follows the scheme applied by Brown in his recent study of flintwork from Cranborne Chase (Brown 1991), with the creation of an extra class of 'shatter fragments'.

Brown's four categories are: preparation flakes, trimming flakes, unretouched flakes, and dressing chips (Brown 1991, 101–2). Shatter fragments can be defined as chunks of flint, usually of sizeable proportions, that exhibit no clear knapping sequence, and appear to have been smashed open as part of a process concerned with assessing their quality. In general, shatter fragments, preparation flakes, and trimming flakes are associated with procurement, while other unretouched flakes and chips are indicative of manufacture.

A number of detailed observations concerning further characteristics of the worked flint were also made and recorded. The flake attributes included: the percussion angle and nature of platform preparation, the form of the distal termination (whether normal, hinged, cortical, or faceted), and the presence, form, and position of any retouch. The details of other traits, occurring on both flakes and cores, were noted. These comprised: weight, length, breadth, and thickness, whether or not the piece was broken or burnt, the extent of cortication, and the degree of patination. In addition, the number of 'mishits' on each core was recorded, registering the quantity of step and hinge fractures in relation to the number of other flake removals. 'Cores' were defined as any piece of flint from which flakes had been struck. Those bearing at least one prepared striking platform (platform cores) were distinguished from pieces on which flaking was conducted from any convenient surface (bashed lumps). Examples of the two types of core are illustrated in Figure 59. Platform cores were further divided into 'specialised' (blade) cores and either 'systematic', or 'unsystematic' flake cores. This distinction was based on the proportion of the striking platform that had been worked; 'systematic' cores were defined as those worked around more than two-thirds of their circumference. The number of platforms and any signs of platform rejuvenation were also noted.

Chronological assessment

The degree of chronological overlap between the sites on Brigmerston Down and Dunch Hill means that the lithic assemblages are likely to be distinguished by differences of emphasis, rather than by absolute contrasts. The ceramics recovered from LDP 102, 080, 081, and 081A consist primarily of Plain Ware, suggesting intensive activity within a relatively restricted part of the Late Bronze Age. It seems probable that the bulk of the flintwork was also derived from this same phase. However, the pottery indicates an extended period of activity at some of the sites, and it is these earlier and later elements that may be partially obscured by the greater quantity of lithic material associated with the Plain Ware horizon. The worked flint from the excavated midden at LDP 081A is of particular value in this respect. It appears to represent a relatively discrete phase of activity and, consequently, it can be used to provide an index of the characteristics of a local lithic assemblage of Late Bronze Age date.

The distribution of percussion angles for all flake types according to site is depicted in Table 35a, Appendix 3. At every site except LDP 104, over 80% of the figures fall between 55° and 69°; at LDP 104, the range is considerably wider between 45° and 74°. These patterns are strengthened by a consideration of the relative proportions of flaking angles above 65° and below 60° within the assemblages from each of the sites (Table 36a, Appendix 3). In general terms, high percussion angles are a more prominent feature of collections from the Northern Core Territory, whereas low percussion angles tend to characterise the assemblages found outside its boundaries. The excavated lithics from LDP 081A are again the most distinct (Table 36a, Appendix 3), with only 19% having angles greater than 65°. It is notable that the worked flints from the sites that represent perhaps the earliest (LDP 102) and latest elements (LDP 081A), on the basis of ceramic evidence, show the strongest contrast. This same evidence identifies an equally late phase at LDP 080, but in the flint assemblage this may be masked by earlier activity at the settlement.

The changing percentage of percussion angles across the settlement sites does not form an even gradient.

Especially anomalous are the high proportion of percussion angles above 65° in the surface collection from LDP 081 (35.5% compared with 19% from the excavated midden (LDP 081A) at the same location) and the unexpectedly large percentage of percussion angles below 60° among the flakes from LDP 102 (28%). The recorded values at LDP 081 may reflect the presence of an earlier chronological element, which was not represented in the assemblage from the midden. The high value for percussion angles below 60° at LDP 102 seems

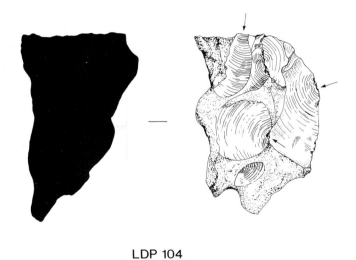

LDP 104

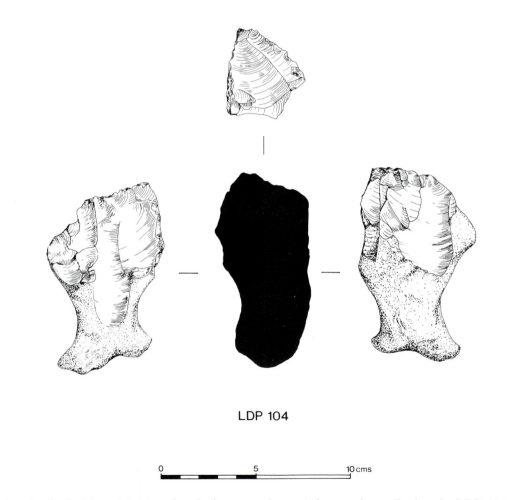

LDP 104

Fig 59   Examples of a 'bashed lump' (top) and a platform core (bottom) from surface collection site LDP 104

likely to be the result of the intensity of Late Bronze Age activity at this site. This is reflected in the relative abundance of Plain Ware sherds, compared with the lower frequency of Middle Bronze Age pottery. Alternatively, these variations might also reflect differences in the proportional representation of trimming and other unretouched flakes in the assemblages from individual sites.

In order to investigate this potential source of bias, the same analysis was carried out on the unretouched flakes, which form the largest single category of lithic material. The results are presented in Tables 35b and 36b (Appendix 3). Again, the sites within the Northern Core Territory have the greatest proportion of percussion angles above 65°. This stands out against the lower values for LDP 081 and 081A and suggests that, although the worked flint from LDP 081 may be later than the assemblages from LDP 102 and 080, the difference is not great. On the other hand, the analysis of unretouched flakes from the midden (LDP 081A) reinforces the impression that this represents a rather later phase of activity not present in the surface collection material from the surrounding area (LDP 081).

In summary, both studies of the percussion angles suggest that the sites in the Northern Core Territory contain an earlier component, although LDP 080 continued in use as late as LDP 081 and 081A. This applies, even if LDP 081 includes an early element not represented in the excavated material. Tables 35a and 35b (Appendix 3) reveal a decline in flaking angle between LDP 102 and 081A. This is seen most clearly in the relatively high percussion angles at LDP 102 and 080 (between 65° and 69°) and in the lower proportion of high percussion angles at LDP 081A. Conversely, the predominance of percussion angles between 55° and 59° at LDP 081A is in marked contrast to the low representation of this group at LDP 080. To a lesser extent, this may be true of LDP 102, where the slightly larger proportion of material in this group could reflect the intensity of later activity. In chronological terms, LDP 081 occupies an intermediate position and this is reflected in the relatively high percussion angles identified in both flake categories. However, the analytical results for LDP 104 are more ambiguous. While the range of percussion angles for all flake types combined suggests that the assemblage is generally late in the sequence, those for unretouched flakes point to a more intense use at an earlier stage. The high percentage of percussion angles above 65° in the unretouched flake category at LDP 104 suggests that the assemblage overall is closer in time to the material from settlements in the Northern Core Territory than to either LDP 081 or LDP 081A. In either case, it seems that the assemblage from LDP 104 is radically different in its composition from the material characterising the settlement sites.

To provide further support for the trends shown by the percussion angle data, breadth to length ratios were measured. Ratios were calculated for complete flakes according to the method devised by Bohmers (1956), and the results for all flake types combined and for unretouched flakes are presented in Table 37 (Appendix 3). Both categories display a decline across the settlement sites in the proportions of elements with a breadth to length ratio below 3:5. In the analysis of combined flake categories, this shift in production appears in the form of a progressive decline across the sites. By contrast, analysis of the unretouched flakes highlights a sharper distinction between settlements outside the Northern Core Territory and those in the interior. The Dunch Hill sites LDP 081 and LDP 081A possess lower proportions of unretouched flakes, with a length to breadth ratio below 3:5, than either LDP 080 or LDP 102 (both within the territory) and notable higher percentages with ratios greater than 5:5.

In other words, the assemblages from the Dunch Hill settlement are distinguished by a stronger component of shorter flakes, suggesting a bias towards a late phase of activity. Conversely, those sites within the Northern Core Territory (LDP 080 and LDP 102) have a higher proportion of long narrow flakes, which indicates that these assemblages contain a more pronounced earlier component. Both analyses show the same relative chronological sequence. However, the results from the unretouched flake category show a sharper contrast between the time span represented in the Dunch Hill material and that implied by the settlement assemblages from within the Northern Core Territory.

The suggestion that LDP 080 and LDP 102 have earlier origins than the Dunch Hill settlements at LDP 081 and LDP 081A is supported independently by the pottery analysis (Chap 4), but we must stress that the flint assemblages from the latter sites are not representative of the entire area of settlement. The tree-hole survey subsequently undertaken at LDP 103 (also on Dunch Hill, Fig 46) produced Middle Bronze Age ceramics, while a single sherd of Beaker pottery was recovered from LDP 111 (Fig 15). For various reasons, this earlier activity on Dunch Hill is not represented quite so strongly in the flint assemblages as it is at the other settlement sites. Undoubtedly, this is a consequence of unavoidable sampling biases, such that the flint assemblages that were available for analysis refer to areas of the settlement with a predominance of later material (LDP 081 and LDP 081A).

As we have indicated, the overall analysis of combined flakes shows a distinction between the elements from LDP 102 and 080 and those from LDP 081 and 081A, with these latter being generally shorter. Most of this decline in the length of flakes is caused by a considerable increase in the proportions of elements between 20 and 39mm at LDP 081 and LDP 081A (Table 39, Appendix 3). The proportions of lengths below 49mm rises from 46% (LDP 102) and 44% (LDP 080) to 68% (LDP 081) and 75% (LDP 081A). At LDP 104, the value for unretouched flakes is 43%. This closely resembles the values from LDP 102 and LDP 080, which lie within the Northern Core Territory.

As with the analysis of percussion angle, these criteria reveal the ambiguous chronological position of LDP 104. It appears to shift its temporal alignment, according to which category of flakes is studied. Using combined flakes, LDP 104 seems to be the most recent assemblage, with the lowest percentage of ratios below 3:5 and one of the highest percentages of elements with ratios greater than 5:5. On the other hand, the analysis of unretouched flakes seems to indicate that the site occupies a chronological position somewhere between LDP 080 and LDP 081A.

The changes in the flake proportions, and in the

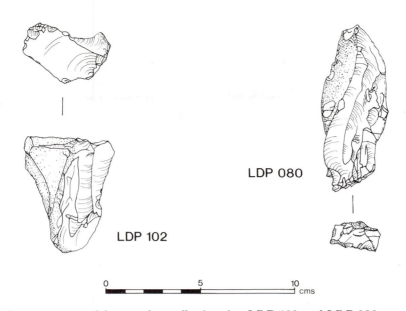

Fig 60   Examples of blade cores recovered from surface collection sites LDP 102 and LDP 080

degree of control exercised in their production, are to some extent reflected in the types of cores recovered from the settlement sites. Two blade cores were recovered from LDP 102 and a single example from LDP 080 (Fig 60). Although these make up a very small percentage of the total number of cores, it is significant that they were the only examples found and that all came from sites within the Northern Core Territory.

No attempt was made to use the retouched artefacts as detailed dating evidence, because the sample size was too small. Instead, it was decided to assess the 'quality' of the 23 scrapers from the assemblages, since these represented the largest single category of regularly retouched tools. It was assumed that the more carefully made artefacts were likely to be earlier than those of poorer quality (Riley 1990, 225–7). This analysis measured the following attributes: the amount of cortex on the artefacts, the extent of regular retouch, the number of edges with evidence of retouch, and the presence or absence of soft-hammer technique (Ohmuma and Bergman 1982). The results are indicated in Table 40 (Appendix 3), while Figure 61 provides a visual impression of the different characteristics of these scrapers.

Taken together, the measurements suggest that more carefully made scrapers tend to be associated with LDP 102 and 104. Both sites possess a relatively high number of non-cortical scrapers. These have regular retouch on two or more edges and also provide evidence for the use of soft-hammer technique. Conversely, at the other sites, higher rates of cortication are associated with irregular retouch along one or two edges of the artefact and with the use of a hard hammer. Although the presence of better quality scrapers may indicate earlier activity, their absence in some assemblages is not necessarily significant, given the small size of the sample.

The single remaining class of evidence that requires consideration is the degree of patination, which might provide an index of relative age, independent of technological attributes. It is only possible to compare assemblages deposited under similar conditions, because patination rates vary locally with geological conditions and rates of groundwater percolation. As all five assemblages came from areas with the same bed-rock, local differences are most likely to result from variations in topography and drainage. While the three surface assemblages from LDP 102, 080, and 081 are from relatively well-drained ridges, LDP 104 is on the edge of the seasonally waterlogged valley of Bourne Bottom (Fig 16), where the soils include a higher clay component. The excavated lithics from LDP 081A may also have been subject to different rates of patination, although the worked flint from the surface of the same field (LDP 081) provides an important point of comparison. Given so much uncertainty, degrees of patination were recorded within individual assemblages. It was hoped that this would provide an index of the duration and intensity of activity across the period of occupation at each site.

Three categories were adopted: 'light patination', 'heavy patination', and unpatinated. A light patina was taken as one that was either mottled or translucent, while a heavy patina had an opaque white appearance. The results of this analysis are presented in Table 41 (Appendix 3). These suggest that the most intensive early activity was at the two sites in the Northern Core Territory (LDP 102 and 080). Their patination profiles are similar, with light and heavily patinated flints each accounting for approximately half the assemblage. By contrast, the assemblages from LDP 081 and 081A contained higher proportions of unpatinated material, fewer heavily patinated flakes, and, in the case of LDP 081A, a higher proportion of lightly patinated pieces. The assemblage from LDP 081 contains slightly more heavily patinated material than that from LDP 081A, which once again suggests that the fieldwalked assemblage contains an earlier element not present in the midden. In contrast to the sites in the Northern Core Territory, the phase of activity represented by LDP 081A seems to have taken place towards the end of the sequence. This is perhaps not surprising, when we recall that this assemblage is associated with the only All Cannings Cross pottery from the Dunch Hill settlement. Indeed, it seems likely that the midden represents an accumulation from a single habitation that was occupied towards the end of this settlement's history.

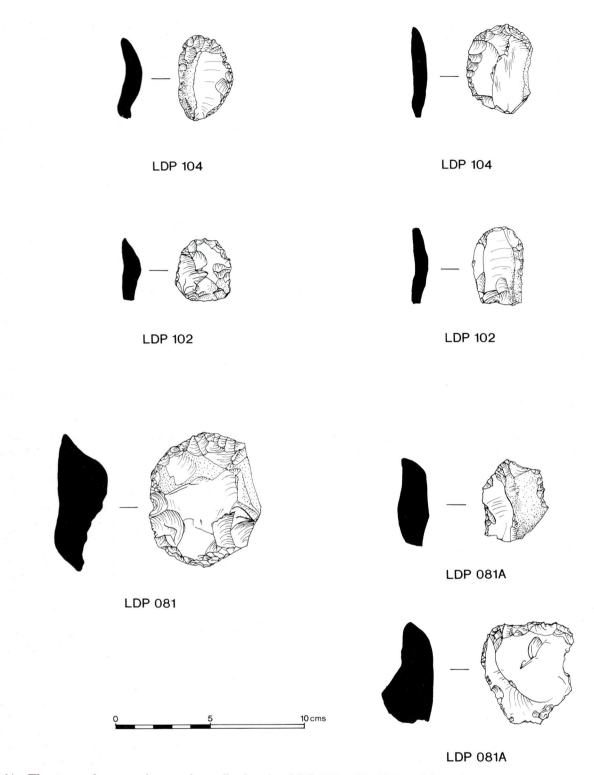

Fig 61   The range of scrapers from surface collection sites LDP 081, 102, 104, and from the excavated midden LDP 081A

The material from the valley site (LDP 104) provides a further perspective, and its most notable feature is the even distribution of worked flint across all three patination categories. It is unfortunate that there is no basis for making a direct comparison between this and the other assemblages. Nevertheless, taken on its own terms, such a patination profile suggests a relatively even distribution of activity over a lengthy period.

To sum up, each of these different analyses puts four

of the assemblages in the same order: LDP 102 is apparently the earliest, followed in turn by LDP 080, 081, and 081A. To a certain extent this is to be expected, because some of the attributes used in these studies are functionally related to one another, but the evidence from the different patination profiles at the various sites provides some independent corroboration of this scheme. Again, it must be stressed that the differences between the assemblages are ones of degree and not of kind and, as the ceramic sequence shows, all the sites experienced intensive activity during the Late Bronze Age. Perhaps the lithic industries show these differences because of earlier activity on some of these sites. On that basis, the assemblages from LDP 102 and 080 would appear to include a greater amount of residual flintwork than the finds from 081 and 081A. Even so, the time interval separating sites in the Northern Core Territory from those outside its boundaries need not be particularly great, and there are signs that the surface material from LDP 081 has closer temporal affinities to sites in that area than it does to the material from 081A.

The chronological position of LDP 104 remains in doubt, for the different analyses have suggested a range of possible dates. Although it is a far from satisfactory approach, we are forced to fall back on the uncertain evidence provided by the patination study. On the basis of the uniform patination profile shown by the material from LDP 104, it is suggested that that assemblage represents a relatively low level of activity taking place over a long period of time. This contrasts with the variable levels of patination observed in the assemblages from the settlement sites and, as we shall see in the following functional assessment, it underlines the distinctive spatial patterns characterising the use of the area.

Functional assessment

In this section, our main aim is to distinguish between assemblages resulting from procurement and those created by domestic activity. The differences implied by these two categories are mirrored by the technological characteristics of flakes, cores, and retouched pieces associated with different stages in the use-life of the artefacts. The first part of the analysis depends on identifying the proportion of shatter fragments, preparation flakes, trimming flakes, dressing chips, and other unretouched flakes in each collection (Table 42, Appendix 3).

According to the criteria set out on pp 91–93, the worked flint most likely to reflect the procurement of raw material is that from LDP 104. The assemblage is unlike those recovered from the other sites, because it contains a much higher proportion of shatter fragments, preparation flakes, and trimming flakes. Conversely, other unretouched flakes account for only 55% of the material from LDP 104 and for more than 80% of the struck flint at the remaining sites. The shatter fragments and preparation flakes should result from nodule testing and primary reduction the earliest stages of the manufacturing sequence. Although trimming flakes are also found at LDP 104, they are not confined to that site and in fact form a significant element among the other collections.

The assemblages from the settlement sites complement the material from LDP 104. In these, unretouched flakes predominate, reflecting the later stages of reduction, and there are few shatter fragments and preparation flakes. This is consistent with a range of technological practices connected with the manufacture and use of tools in a domestic setting. The contrast between LDP 104 and these other sites can be recognised in the amount of cortex present in each group of flakes. The most pronounced variation concerns the proportion of flakes with cortex on more than a third of their dorsal surface. Examples in this category account for more than 35% of flakes from LDP 104, compared to between 7% and 19% at the other sites. These figures imply that a greater proportion of flakes at LDP 104 were produced during the early stages of reduction, and this is consistent with the functional distinctions that we have proposed.

These are reflected by other characteristics of the flakes, notably the degree of care exercised during the various stages of knapping. There are several ways in which this can be illustrated. Table 44 (Appendix 3) records the proportions of flakes with normal (feathered), hinged, cortical, and faceted distal terminations among the five assemblages. Flakes with feathered edges possess the greatest potential for retouch, while the other types of distal termination offer more limited possibilities. In fact, LDP 104 has the lowest proportion of normal terminations and the highest value for distal ends with cortex. Normal, or feathered, distal terminations occur on only 15% of the flakes from this site, compared to 25% at LDP 080 and over 37% at the remaining sites. Since it is easier to retouch a flake, if the edge is free from cortex, the degree of preparation at LDP 104 seems to have been concerned more with preliminary reduction than with tool manufacture.

Table 45 (Appendix 3) records the types of distal termination according to each flake category. In general terms, debitage representing the later stages of reduction appears to be characterised by a higher proportion of flakes with normal terminations. Both the trimming flakes and other unretouched flakes have a majority of normal terminations, although it must be emphasised that the numbers are small in some of the groups. Tables 44 and 45 (Appendix 3) also record variations in the amount of control exercised during the equivalent stage of reduction at different sites. Most notable is the less systematic working that appears to be represented at LDP 104, compared with the other locations. This is indicated by a lower proportion of trimming flakes and other unretouched elements with normal terminations.

We might expect to find similar distinctions between the cores on these sites. In particular, if our hypothesis is correct, those from the settlements ought to be more systematically worked than the cores from LDP 104. They should also be worked down to a greater extent. Tables 46 and 47a (Appendix 3) record the numbers of cores in each assemblage along with the mean weight. In fact, there is a high proportion of cores among the finds from LDP 104 and their mean weight is greater than those from the other assemblages. On the basis of this, we can surmise that those recovered from domestic contexts were being worked down to a greater extent than those at LDP 104. Once again, this is consistent with the interpretation of LDP 104 as a flint procurement site. Further corroboration is provided by the relative frequency of bashed lumps and platform cores in the various assemblages. The former account for 29% of the total number of cores from LDP 104, compared with much smaller numbers in the other collections (Table 47b, Appendix 3). On the other hand, platform cores were more numerous on the settlement sites. This seems to indicate the more controlled and systematic working of flint at the latter, and is consistent with the higher proportion of debitage from the later stages of reduction that characterise these assemblages.

A similar variation in the working of cores is suggested by differences in the range of patination exhibited by individual examples. Flake scars created more or less simultaneously are likely to show less variation in the degree of patination than those produced over a longer period of time. Table 47c (Appendix 3) records variations in the distribution of patination across different flake scars on the cores. More of those from LDP 104 show differences in the degree of patination, apparently reinforcing the earlier suggestion that this site experienced a more variable pattern of working over a long period of time. Those cores that displayed a relatively uniform distribution of patina came mainly from the settlement sites, suggesting that at those locations flintworking was more intensive and short term.

A further contrast between the assemblage from LDP 104, and those from the other sites, is indicated by differences in the frequency of step or hinge fractures among the platform cores. The figures set out in Table 47d (Appendix 3) show step/hinge fractures as a proportion of all flake scars. The cores were divided into three groups: those with less than a third of the flake scars showing this type of fracture, those with between one and two-thirds, and a last group where more than two-thirds of the flake scars had this characteristic. The frequency of cores in each category was then calculated, as a proportion of the total number of cores from each site. As the table shows, the percentages of these fractures characterising over a third of the flakes scars are somewhat higher on the cores from LDP 104. Once again, this implies that a greater degree of control was being exercised over flintworking at the settlements, with far fewer 'mis-hits' occurring.

The remaining contrasts between these assemblages concern the amount of cortex on the cores and higher rates of platform rejuvenation. Of those recovered from LDP 104, 49% had more than a third of their surface covered by cortex, whereas among those from the settlement sites the values are much lower, reaching a maximum of 14% at LDP 102 (Table 47e, Appendix 3). The domestic assemblages reveal higher rates of platform rejuvenation than were present at LDP 104. These range from 50% at LDP 080 and LDP 081 to 33% at LDP 081A, compared to only 14% at LDP 104. On the settlement sites, between 60% and 70% of the individual platforms had been worked around more than two-thirds of their circumference, in contrast to only 28% of those at LDP 104. Taken together, these features further strengthen the argument for a more systematic working of flint on the settlements. In conjunction with the other evidence that has been discussed, this provides a fairly clear indication that cores were being prepared at LDP 104, before they were taken to the settlements for subsequent reduction and tool manufacture.

This interpretation would account for the differences in the proportion and range of retouched pieces represented in each of the assemblages (Table 48, Appendix 3). The sample is a small one, but the percentage of retouched pieces from the domestic sites is generally higher than it is among the assemblage from LDP 104. Moreover, those from LDP 102, 081, and 081A contained a wider range of implements than either LDP 104 or LDP 080. These are represented by several tool types, including a variety of scraper forms together with different kinds of composite implements, such as scraper-notch combinations and borers. In comparison, the material from LDP 104 and LDP 080 was more impoverished, consisting of a few scrapers and a composite tool from LDP 104. Two hammerstones were also recovered from this latter site, one broken and the other complete. The only other hammerstone was a broken example from LDP 102. The range of retouched forms and a hammerstone from LDP 104 are illustrated in Figure 62.

Discussion

We have seen that of the domestic assemblages, those from within the Northern Core Territory (LDP 080 and LDP 102) give the impression of a greater time-depth than either of the Dunch Hill sites (LDP 081 and LDP 081A), which lie outside the bounded area. On the basis of the flintwork alone, it is impossible to assign an absolute date range to the activity represented at these various sites, but the presence of Deverel-Rimbury pottery at LDP 080, LDP 102, and the Dunch Hill site LDP 103 suggests that it stretched back into the second millennium BC. Beaker pottery was recovered from several sites in and around the Northern Core Territory (LDP 102, 103, 109, 111, and 112). Only a few sherds are represented in the individual assemblages, and it seems unlikely that any continuity of settlement pattern is implied by this material.

A comparison of the Late Bronze Age flint assemblage from the midden excavation (LDP 081A) with that from the surrounding area, while indicating an overlap in time, suggests that the material from the midden belonged to a later stage in the settlement on Dunch Hill. A rather more significant difference exists between the midden assemblage and those from LDP 080 and LDP 102. This is most clearly visible in the higher flaking angles and the lower breadth to length ratios reflecting the longer length of flakes from the latter sites. The distinction is paralleled by the presence of blade cores and the 'better' quality of the scrapers recovered from the two sites within the Northern Core Territory. The scale of these differences, particularly among the unretouched flakes, highlights the early activity at LDP 080 and LDP 102 and may provide some indication of its intensity.

The chronological position of the procurement site (LDP 104) presents a further contrast. As we have seen, the characteristic that most distinguishes it is the relatively low level of activity over a protracted time scale. This is most clearly visible in the patination data for this site. However, it may also be implicit in the failure of the other chronological indicators to provide the complementary results necessary for consistent dating of the assemblage, although this could also be a product of the less systematic flint working associated with the site.

While the chronological assessment of the flint assemblages discussed in this chapter has provided useful evidence, it is the functional analysis that is perhaps the most illuminating. The technological changes that have temporal implications are not in themselves sufficiently sensitive, or clearly represented, to add significant detail to the picture formed by the pottery study. However, even within the limitations set by the small sample size, the functional analysis has shed some light on the spatial

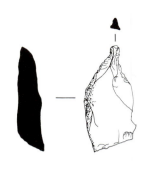

LDP 102

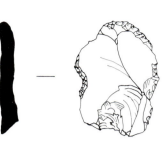

LDP 102

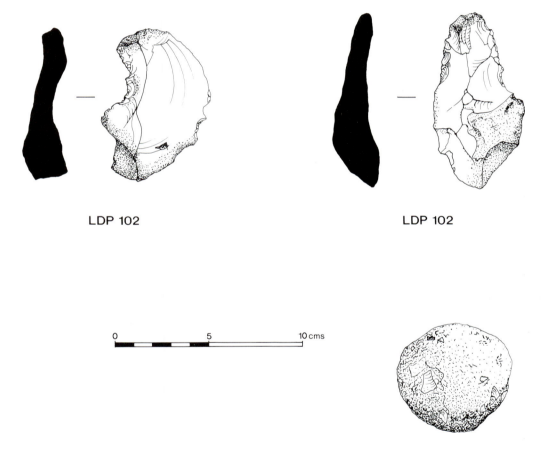

LDP 102

LDP 102

LDP 104

Fig 62   A range of retouched forms from surface collection site LDP 102 and a hammerstone from the procurement site LDP 104

organisation of lithic production, which echoes the patterning of other aspects of material culture.

In conclusion, let us examine the evidence from these flint assemblages in the wider context of the spatial organisation of settlement and resource exploitation. We have already identified LDP 104 as just one of a number of procurement sites located within the Upper Study Area (Fig 16). It was regarded as being outside the brief of this project to examine these other sites in any detail,

but in the case of LDP 104 it was thought possible to establish a fairly clear relationship between the exploitation of raw material and its use on Late Bronze Age settlements.

The setting of LDP 104 is revealing in two ways. First, we can recognise an obvious reason for its location. Like the other procurement sites, it is positioned close to a plentiful supply of flint readily available at the surface: in this instance, the Pleistocene river gravels along

Bourne Bottom. This wet coombe is part of the upper drainage of the Nine Mile River (Fig 16), and during the Late Bronze Age it may have carried running water for at least part of the year. As we shall see in the following chapters, the Nine Mile River and Bourne Bottom were the focus for a range of activities that seems to suggest that the location had a special significance during the Middle and Late Bronze Age (Chap 8). It is an area that lies outside the structured landscape defined by the linear ditches of the Northern Core Territory and, for the most part, it does not appear to have been settled. That might indicate that this part of the landscape, and in particular the river corridor, was viewed as a resource to be shared by a number of different communities. We can see this distinction mirrored in other aspects of material culture (Chap 8), which add further emphasis to the contrast between the settled area and the environs of the Nine Mile River. In view of the broader contrasts, perhaps it should come as no surprise to find that the exploitation of such an important natural resource as flint should also be located in an area accessible to all communities.

There is no evidence to suggest how the procurement of flint might have been integrated into the broader range of subsistence activities, but there are clues. First of all, it is important to recognise that the Nine Mile River would have represented the only abundant supply of water accessible to all the communities occupying the settlements around the Northern Core Territory. As far as we are able to extrapolate from the environmental data (Chap 6), it appears that the margins of the Nine Mile River mainly supported open grassland during the Late Bronze Age, which implies a sustained pressure preventing woodland regeneration. It is possible that this took the form of grazing on common pasture outside the bounded landscape defined by the linear ditches. The bone assemblages from the various project sites are generally of poor quality, but they do point to a dependence on grazing animals, and these would require access to an all-year-round supply of water. Although it can be no more than conjecture, we can envisage practices concerned with the management of livestock that also involved the procurement of flint, as well as other embedded activities that appear to have been confined to the margins of the principal areas of settlement (Chap 8).

6   The environmental setting of the linear ditches system

by Roy Entwistle

Introduction: a review of the environmental background to the prehistoric settlement of the southern chalklands

The most detailed information for the early environmental history of the Wessex chalk mainly comes from the major monument complexes at Avebury, Stonehenge, and around Dorchester in Dorset. The molluscan studies, which have been the principal source of evidence, suggest that these areas shared a common history of progressive woodland clearance, ultimately giving rise to open grassland conditions during the Early Bronze Age. Local variations involving regeneration are plainly visible at some sites, but these do nothing to undermine the general trends that appear to characterise these areas. However, it is far from clear how widely we can extrapolate from this evidence to include other areas that lack similar concentrations of monuments. There are signs that, in different parts of the southern chalklands, clearance may have been less intense during the Neolithic and that woodland continued to be a prominent feature of the landscape until the Late Bronze Age (for example at Bridget's and Burntwood Farms: Fasham 1980).

Pollen diagrams relating to the vegetation of the southern chalklands show some of this variation, albeit at an uncertain scale. Those compiled for the Lewes area of Sussex (Thorley 1971; 1981) indicate a series of minor clearances during the Neolithic and Early Bronze Age, with significant clearance taking place towards the end of the second millennium BC. This is broadly in agreement with the molluscan data from causewayed enclosures on the South Downs (Thomas 1982). A similarly late pattern of clearance is revealed in the pollen diagram for a peat deposit at Snelsmore Bog on the Berkshire Downs (Waton 1982). In the vicinity of this site, major woodland clearance did not take place until the first millennium BC, after which the landscape remained open with only periodic signs of scrub regeneration.

An exhaustive account of the work done on the vegetation history of the southern chalklands would be out of place in this report. Some of the more recent studies indicating areas of late woodland clearance have been mentioned already, but there are others, which point in the opposite direction (Bell 1983). We have dwelt on those studies that indicate late patterns of permanent clearance, merely to emphasise the degree of variation that appears to have characterised the prehistoric ecology of the chalk. The grassland environments suggested for the major Wessex monument complexes may well have been anomalous. Away from these areas, the duration and scale of woodland clearance is less well known, but, undoubtedly, the impact of human communities was not everywhere the same.

As far as we can tell from the limited information available to us, the landscape of Salisbury Plain was largely cleared of woodland by the time that the linear ditches system was founded during the Late Bronze Age.

However, we cannot clarify the background to this, let alone determine the period in which major woodland clearance began. Was it an early, but progressive development punctuated by periods of regeneration, as was apparently the case in the Stonehenge area? Or was the main period of clearance much later and perhaps connected with Middle Bronze Age exploitation of an area, where woodland had remained a dominant feature since the Neolithic? The only evidence that might have a bearing on these questions comes from the eastern buried soil at LDP 092. This takes the form of an Early Neolithic date on unidentified bone from the base of the buried soil where it overlay a fossil tree cast (Table 22, OxA3045). The date of *c* 3700–3370 cal BC seems rather too early to refer to the clearance episode shown in the molluscan sequence, and it is more likely that it belongs with the woodland conditions preceding this stage. Although largely un-resolved as yet, the questions posed above have an important bearing on how we regard the first appearance of farming communities in the Upper Study Area: whether it should be considered as part of a continuous evolutionary process emerging from the Early Bronze Age utilisation of the area, or as a pioneering phase of colonisation leading to the domestication of a landscape perceived as 'wild'.

The environmental study of the linear ditches system

This study is based on research concentrated in the Ministry of Defence Estate of Salisbury Plain Training Area East. In Chapters 2 and 3, we drew attention to the unique survival of tracts of ancient downland in this area, which has seen little cultivation since the Roman period. The exceptional preservation of earthworks offered the opportunity to provide a greater time depth to the environmental study, by augmenting the molluscan data from relatively undisturbed ditch silts with buried soil sequences from beneath adjoining banks. This has enabled the landscape history associated with the ditch system to be reconstructed more confidently, and in more detail, than would have been possible elsewhere in the Upper Study Area.

Contrasting conditions prevail in the predominantly arable landscape surrounding the Training Area, where ploughing has destroyed the topmost ditch stratigraphies and banks at the majority of sites. Almost without exception, this has erased traces of vital stratigraphic relationships, such as those between ditches and 'Celtic' fields, which are essential to any detailed understanding of later landscape evolution. The reworking of upper ditch silts by cultivation also has had the effect of truncating environmental sequences, while the inevitable destruction of banks and buried soils has further contributed to the loss of environmental potential.

At one level, the choice of sample area reflected the need to take full advantage of the enhanced preservation offered by conditions in the Training Area, but another, and equally important, requirement was that the range of palaeoenvironmental data should come from sites that were not too widely spaced, since this would have introduced difficulties from the point of view of interpolation. For that reason, most of the sequences that have been analysed are from sites located in a relatively confined area, but selected as far as possible to represent the principal topographic zones.

Although the main aim of this research was to enhance the archaeological interpretation of the linear ditches system by providing an environmental framework, it is important in its own right as a study of the evolution of a late prehistoric landscape. In the service of this more general theme, the provision of detailed and focused information will help to facilitate comparisons with other areas, especially that around Stonehenge where the prehistoric landscape has been the subject of recent palaeoenvironmental research (Allen *et al* 1990; Bell and Jones 1990; Entwistle 1989; Evans 1984).

Apart from the evidence from the Stonehenge area, comparative environmental data are available locally from a series of linear ditches excavated in advance of road improvements just north of Quarley Hill (Allen 1992) and from a linear ditch on Copehill Down near Shrewton (Allen 1989). Evidence for the earlier prehistoric landscape in the Military Training Area is sparse. Molluscan data from an isolated Neolithic pit on Copehill Down suggest an environment of broad-leafed deciduous woodland, which several millennia later had given way to open, short-turfed grassland, when the linear ditch was constructed. For the intervening period, from the Late Neolithic and throughout the Early Bronze Age, there is no palaeoenvironmental evidence at all from the Training Area. We can only infer from the density of Early Bronze Age round barrows that tracts of open country existed, although it is not possible to estimate their extent. Close to our own Study Area, several sites in the vicinity of Stonehenge have produced evidence for grassland during this period (Evans 1984), but there are also indications of woodland and scrub regeneration, which might point to a rather more complicated environment. This is suggested for other parts of the chalk uplands by a number of molluscan studies (Bell 1983; Fasham 1980; Thomas 1982) and by several pollen diagrams for Sussex (Thorley 1971; 1981), Hampshire, and Berkshire (Waton 1982).

In the absence of suitable pollen bearing deposits in the Upper Study Area, the reconstruction of the prehistoric and Romano-British environment relies almost exclusively on molluscan data. However, some additional information has been furnished by charcoal samples from sites LDP100 and 101 on Sidbury Hill and by the carbonised cereal remains from LDP 092 on Brigmerston Down (Table 26). The overall environmental framework is based on the analysis of five complete ditch columns (LDP 027A, 083, 092, 097, and 101), all of which have provided detailed and well-dated sequences. In the case of the Devil's Ditch (LDP 052), the secondary and tertiary silts were disturbed so thoroughly by tree-root penetration that only four samples from the basal silts were analysed. Two samples from the ditch basal silts of site LDP 091 were also analysed, as well as a complete sequence through the bank and buried soil. Other buried soils were preserved at LDP 027, 092B and C, and LDP 020B, and these have provided additional comparative information pertaining to pre-ditch environments. The location of project sites with environmental data is shown in Figure 70.

The sampling procedures and analytical techniques were based on those recommended by Evans (1972). All samples were taken from freshly cleaned sections and those selected for analysis were air-dried. A standard 1.5kg sub-sample from each was taken for extraction in water, using dilute hydrogen peroxide to aid disaggregation where necessary. The sediment was then wet-sieved through a nest of three sieves of 5.6, 2.0, and 0.5mm mesh. The dried sieve fractions were weighed and the values used to provide a crude index of the particle-size distribution for each sample. In the snail diagrams, the 5.6mm mesh fraction only has been plotted. To some extent, the particle-size histogram merely corroborates context descriptions made in the field. However, it can be useful for identifying incipient sorted horizons that may not have been visible in section, as for example in the secondary silts at LDP 083 (Fig 65).

The behaviour of individual species and the ecological groupings are also based on Evans (1972), although certain revisions suggested by more recent studies have been incorporated. These are principally: Bell (1983, 1987, and 1989), Evans (1984), Evans and Vaughan (1985), and Thomas (1985). In the main snail diagrams, individual species and synecological groups have been plotted as percentage frequency histograms in the conventional manner. There are ecological objections to the use of percentage frequency diagrams (Thomas 1985), but the chief disadvantage is that wide fluctuations in the abundance of a single species can give a false impression of change in the proportional frequency of other species (Evans and Jones 1979).

For this reason, percentage frequency and absolute values have been plotted for the sequence at LDP 083, which was dominated throughout the secondary silts by large numbers of *Pupilla muscorum*. The percentage frequency curves for this site (Fig 65) reveal a very different pattern from that produced by absolute shell numbers (Fig 66). If the percentage histogram alone had been used for interpretation, a misleading impression of the sequence would have been formed, especially of the ecological transition from secondary to tertiary silts.

The diversity indices, which form an integral part of the ecological interpretation throughout this chapter, have been adapted from Gordon and Ellis (1985) and are based on Hurlbert (1971). The two indices are measures of the probability of non-lethal interspecific encounters (D2) and the ratio of interspecific to intraspecific competition (D4) – both formulae are given in the aforementioned papers. Gordon and Ellis have argued that these species composition parameters are more applicable to biological populations than those derived from Information Theory (such as the Shannon-Weaver 'H' or Pielou 'J' indices). In view of the persuasive arguments put forward by Gordon and Ellis (1985), we have chosen to use the Hurlbert indices in this study, especially since these measures are demonstrably independent of changes in absolute shell numbers and appear to be sensitive indicators of environmental change (ibid).

The diversity statistics also have been used, in conjunction with species composition changes, to define local 'site zones', which summarise the principal ecological stages in the environmental history of each site. The 'site zones' reflect complex processes, which are partly the result of localised changes in patterns of landuse, but are modified by the taphonomic and contextual conditions at the individual site.

The archaeology of the following sites was discussed in Chapter 3 and their locations are shown in Figure 70. This section focuses on the environmental sequences; it includes only a limited discussion of site stratigraphy, where this is relevant to the interpretation of ecological change. The species lists for the following sites are set out in Appendix 4, Tables 49 to 58.

The molluscan sequences

LDP 101: The Sidbury Double Linear Ditch (SPTA no 2232)

The earliest molluscan fauna, from context 34 (the primary ditch silt), is dominated by shade-loving species, which comprise over 54% of the total assemblage (Fig 63). Some of the species making up this group, such as *Carychium tridentatum*, *Vitrea contracta*, and *Aegopinella pura*, are characteristically present in tall ungrazed grassland (Cameron and Morgan-Huws 1975). However, also present in context 34 were *Discus rotundatus*, *Aegopinella nitidula*, *Oxychilus cellarius*, and the rupestral group Clausiliidae, none of which are associated with grassland habitats (Bell and Jones 1990). The relative abundance of these species throughout the primary silts (contexts 34 and 27) indicates that the shaded conditions at LDP 101 were created by woodland, rather than by tall grass or open scrub. True woodland conditions were confirmed independently by species identification of charcoal recovered from the primary silts of sites LDP 100 and LDP 101. This showed that oak, ash, elder, and hazel were all present on the hilltop prior to the construction of the double earthwork (see p 115). There is no reason to suppose that the charcoal was derived from a settlement in the immediate vicinity of the site. It is much more likely that it originated from an extensive clearance in the area, presumably in preparation for construction of the linear earthwork, which preceded the hillfort.

Although this clearance represented a major stratigraphic episode, the magnitude is difficult to estimate. There was no evidence to suggest that it extended as far as LDP 020, at the base of the hill and only 150m away (Fig 26). In all probability, the affected woodland was confined to the summit of the hill (as it is at present, except for a modern conifer plantation), where it survived in a generally cleared landscape, either by virtue of its topographic isolation, or because the moisture retentive Tertiary geology favoured dense vegetation. Whatever the reasons for the anomalous ecology of Sidbury Hill, they cannot be attributed to a lack of human activity. We have already noted that the Clay-with-Flints drift on the hill was attracting attention as a

Table 25   Snail species from LDP 020A (nomenclature follows Kerney 1976)

depth (cm)	0–17	17–22	22–27	27–33	33–40
context	1	2	3	4	A/C
P. elegans (Müller)	8	1	2	9	18
C. tridentatum (Risso)	2	–	–	–	–
Cochlicopa spp.	1	–	–	–	2
V. pygmaea (Draparnaud)	3	–	3	5	3
P. muscorum (Linnaeus)	17	2	12	9	18
V. costata (Müller)	1	–	–	2	–
V. excentrica (Sterki)	5	1	7	5	6
P. pygmaeum (Draparnaud)	2	–	–	3	6
D. rotundatus (Müller)	–	–	–	1	1
Limacidae	2	–	–	2	1
V. pellucida (Müller)	–	–	3	–	–
V. crystallina (Müller)	2	–	–	–	–
V. contracta (Westerlund)	2	–	–	–	–
N. hammonis (Ström)	2	–	–	1	–
O. cellarius (Müller)	–	–	–	1	–
Clausiliidae	1	–	1	–	–
C. intersecta (Poiret)	–	+	2	–	–
H. itala (Linnaeus)	5	–	20	6	5
T. hispida (Linnaeus)	13	6	59	5	6
Cepaea/Arianta spp.	2	1	1	3	4
total shells	68	11	129	52	70
number of taxa	16	5	13	14	12
D2	0.87	0.64	0.74	0.89	0.84
D4	6.54	1.72	2.80	8.30	5.16
% shade-loving spp.	16.2	0.00	4.70	11.5	10.0
% catholic spp.	38.2	72.2	48.1	51.9	45.7
% open-country spp.	45.6	27.3	47.3	51.9	45.7

+ = present as a non-apical fragment

readily available flint source from at least as early as the Neolithic and probably continued to do so into the Late Bronze Age (Chap 3).

Open-country species form just over 8% of the total from context 34. They include the xerophile *Helicella itala*, which seems out of place in what must have been a densely vegetated environment. *Vallonia costata*, *Vallonia excentrica*, and *Pupilla muscorum* are all present in very small numbers. The latter species also seem rather anomalous in this setting, generally preferring grassland habitats or areas bare of vegetation (Evans 1972).

Although mature woodland appears to have been the dominant vegetation in the vicinity of sites LDP 100 and LDP 101, a more open aspect must have existed somewhere close by. The absence of charcoal from the ditch silts at LDP 020 (Fig 26), and the open-country conditions suggested by the fauna from the Ah horizon of the buried soil at 020A (Fig 28 and Table 25), may imply that the termination of the double linear was on a woodland margin. In view of the obvious 'false cresting' of the double earthwork (see Chap 7), this would make sense. The termination does in fact occur at the height of maximum visibility from below, but, since the hillside was wooded, it would have been necessary to clear vegetation in order to take advantage of the preferred topographic location.

The transition from primary to lower secondary silts (context 5, sample 75–90cm) is marked in the environmental sequence by a dramatic rise in open-country species, accompanied by an equally abrupt decline in catholic species. Shade-loving taxa still make up 28% of

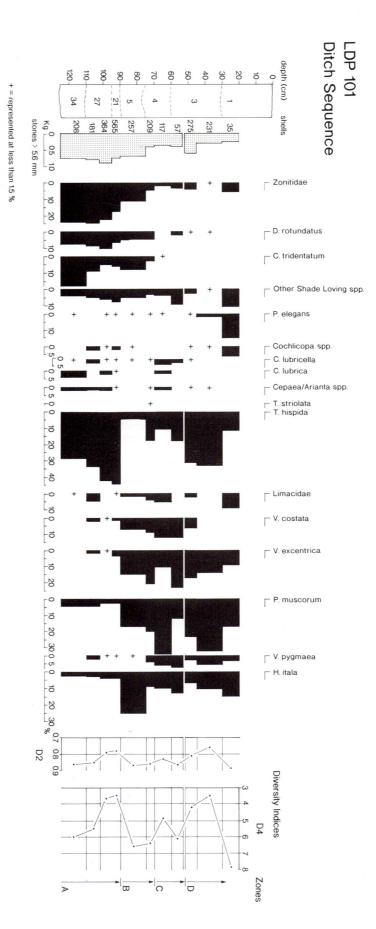

Fig 63   Molluscan diagram for LDP 101: percentage frequencies

the total, and this ecological complexity is reflected by a sharp increase in both diversity indices – D2 rises from 0.78 in the previous sample (90–95cm) to 0.87, and D4 from 3.50 to 6.59. The slower silting during this phase was probably accompanied by the development of a predominantly autochthonous snail population under relatively stable conditions. The time-scale represented by this transition may have been relatively short, perhaps less than a decade for vegetation to become established (Bell 1990). Ecological change is shown by the disappearance of Oxychilus cellarius and Oxychilus alliarius, and the decline of Discus rotundatus, Aegopinella nitidula, and the Clausiliidae. These changes result in an apparent increase in Carychium tridentatum, yet in absolute terms this species also declines. With the exception of Vertigo pygmaea, all of the open-country taxa increase sharply during this stage, although the proportional change for Vallonia costata is less prominent than for the other species.

Shade-loving species still make up a significant proportion of the assemblage from the lower secondary silts, though the rather different species composition suggests that the shaded aspect by this stage was mostly created by tall grass or scrub colonising the ditch. Patches of bare earth and weathered chalk on the bank and sides of the ditch were probably the source of much of the slowly accumulating sediment during this stage. Rather dry and open conditions are indicated by the sharp decline of Trichia hispida and the rise of Helicella itala, but this may be a reflection of very localised habitats, rather than more general conditions. Indeed, the persistence of Discus rotundatus, the Clausiliidae, and Acanthinula aculeata would seem to indicate a rather complex range of habitats. In all probability, woodland refugia still survived close to the site, and there may have been a significant degree of regeneration following the earlier clearance.

The later stages of the environmental sequence are without exception dominated by the open conditions established at 75–90cm. The stratigraphy from this level to the base of the modern soil profile is essentially a colluvial deposit incorporating two buried soils. The lower, represented by context 4, had a weakly defined stone accumulation at its base. There is no significant change in the diversity values corresponding to this horizon, and there are only slight indications of associated ecological change. In the lower of the two samples from the Ah horizon, 60–70cm, there is a proportional increase in Pupilla muscorum and Vertigo pygmaea, both indicative of relatively stable conditions.

By 53–60cm, a slight increase in shade-loving and catholic species, along with a decline in Pupilla muscorum, point to a denser vegetation cover. At 52cm, the lower boundary of site Zone D, there is an abrupt ecological change, and this is marked by a drop in both diversity indices. This is the sorted horizon of the second buried soil, which had formed in the lower part of a positive lynchet spreading across the top of the ditch. The principal changes in species composition are an increase in Pupilla muscorum and Trichia hispida, accompanied by a decline in Helicella itala, the two Vallonia species, and Vertigo pygmaea. Similar faunal associations have been recognised in colluvial deposits elsewhere on the chalk (Bell and Jones 1990). They are often characterised by a predominance of Vallonia excentrica over Vallonia

costata, and indeed this latter species is virtually absent from the upper stratigraphy of LDP 101.

Above this, in the Ah horizon of the buried soil (sample 30–45cm), both Helicella itala and Pupilla muscorum numbers recover. These, together with a slight increase in Vertigo pygmaea, indicate rather dry grassland conditions, which might well have been maintained by grazing. At the base of the modern soil profile, both diversity indices rise, reflecting an increase in shade-loving species. This was probably a response to the cessation of cultivation on the hillside and the establishment of the present-day environment of tall, unmanaged grassland and scrub.

Summary

Zone A (125–90cm) Predominance of shade-loving species in the primary silts. Although some snail colonisation may have taken place during this stage, it seems most likely that the majority of shells represent a relict woodland assemblage eroded from adjacent land surfaces. The low diversity values for context 21 (sample 90–95cm) may be a response to the disruption caused by a shallow scoop (cut 20) excavated at this level.

Zone B (90–70cm) Helicella itala, Pupilla muscorum, and Vallonia excentrica are the dominant species during this stage. Changes in the composition of shade-loving taxa suggest some colonisation by tall grass and scrub.

Zone C (70–52cm) Onset of colluviation, with the subsequent formation of a buried soil. The stable conditions that prevailed during soil formation are reflected by the increase in Pupilla muscorum and Vertigo pygmaea.

Zone D (52–30cm) Lynchet deposit. This is one of a series of lynchets in the vicinity of the site; the formation of a buried soil represents a period of stability separating two major stages of cultivation. This is characterised by a predominance of Pupilla muscorum and Trichia hispida, accompanied by significant proportions of Helicella itala, Vallonia excentrica, and Vertigo pygmaea, all of which are common in short-turfed grassland. The virtual disappearance of Vallonia costata during this period is consistent with evidence from colluvial deposits elsewhere (Bell 1983) and is undoubtedly a response to intensive cultivation between the grassland episodes (Evans 1972).

LDP 027: The Sidbury Double Linear Ditch (SPTA no 2232)

LDP 027 was located on the edge of a military trench cut into the eastern ditch (027A) and central bank (027B) of the earthwork (Figs 14 and 29). Despite the superficial impression of a well-preserved bank, the section revealed that considerable erosion had occured, leaving no more than a few centimetres of loose chalk rubble in situ. A comparable degree of erosion had taken place at sites LDP 020A and LDP 026 (this latter sequence was not analysed) and was undoubtedly caused by the encroachment of Iron Age and Romano-British cultivation (Chap 7). Although it does not appear that tillage had penetrated through to the buried soil at any of these sites, such severe erosion must call into question the integrity of the molluscan fauna from the upper buried soil horizon. Shells of more recent origin may have been incorporated at this level through the action of earthworms and root penetration: these processes would explain the somewhat anomalous appearance of the introduced species Candidula intersecta (Kerney 1966) in the buried Ah horizon at LDP 020A.

The buried soil sequence (027B)

The earliest environmental evidence from LDP 027B comes from a shallow, irregular feature at the base of the buried soil (Fig 29). It was filled with a loose humic sediment (context 12, samples 50–70cm) and was interpreted as a fossil tree hollow. This was confirmed by the predominantly shade-loving molluscan fauna (Fig 64), which made up between 52.2% (65–70cm) and 65.8 % (50–55cm) of the total. Nevertheless, open-country species are present throughout in significant proportions, although there is a general decline to a minimum of 6.1% in the uppermost sample.

The *Zonitidae*, *Discus rotundatus*, and *Carychium tridentatum* together account for most of the shade-loving taxa, although numbers of other shade-loving species, such as *Acanthinula aculeata*, *Clausilia bidentata*, and *Cochlodina laminata*, are also present. Of the catholic species, *Pomatias elegans* is the most numerous in all the samples from context 12. This is a species that thrives in disturbed ground, and its abundance must reflect the favourable conditions created by the loose silting of the tree hollow.

No independent evidence is available to date the ecological conditions represented in the fill of the subsoil hollow. However, the presence of the open-country species *Helicella itala*, *Pupilla muscorum*, and *Vallonia excentrica* suggest that they were created by relatively light woodland. The species composition contrasts with the molluscan fauna from the Neolithic pit on Copehill Down (Allen 1989), perhaps indicating that the tree hollow belonged to a later stage of secondary woodland. Some regeneration appears to have taken place during the final silting of the hollow, but this may have been fairly restricted.

Interpretation of the ecological transition to the overlying sorted horizon is made difficult by the complex processes influencing the age stratification of snail shells in buried soils (Carter 1990). In broad ecological terms, the fauna from the lower sorted horizon (sample 43–47cm) suggests that the earlier shaded conditions persisted with little change in proportional species composition. The diversity curves reach maximum values at this level, perhaps indicating a more stable environment in the immediate vicinity of the hollow, which was completely silted by this time.

Higher in the sorted horizon (sample 38–43cm), there is an abrupt change involving an increase in the proportions of all open-country taxa and *Pomatias elegans*, accompanied by a decrease in most of the shade-loving taxa. This could represent a clearance phase (Evans 1972), although, as Carter (1990) has argued, the differential size sorting and destruction of shells in sorted horizons calls into question the validity of such interpretations.

The fauna from the thin Ah horizon of the buried soil (sample 32–38cm) is a more reliable guide to the pre-bank environment, perhaps reflecting the final 20 to 30 years before burial (ibid). The environment during this period was predominantly open. Shade-loving species make up just over 9% of the fauna and are represented mainly by the more catholic species, such as *Punctum pygmaeum* and *Carychium tridentatum*. Worn apices of the *Clausiliidae* suggest that these are residual elements,

so too perhaps are the single example of *Aegopinella nitidula* and the non-apical fragment of *Discus rotundatus*. We can infer, therefore, that the shaded aspect of the pre-bank environment was probably created by tall grasses and herbaceous vegetation, with little or no trace of woodland in the immediate vicinity.

The ditch sequence (027A)

There is close agreement between the diversity indices and faunal composition of the lowest sample from the ditch silts (90–100cm; Fig 64) and those for the Ah horizon of the buried soil. However, this impression of ecological continuity is rather at odds with the stratigraphic evidence from the ditch, which suggests that the original primary silts were scoured out (see Chap 3). If the basal silts do belong to a later stage in the history of the ditch, it is rather surprising to find little or no evidence for environmental change in the molluscan sequence.

Perhaps the most plausible explanation is that the interval between the cutting of the original ditch and the removal of accumulated silts was very short. If only a limited time had elapsed, shells might have continued to be eroded from the buried soil, and recolonisation would have taken place from a range of habitats broadly similar to those present in the pre-bank environment. The only significant difference between the fauna from the upper buried soil and the lower ditch silts is the presence of a rather more shaded aspect in sample 90–100cm. However, this can be attributed to the unique micro-habitat of the newly cleared ditch and is unlikely to be representative of wider conditions. Indeed, the most abundant shade-loving species are *Nesovitrea hammonis*, *Punctum pygmaeum*, and *Vitrina pellucida*, which characterise the early stages of ditch colonisation by plants (Evans 1972).

The following part of the sequence (down to 52cm) shows a steady overall increase in open-country species. Along with the decline in the diversity indices, this indicates a much more restricted range of habitats in a generally dry environment. Such conditions could have been created by intensive arable or pastoral land-use, but, for various reasons, it can be extremely difficult to distinguish between the two (Bell 1990). Nevertheless, there are aspects of the environmental sequence at this and other sites that, together with unusual silting sequences, suggest that changes in the ratio of arable/pastoral landuse might be identified.

Between 90 and 75cm, the diversity indices are relatively stable. Higher shell numbers and the increase in stones greater than 5.6mm are indicative of continuous erosion, mostly from exposed chalk on the edge of the ditch and perhaps also from the bank. The presence of areas with sparse vegetation cover, which would have been susceptible to erosion, is confirmed by the relative abundance of *Pupilla muscorum* and *Helicella itala*, both common in dry exposed habitats (Evans 1972). A single shell of *Candidula intersecta* was recovered from sample 80–85cm. Since this species is a medieval introduction (Kerney 1966), its appearance in the lower ditch silts is difficult to explain, unless it was introduced through contamination during sampling.

From 75 to 58cm, a number of ecological changes occurred. Both diversity indices decrease, although shell

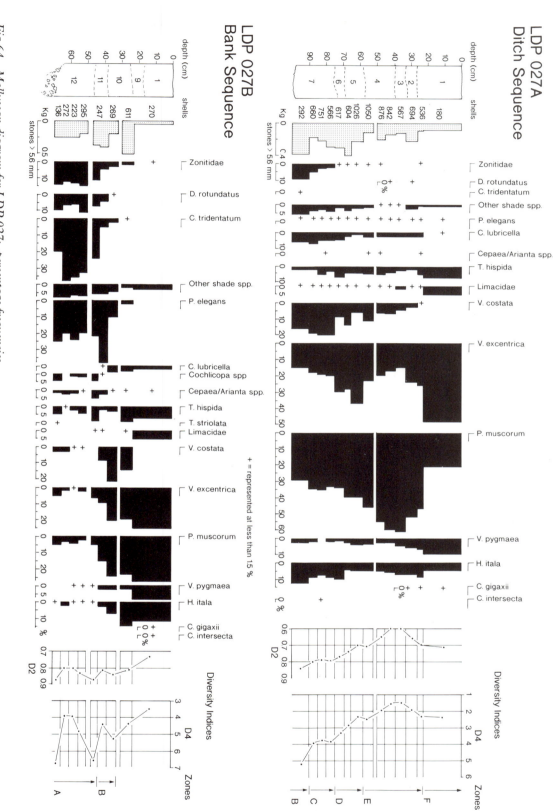

Fig 64   Molluscan diagram for LDP 027: percentage frequencies

numbers remain high. *Vallonia costata* declines erratically as *Vallonia excentrica* becomes more numerous; the *Zonitidae*, along with other shade-loving species, also decrease. This low-diversity fauna is reminiscent of the restricted assemblages from arable soils in lynchets (Evans 1972; Thomas 1977) and dry-valley deposits investigated elsewhere on the chalk (Bell 1981). The colour (10YR 5/4–10YR 6/4) and composition of the silts (contexts 5 and 6) also suggests that they were derived at least partly from arable soils. LDP 027 lies just to the north of the pastoral enclosure bounding Snail Down (Chap 7) in an area crossed by several lynchets, and it is entirely possible that these belong to the period of cultivation during which contexts 5 and 6 accumulated. The only ecological anomaly at this stage is the abundance of *Pupilla muscorum* throughout the secondary silting, which does seem to conflict with its reported intolerance of cultivation (Evans 1972). However, the species is not uncommon in colluvial deposits (Bell 1990), and it is abundant in the silting sequences at sites LDP 083 and LDP 097, where arable cultivation seems also to have played a major role in sedimentation.

At 69cm (context 12), the rate of silting slowed down, allowing a soil to form. *Vallonia costata* made a temporary recovery as a result of the more stable conditions, but there is no sign of any significant ecological change. A truncated Ah horizon was identified between 58 and 65cm. It is associated with an abrupt rise in the absolute numbers of *Vertigo pygmaea*, which indicates a relative degree of stability during this phase. A similar, though less prominent, stabilisation occurred between 52 and 58cm and was associated with an increase in *Vallonia costata* and *Vertigo pygmaea*.

Above 52cm, there is a continuous accumulation of colluvial sediment, interrupted only by a layer of chalk rubble (context 3), which was derived from ploughing over the bank. *Vallonia costata* declined throughout this deposit, finally disappearing at 26cm. *Vertigo pygmaea* initially followed this decline, but then recovered as more stable conditions returned at the base of the modern soil. This level is also characterised by the first appearance of the introduced species *Candidula gigaxii*.

The characteristic diversity curve for the tertiary silts is similar to that at the equivalent horizon at LDP 083. In both sequences, it precedes an abrupt reduction in the numbers of *Pupilla muscorum*, although the decrease is not quite so pronounced at LDP 027. For reasons discussed in the environmental report on LDP 083, this is interpreted as marking the onset of a more intensive Romano-British cultivation extending over the ditches.

Summary

Zone A (70–50cm at 027B)   The fauna from the subsoil hollow. This reflects a predominantly shaded environment, although a significant proportion of open-country species are present throughout the silting. The persistence of open-country species, albeit in low numbers, suggests that these conditions were created by secondary woodland (cf Evans and Vaughan 1985, 18).

Zone B (from 50–38cm at 027B; 100–90cm at 027A)   Open-country aspect in the upper part of the buried soil and present in the lower silts of the ditch. Essentially a period of ecological continuity, probably within a grassland environment. The shaded aspect reflected in the fauna of the ditch primary silts is due mainly to the presence of *Nesovitrea hammonis*, *Punctum pygmaeum*, and *Vitrina*

pellucida, all of which are associated with the initial stages of plant colonisation.

Zone C (90–75cm)   The conditions suggested for Zone B continue. The xerophilic elements in the assemblage reflect the exposed chalk and patchy vegetation that existed on the margins of the ditch and on the bank.

Zone D (75–58cm)   The onset of cultivation, probably of Iron Age date. Around 69cm, there was a major interruption, during which sedimentation relaxed sufficiently to allow a soil to form. This may be a response to adjacent field plots being taken out of cultivation on a temporary basis, or it might indicate a more widespread reduction in the amount of cultivated land. A second, though less prominent, stabilisation horizon was present at 58–65cm, indicating another cycle of cultivation followed by grassland.

Zone E (58–23cm)   The lower part of this zone marks the transition from secondary to tertiary silts. The relatively stable conditions in the upper secondary silts were disrupted by a further period of tillage. Initially, this is associated with increasing numbers of *Pupilla muscorum*, which were probably derived by erosion from the previous grassland episode. The decline of this species in the upper part of Zone E, along with the disappearance of *Vallonia costata*, and the increased proportions of *Trichia hispida* and the *Limacidae*, may be associated with rather more intensive cultivation during the Romano-British period (Chap 7).

Zone F (23–0cm)   This is the modern soil profile. The contemporary environment of tall, ungrazed grassland is clearly reflected in the species composition at both subsites. The fauna is characterised by the dominance of *Vallonia excentrica* and the introduced Helicellids, *Candidula intersecta* and *Candidula gigaxii*.

LDP 083: The Weather Hill Linear Ditch (SPTA no 2234)

LDP 083 is situated on the southern edge of a fragmentary field system that may be part of the same network of lynchets stretching to LDP 027 (Figs 10 and 14). The ditch is one of several that define two large enclosures abutting the Sidbury Double Linear Ditch. On the basis of the evidence discussed in Chapter 7, we suggest that these were set out during the Early to Middle Iron Age as stock enclosures within a largely cultivated landscape. The site was one of a number exposed during the resurfacing of the Old Marlborough Coach Road. This involved the removal of the topsoil and a variable depth of chalk, and, consequently, the excavated section shown in Figure 37 is considerably truncated. In order to sample the full depth of the profile, samples were taken from the oblique section formed by the edge of the track cutting. No bank survived at LDP 083, therefore only a minimal reconstruction of the pre-ditch environment can be attempted.

Two diagrams have been prepared for this environmental sequence. The first (Fig 65) displays species composition in the conventional manner, using percentage frequency histograms. The second diagram (Fig 66) is based on absolute shell numbers and has been included in order to highlight some of the more subtle detail masked by the percentage frequency calculations.

Very few shells were recovered from the primary silts (120–140cm: context 6), but they were all from species common in open-country settings. The uppermost sample from the same context contained a more viable assemblage, which reinforced the impression that the ditch was constructed in an open and rather dry landscape. Unlike the eastern ditch of the Sidbury Double

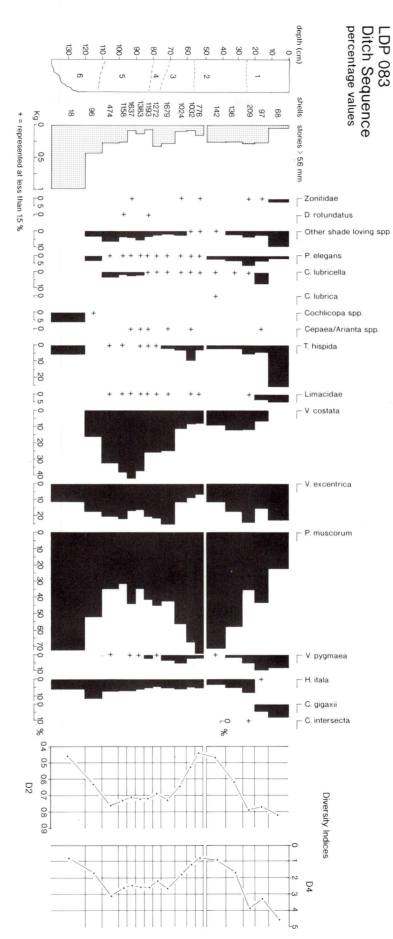

Fig 65   Molluscan diagram for LDP 083, based on percentage frequencies

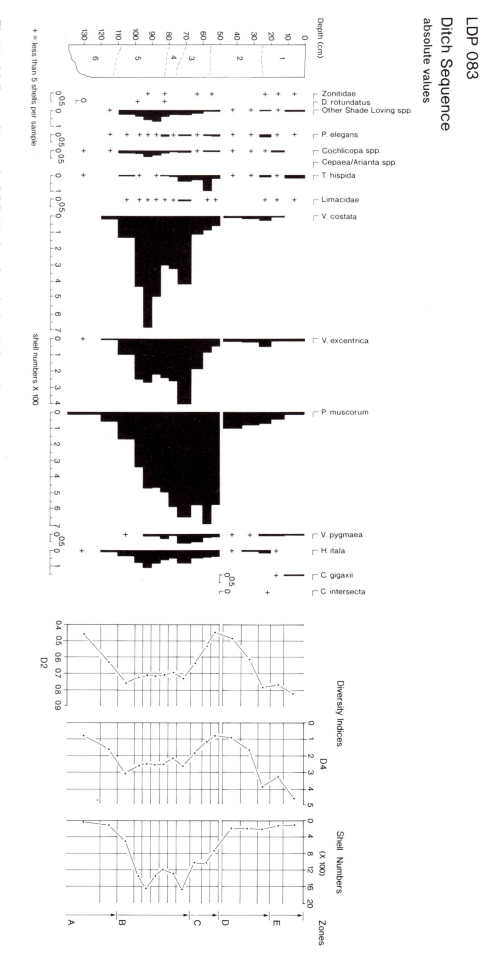

Fig 66 Molluscan diagram for LDP 083, based on absolute shell numbers

Linear at LDP 027, the basal silts at this site are composed of the more usual coarse chalk rubble. There are two pertinent observations on the date and landscape setting of these two ditches, which may explain this difference.

First, it was suggested that the ditch at LDP 027 had been scoured out, and that this may have been connected with a later phase of reuse in an arable setting. Ditch 2234, sectioned at LDP 033 and 083, had a symmetrical 'V'-shaped profile, which is characteristic of recut Late Bronze Age ditches and subsequent Iron Age additions to the original system. One possible explanation for the different silting sequences might be found in the contrasting histories of the two ditches. Since the ditch at LDP 027 was a remodelled one, subsequent silting would have been initiated by the weathering of a profile that had already achieved a degree of relative stability. Ditch 2234, on the other hand, was a new ditch constructed to serve as a boundary between a cultivated area and a pastoral enclosure (Chap 7). Consequently, this ditch would have been susceptible to primary erosion from the freshly exposed chalk for a period before the adjacent field system was fully developed. The second relevant point is that ditch 2234 forms the upslope boundary of the field system, thus for a time ploughsoil may have moved away from the ditch, rather than towards it.

In section, the slower secondary silts (which began to accumulate from 100cm) appeared to be relatively undifferentiated, but the particle-size graph shows several paired peaks and troughs that might represent stabilised soil horizons. Alternatively, it is possible that these represent periodic accumulations of more vigorous silting, produced by seasonal climatic effects. However, this seems unlikely in view of the uniformly high shell numbers present throughout the sequence, and the more or less constant diversity values. Perhaps a more satisfactory explanation is that the secondary silts were derived mainly from the adjacent arable land and that, over this period, there were intervals when cultivation was relaxed or ceased altogether. Between 70 and 80cm, cultivation was encroaching on the bank, resulting in the formation of context 4. This horizon is not marked by any significant change in diversity or shell numbers, and there seems to be no sign of ecological alteration.

Similarities can be recognised with other colluvial ditch sediments discussed in this chapter and at other sites (for example, Coneybury Henge: Bell and Jones 1990). This is most noticeable in the especially high numbers of *Pupilla muscorum* and the relative abundance of *Helicella itala*, the two *Vallonia* species, and *Trichia hispida* (Evans and Vaughan 1985, 25). However, given the rather unstable conditions implied by the proposed origin of the secondary silts at LDP 083, it seems somewhat incongruous also to find increased numbers of *Vertigo pygmaea*.

An explanation for this apparent anomaly is suggested by the absolute diagram (Fig 66), which shows that the variation in *Vertigo pygmaea* numbers was probably related to phases of stabilisation not visible in the section, but indicated by the particle-size graph. The relationship is far from perfect. However, bearing in mind that these horizons were not visible in the stratigraphy (hence the sampling interval does not coincide exactly with the pedological boundaries), it is strong enough to suggest that the peaks in *Vertigo pygmaea* represent periods during which colluviation relaxed and some vegetation cover was being established. The correspondingly high numbers of *Punctum pygmaeum* appear to support this conclusion, and its rather earlier increase may reflect the initial stages in the process.

The absolute numbers histogram for *Pupilla muscorum* shows some slight alternation with that for *Vertigo pygmaea*. This is an interesting contrast, since the abundance of *Pupilla muscorum* in colluvium is thought to result from the erosion of stabilised land surfaces, which had formed between periods of cultivation (Bell and Jones 1990). If these were too short to permit complete vegetation cover to become established, the resultant conditions, consisting chiefly of broken ground, might favour *Pupilla muscorum* (Evans and Vaughan 1985). However, a more complete vegetation cover is suggested by the numbers of *Vertigo pygmaea*, a species that prefers short-turfed grassland. Such conditions are likely to have existed within the area enclosed by ditch SPTA 2234 and its counterpart (SPTA 2236), since these appear to have reserved a tract of pasture (see Chap 7). Given the ecotonal setting of ditch SPTA 2234, we can explain the alternating numbers of the two species in the following way. The *Pupilla muscorum* shells may reflect the intermittent cultivation on one side of the ditch and were probably incorporated mostly by colluviation. On the other hand, the *Vertigo pygmaea* shells could represent an autochthonous population more closely reflecting the grassland ecology on the other side, with their numbers in the ditch increasing during periods of relaxed sedimentation.

We can envisage, therefore, a long period of cultivation adjacent to LDP 083, during which the secondary silts accumulated, but punctuated by several fallow episodes allowing soil formation in the ditch. The time-scale represented by the stabilisation horizons is difficult to estimate, but recent research on soil formation processes suggests that these episodes lasted decades, rather than years (Carter 1990).

The transition from secondary to tertiary silts (context 2) is accompanied by an initial decline in diversity indices, followed by a recovery at the base of the modern soil (context 1). The associated ecological change is similar to that in the equivalent horizon at LDP 027A (Fig 64). It is chiefly characterised by a sharp decline in the absolute numbers of *Pupilla muscorum*, a somewhat erratic increase of *Vallonia excentrica* over *Vallonia costata*, and a more consistent decline in *Vertigo pygmaea*. These changes reflect the locally widespread influence of Romano-British cultivation, which appears to have had a more profound ecological impact than earlier arable episodes.

Summary

The local site zones are based on the absolute diagram (Fig 66).

Zone A (140–110cm)   The fauna of the primary silts is predominantly allochthonous. Some initial colonisation may be represented by *Vallonia costata* and the appearance of *Punctum pygmaeum*. The environment initially was probably short-turfed grassland in the process of being converted to arable.

Zone B (110–67cm)   The fairly restricted fauna of the secondary silts, mostly the two *Vallonia species*, *Pupilla muscorum*, and *Helicella itala*, indicates an arable environment. Fluctuations in the numbers of *Vertigo pygmaea* suggest a series of stabilisation horizons during which a vegetation cover became established in the ditch.

Zone C (67–48cm)   Both diversity indices decline during this zone, and there is a steady reduction in *Vertigo pygmaea* and the *Vallonia* species. Cultivation appears to have continued intermittently throughout this period, although the changes noted already may indicate increasing instability.

Zone D (48–20cm)   This zone begins with a marked ecological change. The most obvious effect is the abrupt reduction in *Pupilla muscorum*, but this is also accompanied by a less pronounced decline in *Helicella itala*, the two *Vallonia* species, and *Vertigo pygmaea*. Together with the very low diversity indices, this indicates greater ecological instability and probably reflects the cumulative effect of intensive Romano-British cultivation.

Zone E (20–0cm)   The higher diversity indices reflect much more stable conditions in the modern soil profile. The time-scale represented by this fauna is unclear, but it undoubtedly contains a mixed assemblage reflecting various episodes of post-Roman land-use. Nonetheless, the overall impression is consistent with the present environment of tall, ungrazed grassland, with no significant evidence for scrub regeneration.

LDP 097: The Sidbury East Linear Ditch (SPTA no 2244)

The primary silts accumulated rapidly in a predominantly dry and open environment indicated by *Helicella itala*, *Pupilla muscorum*, and the two *Vallonia* species (Fig 67). According to a recent study of ditch sedimentation rates by Bell (1990), the time-scale involved may have been less than a decade. The single shell of *Discus rotundatus*, and the non-apical fragment of *Clausilia bidentata*, probably represent a relict element derived from the base of the adjacent topsoil, as it eroded into the ditch. Some evidence for an autochthonous fauna is furnished by shells of *Nesovitrea hammonis* and *Punctum pygmaeum*. As the ditch profile stabilised, a period of slower silting was initiated (context 8), during which these species became well established along with *Vallonia costata*.

The subsequent layer (context 5) was an unusually humic sediment (10YR 4/4), which might indicate a colluvial origin, but, unlike the corresponding deposits at site LDP 027, there were no indications of stabilisation horizons, nor can these be detected in the particle-size graph. The particle-size histogram and the uniformly high shell numbers point to a slow and continuous process of accumulation, but once again the relative instability implied by this process appears to be contradicted by the increasing numbers of *Vertigo pygmaea*. It is possible that there were periods of incipient stability even more transient than those at LDP 083, but if so they have left no identifiable trace.

Above this level, the tertiary silts showed a composite structure incorporating two major soil horizons. The fall in diversity and the changes in species composition resemble similar trends in the sequences for LDP 027A and LDP 083, although the detail is rather more complicated. In the sorted horizon of the lower buried soil (context 4), the restricted fauna is probably representative of species characterising the preceding colluvial phase and is composed chiefly of *Helicella itala*, *Trichia*

hispida, the two *Vallonia* species, and slightly reduced numbers of *Pupilla muscorum*. In the Ah horizon, stable conditions are reflected by a slight numerical rise in *Vertigo pygmaea* and a proportional increase in *Pupilla muscorum*.

A second episode of colluviation occurred above context 4, eventually giving way to another period of stability (context 3). The fauna preserved in this buried soil is characterised by reduced numbers of *Vertigo pygmaea*, the *Vallonia* species, and *Pupilla muscorum*, and a minor recovery of shade-loving species. This latter group is composed entirely of species commonly found in grassland. Abraded non-apical fragments of *Discus rotundatus* and apices of the *Clausiliidae* were present in the Ah horizon, but these are undoubtedly residual elements from a relict soil assemblage.

Apart from traces of a sorted horizon between 20 and 12cm, most of the upper stratigraphy had been mixed by recent cultivation; therefore, the samples from above this level were not analysed.

Summary

Zone A (108–87cm)   The fauna at this stage is predominantly allochthonous, derived from erosion of the ditch sides, bank, and adjacent topsoil. Towards the end of this stage, reduced silting permitted an autochthonous fauna to become established. This is typified by the rising numbers of *Nesovitrea hammonis* and *Punctum pygmaeum*.

Zone B (87–52cm)   This zone represents a period of sedimentation that seems to have a colluvial origin. This could be of Late Bronze Age or Early Iron Age date, and, in fact, it may have been broadly contemporary with the similar silts at LDP 027. There were no signs of stabilisation in the stratigraphy, although it might be suggested by the relative abundance of *Vertigo pygmaea* at this level.

Zone C (52–37cm)   A major episode of colluviation, with intervening buried soils, resulting in the formation of a two-phase lynchet in the top of the ditch. This broadly corresponds to similar episodes at sites LDP 027A and 083, and is probably Romano-British. *Candidula gigaxii* appears in the Ah horizon of the lower buried soil (context 4), but the fresh condition of the shells suggests that they may be intrusive elements.

Zone D (37–20cm)   Some increase in shaded conditions is indicated by the fauna from the upper buried soil (context 3), but this was mostly reflected by species common in grassland. There is no indication of scrub or woodland regeneration, and it seems likely that the adjacent field system had been abandoned to rough pasture.

LDP 092: The Brigmerston Down Linear Ditch (SPTA no 1971)

The eastern bank section and buried soil (092C)

The ecological setting of 092 is rather complicated. It was constructed along the edge of a field in such a way that the western bank covered an undisturbed grassland soil (context 3), while the eastern bank sealed an unsorted ploughsoil (context 3A). A subsoil hollow at the base of the buried soil beneath the eastern bank contained a predominantly shade-loving fauna in the lowest sample (Fig 68). Like the subsoil hollow at LDP 027A (Fig 64), this feature was interpreted as a fossil tree cast and it contained a similar faunal assemblage, but of lower diversity. Such differences as do exist, for example the higher numbers of *Discus rotundatus* and the presence of

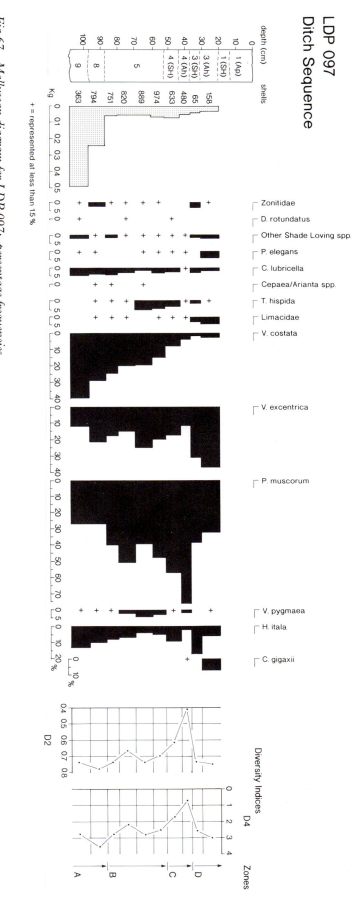

Fig 67   Molluscan diagram for LDP 097: percentage frequencies

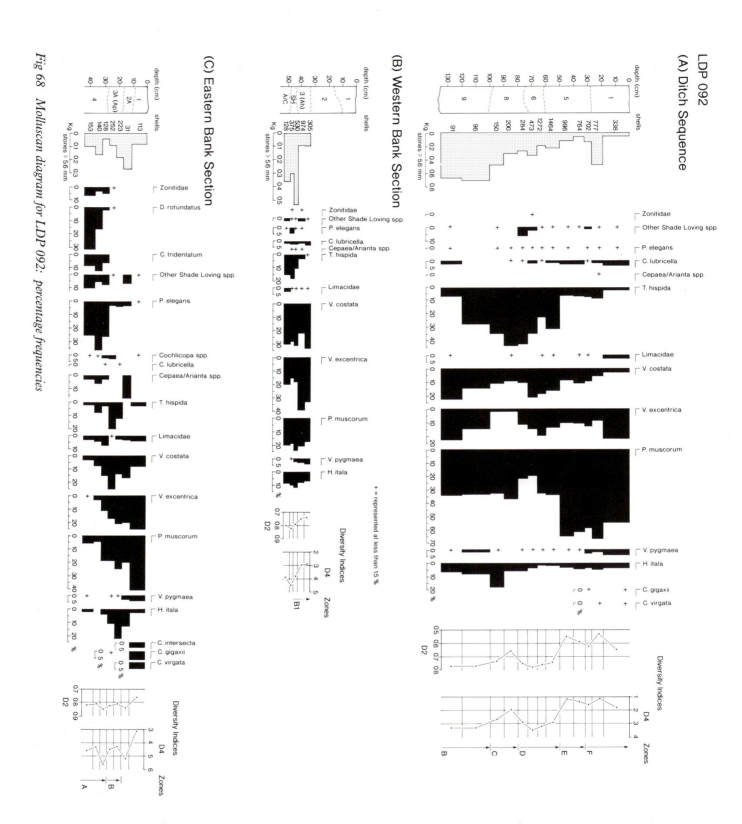

Fig 68   Molluscan diagram for LDP 092: percentage frequencies

Helicigona lapicida at LDP 092C, are difficult to interpret in purely ecological terms. However, unlike the subsoil sequence from LDP 027, the overall trend is towards more open conditions, which attain 43% of the total species in the uppermost sample (27–32cm). It is possible that this is directly associated with the clearance of the area for cultivation, which would have prevented regeneration, but we cannot discount the possibility of a break in the sequence at this level (Carter 1990). A single radiocarbon determination on bone from the base of the buried soil gave a date of *c* 3700–3370 cal BC (Table 22, OxA3045), which seems rather early for major clearance. It may instead refer to the preceding woodland conditions, but, owing to the disturbance caused by subsequent cultivation, we cannot be more specific.

Reduced numbers of *Carychium tridentatum* and *Discus rotundatus* persist into the lower horizon of the buried soil, but this seems unlikely to represent ecological continuity. Instead, these shade-loving species probably make up a mixed residual assemblage, derived from relict woodland contexts during cultivation. The long-term decline of shade-loving species during the silting of the subsoil hollow clearly reflects the general trend towards more open conditions, but it is impossible to relate this directly to the overlying ploughsoil (context 3A). No hint of woodland conditions or major clearance survives in the equivalent buried soil under the western bank, therefore we must conclude that the subsoil sequence is truncated and belongs to a very much earlier period, as the radiocarbon date suggests.

The taxa present in the buried ploughsoil are typical of the low-diversity faunae associated with cultivation. They consist chiefly of *Helicella itala*, *Trichia hispida*, *Vallonia costata*, *Vallonia excentrica*, the *Limacidae*, and *Pupilla muscorum*. However, compared with the buried Rendzina profile below the western bank, the buried ploughsoil contains far fewer shells of this latter species, which is in accordance with its reported intolerance of cultivation (Evans 1972). *Vertigo pygmaea* is also poorly represented by comparison with the western buried soil, and this too can be attributed to its preference for stable conditions (ibid).

The western bank section and buried soil (092B)

The buried soil below the bank showed a typical grassland Rendzina profile with a stone-free mull humus horizon (Ah) overlying a sorted horizon (SH). The fauna from both spits of the Ah horizon are dominated by the two *Vallonia* species, *Helicella itala* and *Pupilla muscorum*. Together with *Vertigo pygmaea* (Fig 68), these indicate a long period during which the environment consisted of short-turfed grassland, possibly maintained by grazing.

A minor, shade-loving element is present throughout the Ah horizon, especially in the lower spit (sample 37–42cm), but this is composed of species such as *Punctum pygmaeum*, *Vitrina pellucida*, and *Aegopinella pura*, all of which are common in grassland habitats. Worn apical fragments of *Pomatias elegans* and the *Clausiliidae* are present in small numbers towards the base of the soil, but these are almost certainly vestiges of much earlier ecological episodes.

The ditch section (092A)

The lowest sample from the primary ditch silts (context 9: 120–135cm) has similar diversity values and species composition to the fauna from the western buried soil (Fig 68). This may indicate that the earliest ditch fauna was derived chiefly from the erosion of the western ditch edge. Some hint of an autochthonous snail population appears in the lower secondary silts (context 8) with the increase of *Vallonia costata* over *Vallonia excentrica*. Between 73 and 80cm, the higher diversity indices and increased shell numbers indicate a period of relative stability. A minor peak in shade-loving species, composed mainly of *Vitrina pellucida* and *Punctum pygmaeum*, might indicate that this was associated with plant colonisation.

The most striking ecological feature of the secondary silts at this site is the abundance of *Trichia hispida*, which rises to almost 42% of the total fauna between 73 and 80cm. This contrasts with the faunal assemblages from the secondary silts at sites LDP 083 and LDP 027A, where it was argued that the ditches occupied arable settings. The contrast may indicate that sedimentation at LDP 092 was taking place in a rather more moist and well-vegetated environment, than was present at the other two sites. Whether or not cultivation continued in the previously cultivated field after the ditch had been constructed is uncertain. If it did continue, it was probably on a very limited scale, or rather more distant than before. The species *Trichia hispida* appears to have been common in grassland environments of late prehistoric date (Evans 1972), and, in all probability, its abundance in the secondary ditch silts at LDP 092 reflects such conditions in the immediate vicinity of the boundary earthwork.

Context 6 (60–73cm) was interpreted in the field as a rather disturbed and weakly sorted buried soil. Both diversity indices increase during this stage and this is accompanied by a dramatic rise in shell numbers. The associated fauna is mainly open country with a strong xerophilic element made up of *Pupilla muscorum* and *Helicella itala*, and it still includes large numbers of the catholic species *Trichia hispida*. A minor, shade-loving element is also present, although in the upper sample (60–66cm) it comprises less than 1% of the total assemblage. With the exception of the worn apical fragments of *Clausilia* spp., all of the shade-loving taxa are consistent with an open-country aspect, most probably created by grassland.

The onset of tertiary silting (context 5: sample 50–60cm) is more difficult to interpret than in the other sequences. The initial stages do not appear to be associated with any major ecological change. Possibly this is because the fauna is of mixed origin, being derived largely from truncation of the underlying palaeosol. However, above 50cm ecological change is clearly visible; there is a characteristic decline in both diversity indices, but, in this instance, it is caused by an abrupt fall in the numbers of *Trichia hispida*, not *Pupilla muscorum* as in the previous sequences.

Pupilla muscorum remains common throughout the tertiary silts, and there are also significant numbers of *Vertigo pygmaea* present, though the latter species is less common than in the modern soil profile (32–0cm). This association is reminiscent of the fauna from the secondary silts at LDP 083, which might indicate that the most recent phase of cultivation on Brigmerston Down was Iron Age rather than Romano-British. There is no direct evidence for later fields adjacent to this site, and it may be that by the Romano-British period the area was peripheral to the main focus of cultivation around Dunch Hill and the Devil's Ditch.

The fauna from the modern soil profile (32–0cm) contains the introduced species *Candidula gigaxii* and *Cernuella virgata*. It is predominantly an open-country fauna, with a minor shade-loving element reflecting the present vegetation of tall grasses and herbs growing in the hollow of the ditch.

Summary

Zone A (092C: 45–27cm)   Shaded aspect created by secondary woodland. These conditions are similar to those in Zone A at LDP 027B and may be part of a more widespread open woodland environment.

Zone B1 (52–33cm at 092B and 135–100cm at 092A)   Grassland environment reflected in the fauna of the western buried soil and the primary ditch silts. Contemporary with the cultivation under the eastern bank (Zone B, see Fig 68 C).

Zone C (100–80cm)   Very restricted fauna dominated by *Trichia hispida*, *Pupilla muscorum*, *Vallonia costata*, and *Helicella itala*. This probably represents an allochthonous assemblage derived from exposed and sparsely vegetated habitats on the margins of the ditch.

Zone D (80–50cm)   Some relaxation in the rate of sedimentation and the formation of a palaeosol (context 6) between 73 and 60cm. This period of stability is marked by a much greater number of shells and higher diversity indices. Shade-loving taxa are present in small numbers, but apart from residual elements they are all species common in tall grassland. During this stage a complete vegetation cover was established in the ditch.

Zone E (50–32cm)   Period of colluviation forming the tertiary silts (context 5). Declining diversity indices, caused mainly by the abrupt fall in *Trichia hispida* numbers, are accompanied by a consistently high proportion of *Pupilla muscorum* and significant numbers of *Vertigo pygmaea*. A similar association was recorded in the secondary silts at LDP 083, where it appears to have been associated with intermittent Iron Age cultivation.

Zone F (32–0cm)   The modern soil profile (context 1). Relatively low diversity indices reflect the predominantly open aspect and dry conditions prevailing throughout this context. Shade-loving taxa are present in very small numbers, but there is no indication that woodland or scrub regeneration took place in the immediate vicinity of the site. The slightly shaded aspect was probably created by tall grasses, possibly interrupted by a period of grazed grassland at 19–27cm.

LDP 052: The Devil's Ditch (SPTA no 1959)

The silting sequence at this site closely resembles that at LDP 027, in that there was no sign of the vacuous chalk rubble usually associated with the initial stages of primary infill. Apart from the topmost horizon, the ditch was filled with a fine and uniform chalk wash (context 5) that showed only minor colour variations (Fig 34). This has been interpreted as evidence for recutting, or at least the scouring out of the original ditch silts (Chap 3). Following this, the accumulation of context 5 appears to reflect a continuous process of erosion with little discernible change in the ecological setting of the ditch. In view of the homogeneity of the ditch infill, only four samples

from the base of the section were taken for analysis.

The fauna from the lowest sample (160–170cm; Fig 69) indicates a predominantly open-country aspect, although a minor shade-loving element is present. This consists of the species *Carychium tridentatum* and *Vitrea crystallina*, both of which occur in grassland habitats. However, also present are *Clausilia bidentata* and *Acanthinula aculeata*, which might reflect the presence of wood or scrub refugia nearby.

None of the species comprising Evans's 'Punctum group' occur in the lower samples (only one specimen of *Punctum pygmaeum* was recovered from 130–140cm), perhaps indicating that no significant colonisation by vegetation occurred during the period represented by context 5. The character of the silts and the extremely low faunal diversity (D2 ranges between 0.51 and 0.66, and D4 between 1.05 and 1.93) are indicative of uninterrupted sedimentation from exposed surfaces on the margins of the ditch.

In the uppermost three samples (from 150 to 130cm), the faunae reveal a remarkably uniform environment of persistently low ecological diversity. The slight recovery of shade-loving species in sample 130–140cm is the only indication of ecological change, but it is represented mostly by apical fragments of the *Clausiliidae* and *Helicigona lapicida*, which are particularly robust and therefore may be residual. However, these could well be intrusive, since context 5 was disturbed extensively by the fibrous roots of the beech trees that now cover the site.

Summary

The overall trend revealed by the four samples seems to reflect increasingly dry conditions over the period during which context 5 accumulated. Faunal composition is consistent with conditions created by intensive arable cultivation close to the ditch and latterly encroaching over the banks. The sequence throughout is dominated by relatively high numbers of *Pupilla muscorum*, but, unlike the sequence at LDP 083 (Fig 66), there is no indication of transient episodes of stability, nor is there any change to the extreme paucity of *Vertigo pygmaea*, which might point to a relaxation in the rate of sedimentation.

Attention has already been drawn to the similarities between LDP 052 and LDP 027A. Aside from the character of the ditch fills, both are associated with field systems and each has produced a low-diversity xerophilic snail fauna. At each site, the faunal assemblages indicate a restricted range of habitats in dry and apparently unstable environments. This implies that the adjacent field systems were in use from the time when the ditches were remodelled, and, in the case of LDP 027, we can link this with evidence suggesting a closer management of the arable landscape (Chap 7).

LDP 091: The Windmill Hill Linear Ditch (SPTA no 2247)

Seven samples were analysed from this site: five from a column through the bank and buried soil, and two from the base of the ditch primary silts (Fig 35). Although the site occupies a peripheral location with respect to the other sites discussed in this chapter (Fig 70), the drift geology and soils closely resembled those at sites LDP 100 and 101 on Sidbury Hill (Fig 16). This introduced the possibility that Windmill Hill might also have supported woodland during the Late Bronze Age.

The ecological aspect represented in the ditch samples compares favourably with that from the buried soil;

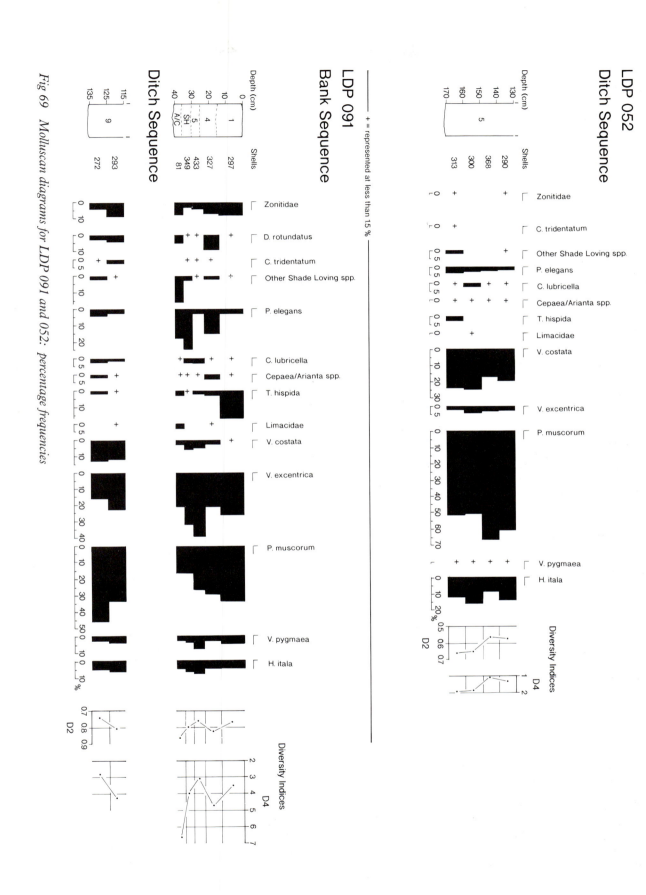

Fig 69 Molluscan diagrams for LDP 091 and 052: percentage frequencies

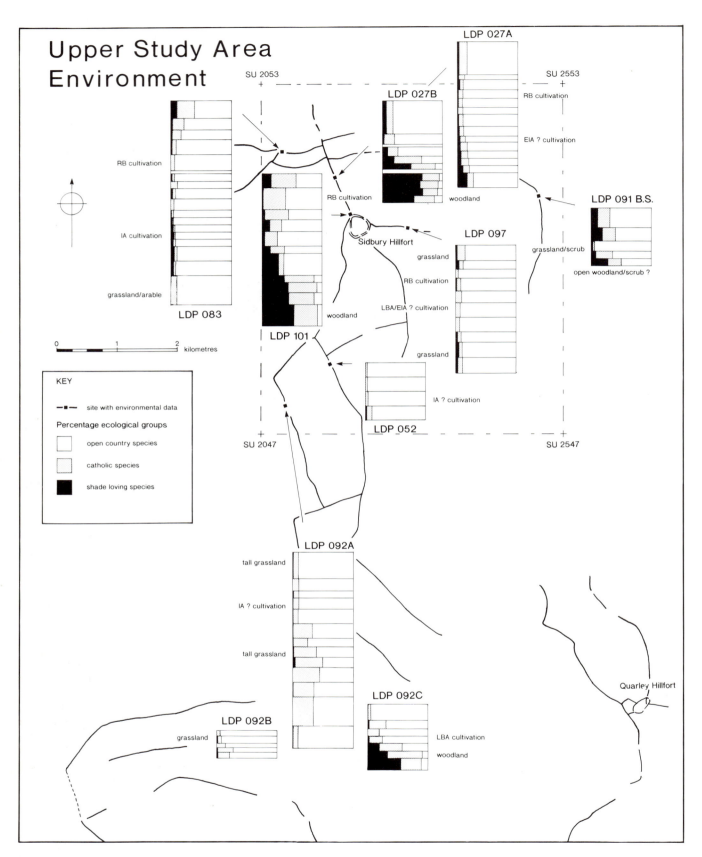

Fig 70   Part of the Upper Study Area, showing the location of sites with environmental data and summaries of the principal ecological episodes relating to changes in the pattern of landuse

shade-loving taxa make up 8.5% of the total in the lowest ditch sample, and between 7.4 (sorted horizon) and 5.3% (Ah horizon) in the buried soil (Fig 69). The tendency towards rather more shaded conditions between 125 and 115cm in the ditch sequence is strongly suggestive of vegetation colonisation, especially the increase in the numbers of *Punctum pygmaeum*. The slightly higher numbers of *Discus rotundatus* in the ditch samples, and the presence of *Ena obscura* and *Acanthinula aculeata* (absent from the buried soil), may denote a measure of scrub colonisation from nearby refugia.

The insubstantial and vacuous residue of the bank contained a surprisingly rich assemblage, amounting to 327 shells. However, since the sorted horizon of the modern soil had become mixed with loose bank material, we must conclude that some, if not all, of these shells were incorporated from the overlying soil. Nonetheless, the fauna preserves traces of a period of scrub regeneration that was probably a continuation of the trend represented in the ditch primary silts. Shade-loving taxa account for almost 18% of the total fauna, but are accompanied by a strong xerophilic element, including *Pupilla muscorum*, *Vertigo pygmaea*, and *Helicella itala*. These latter may indicate that regeneration was patchy, and the bank itself, at least in the early stages, remained free of vegetation.

Although there were substantial differences between the environmental setting of LDP 101 and LDP 091, the sequences for the two sites share similarities that distinguish them from any other of the sequences in the Upper Study Area. It is perhaps unwise to make too much of these similarities, but it may be more than a coincidence that the common topographic and drift geologies at the two sites are mirrored by evidence for a similar ecology. The woodland conditions prevailing on Sidbury Hill are directly attested by the charcoal identifications, as well as being clearly reflected in the molluscan fauna. At LDP 091, the evidence is not as strong. However, this may be a consequence of the peripheral location of LDP 091 with regard to the distribution of Clay-with-Flints and Plateau Gravel, which stretches mostly to the south along the ridge of the Bourne Valley. If this supported woodland, the signs of regeneration at LDP 091 could be seen as a marginal response to clearance and regeneration affecting a larger area.

Charcoal identification

by Rowena Gale

Two samples of charcoal were submitted for identification prior to radiocarbon dating. Both samples consisted of a number of fragments. Many of these measured less than 1mm in transverse section and therefore did not contain sufficient anatomical detail for identification purposes.

The larger fragments were initially sorted into groups based on the anatomical features visible using a ×20 hand lens. Representative pieces from each group were selected for examination using an epi-illuminating microscope at magnifications up to ×400. These fragments were fractured to reveal clean, flat surfaces in transverse, radial longitudinal, and tangential longitudinal planes and supported in sand. The anatomical features were matched to authenticated reference material.

LDP 100: The Sidbury Double Linear Ditch (SPTA no 2232)

The charcoal in this sample was structurally in very poor condition and extremely friable. It was only possible to examine 12 fragments, all of which matched *Fraxinus* spp. (ash).

LDP 101: The Sidbury Double Linear Ditch (SPTA no 2232)

Forty fragments were examined:

> 28 *Corylus* spp. (hazel)
> 9 *Quercus* spp. (oak)
> 3 *Sambucus* spp. (elder)

The minimal size of the fragments makes it almost impossible to comment on the maturity of the wood. However, none of the fragments examined appeared to be twiggy, that is with a diameter of less than 1cm.

Carbonised cereals

by Wendy Carruthers

LDP 092: The Brigmerston Down Linear Ditch (SPTA no 1971)

On microscopic examination, four of the molluscan samples from the western buried soil (context 3) were found to contain carbonised plant remains. In each case, the original sample size was 1.5kg (dry weight), and the minimum mesh used for sieving was 0.5mm. The carbonised plant remains recovered are listed in Table 26.

Small assemblages of this nature are of little interpretive value except, as in this case, to suggest the cultivation of hulled barley. Hulled six-row barley is the predominant cereal recovered from sites of the Late Bronze Age in Britain, but, because no twisted lateral grains were present in the samples from LDP 092, it cannot be confirmed in this instance. However, since no two-row barley has yet been identified from prehistoric contexts in Britain, it can be assumed that the cereal remains from this site are in fact from the hulled six-row variety.

The source of the carbonised cereal grains is uncertain, but it seems most likely that they were derived from *in situ* domestic activity, rather than from manuring. This suggestion is strengthened by the spread of pottery and burnt flint in the buried soil profile under both banks, and perhaps also by postholes that clearly predate the linear boundary by some considerable period and may have formed part of a structure (Chap 7).

Table 26 Carbonised cereal remains from LDP 092B, the western buried soil

depth (cm)	context	identification	number
33–37	(3) Ah	indeterminate seed fragment	1
42–45	SH	*Hordeum* spp.	3
		indeterminate cereal fragments	12
45–48	A/C	*Hordeum* spp.	7
		Hordeum spp.	1
		indeterminate cereal fragments	16
48–52	A/C	indeterminate cereal fragment	1

Discussion

All of the linear ditches discussed in this chapter belong to a common tradition of landscape organisation, and, although there are functional and chronological differences, these can be shown to have a direct and clearly recognisable relationship to the contemporary environment. The archaeological evidence recovered from the numerous excavations has provided an insight into this complex relationship, but for the more subtle detail we must rely on the molluscan data. The contribution made by the molluscan research has been enhanced because it was regarded as a central part of the study from the outset. As a result, the selection of sample sites, and the scale of subsequent analysis, was determined first and foremost by environmental criteria.

The close proximity of the sample sites and the formal similarity of the earthworks to some extent have alleviated the difficulty of relating changes in the composition of molluscan faunae to specific types of landuse. Certain recurrent associations in the molluscan sequences suggest broader ecological patterns, which in turn correlate well with the chronological and functional development of the linear ditches system. Perhaps the most significant gain has been a clearer understanding of the relative scale and intensity of arable cultivation from the later second millennium BC down to the Romano-British period.

The earliest reliable evidence for arable cultivation comes from the eastern buried soil at LDP 092. The carbonised cereal remains from here were distributed throughout the profile, which contained both Middle and Late Bronze Age pottery. A radiocarbon date of c 3700–3370 cal BC (Table 22, Chap 3) was obtained on bone from the base of the soil, but this undoubtedly refers to a much earlier episode, probably incorporated from the subsoil hollow during later cultivation. All this evidence really tells us is that at some time over the course of the Middle or Late Bronze Age part of the adjacent field system was in use for the cultivation of barley. The interpretation of the evidence from LDP 081A must be similarly circumspect. It is possible that the Deverel-Rimbury sherd from the field ditch at this site dates an early stage in the development of the field system, but there remains a chance that the sherd could be residual. Apart from the evidence from LDP 092, there is nothing to suggest a widespread change involving the imposition of linear ditches on pre-existing fields. At LDP 020, 027, 091, and 092B, the structure of the contemporary buried soil horizons and the associated molluscan faunae show no trace of previous cultivation. But signs of somewhat later cultivation do appear at LDP 027 and LDP 097. At the first of these sites, it seems to have been under way by the time that the Sidbury Double Linear Ditch was built to replace a previous boundary. This might have been as early as the beginning of the eighth century BC. A similar date could apply to the accumulation of secondary silts at LDP 097, which also show signs of being derived from arable cultivation. These sediments accumulated after a period of stability (represented by context 8) of unknown duration, but possibly lasting several centuries. Although problems of residuality do affect the artefact dating of this site, the hiatus between primary and secondary silting and the

incorporation of abraded sherds of Late Bronze Age Plain Ware all point to a considerable time lapse before cultivation began.

The impression of the Late Bronze Age landscape at the time that the linear ditches system was established is of a predominantly open environment, chiefly of grassland. Even close to the Nine Mile River, at LDP 092, where we might have expected some residual woodland to persist, conditions seem to have been similar to those in other parts of the Upper Study Area. Within this broad setting, we can recognise traces of arable farming, albeit on a rather limited scale, which does not appear to have brought about any radical or widespread ecological change. So far as the evidence allows, we can surmise that the Late Bronze Age settlements were dependant on a mixed farming economy, involving cereal cultivation (perhaps mainly of barley: Table 26) within a patchwork of permanent fields, with their attendant settlements and trackways (LDP 081A). Although the evidence for animal husbandry is too slight and variable to permit quantification, it certainly involved the exploitation of sheep, pig, cattle, and horse (Chap 3). The absence of wild species in the bone assemblages (except for a red deer antler used as a pick from LDP101) points to an overwhelming reliance on domesticated and predominantly grazing animals. It was undoubtedly this aspect of subsistence, with the implied emphasis on pasture, that helped to create and maintain the widespread grassland conditions.

The environmental sequences from Sidbury Hill (LDP 101) and from Windmill Hill (LDP 091) have introduced some evidence for ecological diversity. During the Late Bronze Age, mixed woodland of oak, ash, hazel, and elder flourished on the Tertiary geology capping Sidbury Hill. To a somewhat lesser extent, similar conditions may have existed in the vicinity of LDP 091 on Windmill Hill. This site is at the northern extremity of a distribution of Clay-with-Flints and Plateau Gravel stretching along a ridge forming the eastern margin of the Bourne Valley. Given its rather peripheral setting, it seems quite feasible that the slight woodland aspect revealed in the environmental sequence at LDP 091 refers to more extensive tracts of woodland further south along the ridge.

Evidence for developments in the later landscape has been recovered from most of the excavated ditches. It has been suggested that the ecological impact of Iron Age cultivation can be recognised in several of the ditch sequences (Fig 70). At present, the limited dating evidence precludes greater precision in identifying the origins of what appears to be an intensification of arable farming. However, there are indications that this trend was already emerging towards the end of the Bronze Age. It was argued that the scouring out of the ditch at LDP 027 followed shortly after its initial construction, and it is quite possible that the inferred cultivation may have taken place in the Late Bronze Age/Early Iron Age. A similar date might also apply to the cultivation around LDP 097. Some of the environmental sequences indicate a relatively long period of intermittent Iron Age cultivation, but the scale and intensity is difficult to judge from the ditch silts alone. In Chapter 7, we suggest that the creation of large pastoral enclosures, such as those on Snail Down, on Figheldean Down, and to the north of

Quarley Hillfort, all indicate that a greater level of control over domestic resources was being exercised at a time when the major hillforts were in use. This may have involved an intensification of arable production, but with the evidence available we are unable to be more specific.

At most of the sites (with the exception of LDP 092), the onset of a final phase of cultivation is marked by major ecological change. A range of early and late Romano-British sherds have been recovered from the tertiary ditch silts at several sites. At LDP 082, a stratified sequence of pottery was excavated from a lynchet that appeared to have accumulated continuously from the Iron Age through to the early Romano-British period. A break in cultivation appears higher up in the lynchet at LDP 082, and at some other sites (LDP 097 and LDP 101) similar interruptions have been recorded. However, despite these fluctuations, the overall impression is of rather intensive cultivation with very rapid colluviation.

Most of the ditches and banks appear to have been ploughed over during the Romano-British period (Fig 70), and no doubt this accounts for the contrasting ecological impact shown by Iron Age and Romano-British cultivation. During the former period, some of the linear ditches functioned as integrated boundaries reserving pastoral areas within the arable landscape, and as such they would have ensured the survival of a relatively sheltered range of habitats. For the most part, however, these boundaries had no part to play in the layout of the Romano-British landscape and were consequently destroyed along with their distinctive ecology. However, the dating for these events remains problematical. Without further research into the chronology and development of the field systems, we are limited to making general statements by period to cover this important stage in the evolution of the landscape. At present, we can only speculate on the origins of the field systems and, from the environmental evidence, identify related patterns of ecological change that await a more refined chronology for their elucidation.

7 Settlements, territories, and 'Celtic' fields: the changing role of boundary earthworks

by Roy Entwistle

Introduction: bounded landscapes

The best preserved and most coherent arrangements of linear ditches in the Upper Study Area lie between the floodplain of the Bourne Valley and Dunch Hill (Fig 10). Between these two locations, long-distance ditches form the boundaries of two large contiguous enclosures, each of approximately 218ha. Although there is no direct stratigraphic evidence to show that the ditches bounding these areas were constructed as a single layout, the interrelationship between the individual elements strongly suggests a unitary plan. It was because of the regularity of this arrangement, and initial assumptions about its primacy, that the two enclosed areas were designated the Southern and Northern Core Territories (Fig 10). Around Sidbury Hill, other territories can be recognised, but in general they are less well preserved, especially in the areas of long-term arable farming found to the north and east of Snail Down. Even though the layout of the Sidbury Hill system is not structured as clearly as that of the Northern Core Territory, the dating evidence is consistent enough to propose a similar chronology and pattern of associated settlement. Viewed together, these boundary ditches give the impression of a network of near contemporary territories, stretching northwards in a strip between 3 and 4km wide along the western margin of the Bourne Valley. This arrangement is one of the best examples of the earliest formal organisation of the landscape, which can still be recognised in the Upper Study Area.

The single radiocarbon determination of *c* 3700–3370 cal BC (OxA-3045), on bone from the eastern buried soil beneath the bank of SPTA 1971 at LDP 092, has no relevance to the date of the earthwork whatsoever, and it is of interest only insofar as it has some bearing on the Neolithic environment (Chap 6). However, the presence of Late Bronze Age Plain Ware sherds in fresh condition at the surface of the western buried soil suggests a *terminus post quem* of 1200 BC (see Chap 4) for the construction of the boundary.

The background to the foundation of artificially delineated territories is perceived less clearly. They appear to represent the formalisation of territories defined already by the disposition of Middle and Late Bronze Age settlement, which in turn may have drawn on much earlier notions of territory implied by the distribution of Early Bronze Age round barrows.

By analogy, similar boundary systems in the Study Area, such as that stretching from the Bourne Valley to Earl's Farm Down, or the rather fragmentary layout to the south and south-west of Quarley, may represent other primary territorial divisions (Fig 8). Although the dating evidence from these areas is less satisfactory, it is consistent enough to argue that the territories belong to the same Late Bronze Age cultural horizon.

Recent work by the Trust For Wessex Archaeology in advance of a Wessex Water pipeline involved the excavation of two of the major linear ditches in the Earl's Farm Down complex – SMR 745 and 746 in Figure 22 (P Harding pers comm). Although neither excavation produced primary dating evidence, the scale of the earthworks resembles those defining the Core Territories, and at least one ditch (SMR 745) was similarly double banked (a short section of standing earthwork is preserved at SU 21244206 in Rollerhouse Belt, see Fig 10). The western end of this territory is shown as incomplete on aerial photographic transcriptions, but information provided by Mick Rawlins confirms that ditch SMR 745 turns sharply southwards on Butterfield Down. Originally, it probably joined SMR 749, completing the territory defined by the boundary ditches SMR 745 and SMR 751.

The exact relationship of ditch SMR 746 to this layout is somewhat problematical. Its morphology suggests a date and function similar to the other two ditches, yet it subdivides the enclosed area axially, forming two unusually narrow strips. The most likely explanation for the siting of this ditch is that it was a subsequent addition used to define separate units within the original territory.

One further example of a possible subdivision occurs to the south of Sidbury Hill, where the area enclosed by ditches 1957 and 1983 is bisected by ditch 1982 (Fig 10). Since none of these features have been excavated, the exact relationship between them remains conjectural. However, all three are double banked (SPTAE records), and, as far as we are able to generalise, this appears to be a characteristic of the Late Bronze Age boundary earthworks. The only other evidence for the dating of these ditches is based on the relationship between ditch 1982 and a large field system stretching across Tidworth Golf Course and Dunch Hill Plantation. In places, there are clear signs that the lynchets of this system supersede the ditch, which forms part of the grouping extending across ditch 1971 at LDP 098. The evidence from this site (discussed later) indicates that the field system probably had Iron Age origins. Although we have no detailed knowledge of the duration of the system as a whole, or the relative chronology of individual fields, there is a case for arguing that ditch 1982 was in existence prior to the Iron Age.

Sometime between the eighth and fifth centuries BC, certain changes to the boundary system, and the abandonment of open settlements following the appearance of Early All Cannings Cross ceramics, indicate a radical restructuring of the previous territorial arrangements. The dating of this stage relies on the radiocarbon chronology for the remodelling of the Sidbury Hill to Snail Down linear ditch in order to create a monumental double earthwork: *c* 795–410 cal BC (OxA-2987 and OxA-2988). Although more tentatively dated, the backfilling of ditch SPTA 1971 at LDP 098 (discussed later) also may have taken place during this period, suggesting that the significance of at least one boundary was being consciously suppressed. Within the same general period, the settlement on Dunch Hill (LDP 081A) seems to have been deserted. The latest pottery from the site is Early All Cannings Cross from the midden, which also produced a radiocarbon date of c 770–395 cal BC (OxA-3048). The absence of any developed All Cannings Cross or Iron Age pottery in the assemblage would seem to indicate that a date in the early part of this range is closest to the true time of abandonment. Taken together, these dates suggest that the system of territorial boundaries, which was established some time after 1200 BC, was undergoing considerable change by the eighth century BC and that this involved the abandonment of the Dunch Hill and Brigmerston Down settlements.

Since the construction and original function of these territories form part of a common tradition emerging during the Late Bronze Age, the excavation evidence will be discussed in the context of a proposed developmental sequence, following the broad chronological framework established for the ditch system as a whole. This approach has been adopted in order to avoid over-detailed discussion on a site-by-site basis and to facilitate the integration of evidence pertaining to wider aspects of associated settlement (Fig 71) and landuse (Fig 70).

The Southern Core Territory

The boundary ditches of this territory were sectioned at two locations (Fig 14): ditch 2061 on the eastern slope of Beacon Hill (LDP 095, Fig 49) and ditch 1959 close to Pearl Wood (LDP 090, Fig 34). Site LDP 095 is currently in an area of 'set aside', and consequently surface collection could not be used to select the optimum location for the excavation. Instead, the site was positioned approximately 175m to the north-west of a field system, spreading across the area through which the ditch passes (Fig 72). A similar problem was encountered with ditch 1959 (the Devil's Ditch), which is in woodland for much of its course. Although an adjacent stretch of arable was fieldwalked (LDP 010, 011, 012, and 013 – see Fig 14), close to an area where elements of a field system appear to encroach on the ditch, access for excavation was difficult and an alternative location was chosen.

Unlike the Devil's Ditch, ditch 2061 has been completely levelled from the perimeter of the Military Training Area to the River Bourne. On the summit of Beacon Hill, within the Training Area, the earthwork can still be traced as a substantial hollow flanked by a bank on either side. The modern boundary separates uncultivated grassland from the former arable area to the south-east, and it appears that the differential survival of 2061 is a reflection of this relatively recent partition. Indeed, some evidence for a recent phase of levelling was detected in the uppermost stratigraphy at site LDP 095 (Fig 49). The modern topsoil was situated directly over a layer of coarse chalk rubble (context 2), which presumably was formed from displaced bank material. This in turn was superimposed on a buried soil containing lenses of charcoal and burnt clay (context 3). Only three sherds

of pottery were recovered from the site: a rim from a Romano-British vessel, dated to the first/second century AD (from the topsoil), and two post-medieval sherds from context 2. There can be little doubt that all three are residual. However, the post-medieval sherds do provide a *terminus post quem* for the phase of clearance and cultivation that was responsible for finally levelling the ditch.

The relationship between ditch 2061 and the adjacent field system is difficult to establish with certainty. Palmer's interpretation of the aerial photographic transcription (1984, fig 29 – reproduced here as Fig 72) for this area maintains that both linear ditches (ditch 2061 and the Devil's Ditch) cut through pre-existing fields and break up 'the unity of the system' (ibid, 112). However, it is far from clear if the relationship is quite so straightforward. There are locations where field corners may simply abut 2061, and other instances where fields appear to respect the ditch (Palmer 1984, fig 29 – SU 2143). Furthermore, the stratigraphy of ditch 2061 at LDP 095 (though outside the mapped area of the field system: Fig 72) contains evidence for a period of colluvial sedimentation, following the accumulation of the secondary silts (context 6). This sediment (context 5) is probably the parent material of the buried soil (contexts 4 and 3), and it began to accumulate from a depth of 50cm below the chalk surface at the centre of the ditch. By this stage, considerable erosion would have widened the ditch, so that, even allowing for the height of a bank, it would have been no more than a shallow hollow and easily cultivated over (cf LDP 098, Fig 48).

Thus, while some fields do appear to predate the ditch and were probably put out of use by it, there are also stratigraphic grounds for arguing that some fields must postdate it. No evidence is available to put a date on the inferred cultivation, but Iron Age and Romano-British pottery have been recovered locally and there are traces of a settlement situated nearby at SU 221437 (Palmer 1984).

The ditch profile at LDP 095 terminated in an unusually pronounced 'V'-shaped base, which sets it apart from the other boundary ditches in the Upper Study Area. On morphological grounds, this profile has more in common with the later recut forms discussed below. However, there was no conclusive evidence to suggest recutting, except for a ledge towards the base of the ditch, which might indicate that it was originally flat bottomed.

The excavation at LDP 090 was altogether more informative (Fig 14). The ditch stratigraphy showed clear signs of massive recutting that had removed almost all of the original silting (Fig 34). The recut passed through the chalk floor of the earlier ditch to form a basal slot. This feature was present in another section of ditch 1959 at LDP 052, but at this latter site no trace of the original stratigraphy survived.

Despite the indications of subsequent remodelling, the relationship of ditch 1959 to ditches 2061 and 1971 (the latter is demonstrably Late Bronze Age) supports the assertion that originally these were contemporary elements in a single territorial layout. The dating of the recut at LDP 090 is based on a single radiocarbon determination of c 395–50 cal BC (Table 22, OxA-3046). Interpreting this date range in the light of the pottery recovered by Thomas from a similarly shaped

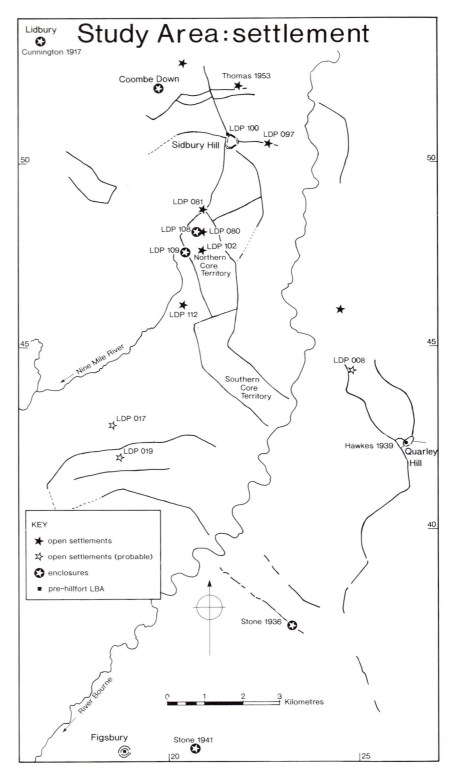

Fig 71   Map of the Study Area, showing the distribution of Middle and Late Bronze Age settlement sites in relation to the linear ditches system

ditch on Snail Down (N Thomas forthcoming; Chap 3), we can conclude that the stretch of the Devil's Ditch bordering the Southern and Northern Core Territories was remodelled during the Middle Iron Age.

There was no sign at either of these two sites of the double banks recorded by recent fieldwork (SPTAE Records, Trowbridge), although there are indications that these may once have existed. The superficial appearance of double banks accompanying the ditch near Dunch Hill is created by a scarp running parallel to the ditch on each side. These were formed by negative lynchets, which developed at the edges of 'Celtic' field plots, but which, in all probability, mark the position of former banks, which were gradually eroded as cultivation

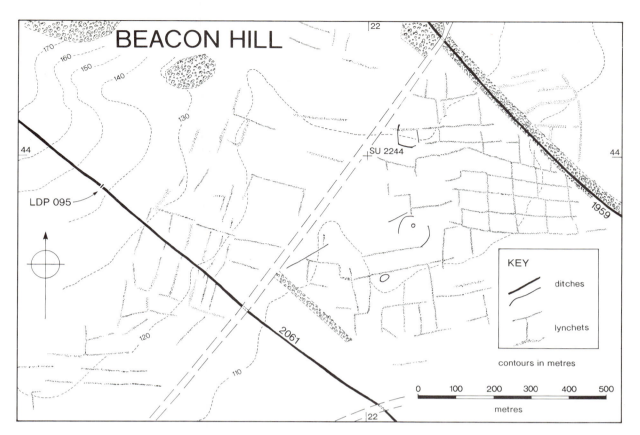

Fig 72   The area to the east of Beacon Hill, showing the distribution of 'Celtic' fields in relation to the principal linear ditches of the Southern Core Territory (redrawn from Palmer 1984, fig 29)

spread over them. At LDP 090, traces of a bank survived on the eastern side of the ditch, but there was no sign of a bank on the opposite side. This could have been missed, since the width of the excavated section barely extended beyond the erosion slope of the ditch on the western side. However, even if a bank had been present originally, it seems unlikely that it would have survived the cultivation that produced the deep positive lynchet over the top of the ditch.

The recutting of the Devil's Ditch, and perhaps also ditch 2061, raises further issues about the chronological relationship between the ditches and adjacent 'Celtic' fields. We have suggested already that ditch 2061 was superseded by some fields, but that other fields probably went out of use when the boundary was established. Similarly with the Devil's Ditch, the distribution of 'Celtic' fields shown by Palmer (1984, fig 29; Fig 72) hints at both possibilities, but whether the Devil's Ditch cuts, or is superseded by, the larger fields to the north of the distribution is a question that is difficult to answer from aerial photographs alone.

Between the Bourne Valley and Dunch Hill, the Devil's Ditch marks the Hampshire–Wiltshire county boundary, and for much of its course it runs through long-established, broad-leafed woodland. Although both of these factors have protected the Devil's Ditch from arable encroachment in recent times, there are long stretches where the earthwork is barely visible. This suggests that certain parts of the Devil's Ditch may have been slighted at an early date, before it was appropriated as a political boundary. Given the proximity of 'Celtic' fields and the evidence for Iron Age and Romano-British

activity nearby, it was probably during this time that the earthwork was substantially reduced by cultivation spreading over it.

Clearly, this was not the case throughout all its length: at LDP 052, the ditch seems to have remained a significant feature and may even have functioned as some form of boundary between 'Celtic' field blocks. Hereabouts, the ditch is abutted by a series of substantial lynchets and, although the banks have been destroyed and ploughwash accumulated in the ditch, there is no indication that cultivation actually spread over it. The relationship of these lynchets to the ditch suggests that the earthwork was deliberately incorporated into the field layout, unlike the arrangement at SU 2243, where the fields are set obliquely to the axis of the ditch. There was also evidence from LDP 052 to suggest that this stretch of the Devil's Ditch had been substantially remodelled. Although the evidence for recutting was inconclusive compared with LDP 090, at the very least it involved scouring out the primary silts in order to restore the boundary. The environmental evidence from the site reflects the intensity of nearby cultivation, yet in contrast to the ditches defining the Southern Core Territory, this part of the Devil's Ditch still remains a prominent earthwork.

There is no direct evidence for Middle or Late Bronze Age fields within the Southern Core Territory to match that available for the Northern Core Territory. However, adjacent to both boundary ditches there are fragmentary fields that appear to respect the earthworks and perhaps are contemporary with them. One such example is the distinctive grouping in the vicinity of surface collection site LDP 013 (Fig 14), where a cohesive block of small fields seems (in contrast to the larger fields adjoining it) to be constrained by the Devil's Ditch. In the absence of any corroborative dating evidence, we can do little more than recognise the possibility that some of these fields represent the vestiges of Middle to Late Bronze Age cultivation, and that they may be contemporary with the more reliably dated examples in the Northern Core Territory (Fig 10).

The impression gained from excavation and surface observations is that the majority of 'Celtic' fields in their final form date from the Romano-British period, and that, while there are undoubtedly traces of earlier fields to be discovered, these are likely to represent a minor part of the observable pattern. This conclusion is in agreement with the wider picture that is beginning to emerge of an extensive arable exploitation of the chalk uplands during the Roman period. The results of field-work on the Berkshire Downs emphasise the scale of arable uptake, especially during the first to mid third centuries AD (Ford *et al* 1988). Regarding the relationship between linear ditches and field systems, other research in the same area echoes the findings of the Linear Ditches Project (Ford 1982a) – while there is evidence for prehistoric fields, shown by the way in which linear earthworks respect pre-existing boundaries, the overwhelming majority of fields belong to a much later stage of landscape development.

The Northern Core Territory

The boundary ditches of this territory were sectioned at three locations. Ditch 1971 was excavated at LDP 092 and 098 (Chap 3, pp 53 and 55), and the common boundary ditch 1959 (the Devil's Ditch) at LDP 052 (Chap 3, p 53). This latter section has already been discussed in relation to the Southern Core Territory.

Ditch 1971 runs from the north-west corner of the Southern Core Territory, across Milston Down to Brigmerston Plantation, where it turns north-eastwards to join ditch 1959 in Dunch Hill Plantation (Fig 8). Like its counterpart bounding the Southern Core Territory, ditch 1971 is double banked. Early editions of the Ordnance Survey 1:2500 sheet show that both banks were once visible along the stretch excavated at LDP 098, but these can no longer be traced on the ground. We have mentioned already the likelihood that the Devil's Ditch (SPTA 1959) was once double banked throughout its length and that this applies similarly to ditches 1957, 1982, and 1983 (SPTAE records), which form an adjacent territory to the north-east (Fig 10). One of the ditches bounding the territory on Earl's Down Farm (SMR 745) also shows traces of double banking, where it has been protected by woodland on Beacon Hill and in the Bourne Valley at Rollerhouse Belt (Fig 10). Further afield, the ditch excavated by Stone on Easton Down (1935; Fig 8) had double banks; moreover, it crosses a similar topographic range to those east of the Bourne Valley, running from the high ground towards the floodplain. Considering these together, we can begin to recognise a consistent pattern, expressed both in the topographic alignment of the Late Bronze Age territories and in the morphology of the boundary earthworks.

Along most of its course, the ditch and both banks of 1971 are clearly visible, but they are particularly well preserved on Milston Down, despite being cut by several trackways and having been damaged in the past by military trenches. One such disturbance was fortuitously located between surface collection site LDP 102 and a well-preserved enclosure (LDP 109; Fig 21). This enabled a section of the ditch and both banks to be excavated adjacent to a dense artefact distribution and at a point where the lynchets of a field system encroached on the eastern bank. In addition to fulfilling archaeological criteria, the location of LDP 092 close to the margin of the Nine Mile River (Fig 14) provided an opportunity to recover a molluscan sequence that could be related to the palaeoecology of the river basin. The analytical results are discussed in detail in Chapter 6, but in summary they demonstrate that the periphery of the river valley was substantially cleared of woodland by the Late Bronze Age.

Buried soils were preserved beneath both banks at LDP 092 (Fig 47), and the contrasting pedological character of these has produced some of the strongest evidence for variations in pre-ditch landuse. Beneath the western bank, the soil profile was typical of a lithomorphic Rendzina, comprising an upper Ah horizon with an underlying stone accumulation over the A/C horizon. By comparison, the eastern buried soil was poorly sorted and had the appearance of having been in cultivation prior to burial.

The lack of any discernible structure in the eastern buried soil profile implies that insufficient time had elapsed between tillage and burial for any visible soil stratification to develop. Estimates given by Atkinson for the formation of stone-free A horizons suggest a rate of 5cm in ten years for the burial of stones (1957). Even allowing for variations in the rate of formation, and post-burial changes in the soil profile (Evans 1972), this would indicate that less than a decade may have passed between cultivation and the construction of the eastern bank. Palmer's aerial photographic transcription shows lynchets on both sides of ditch 1971 in the vicinity of LDP 092. Those on the western side reach towards the enclosure LDP 109 and are depicted as being very much slighter features (Palmer 1984; see also Bowen 1975). The SPTA 1:25000 archaeological overlay omits the western lynchets, which are not visible on the ground. If we accept Palmer's evidence, these lynchets must represent a very much earlier phase of cultivation than the ploughsoil preserved beneath the eastern bank of ditch 1971. Indeed, it is possible that these lynchets, if they are real, relate to Middle Bronze Age cultivation, and we are reminded of the instances where enclosures of the period were set within fields.

On the weathering slope at each side of the ditch, two single postholes were discovered (Fig 47). These were not visible at the surface of the corresponding buried soils, nor was there any indication that the posts had been inserted through the bank. However, since both buried soils and banks had been subjected to erosion on the margins of the ditch, there was some doubt about the exact phasing of these features. We were also aware that these two isolated postholes might be part of an alignment, such as that accompanying the ditch excavated by Stone at Winterbourne Dauntsey (1934). In the face of this uncertainty, a 2 × 1m extension was excavated along the axis of the western bank, where the higher elevation suggested that the stratigraphy might be better preserved.

Despite careful excavation, the extension failed to locate further postholes, and so the question of phasing remains in doubt. Bearing in mind that the postholes uncovered by Stone were set at intervals of 5ft (1.5m), we must acknowledge the possibility that those at LDP 092 formed part of a similarly widely spaced alignment, and evaded detection. Yet, even if we allow for the somewhat disturbed stratigraphy surrounding the two excavated examples, it seems unlikely that substantial posts could have been set into sockets penetrating through the banks into the chalk subsoil without leaving some trace in the bank section.

Viewed overall, the balance of the evidence seems to weigh in favour of the postholes belonging to a pre-ditch structure, perhaps connected with the nearby enclosure (LDP 109). Debris from the occupation around this site extended beneath the western bank of site LDP 092. This included carbonised cereal remains, recovered from the samples taken from the western buried soil for molluscan analysis (Chap 6, p 119), and an unusual quantity of burnt and struck flint in the buried soil and the ditch silts.

LDP 109 has produced a collection of pottery from animal disturbances in the ditch and the interior of the enclosure (recovered by members of the SPTA Conservation Group). Though small (59 sherds), the assemblage is composed principally of Late Bronze Age Plain Ware and Deverel-Rimbury pottery; Early Bronze Age fabrics are a very minor component indeed, while Iron Age fabrics are entirely absent (Chap 3, Table 2). In size and shape, the earthwork resembles some of the enclosures with Deverel-Rimbury associations on the Marlborough Downs (Piggott 1942) and on the South Downs (Piggott 1950), and we know that the excavation of two nearby round barrows produced secondary urned cremations (Milston 2 and Milston 23, Grinsell 1957, 183). Those from the latter barrow (Hawley 1910; Fig 21), which is less than 300m from LDP 109, are almost certainly Middle to Late Bronze Age in date. Among the Marlborough Downs enclosures, it is the group on Ogbourne Down that provides the nearest parallels for LDP 109. These are not closely associated with pre-existing fields, which in the case of the enclosures on Preshute and Ogbourne Maizey Down appear to have determined their rectangular shape (see Grinsell 1958, fig 15). It would of course be unwise to push this evidence too far, but it does seem to be a plausible basis for arguing that the enclosure was built during the Middle Bronze Age. Its subsequent history is uncertain, but it may have continued in use into the first millennium BC. However, since unenclosed sites seem to typify the settlements of the Late Bronze Age in this area, the Plain Ware pottery from LDP 109 probably relates to an open settlement, which replaced the enclosure.

The evidence from LDP 092 and the adjacent enclosure (LDP 109) reveals an intriguing situation in which the linear ditch cuts through an existing settlement, isolating it from nearby fields. Unfortunately, it is difficult to move beyond this observation to elucidate the specific relationship between the occupation of the settlement, the use of the fields, and the effect of the boundary ditch. Although the pottery evidence suggests that the Late Bronze Age occupation around LDP 109 was contemporaneous in part with that at LDP 102, within the Northern Core Territory, our chronology is not sufficiently sensitive to determine if both were occupied at the time that the ditch was constructed. One possibility, but again almost impossible to substantiate, is that LDP 109 and LDP 102 were part of a continuous spread of occupation across Brigmerston Down produced by settlement drift through time. Treating them separately might be a perspective conditioned by the limited extent of surface collection; in reality, we could be confronting the archaeological record of different parts of the same settlement, which were not necessarily functioning at precisely the same time.

However, in the case of the Milston Down site (LDP 112; Fig 20), we have no reason to suppose that it was anything other than a quite separate settlement lying outside the Northern Core Territory. The pottery assemblage supports this idea and conveys the impression that the settlement was contemporary with those on Brigmerston Down and at Dunch Hill. Although subtle differences can be recognised in the range of fabrics and technical practices, these appear to be connected with the traditions and identities of distinct communities, rather than being a reflection of chronological differences.

On the basis of this evidence, we can argue that ditch 1971, and by implication the other boundaries of the Northern Core Territory, were laid out in a landscape with an established pattern of settlement stretching back at least to the Middle Bronze Age. In the vicinity of LDP 092, the boundary clearly separated a settlement from an adjacent field system, skirting the edge of one field which had been in recent cultivation. This is one of the clearest illustrations of the relationship between the linear ditch layout and Late Bronze Age settlement. It demonstrates that the system of formal territorial boundaries was imposed on an existing pattern, and that this process of delineation appears to have involved the exclusion of some settlements.

Further to the north, a second section of ditch 1971 was excavated at site LDP 098 (Fig 21). This site was located within a field system, and the precise location was chosen to examine the intersection of the ditch and a well-preserved lynchet which appeared to overlie it (Fig 48). Excavation confirmed the superficial impression, showing that the upper stratigraphy of the ditch (context 3) was formed from a flinty ploughsoil derived from the adjacent field. A mixed pottery assemblage was recovered from this deposit, comprising sherds of Deverel-Rimbury, Late Bronze Age, and Iron Age wares. All of this material is residual, but, in view of the recurrence of small quantities of Iron Age pottery associated with colluvial ditch silts at other sites (eg LDP 083 and Raymond forthcoming, Snail Down site IV), we are inclined to accept this as dating evidence for the inception of the field system.

The lower stratigraphy at this site was rather unusual. Apart from a slight accumulation of loose chalk rubble on the floor of the ditch, the overlying stratigraphy, to the base of the lynchet (context 8), was characterised by interleaving tips of exceptionally humic sediment (contexts

11 and 12). These were sealed by context 10, which appeared to be a weakly developed and somewhat disrupted palaeosol.

The disposition of contexts 11 and 12 and their texture and colour (10YR 5/4) suggest deliberate backfilling involving material from the banks and surrounding soil. Given the proximity of the field system, the immediate explanation which comes to mind is that the ditch was levelled to facilitate ploughing. However, there are difficulties with this idea. First, the ditch was only partly filled, leaving a considerable hollow which would have remained an obstacle to cultivation. Second, contexts 11 and 12 were overlain by a buried soil, which implies that a long period of stability followed backfilling. The first trace of cultivation came later, with context 8. This was a colluvial sediment filling the top of the ditch, and it in turn gave way to the main lynchet deposit which spreads across the site. Since there was no trace of secondary silts over the rapidly formed primary chalk rubble, the backfilling must have taken place at a relatively early stage in the history of the ditch.

Just beyond this stretch of ditch 1971 lay one of the principal areas of Late Bronze Age settlement outside the Core Territories. The extent of the site was established by fieldwalking (LDP 081) and by the recovery of pottery, burnt flint, and bone from recent tree casts on the edge of Dunch Hill Plantation (LDP 103). The distribution of this material (Fig 46) demonstrated that the settlement had occupied a narrow strip of land on the south-west facing slope of the hill, overlooking the seasonally flooded coombe known as Bourne Bottom (Fig 16). Sites LDP 081 and 103 are less than a kilometre from LDP 080, the most northerly settlement in the Northern Core Territory. Between the two there is a clear fall-off in the concentration of pottery, and it is through this area that ditch 1971 passes. The low frequency of pottery in the vicinity of the excavated section at LDP 098 is probably an indication of earlier settlement drift, but, by the time the ditched boundary was established, these sites were quite separate and at some distance from the boundary.

We have intimated that the spread of settlement debris from the Dunch Hill site and LDP 080 respects the boundary ditch separating the two sites. There is another aspect to the boundary zone which bears directly on the perception of territory edges by communities in adjacent settlements. In 1980, an unaccompanied crouched inhumation was recovered under rescue conditions from a position 30m to the south of ditch 1971 (SPTA 1908). The burial is undated, but, given the density of Late Bronze Age occupation, there is a strong chance that it was broadly of the same period. Just to the north of the ditch, one of the tree hollows (LDP 103) produced a fragment of human jaw bone, which may have been from a burial, but no signs of a grave cut could be recognised in the disturbed ground. Although these remains might predate the construction of the boundary ditch, this does not rule out the possibility that burials were being purposefully sited at the edges of territories. As we shall see, human and animal remains were deposited in boundary ditches at a later stage, and it may well be the case that the tenuous evidence from Dunch Hill is an early echo of this tradition.

Dunch Hill and the Nine Mile River

Some insight into the relationship between settlements was gained from the excavations at LDP 081A (Figs 14 and 46). This site was located within a small ploughed field, which was crossed by a prominent hollow passing between a series of lynchets (Fig 73). A resistivity traverse across the linear feature at several points was rather inconclusive, but seemed to indicate a shallow ditch. This appeared anomalous at the time in view of the substantial hollow showing on the surface, but it was thought that this might be the result of a trackway superimposed on the line of the ditch.

Subsequent fieldwalking revealed a distribution of Late Bronze Age Plain Ware sherds which was concentrated towards the south-western edge of the field (LDP 081). An examination of tracked-vehicle damage in the grassland adjacent to the field showed that the pottery concentration continued for a short distance beyond the western field edge, but was more widespread to the south-east. At a later stage, the south-eastern extent of the settlement was defined more precisely by sherds recovered from recent tree hollows in Dunch Hill Plantation (LDP 103).

The excavation confirmed the presence of a ditch and a hollow-way, but instead of the latter being superimposed on the ditch it actually paralleled it (Fig 45). Overlying the silted up ditch, and filling the hollow-way, there was a truncated midden that was the source of much of the pottery concentrated in this part of the field. The midden (context 3) produced a considerable amount of Late Bronze Age Plain Ware, bone, and a rather smaller quantity of struck flint. A short distance away, a similar feature was discovered (LDP 087). This was a shallow hollow exposed in the side of a rainwater gully on the edge of a trackway. It was filled with a large quantity of burnt flint, some sherds of Late Bronze Age Plain Ware, and a few fragments of bone. It is possible that this deposit represents another accumulation in the same hollow-way sectioned at LDP 081A. The aerial photographic transcription shows that this turned southeastwards on the edge of the fieldwalked area (LDP 081), taking up an alignment, which approximates with the direction of LDP 087. From the surface, it was impossible to confirm this, for the area is crossed by a large field system, and one of the lynchets actually lies along the conjectured alignment. Between the two sites, there are two or three small subcircular terraces, which might be house platforms, but again these features are poorly defined because of the superimposed lynchets.

The date of the field system is difficult to establish with certainty. On the ground, it is possible to trace individual lynchets through Dunch Hill Plantation, where they join elements of the layout spreading across North Tidworth Golf Course. Other lynchets are clearly part of the field system superimposed on ditch 1971, which is itself part of the Dunch Hill Plantation and Golf Course layout. In its developed form, this extensive field system probably belongs to the Romano-British period, though the possibility of an Iron Age origin has been considered already with regard to site LDP 098.

Fig 73   A view eastwards across LDP 081, showing the hollow-way and, in the centre foreground, a dark patch marking the position of the Late Bronze Age midden, LDP 081A

The excavation at LDP 081A produced evidence relating to the development of the field system during the Bronze Age. The shallow ditch (cut 7) is stratigraphically earlier than the midden, and so is the hollow-way running parallel to it (cut 2). Both follow a major axis of the field system and were probably near contemporary elements connected with the organisation and use of the fields. Indeed, ditched boundaries and trackways are a common feature of Lowland Zone field systems, and they are known to delineate both field blocks and individual plots (Fowler 1983). Other sites in the Upper Study Area have revealed a range of boundary features, including trackways and postholes (LDP 084, Fig 40), a ditch and trackway (LDP 056, Fig 74), a ditch at SU 21715102 (LDP 110), and postholes at LDP 082 (Fig 75). A residual sherd of Deverel-Rimbury pottery recovered from the primary silts of the ditch at LDP 081A is the only evidence for Middle Bronze Age activity in the vicinity. However, the worked flint from surface collection contains an earlier component that was not present in the flint from the midden (Chap 5). Certain elements in the pottery assemblage also suggest a chronological distinction, and it seems that the midden, at least in part, was a late accumulation (Chap 4). This is confirmed by the radiocarbon assay, which produced a date range of *c* 770–395 cal BC (Table 22, OxA-3048). For reasons discussed in the introduction to this chapter, a date in the earlier part of this range would be the most accept-

able. Although the evidence for the Middle Bronze Age is tenuous, it does suggest that the Dunch Hill settlement, like others in the Upper Study Area, may have originated before the first millennium BC (Chap 4), but there is insufficient evidence to develop this further.

The dating of the field system from this evidence relies on the phasing of the midden with respect to the hollow-way and field ditch. Both of these clearly predate the domestic activity implied by the accumulation of debris in the midden. Since this slighted the ditch and hollow-way, these must have been part of a previously established field system that was no longer functioning in its original form. What fields were still in use, and how the system as a whole had changed, are questions that cannot be answered using the existing evidence. We know from the surface evidence that the settlement was unenclosed and fairly extensive, and we may reasonably surmise that it depended for its survival upon a considerable tract of arable land. Similar unenclosed sites associated with extensive field systems are not uncommon in the chalklands of southern England (Barrett *et al* 1991, chap 5). The Dunch Hill settlement is less well preserved than some of the better known sites, and it is more difficult to identify the extent of contemporary cultivation. This is a consequence of the subsequent expansion in the scale and intensity of arable cultivation. As we have mentioned already, this probably began during the Iron Age, but its maximum extent was at-

Fig 74 Section at site LDP 056, showing two parallel trackways separated by a field ditch, running along the edge of a lynchet which is just visible in section at the far end of the trench (the scale is 1m)

tained sometime during the Romano-British period.

Unenclosed sites typify the settlement pattern of the Late Bronze Age in the Upper Study Area. Yet, as far as we are able to determine from the limited evidence, this stands in contrast to the Middle Bronze Age, when small earthwork enclosures appear to have been a characteristic, though perhaps minor, feature of settlement. In the vicinity of the Dunch Hill and Brigmerston Down Late Bronze Age settlements, the two enclosures (LDP 108 and LDP 109) are both associated with Deverel-Rimbury pottery, and at the latter site this makes up 46% of the total assemblage. Within the surface collection site LDP 102, soil marks suggest the former presence of two other enclosed sites (Figs 21 and 76). Although neither of these enclosures is visible on the ground, they are adjacent to a concentration of pottery that includes sherds of Deverel-Rimbury pottery (Chap 3, Table 2). If this is evidence of a real change in the character of settlement, how do we explain it? The trend towards open settlement was under way before the establishment of formalised territorial boundaries, therefore we cannot postulate a direct causal link between the two. However, we may be witnessing a change in demography that involved a degree of settlement nucleation in a substantially cleared and recognisably domesticated landscape (Chap 6). The differences in the character and density of settlement between the Middle and Late Bronze Age

may be inextricably bound up with changing attitudes towards the landscape, as this came increasingly under the control of individual communities. The creation of formal boundaries at a later stage may be an overt expression of society's traditional, yet evolving relationship with the land, but, as we will see, this was not articulated by all Late Bronze Age communities in the same way.

Before we look at settlement and the bounded landscape, some thought needs to be given to aspects of Middle and Late Bronze Age occupation that exist on the margins of the settled area. Some of the more intriguing evidence for the period comes from the spring line of the Nine Mile River, between Milston Down and Brigmerston Down. This is a part of the Upper Study Area that received little attention because of restricted access – it lies within the danger area of the Bulford rifle ranges. However, despite the limitations, some fieldwork was undertaken on the floodplain and adjacent river terraces.

There is a singular absence of Middle and Late Bronze Age pottery in the valley. Although there are small arable fields and extensive tracked-vehicle disturbances, only a few sherds were recovered from the area between Milston and Brigmerston Downs, but none of these came from the river basin. This is rather surprising in view of the amount of pottery recovered by surface collection from the Milston and Brigmerston sites, and the frequent discovery of sherds in track edges and animal disturbances above the eastern margin of the river. The lack of extensive systematic collection in the area must cast some doubt on the validity of this conclusion, but it is based on repeated observations throughout the period of fieldwork.

In contrast to the paucity of pottery, there are extraordinarily dense concentrations of burnt flint, both along the floodplain and on the lower terrace. Close to the ponds where the Nine Mile River now rises, there are several concentrations of burnt river gravel, and one of these is associated with an irregular 'D'-shaped enclosure, itself formed from burnt flint and soil charged with charcoal (SU 19904761). The enclosure is difficult to define exactly because it lies in dense woodland, but superficially it has the appearance of being formed from dumps of burnt flint. There is little doubt that this, and the dispersed material round about, is a 'burnt mound' of the type characteristically located in riverine settings. These have a widespread distribution in Britain and Ireland, and they are mostly dated between the end of the second millennium and the middle of the first millennium BC – although some of the Welsh examples are significantly earlier (Williams 1990). More relevant to the local situation is the 'burnt mound' by the edge of the River Avon near Amesbury, which was dated to before *c* 1520–1052 cal BC (OxA-1399) by bone from an intrusive burial (Entwistle in prep).

It is important to make a distinction between concentrations of burnt flint associated with settlement and the phenomenon of 'burnt mounds' (Buckley 1990). The former are usually smaller (perhaps LDP 087 falls into this category) and sometimes associated with pits filled with burnt flint which are interpreted as cooking holes. The small pit (LDP 110) discovered during the upgrading of a military trackway at SU 18605059 may fall into this category: it was roughly circular, about 1×0.75m in

Fig 75   Section through a lynchet at LDP 082, showing the postholes of a fence line (scale in centimetres)

plan, and between 0.15 and 0.2m deep, containing approximately 19kg of burnt flint. By contrast, 'burnt mounds' are invariably associated with rivers, seldom produce artefacts, and are often located on marginal land at the periphery of the main settlement pattern (Williams 1990).

We have established the evident isolation of the 'burnt mound' by the Nine Mile River, at least in terms of the settlement pattern. Yet, there is confirmation of other activities in the river valley, although these too seem to be rather distinctive in terms of the archaeological record for this part of the Upper Study Area. The only two examples of Late Bronze Age metalworking in the area both come from the Nine Mile River – a syenite mould for socketed axes (SMR no SU 24NWU03) with a doubtful provenance of SU 180460 and a hoard of axes from SU 192493 (SMR no SU 14NE152).

Despite the suitability of large river pebbles for knapping, the concentrations of burnt flint around the spring line of the Nine Mile River contained very few worked pieces. However, slightly further north in Bourne Bottom, which is part of the river drainage, one of the major procurement sites was discovered (LDP 104; see Chap 5 and Fig 16). This lies quite close to the settlement on Dunch Hill, but it is clearly outside the settled area. Some connection between the settlement and the procurement site is implied by the flint study, and by the appearance on the Dunch Hill site of waterworn sarsen pebbles with traces of polishing. The analysis of the flint from LDP 104 and from a number of the settlements has revealed an interesting spatial pattern, which reinforces

the distinction between the settled area and the region beyond it (Chap 5).

The contrast between the various activities focused on the Nine Mile River and those recognised in areas of settlement may reflect real differences in the perception of the landscape, which became more emphatic with the setting out of formal boundaries. Undoubtedly, the use of the river valley had a long history of mutual exploitation. It is after all the most accessible local source of water, and it seems inconceivable that the formal bounding of territories denied some settlements access to water and other riverine resources. Perhaps a rather more subtle distinction was emerging, in which some communities were defining the extent of their domesticated resources in contradistinction to those that were perceived as being natural. In this connection, we have avoided the term 'wildscape', because in a sense both elements in this opposition are culturally determined, and it seems improbable that any part of the landscape was truly primordial. This opposition was not made explicit in the same manner by all Late Bronze Age communities. Those occupying the settlements on Milston Down and Dunch Hill apparently lacked a formal concept of territory and may well have maintained a sense of place that was physically defined by natural features and the earlier works of man, such as the numerous round barrows. It seems that at this very local level we can recognise varying attitudes towards landscape and the human environment, in which the exploitation of domesticated resources was viewed rather differently than the exploitation of non-domestic resources.

Sidbury Hill and the surrounding area

The pottery assemblages from LDP 080 and LDP 081A (excavated site within LDP 081) are dominated by Late Bronze Age Plain Ware. However, they are distinguished from LDP 102 and LDP 092 by the presence of Early All Cannings Cross pottery, indicating that their occupation continued through to the eighth century BC. The only other site associated with the Northern Core Territory where this pottery appeared is LDP 112 (Table 2), on Milston Down, which lies outside the area defined by the boundary ditches. Early All Cannings Cross pottery is a minor component in the assemblages from these sites and, for several reasons discussed in Chapter 4, its appearance on some sites, but not on others, may be a less than reliable guide to its original distribution. However, it does appear to represent a real distinction between the pottery styles employed contemporaneously at different settlements, and hence it gives us some insight into the later evolution of the Northern Core Territory. This appears to have been a time of transition for some settlements. A new ceramic style was beginning to emerge from the local technological tradition of Late Bronze Age Plain Ware, and this may be a reflection of an early stage in the decline of parochial cohesion implied by the territorial boundaries.

The introduction of Early All Cannings Cross pottery styles at LDP 081A, 080, and 112 points to an affinity between these sites, and indeed this is prefigured in the earlier relationship of two of these sites to the Northern Core Territory. Both the Dunch Hill and Milston Down sites lay outside the bounded area, apparently from its inception, and we can recognise similarities within the distribution of Plain Ware fabrics that distinguish these sites from neighbouring settlements inside the territory. There is a strong impression that the sites on Milston Down and Dunch Hill shared mutual pottery characteristics, which were not related to their proximity, for they lie at opposite ends of the settled area, but seem rather to reflect their common exclusion from the Northern Core Territory.

The appearance of an Early All Cannings Cross component in the assemblages from these two sites represents a continuation of differences reflected in their exclusion from the Northern Core Territory. However, during this later period the settlement at LDP 080 was also distinguished by the presence of Early All Cannings Cross pottery, even though it was one of the settlements within the bounded landscape. To explain this paradox, we need to refer to the interpretation of the ditch sequence at LDP 098. It was argued that ditch 1971 had been backfilled at an early stage in the silting sequence, and that this was not a preparation for subsequent cultivation. In the light of what has been said about the introduction of Early All Cannings Cross pottery styles at LDP 112 and 081A, we propose that the backfilling of ditch 1971 (where it runs between the two sites) occurred during the time when this new ceramic style was being adopted, and that it was undertaken in order to nullify the boundary. Although this may have been only a token backfilling, its symbolic intent would have been clear enough. By negating the significance of the

boundary, local communities were asserting that it no longer marked them out as separate groups, occupying and using by tradition different parts of the landscape. At another level, it may represent a progression away from a sense of unity focused inwards on individual settlements, towards the closer integration of a much larger group drawing on a new ceramic style zone; certainly, this was a trend that appears to be defined more clearly by the time that evolved All Cannings Cross assemblages were in use.

Whether this signalled a breakdown of the original territorial arrangements embodied in the linear ditches system, or whether we are witnessing an expansion of separate units to accommodate wider spheres of interaction, is a question we are unable to answer conclusively. Perhaps the question is too crudely framed, though this is a condition imposed almost inevitably by the limitations of our chronology. It is possible, however, to make certain general observations about the settlements in the Dunch Hill and Brigmerston Down area towards the end of the Bronze Age. Despite the appearance of Early All Cannings Cross styles on some of the sites, the fabrics and stylistic criteria give the impression that the new pottery was being introduced rather tentatively into a pre-existing technological framework. All of the vessels with All Cannings Cross attributes were being constructed from traditional fabrics, but, with the possible exception of a single sherd from Dunch Hill, there are no signs that these developments continued into the evolved All Cannings Cross tradition (see Chap 4). The distribution of this style in the Upper Study Area is markedly different from the distribution of Late Bronze Age Plain Ware. Between these two traditions there appears to have been a shift in the focus of settlement towards Sidbury Hill, the north-west, and in particular the margins of the Avon Valley. But, before we discuss these later developments, we need to trace the origins of the territorial arrangements in the Sidbury area and highlight certain parallels with the Northern Core Territory.

As we move northwards to examine the evidence from the Sidbury Area, there are frequent, but tantalisingly elusive signs that the ditch system had evolved through a rather complex sequence of recutting. A physical link between the Northern Core Territory and Sidbury Hill is made by ditch 1957, which can be traced almost as far as the termination of the Sidbury Double Linear (SPTA 2232, site LDP 101). This forms the western boundary of the territory defined to the east by ditch 1983. Since neither of these ditches were sectioned, we are unable to assign them to a specific phase in the evolution of the territories south of Sidbury Hill. However, the excavation at LDP 101 (the western ditch of the double linear) revealed the truncated remains of an early ditch on the line of 1957 (cut 30). A similar cut appears in section 11 of Thomas's site VII on Snail Down, although at this location it is present in the eastern ditch (Thomas forthcoming; Fig 32). This anomaly will be discussed later, but for the moment let us consider the possibility of an early ditch running from Snail Down, across Sidbury Hill, to join up with the Northern Core Territory. This link appears to be part of a penultimate development in the Late Bronze Age territorial arrangement, and it accentuates the significance of Sidbury Hill which, like

Quarley Hill, carries a major intersection of linear ditches. However, it may have been preceded by another ditch which appeared in section at LDP 101. This would imply that ditch 1957 is a refurbished boundary, rather than a new development associated with the expansion of the Northern Core Territory. If such was the case, these changes to the existing arrangements might have involved the amalgamation of two established territories, and not merely an expansion of the Northern Core Territory. In terms of our overall understanding of the Late Bronze Age settlement in the area, this is a far more satisfactory explanation, for it provides a direct sequential link between the Core Territories to the south of Sidbury Hill and the rather more complicated developments to the north.

The precise relationship of the ditches converging on Sidbury Hill could not be established with certainty, since their meeting point, if such was the case, has been obliterated by the earthworks of the hillfort. The Sidbury West Linear Ditch (SPTA 2242) was excavated at several points, but no dating evidence could be found. It was established that the ditch was partly recut to form a pit alignment, which extended its course westward across Haxton Down. The radiocarbon date of c 760–190 cal BC (OxA-3042) for the pit excavated at LDP 099 provides a *terminus ante quem* for the ditch, but there is no indication of how much time elapsed before the pit alignment replaced it. The Sidbury West Linear Ditch is much slighter than those others making up the Late Bronze Age boundary system, and, in all probability, it is a late element unconnected with the original layout. In connection with this suggestion, it is worth mentioning that Hawkes commented on a similarly slight ditch at Quarley (1939, Ditch 2), which he suggested was a subsidiary feature added later in the sequence. Apart from the few sherds of Plain Ware from the base of the lynchet at LDP 082 (Fig 14), there was no evidence for settlement in the area between Sidbury Hill and Haxton Down, which contrasts sharply with the density of material from around the Northern Core Territory. This reinforces the impression that the land along the Nine Mile River, including Bourne Bottom and Haxton Down (Fig 10), lay outside the main area of occupation during the Late Bronze Age.

Between Sidbury Hill and the Bourne Valley, ditch SPTA 2244 forms the upper boundary of a territory defined by the river to the east and possibly by the Devil's Ditch to the south. This encompasses a much larger area than has been proposed for the other Late Bronze Age territories, and in reality the southern boundary may lie somewhere beneath the built-up area of North Tidworth. The Sidbury East Linear Ditch (SPTA 2244) was excavated at two locations. The ditch in its original form was revealed at LDP 097, which produced a small Plain Ware assemblage scattered throughout the ditch fill. There was a residual element in the primary silts and the upper tertiary silts, but the otherwise uniformly Late Bronze Age assemblage seems a reasonable basis for dating this ditch. As in the case of SPTA 1971 at Dunch Hill, these sherds were probably derived from a nearby settlement, but in this instance we have only the vaguest notion of its extent and density (see Chap 3).

The second excavation on SPTA 2244 (LDP 096) was on the flank of Sidbury Hill, less than 200m from the hillfort. At this location, the ditch had been recut to form a stepped 'V'-shaped profile. Although no dating evidence was recovered from this site, the recutting must predate the hillfort, which is superimposed over the ditch.

A parallel sequence was recorded at LDP 101 (cut 2A), where the original ditch also had been recut. The selective treatment of these ditches towards the summit of the hill may be connected in some way with the pre-hillfort occupation, attested by a single sherd of Plain Ware recovered from LDP 100. Some concern for enhancing the visibility of these earthworks is implicit in the 'false cresting' that characterises their aspect on hilltops and ridges. It might also have been the motivation for recutting. For in order to maintain the maximum visibility of the banks from a distance, additions of fresh chalk would have been necessary, and of course the most accessible source would have been the ditch itself.

The primary territorial layout to the north of Sidbury Hill is tentatively reconstructed from the excavations of the double linear ditch at LDP 100 and LDP 101 and from unpublished information on the Snail Down excavations made available by Nicholas Thomas. We have already mentioned that ditch SPTA 1957 continued along the western scarp of Sidbury Hill, eventually following the line subsequently taken by the double linear ditch. It was preceded by a shallow ditch surviving only as a small ledge (cut 30) in the side of cut 2A at LDP 101. A second early ditch that had been backfilled terminated just short of the southern trench section (cut 16). The projected alignment of this ditch would have taken it under the central bank of the earthwork and across the course of the eastern ditch of the double linear. On the surface, there was no trace of it emerging on the other side of the eastern ditch, nor was there any indication further down the hill of a ditch following this course. Neither one of the two earliest ditches was recorded in the excavation at the foot of Sidbury Hill (LDP 020), nor was there any indication of an earlier ditch at LDP 027.

The significance of the early cuts at LDP 101 would not have been appreciated had the additional evidence from Snail Down not been available. Thomas's excavation of the eastern ditch on the double earthwork showed an equivalent sequence, involving two early ditches of similar dimensions to those identified on Sidbury Hill (Fig 32; section VI, cuts 1 and 2). However, the precise phasing of the Snail Down ditches is as elusive here as it was at LDP 101, for once again the massive recutting obscured the earlier sequence. It is clear, however, that one of the early ditches had continued north beyond Snail Down on the same alignment subsequently followed by the double linear ditch. The second had turned eastwards towards the Bourne Valley, bounding Snail Down barrow cemetery on the northern side. Some time after the construction of the double earthwork, this second ditch was replaced by a much larger 'V'-shaped form with a basal slot (SPTA 2238).

The absence of arable fields around Sidbury Hill prevented the recovery of the local settlement pattern associated with the linear ditch system. The small amount of Plain Ware and Deverel-Rimbury pottery recovered during Thomas's excavations (ditch SPTA 2238), and a few sherds from the surface of a track at SU 220523 (SMR SU25SW152), are the only evidence for

Middle and Late Bronze Age occupation north of Sidbury Hill. Bearing in mind the peripheral location of the linear ditch with respect to the settlements on Dunch Hill and Brigmerston Plantation, the pottery from around Snail Down probably represents the edge of a settlement to the north of SPTA 2238. Although the pattern is perceived less clearly here and in the vicinity of the Sidbury East Linear Ditch (SPTA 2244) than it is to the south, still we are confronted with the association between territorial boundaries and Late Bronze Age pottery. This is a recurrent feature and, although at individual sites the quality of the evidence is variable, such a repeated association must strengthen the chronology for the emergence of formal ditched territories.

Any interpretation of the early sequence between Sidbury Hill and Snail Down is bound to be highly speculative, and we cannot even confirm whether the original boundary was single or double ditched. But as far as later developments are concerned, we can be more confident. In the reconstruction of this boundary, it is possible to recognise a change in the perception of the previous territorial arrangements. Attention apparently shifted from the boundary in its entirety, to Sidbury Hill and the stretch of ditch to the north. This involved the building of an impressive double linear ditch with a central bank, terminating at a point of maximum visibility just below the crest of the hill. It was preceded by woodland clearance, which may have affected more than the limited area around the earthwork. Indeed, it is possible that a major clearance was undertaken in preparation not only for the double linear ditch, but also for a pre-hillfort setlement. This episode is dated between the eighth and sixth centuries BC by radiocarbon assay on charcoal from the primary ditch silts.

After the primary silts had accumulated, shallow features were cut into both terminals. In one of these (LDP 101, cut 20), a cattle skull was buried, which has produced a date of *c* 795–400 cal BC (Table 22, OxA-3044). At LDP 100, fragmentary human remains, including a skull, were deposited at the later date of *c* 365 cal BC–AD 60 (Table 22, OxA-3043). In the case of LDP 101, the burial must have occurred shortly after the construction of the double earthwork, and in all probability it was connected with some form of pre-hillfort occupation. That the significance of this part of the double earthwork was not lost in later times is implied by the date of the human remains buried at LDP 100, suggesting a continuing respect for the site during the hillfort phase. Although these deposits span many centuries, they clearly belong to a tradition of burial associated with a late stage in the development of the boundary system, and to support this we can cite similar deposits in secondary contexts at other sites, such as LDP 090 and 091, dated to *c* 395–50 cal BC and *c* 385 cal BC–AD 5 respectively (OxA-3046 and OxA-3047, Table 22).

We have no structural evidence for a pre-hillfort settlement, but the possibility is raised by a study of early hillfort developments in Hampshire (Cunliffe 1990). There is, however, pottery evidence for activity on Sidbury Hill prior to the hillfort. The single sherd of Late Bronze Age Plain Ware has been mentioned already, but, in addition to this, 11 sherds of haematite-coated pottery belonging to the All Cannings Cross tradition were recovered from several contexts at LDP 100. Although these cannot be assigned to an exact period, they are consistent with the date range for the construction of the double linear ditch, and they must have originated from an existing settlement on the hilltop. In the absence of excavations at Sidbury Hillfort on the scale of those conducted at Danebury (Cunliffe 1984b and c), the presence of an early enclosure can neither be confirmed or denied. Nonetheless, the reconstruction of the boundary earthwork, so as to emphasise the location subsequently occupied by the hillfort, must strengthen the possibility that one remains to be discovered.

Quarley Hill and the Bourne Valley

The so-called Quarley High Linear (Palmer 1984) was excavated just to the north of the Andover to Amesbury trunk road (A303) on Thruxton Hill (LDP 008A). No primary dating evidence was recovered from this section. The only sherds of pottery came from the upper stratigraphy and were principally Romano-British and Iron Age. An attempt was made to trace a connection between this ditch and SPTA 2247, but this proved fruitless, because of the dense areas of woodland interspersed with intensively cultivated farmland between Thruxton Hill and North Tidworth. Despite the failure to establish a physical connection between the two, the alignment taken by both ditches along the ridge of the Bourne Valley is a reasonable basis for arguing that they were in fact parts of the same boundary. The settlement pattern associated with this linear ditch is less clear than it is around Dunch Hill. However, recent fieldwork has identified an extensive Plain Ware site just to the east of this boundary (Fig 71).

A section of SPTA 2247 was excavated on Windmill Hill (LDP 091). Again no primary dating evidence was recovered, but the horse skull placed in the top of the secondary silts (Chap 3) produced a radiocarbon date of *c* 385 cal BC–AD 5 (Table 22, OxA-3047), relating to a subsequent use of the boundary. In addition to LDP 091, a number of other sites produced evidence for secondary activity involving the deposition of human and animal remains in shallow graves (for example, a human burial in the ditch at site LDP 100 and animal burials at sites LDP 090 and 101). These examples all belong to a later stage in the development of the linear ditches system, and they indicate that parts of the original layout were being incorporated into a new and apparently more expansive expression of territory. In the case of the deposits at sites LDP 090, 091, and 100, these relate to a period following the restructuring of the linear ditches system and would seem to be examples of the widely recognised practices on Iron Age sites, involving the burial of fragmentary human and animal remains (Wait 1985; Hill 1989). Current fieldwork has reinforced this pattern. The excavation of a number of enclosures in the Training Area has revealed human and animal remains placed in the ditches during the Early and Middle Iron Age.

There is no evidence for substantial recutting at LDP 091, but the deep 'V'-shaped profile at LDP 008A, and in Hawkes's section of the same ditch, might indicate a remodelling of the southern part of the boundary. Certainly, the profile contrasts with that of ditch 2 at Quarley, which is shallower with a broad, flat bottom and apparently of the same date (Hawkes 1939). Moreover, the silting pattern is different: ditch 1 has the unusually uniform silting characteristic of the Iron Age ditches on Snail Down and Weather Hill, whereas ditch 2 has a silting pattern typical of sequential weathering. We will return to this point later; here, it is sufficient to point out that these subtle distinctions are often the only evidence for subsequent remodelling of the Late Bronze Age ditch system.

Final developments

The subsequent history of the linear ditches system in the Upper Study Area is most clearly seen in the vicinity of Sidbury Hill, on Snail Down, and in the area to the north-west. Later activity on Dunch Hill and Brigmerston Down seems to be limited to the recutting of the Devil's Ditch and the development of more extensive field systems. There is no evidence that the settlements associated with the Northern Core Territory continued into the Iron Age, indeed these Late Bronze Age sites may well have been abandoned shortly after the appearance of Early All Cannings Cross pottery. Further to the south, the area around Earl's Farm Down and Butterfield Down became a major focus of Iron Age and Romano-British settlement, and at Boscombe Down West an extensive Iron Age open settlement (SU 188393–189397) was superseded by a hillfort at SU 190391 (Richardson 1951). Late Bronze Age Plain Ware was recovered from the fieldwalking on Earl's Farm Down (surface collection sites LDP 017, 018, and 019), demonstrating a consecutive, though not necessarily continuous, pattern of settlement.

A more complicated pattern is evident in the transition from the Late Bronze Age to Early Iron Age in the Military Training Area. We have mentioned already the desertion of the Dunch Hill and Brigmerston Down sites, but this is only part of the story. The Plain Ware and haematite-coated pottery from Sidbury Hill shows that it continued to be an important focal point from the Late Bronze Age onwards. But overall there appears to have been a geographical shift in the focus of settlement, such that a greater emphasis was placed on the Avon valley, rather than the Bourne Valley/Nine Mile River interfluve.

The Upavon area in particular seems to have been at the centre of this reorientation. Sizeable assemblages of Early All Cannings Cross pottery were recovered from Upavon Aerodrome (Grinsell 1957) and from the midden at East Chisenbury (D McOmish pers comm), and later styles from the old land surface beneath the bank at Chisenbury Trendle (Cunnington 1932). The pottery from Lidbury suggests some continuity from the Late Bronze Age through to the Early Iron Age, as exemplified by a fine, black-burnished bipartite bowl and All Cannings Cross-Meon Hill pottery from a pit in the interior of the enclosure (Cunnington and Cunnington 1917; Chap 4).

Returning once more to the Sidbury Hill area and following the building of the double linear earthwork, subsidiary ditches (SPTA 2234, 2236, 2238, and 2240)

were added to create two adjacent enclosures on either side of the monument (Fig 10). That to the east is Thomas's Enclosure A, and, though it is incomplete, the ditches encompass an area of approximately 36ha. To the west is his Enclosure B, which is rather smaller at approximately 21ha. Two of the ditches delineating these enclosures (SPTA 2234 and 2238, Fig 33) are of the symmetrical 'V'-shaped type. The first, excavated at LDP 083, produced the anomalously early radiocarbon date of c 1255–815 cal BC (OxA-3130; Table 22), while the second is dated by the Middle Iron Age pottery recovered from the base of the secondary silts (Raymond forthcoming). The reasons for discounting the radiocarbon date for SPTA 2234 were discussed in Chapter 3 (p 68), and on balance we are inclined to consider the pottery evidence from Thomas's section of ditch SPTA 2238 to be the more reliable guide to the date of the enclosures.

Some mention has been made in Chapters 3 and 6 of the rather unusual silting sequence recorded in both of these ditches and in the eastern ditch of the Sidbury Double Linear at LDP 027. The physical character of the silts and the molluscan data both suggest derivation from an intensely cultivated environment, and this is borne out by the numerous lynchets in the vicinity of the enclosures. However, there is an important detail that enables us to develop this interpretation. Thomas's excavations and the geophysical surveys undertaken as part of this present study have shown that all of the linear features running north-east and south-west across enclosure A are trackways. All of the confirmed lynchets in the area abut or stop short of the enclosure ditches, leaving the interior free from any trace of cultivation. This is repeated for Enclosure B, although here the full extent of the field system is more difficult to discern. Another example of the apparent exclusion of 'Celtic' fields from an enclosure was first noted by Crawford on Figheldean Down (1924; Fig 10), the area later studied by Appelbaum (1954). The enclosed area in this example is much larger than on Snail Down or Weather Hill (enclosures A and B, Fig 10), but the pattern is even more striking. With the exception of one isolated element, all of the lynchets abut the ditches from the exterior, and they do so in a manner that allows space for complete fields next to the boundary. Finally, there is the enclosure to the north-west of Quarley Hillfort defined by two linear ditches and a cross ditch. Hawkes (1939) commented on the exclusion of 'Celtic' fields from this area, and the more recent mapping of aerial photographic information has done nothing to negate his observations (Palmer 1984). It is significant that the ditches excavated by Hawkes in connection with Quarley Hillfort have profiles resembling those on Snail Down and Weather Hill. Moreover, the section of Hawkes's ditch 1 shows the same singular paucity of primary silting.

Taken together with the evidence of the ditch silts, the repeated exclusion of 'Celtic' fields from these enclosures suggests that areas were being reserved for pasture in a landscape that was intensively cultivated. The idea that linear ditches had a function in defining areas of pasture is hardly new (see Fowler 1983), but in reviving the suggestion we are drawing attention to a more selective use of linear ditches with a specific period in mind. It is selective in the sense that elements of the Late

Bronze Age boundary system were being appropriated as part of a large-scale reorganisation of the landscape. As regards the dating of these events, all of the available evidence points to the Early and Middle Iron Age. The process may have been under way before this time, but it is in the nature of the evidence that physical traces of the very earliest stages are effaced by later developments. We can, however, draw attention to an underlying trend during the course of the first millennium BC that might suggest mounting pressure on cultivated resources. This involved an increase in the scale of arable production, accompanied by an expansion onto a wider range of soils and a diversification in the type of crops being grown (Jones 1984).

It can be no mere coincidence that landscape reorganisation should be recognised at a time when the first hillforts appeared. The storage facilities at these sites are a well-documented characteristic, and it comes as no surprise to discover that, in the hinterland of a major hillfort, there are signs of intensive arable cultivation, as well as evidence for a closer management of livestock.

Detailed research into these aspects of later prehistoric settlement in the eastern Military Training Area was never part of our brief, and they have been studied only insofar as they throw light on the later evolution of the linear ditches system. This also applies to the Romano-British period. The Training Area abounds with evidence for settlement during this time, ranging from well-known village settlements, such as Chisenbury Warren (Cunnington 1930), to lesser known sites, such as Beach's Barn (Cunnington 1895) and Rainbow Bottom (Cunnington 1930). With regard to our principal subject, however, there is little, if any evidence to show that the linear ditches system continued to play a structural role in the organisation of the landscape. While many of the ditch excavations have produced Romano-British pottery, it was mostly associated with sediments derived from arable cultivation, which by that time was effectively destroying the structural components of the earlier landscape.

PART III   THE EVOLUTION OF THE LINEAR DITCHES SYSTEM IN THE UPPER STUDY AREA AND ITS WIDER IMPLICATIONS

In this concluding part, some of the issues raised by previous studies of linear ditches are reviewed in the light of this latest research. We are concerned with certain observations, such as topographic setting, the relationship of linear ditches to 'Celtic' fields, and the morphology of ditches, which have contributed to the idea of Late Bronze Age 'cattle ranches'. The reader has been shown that the linear ditches system evolved through different stages and that at different times its function varied. It is important that we now consider from a more theoretical perspective the implications of formal boundaries in the light of this functional variation. In particular, we must give some thought to the related concepts of domestication and intensification. In the evolution of the linear ditches system, it is the character and perception of the landscape that changes with regard to demography, settlement, and cultural interaction. This in turn is linked to subsistence productivity, land ownership, and the scale of domestic production. Shifts in the balance of these ingredients are at the root of the changes that we have recognised in our study of boundaries.

8   Discussion and conclusions

by Richard Bradley, Roy Entwistle, and Frances Raymond

Introduction

In the opening chapter, we discussed some of the problems affecting the interpretation of prehistoric land divisions and set out our reasons for mounting a new investigation of these earthworks. Having described the progress of that fieldwork and examined its local implications, we must now return to those broader issues. Before considering these, however, we need to review the principal conclusions based on the fieldwork and contrast these with the results of previous work.

To begin with, it is important to stress the long sequence of construction and reuse that has been established. Although there is no evidence whatsoever to indicate that the linear ditches system was established in the Middle Bronze Age as was once supposed, it may have drawn on notions of territory already current during that period. The construction of linear ditches may not have been a significant departure in the sense of laying claim to territories, but the definition of these by the establishment of formal boundaries almost certainly was. These first appeared during the Late Bronze Age, in a landscape already characterised by a pattern of Plain Ware open settlement, which to some extent appears to have replicated that of the Middle Bronze Age. We cannot be sure if the boundaries were laid down more or less at the same time, or if they evolved by incremental additions taking in an ever increasing area of land. This uncertainty has its origins in our chronology, which is too insensitive to resolve the fine detail required to answer such questions.

From the eighth century BC, we can recognise evidence that suggests that the pattern of settlement, integral with the original arrangement of territories, was undergoing a number of changes. Some parts of the ditches system were also being modified at this time. There are indications that larger territorial divisions were evolving and that this eventually gave way to a reorientation of settlement, involving a shift away from the primary focal area. These changes seem to have been under way before the foundation of hillforts, and in a sense they may reflect the emergence of the social and economic structures out of which the hillforts and ditched enclosures developed. In the final stages of this process, much of the Late Bronze Age linear ditches system appears to have become redundant, but there were exceptions. During the Iron Age, some boundaries were refurbished and new ones created, yet it appears that they now served a different purpose. Boundary ditches became closely integrated into a landscape of organised fields and pasture, in a way that suggests that domestic resources were being much more intensively managed. Such systems developed and expanded at the expense of earlier territorial divisions, so that by the Roman period the evidence from lynchets and the ditches themselves suggests that their significance was lost.

If this work goes some way towards establishing a new chronology for linear ditches, it also has implications for their interpretation. Their extended history makes it much easier to appreciate their role in the changing exploitation of the landscape. There is nothing to indicate the drastic shift from arable to pasture that the name 'ranch boundary' suggests and, in view of this, we can no longer maintain that their establishment involved a major agricultural change. The linear ditches clearly define areas of settlement, and all the evidence suggests that this included arable fields and pasture. What they exclude are other settlements, and parts of the landscape where the exploitation of resources may have been relatively unstructured.

Earlier suggestions of agricultural change now seem unwarranted. They were based on the observations that linear ditches might run obliquely across 'Celtic' fields, in such a way that the two could not have been in use together. We now need to reconsider the chronological implications of this argument. When these observations were first made, one sequence seemed inescapable: the linear ditches cut across large tracts of organised arable land and put them out of use. Our fieldwork has shown that this was rarely the case. Such observations have proven to be deceptive, and in almost all instances the fields are later than the ditches. This has been confirmed by excavation at a number of locations in the Upper Study Area, and similar results have emerged from other studies (Ford *et al* 1988). Although we would agree that the relationship between fields and ditches may sometimes represent changes in the relative proportions of arable land and pasture, the sequence generally runs in the opposite direction to that usually proposed.

There is a further sense in which perceptions of the linear ditches system are changed by this programme of fieldwork. Until recently, the pattern of land divisions was reconstructed almost entirely from the evidence of aerial photography. Our own research tested these projections on the ground, with the result that the overall layout has been greatly simplified and its coherence is now much easier to appreciate. A number of linear features are now known to be trackways of Roman or later date, while previously unrecognised stretches of ditch have been identified through a combination of augering and geophysical survey. Not only has this eliminated a number of spurious linear ditches, but it has also refined the picture of valley-based territories first hinted at by Hawkes (1939). The pattern of linear ditches now shows a more consistent relationship with the topography than was apparent when the project began. At the same time, more detailed surface survey has also shed light on the relationship between linear ditches and other monuments, especially round barrows and hillforts. This is particularly important with regard to round barrows, for in some cases these monuments may have exerted an influence over the layout of the boundary system that could not have been predicted from aerial photographs. The surface surveys have also clarified some of the complexity that would have been impossible to unravel by excavation alone.

These revisions to the widely accepted view of the linear ditches system have important consequences. The better understood chronology calls for a new interpretation of their place in the landscape history of the chalk, especially now this can be linked with the rapidly changing circumstances of Late Bronze Age and Iron Age society. At the same time, our more detailed knowledge of how linear ditches relate to the better known archaeological sites on the chalk suggests a history of landscape development involving more complexity than has been allowed for in the past. In both respects, the implications are the same. We can no longer discuss the history and function of the linear ditches system as though it represented a unitary phenomenon. It is clear that distinctions must be made to allow for its changing operation over a long period, especially in relation to some of the better documented developments in the archaeology of Wessex.

The development of the linear ditches system: the Middle to Late Bronze Age

One of the paradoxes of Wessex archaeology was discussed by Stuart Piggott (1973) in his contribution to the Victoria County History of Wiltshire. There is abundant evidence for Early Bronze Age barrow cemeteries and for settlements and cemeteries belonging to the Middle Bronze Age. Some settlements contained substantial timber buildings and were enclosed by earthworks or palisades, and a few were associated directly with small groups of 'Celtic' fields. In some ways, these are features that also characterise the settlements of the Early Iron Age, but in between the two periods there is a virtual hiatus in the archaeological record. The Late Bronze Age lacks many settlements, and those few that are known, such as Potterne, are found around the edges of the chalk uplands (Gingell and Lawson 1984a and b; Gingell 1992, 157–8). In contrast to the paucity of settlement evidence, the Late Bronze Age is represented by a distribution of diagnostic metalwork that extends across the county as a whole.

Exactly the same problems were identified by fieldwork in Cranborne Chase, where once again we find settlements and field systems in both the Middle Bronze Age and the Iron Age, but little sign of Late Bronze Age activity apart from metalwork (Barrett *et al* 1991, 228). This can no longer be attributed to the vagaries of ceramic chronology, as there are other parts of southern England, in particular the Thames and Kennet valleys, where Late Bronze Age settlements are commonplace. Here any case for 'continuity' breaks down, as these have little in common with Deverel-Rimbury sites and are much more akin to settlements of the Early Iron Age (Bradley 1986).

One benefit of concentrating our work in the Upper Study Area was described in Chapter 3. We made the point that unlike most parts of southern England, this is an area where only limited cultivation is practised. As a result, a variety of prehistoric pottery still survives in the ploughsoil, when elsewhere this material has been destroyed by widespread intensive cultivation. The contrast is immediately apparent, when we compare the results of surface collection in the Military Training Area (Chap 3, Table 2) with the assemblages from our work in the farmland to the south and east (Chap 3, Table 1). In both areas, worked flints have been recovered in large quantities, but, without the pottery that accompanied these finds at surface collection sites in the Military Training Area, there is little prospect of dating such assemblages closely. It is because of this uncommon degree of preservation that the 'missing' phase of Late Bronze Age settlement can be identified. In other parts of the chalk uplands that are farmed more intensively, sites of this period are irretrievably lost.

However, not all the problems result from the destruction of Late Bronze Age pottery. The evidence from our Study Area shows that there was also a change in the physical character of occupation sites. One reason for the apparent hiatus in the settlement record was a shift from enclosed to open sites and, in consequence, most settlements have left no distinctive earthworks behind them. We are in the fortunate position of being able to recognise Middle and Late Bronze Age sites in the Training Area, and this permits us to make direct comparisons between the settlement patterns of both periods.

In the first chapter of this report, we emphasised how Deverel-Rimbury settlement is unevenly distributed in Wessex. There are areas, such as Cranborne Chase, with major concentrations of field systems, settlements, and enclosures, while there are other regions in which such evidence is limited or absent altogether. The same contrast affects different parts of the Study Area. To the east, where agricultural damage has been most severe, is a major concentration of activity first investigated by Stone (1936 and 1941). In the Training Area, there is less evidence for Middle Bronze Age settlement, but against this we must balance the possibility that some of the many unexcavated enclosures might belong to this period (for instance, the levelled enclosures A and B near LDP 102, see Figs 15, 21, and 76). Even so, the few recognised traces do point to the existence of a wider pattern. There are two extant subcircular enclosures with Deverel-Rimbury pottery (LDP 108 and LDP 109), both of them similar in plan to excavated sites on the Marlborough Downs (C Piggott 1942; Gingell 1992) and in central Sussex (Ellison 1978). One of these (LDP 109) may be accompanied by a contemporary cemetery (Hawley 1910; Fig. 21), a relationship most clearly documented in Cranborne Chase (Barrett *et al* 1991, chap 5).

There is also the slight evidence for arable cultivation during the Middle Bronze Age, which was discussed in the previous chapter. Nevertheless, as we have already commented, there are no indications that this reflects widespread arable cultivation, and, by demonstrating that none of the linear ditches belong to this period, we have removed a further element that might have suggested large-scale land management. The low level of arable landuse suggested by the environmental data carries with it an important implication: far from being a period that saw a rapid expansion of settlement on the chalk, the Middle Bronze Age was a time when the chalk uplands were occupied on a limited scale. In this respect, the closest counterpart may be the Berkshire Downs, another region with linear ditches in which fieldwork has found very little material dating from the Middle Bronze Age (S Ford pers comm). But we must be cautious in making such parallels, for this too is an area where intensive cultivation may have affected the survival of material.

We can recognise another way in which the evidence from our Study Area conforms to a wider pattern. Although the sample is limited, detailed analysis of the Deverel-Rimbury pottery suggests that different settlements were linked by a fairly uniform repertoire of fine ware, but maintained their independence in the production of coarse ware. This precisely echoes the results of a programme of neutron activation analysis carried out on Deverel-Rimbury pottery from Cranborne Chase (Barrett *et al* 1978); indeed, the case is strengthened additionally by the analysis of other pottery from that area, which has yet to be published. The extension of this pattern to our Study Area is intriguing, since it suggests

that different communities were emphasising their separate identities before these took on a more explicit form through the creation of formalised land boundaries. At this stage, these may have depended on a more implicit sense of territory, centred on natural landscape features and on the distribution of monuments already in existence.

While there is evidence that seems to suggest a change in the character of individual settlements from the Middle to Late Bronze Age, the transition to Plain Ware did not involve any drastic change in settlement distribution. There appears to have been a continuity of occupation at several sites, but the small enclosures with Deverel-Rimbury associations (LDP 108 and LDP 109, and possibly LDP 102 sites A and B, Figs 15, 21, and 76) seem to have gone out of use and were apparently replaced by large unenclosed sites. Indeed, the levelling of sites A and B may have resulted from cultivation associated with the Late Bronze Age settlement that subsequently developed nearby. In other parts of Wessex, enclosed settlements do decline, and in their place we find extensive spreads of Late Bronze Age domestic material representing open settlements. Yet, we must avoid overemphasising this point, for it is far from clear how typical of Middle Bronze Age settlement in the Upper Study Area these enclosures were. We know that some of the open sites of predominantly Late Bronze Age date have small amounts of Deverel-Rimbury pottery (for instance, LDP 081/103 and LDP 112), but there are no signs of enclosing earthworks on the scale of those recognised in other parts of southern England.

Such changes that do appear seem rather subtle and might have involved a decline in only the most structurally visible type of site, while isolated habitations or small, open settlements may have continued in use. In fact, it is the greater density of settlement that seems to distinguish the Late Bronze Age in the Northern Core Territory. But since we lack a refined chronology for the Plain Ware ceramics, it is not possible to say with certainty whether all the settlement sites were in use at the same time, or whether they represent successive occupations at different locations (Chap 4). Nevertheless, the contrast in density between Middle and Late Bronze Age settlement is striking and may suggest that in this latter period more extensive nucleated settlements were emerging. The evidence from LDP 092 and LDP 102, on Brigmerston Down, indicates that this trend was already under way before the construction of formal territorial boundaries. Whatever the motivation for building these extensive ditch networks, they represent an impressive moulding of the landscape. It clearly was not a pioneering response, since it involved communities with a well-established tradition of settlement and no doubt with a strong cultural awareness of their place in the landscape.

It is difficult to suggest precise analogies for these developments, especially because open settlements are normally so difficult to locate. Even so, the change from enclosed to open settlement can be recognised elsewhere in the chalk uplands of southern England. There are at least four areas, where a similar development is documented. At the classic site on Plumpton Plain in Sussex, a series of Middle Bronze Age enclosures was replaced

Fig 76   Brigmerston Down, showing the enclosures LDP 108 and LDP 109, the location of the round barrow excavated by Hawley, and the two soil mark sites, A and B, at LDP 102 (reproduced by courtesy of the RCHME)

by an open settlement of uncertain extent nearby (Holleyman and Curwen 1935). Much the same development may have taken place on the Marlborough Downs (Gingell 1980; 1992). It can also be seen in Cunliffe's detailed survey of the settlement pattern at Chalton in Hampshire, which has revealed a large open settlement of Late Bronze Age date (1973, 178). Closer to our own Study Area, extensive artefact scatters of Late Bronze Age origin were identified by the Stonehenge Environs Project (Richards 1990, 240–6 and fig 154). Although in that area we do not know the exact nature of these sites, they do coincide with concentrations of Deverel-Rimbury material that may belong to a late phase of the Middle Bronze Age.

It is much less common for these changes to be linked with the subsequent creation of formal land boundaries, although there are occasional instances in which a parallel sequence might be recognised. This may be the case on the Marlborough Downs (Gingell 1992, 156), and the same pattern has been traced by survey and excavation at several sites on the Berkshire Downs (Ford 1982a and b). In the Stonehenge area, there appears to be a similar relationship between areas with Late Bronze Age artefact concentrations and the local network of linear ditches (Richards 1990, fig 154). The recent excavations at Easton Lane, Winchester, document in rather more detail the contrast between enclosed and open settlement (Fasham et al 1989), and, as we suggested in Chapter 1, the sequence on this site also traces the creation of ditched land units of steadily increasing size (Fig 4).

Although such evidence provides faint echoes of the sequence in the Upper Study Area, it is only in the Military Estate that the pattern can be explored in greater detail. The topographic alignment of linear ditches takes in ridges and valley bottoms, and invariably the ditches are false crested where they cross the higher ground. Although this is a common feature and well documented in other parts of the country, the recovery of the associated settlement pattern in the Upper Study Area makes it possible for us to qualify the observation. In several places, the topographic siting of boundaries appears to emphasise their visibility from within the territories, rather than from outside. The clearest example of this occurs in the Northern Core Territory, where the greatest extent of the territorial boundary can be seen from the settlements at LDP 080 and LDP 102. From LDP 081A, the closest settlement outside the territory, the boundary ditch SPTA 1971 is not visible at all, since it lies below the crest of Dunch Hill. There are other examples that can be cited: the western terminal of the Earl's Farm Down territory is false crested so as to be visible from within, and likewise the boundary ditches SPTA 1957 and 1983 are visible in their greatest extent from inside the enclosed area.

In many ways, the layout of the linear ditches system emphasises the alignment of the main ridges and watersheds. The same can be said of the distribution of round barrows, which often cluster on high ground and along ridges, and there are many instances where linear ditches appear to be aligned on prominent barrows or on barrow cemeteries. This relationship has been commented on many times, and most authorities have suggested that the burial mounds were used merely as conspicuous land-

marks upon which to align particular stretches of ditch. Yet, a closer inspection of the visibility of individual mounds reveals a more complicated relationship that does not always conform to this interpretation. In many instances, linear ditches do run up to individual, prominently sited barrows, and there are even examples of ditch junctions that are marked by a barrow mound. However, there are also frequent instances where linear ditches avoid the most conspicuous landmarks and approach barrows that are much less prominent. Indeed, some examples of the mounds associated with stretches of linear ditch could not have been seen from far enough away for them to be useful as sighting points.

Given this rather more varied picture, we wonder if the expedient use of barrows as sighting points is only part of the reason for their frequent inclusion in ditch alignments. These funerary monuments may have been part of an already existing territorial system, albeit a system with a less formal mode of definition, but one in which the dead and the supernatural played an important role (cf Spratt 1982b, 158–66). This suggestion might be strengthened, if we knew more about the structural history of the barrows most closely associated with the linear ditches system. We have already cited, rather tentatively, the evidence from the Northern Core Territory that might indicate an association between boundaries and burials, a trend that re-emerges more clearly at a later stage in the evolution of the linear ditches system (Chap 7). It is not outside the bounds of possibility that another expression of this same association was the incorporation of the dead from an earlier period.

Unlike the notion of territory implied by the distribution of round barrows, its expression during the Late Bronze Age was intimately connected with the physical presence of a continuous boundary. The function of these earthworks remains elusive, but we can no longer regard them as a device solely for the management of livestock, made necessary by a greater emphasis on pastoral resources. At best, it seems unrealistic to regard them as a physical barrier to the movement of people, nor would our study suggest that they were any more effective as a barrier to cultural interaction. Although the pottery evidence from the Brigmerston, Milston Down, and Dunch Hill sites points to differences between settlements separated by a boundary, it also suggests the sharing of common traditions (Chap 4), with all that this implies in terms of the frequency of contact and the exchange of ideas. A further point, which needs to be underlined is that not all of our settlements occupied bounded territories. Some apparently remained outside this system, but, as far as we are able to judge from the limited evidence, these communities were culturally indistinguishable from their contemporaries living inside the territory.

Broadly stated, the central significance of the boundary earthworks to communities living in and around the Northern Core Territory seems to have been the opposing principles of interaction and independence. Though these earthworks divided separate territories, their meaning appears to have been directed inwards. At the same time, these settlements were sharing a common ceramic tradition with neighbouring communities, who for one reason or another, chose not to define their territory with linear ditches. Technological differences do exist between included and excluded communities, but they have also been recognised between those within the territory. Despite the deficiencies of our evidence, a subtle interplay is indicated, which unites communities at one level, while stressing their separate identities at another.

We can see the same mixture of interaction and independence in the wider exploitation of the landscape, where settlements divided by boundary earthworks may have utilised unenclosed resources in common. Outside the strip of contiguous territories stretching along the western ridge of the Bourne Valley, there are tracts of open country that appear to have remained unenclosed during the Late Bronze Age. Indeed, in this western part of the Upper Study Area the only trace of enclosure is to be found on Figheldean Down (Figs 10 and 16), and this may belong to a later stage in the evolution of the landscape. Mostly, we are confronted with an area that was apparently devoid of major settlement during the Late Bronze Age. Isolated sites, such as LDP 081A and LDP 112, are to be found, but these lie close to the boundaries of the Northern Core Territory. Few arable fields were available in this area for surface collection – only LDP 104, 105, and 106 were investigated. However, the paucity of pottery from track cuttings and vehicle damage contrasts so sharply with the density of material between Sidbury Hill and Milston Down that Late Bronze Age settlement on any scale seems highly unlikely.

This area includes the Nine Mile River and Bourne Bottom (Fig 16), and it has several characteristics that distinguish it from the main areas of settlement. Towards the present source of the river, there are the concentrations of burnt flint mentioned in the previous chapter. Sites of similar aspect and character in other parts of Wessex have produced Middle or Late Bronze Age dates. Examples investigated recently include: Everley Water Meadow (Mercer 1984), sites in the Gussage (M Green pers comm) and Avon River valleys (S Shennan pers comm), and the burnt mound at Countess Farm (Entwistle in prep; Chap 7). None of these sites is associated with any evidence for domestic activity. This also applies to the deposits of burnt flint around the source of the Nine Mile River, but here their sheer extent suggests that the area was used over a long period of time and probably by a large number of people.

A further use of this area was as a source of raw material. In Chapter 5, Whitehead showed how the flintwork from LDP 104 differs from that recovered from nearby settlements. There are major technological differences, resulting from the preparation and 'testing' of flint nodules, and the site lacks the concentrations of pottery and burnt flint that characterised the domestic assemblages. By contrast, flint collections from nearby settlements show a quite different range of attributes, indicating the reduction of partly prepared raw material brought in from procurement sites. The valley of the Nine Mile River must have provided one of the most accessible sources of good quality flint in the Upper Study Area and, like the Plateau Gravels on Sidbury Hill, it probably met the needs of more than one community.

Lastly, there is the evidence for bronzeworking along the Nine Mile River valley. A stone mould piece with two matrices used for the casting of Late Bronze Age sock-

eted axes was recovered close to the river during the nineteenth century. It is poorly provenanced, but appears to have come from the river valley somewhere to the north of Bulford (Passmore 1931; SMR no SU24NWU03; Needham 1981, 12–15). More recently, a hoard of socketed bronze axes was discovered on Figheldean Down just above Bourne Bottom at SU 192493 (Coombs 1979). Many of the axes in this group came from a single mould (of a different type to that from the Bulford mould), and a number were unsharpened. These discoveries provide evidence for bronze production, and it is worth recalling that moulds or other evidence for bronzeworking have been recorded in the vicinity of burnt mounds in other parts of the country (Mercer 1984; M Green pers comm; C Young pers comm). Such evidence is often found in locations that are peripheral to the main focus of settlement.

This is a pattern repeated at the local level in the Upper Study Area, where bronzeworking might have been yet another activity that took place beyond the limits of enclosure. Even though such evidence is slight, it provides an important contrast with the domestic use of space implied by the bounded settlement areas. Thus a range of activities, including raw material procurement and bronzeworking, seem to have taken place outside the territories in an area that lay beyond the control of any one community. This might suggest that opposing concepts of space characterised the different regions, and to some extent determined their use.

We have already seen how the Middle Bronze Age reorganisation of the landscape extended into some areas of Wessex, but not into others. On a smaller scale, the contrasting treatment of different parts of the landscape in the Upper Study Area may have its origins in the traditions and settlement pattern of the second millennium BC. Although individual settlements seem to have become larger during the Late Bronze Age, there is no sign that the landscape was becoming more widely settled. Extensive tracts of potentially productive land remained outside the territorial structure imposed by the linear ditches system, and consequently there is no reason to suppose that population pressure motivated the establishment of formal boundaries.

Even within the territories, the pressure on resources seems to have been modest. The environmental evidence discussed by Entwistle in Chapter 6 suggests that the extent of arable cultivation was limited and that the open-country aspect revealed in most sequences was largely composed of grassland, probably maintained by grazing. The first evidence for intensification comes later, towards the end of the Late Bronze Age, and from this time onwards we can recognise signs of arable farming on an increasing scale, culminating in the Romano-British exploitation of the area.

The later history of the linear ditches system: the Late Bronze Age to Iron Age

The first signs of a major change in the territorial arrangement established during the Late Bronze Age came during the eighth century BC, at a time when Early All

Cannings Cross pottery made its appearance. The subsequent development of this ceramic style has its own significance, for it provides evidence for spatial patterning at a quite different scale. Raymond's analysis of the pottery in Chapter 4 demonstrates that the earliest All Cannings Cross ceramics developed out of established technological practices and styles, although the appearance of new formal and decorative attributes suggests a break with tradition. Previously, the pottery at different settlements showed an idiosyncratic use of widely distributed fabrics and decorative techniques, yet across the Upper Study Area there was a broad level of unity. The appearance of the earliest All Cannings Cross style prefigures a new range of cultural contacts connected with a very different settlement pattern.

The earliest material had a limited distribution on sites around the Northern Core Territory, and its appearance seems to coincide with a dissolution of the local territorial boundary. Later, in place of the subtle local distinctions, a single tradition unites a very large area, and by this time the Late Bronze Age settlements of the Northern Core Territory were abandoned. Stylistic contrasts during the Early All Cannings Cross phase may signal differences between whole regions (Barrett 1980a and b; Cunliffe 1984a, 12–18 and 39), and there may have been a lesser emphasis on differences between individual settlements. The same is also true of the scratched-cordoned bowl tradition, which succeeds this material (Cunliffe 1984a, 12–18 and 39–40). However, because so much of the pottery from the Upper Study Area is too fragmentary for precise phasing, the earlier and later material is considered together unless otherwise stated.

As we have intimated, the change in the character of the pottery assemblages is reflected by important changes in the distribution of settlements. Without exception, the open settlements that characterised the pattern associated with the foundation and primary use of the linear ditches system went out of use. The sites that replace them have a rather different character and distribution, with a major emphasis on two distinct regions. To the north-west, this material is found in new locations around Lidbury and the Avon Valley, while on Sidbury Hill it appears alongside changes that suggest that this location had taken on a new significance. The enclosure at Lidbury is abutted by two sections of a longer earthwork (Cunnington and Cunnington 1917), possibly indicating that it was integrated into a new territorial system with its emphasis on the Avon Valley and the area around Upavon. Conversely, recent work to the north-west of Coombe Down has revealed a ditched enclosure of Early Iron Age date linked to an older linear earthwork. On Sidbury Hill, an existing boundary ditch running down the northern slope of the hill was replaced by a much more substantial double-ditched earthwork. This was the only existing boundary to be reconstructed, and it is particularly significant that the new earthwork was built on a monumental scale.

The importance of Sidbury Hill as a landmark and nodal point in the layout of the Late Bronze Age linear ditches was mentioned in the previous chapter. This was emphasised by the recutting of the Sidbury East Linear Ditch, where it mounts the hill from the east, and the similar treatment of the ditch (cut 2A) at LDP 101,

which runs just below the western crest of the hill. Neither of these are recuts of the kind that were undertaken to create the 'V'-shaped morphology characteristic of Iron Age ditches. In both instances, it seems more likely that the recutting was intended to re-establish the boundary, in a physical and symbolic sense, by providing extra chalk to enhance the visibility of the bank.

Such scattered observations take on more substance when we recall that it was during this general period that the earliest hillforts and the precursors of others appear (Cunliffe 1984a, 13–23). The chronology for the first hillforts poses many problems, but in a number of cases they, or their immediate predecessors, developed at significant points in the layout of the linear ditches system (Cunliffe 1990). In our own Study Area, it is unfortunate that the most promising evidence comes from the earliest excavation. Nonetheless, enough can be recovered from Cunnington's work at Lidbury to establish that the oldest enclosure was associated with an All Cannings Cross furrowed bowl, and that two lengths of linear ditch were linked to the enclosure earthwork at an early stage in its history (Cunnington and Cunnington 1917). At Danebury, the chronological evidence is of a similar order, and here a double linear earthwork, like that approaching Sidbury, was joined to a large enclosure that preceded the hillfort by an uncertain period of time (Cunliffe 1990, 323–6; Cunliffe and Poole 1991, 20–22). A similar configuration exists at Woolbury, in Hampshire, where a double linear earthwork runs up to the hillfort in a manner reminiscent of Danebury (Cunliffe 1990, 323–6). On two other sites in Wessex, a single linear ditch runs up to the defences of an early hillfort, but in each case their precise chronological relationship remains uncertain. This applies more to Uffington Castle on the Berkshire Downs (Ford 1982a; S Palmer pers comm), than to Liddington Castle, the next hillfort to the west, where the boundary ditch may run under the defences (M Corney pers comm). The evidence from this site is rather better, taking the form of a large amount of Early All Cannings Cross pottery and a pin dated to the Late Bronze Age/Early Iron Age transition (P Rahtz pers comm). Finally, a recent survey of Ladle Hill in Hampshire, which is also associated with a single linear ditch, has identified traces of an earlier ditch circuit partly obscured by the later hillfort defences (Fig 77).

We have seen already that the small hillfort at Lidbury was built during this same general period, and that it is linked directly to a boundary ditch. It is most unfortunate that we cannot achieve a similar precision with regard to the other hillforts in our Study Area, those at Quarley and Sidbury. Despite the quality of Hawkes's work at Quarley, the fact remains that the earthworks are still poorly dated (Hawkes 1939). As we saw in Chapter 1, the defensive circuit overlies the junction of a number of ditches, while a later addition links elements of the boundary system to the hillfort earthworks. Hawkes envisaged a fairly short sequence on the site, starting with a palisaded enclosure and ending with an unfinished hillfort. The excavated pottery included scratched-cordoned bowls from a single deposit bracketing the tail of the hillfort rampart. In fact, the sequence at Quarley may have been longer than Hawkes supposed. There seems little reason to accept that the hillfort defences were left unfinished. Although parts of the earthwork have sus-

Fig 77 A view of the incomplete ditch circuit at Ladle Hillfort, showing traces of an earlier ditch preserved in one of the causeways

tained quite recent damage, the remains of an unrecorded series of quarry scoops are plainly visible behind the ramparts. None of these appear on Hawkes's site plan, although he did identify one example during the excavations (1939, fig 11). These would normally be interpreted as secondary features, postdating the initial construction of the rampart. Hawkes's own section of the defences seems to depict a two-phase earthwork (ibid, fig 11), and some of the posts in the entrance had certainly been replaced (ibid, fig 12). The key group of pottery appears to have been associated with the final refurbishment of the rampart, and much of it could have come from the bottom of a quarry scoop (ibid, fig 5). The implication of this reinterpretation is obvious. The only diagnostic material comes towards the end of a lengthy sequence, and the earliest defensive circuit might be of the same date as that at Lidbury.

Although we can build on the work of earlier archaeologists to reassess Lidbury and Quarley, we have no such advantage where Sidbury Hillfort is concerned. Some clues as to the construction sequence do exist, but these are far from satisfactory. A partial section through the inner rampart close to the south-east entrance was published by Megaw (1967). This suggests that the earthwork comprises at least two phases, the last of which was associated with pottery of Middle or Late Iron Age facies. The paired ditches of the double earthwork run up to the ramparts of the hillfort, stopping some 80m

short of the outer ditch circuit. The relationship of this earthwork to the hillfort is better understood than at the other sites where similar configurations have been recognised.

The radiocarbon dates (Chap 3, Table 22: OxA-2987 and 2988) show that the double earthwork was constructed sometime between the eighth and fifth centuries cal BC. The stratigraphic sequence at LDP 101, the section of the western ditch, suggests that a relatively short interval had elapsed, before the preceding boundary ditch (Fig 31, cut 2A) was replaced. On the basis of this interpretation, we conclude that the date for the reconstruction of the earthwork is most likely to lie towards the earlier part of the radiocarbon range.

It seems as if all these developments were linked. The earliest hillforts and related enclosures emerge during the period following the demise of open settlement, while over the same period, the territorial arrangements established earlier in the Late Bronze Age seem to break down. These same changes are mirrored by a transformation in pottery styles, which suggest that a wider sphere of interaction and cultural exchange was emerging. Coupled to this is the evidence for a selective remodelling of the linear ditches system. Some boundaries, such as that closing the upper end of the Northern Core Territory, were slighted. The Sidbury boundary was rebuilt on a monumental scale, further enhancing the importance of the hilltop, while at a broader scale, other linear ditch junctions may have had enclosures attached to them.

The elaboration of hilltop linear ditch junctions may be particularly significant, for it suggests that regional visibility was becoming an important concern. We can contrast this with the rather more local preoccupations that appear to have dictated the siting of the Late Bronze Age boundary ditches. Of course, these too ran across hilltops and ridges, and it is at these locations that we encounter the major junctions between territories. Where territories adjoined, we might expect to detect a greater concern for wider visibility, but for the most part Late Bronze Age boundaries appear to have conveyed a sense of place to those who occupied the interior of a territory. Generally, they would have been less effective in conveying messages to the outside.

The apparent concern with wider visibility that characterises developments during the eighth century BC may have been connected with an emerging sense of regional identity (see Chap 4). In connection with this, we must stress the significance that appears to have been attached to the Avon Valley. This is implicit in the shift of settlement pattern that occurred in the Upper Study Area, as the All Cannings Cross tradition developed. It may be that the river itself formed a major communication route, articulating the movement of ideas and cultural influences. In the context of this argument, it is surely significant that both All Cannings Cross and Potterne lie close to the Avon and that the excavated material from the latter included imported objects of amber and Kimmeridge Shale (Gingell and Lawson 1984a and b). A newly discovered site at East Chisenbury (D McOmish pers comm) occupies a similar location on a spur above the river valley.

One of the most important trends suggested by the previous discussion is the transformation in the character and distribution of settlement, which includes the development of hillforts. We have pointed out that the open settlements of the Late Bronze Age went out of use and that a new pattern was established centred on a number of sites, most of which have no evidence of Plain Ware settlement. It is less clear how the hillforts fitted into this new pattern. Chisenbury Trendle has produced later styles of All Cannings Cross pottery from the old land surface beneath the bank (Cunnington 1932), and at Sidbury Hill the presence of haematite-coated ware might be indicative of either an early hillfort, or some form of pre-hillfort occupation. Combined with the early pottery from Quarley Hillfort, this seems to suggest that these sites were continuously occupied from the end of the Bronze Age and that the hillfort stage was the culmination of this development. Having said this, we must emphasise that there is little to show how the occupation of hillforts related to wider aspects of contemporary settlement. There are numerous small enclosures in the Training Area, and preliminary results of current fieldwork suggest that some of them originated in the Early Iron Age. There is no conclusive evidence for contemporary open settlement, and we are left with the impression that these earthworks developed at the expense of open sites. This unbalanced picture characterises the archaeological record well into the Iron Age.

It is quite possible that similar circumstances prevailed in the area around Stonehenge. As we have seen, the work of the Stonehenge Environs Project (Richards 1990) also identified a series of open settlements of Late Bronze Age date, and, similarly, these also produced evidence for Deverel-Rimbury origins. But once more the archaeological record is truncated at the very end of the Bronze Age, and in this case there are few earthwork enclosures after that time. Indeed, the paucity of Iron Age material is made all the more striking by the overall sense of continuity that appears to have characterised the area up until that time.

It is always possible that the landscape around Stonehenge was avoided because of its unique monument complexes, but this seems unlikely in view of the ample evidence for farming throughout the Middle and Late Bronze Age. It is unfortunate that we know so little about the chronology of the hillforts nearest to this area. There is, however, evidence for cordoned bowls from the first enclosure at Yarnbury, 9km to the west of Stonehenge (Cunnington 1933), and 'earlier Iron Age' pottery was recovered from Vespasian's Camp, just 3km away (RCHME 1979, 20).

A similar situation to the Stonehenge area has been revealed by survey and excavation close to Maiden Castle, in Dorset (Sharples 1991a, 257–64). There is limited evidence for Middle and Late Bronze Age settlements in the area, but, by the Early and Middle Iron Age, the hillfort seems to have been the only occupation site in use. There is also a series of Late Iron Age sites, which belong to the period during which the character of the hillfort changed (ibid). Other regions with a rather similar sequence are the Marlborough Downs (Gingell 1992) and the Berkshire Downs (S Ford pers comm). In both areas, we find open settlements and linear ditches characterising the Late Bronze Age, but almost all the evidence for Early Iron Age settlement comes from the hillforts.

It is clear that there were certain contrasts between local sequences in different parts of Wessex, but in every case the development of hillforts forms a distinct horizon. Even here, the evidence is not as straightforward as it might appear. The early enclosures were built on much the same scale as some of the first hillforts and there may be little difference between the two classes of monument. This becomes evident when we compare the size of the enclosure at Old Down Farm (Davies 1981) with that at Lidbury: the distinction is largely created because one earthwork still survives, while the other has been destroyed by ploughing. At the same time, we must also remember that at sites such as Quarley the defensive structure replaced a less substantial enclosure. During the Early Iron Age, enclosures and hillforts form a continuum and it is only later, when some of the 'hillforts' grow in scale, that a sharp division is possible. This point is emphasised by the results of recent fieldwork in the Training Area.

The real contrast may be between areas of open settlement and areas with earthwork enclosures of any kind. The available figures from Hampshire, Wiltshire, and Berkshire are rather revealing. In the Early All Cannings Cross phase – the period that sees the last occupation of the open settlements in the Upper Study Area – just over half the sites producing diagnostic pottery are enclosures or 'hillforts' (this information is extracted from Cunliffe 1984a, appendix 1). By the time that scratched-cordoned bowls were in use, the proportion rises to three-quarters (ibid). Such statistics are striking, but they are subject to many biases. The true relationship between enclosures and open settlements can only be investigated by a programme of carefully planned fieldwork.

It is by no means clear how the early hillforts should be interpreted. A few show signs of destruction by fire (Bradley 1984, 134–6), but this does not mean that they were 'forts' in the modern sense (Sharples 1991b). Nor is it certain that they were even high-status settlements (Stopford 1987; Hill in press), although the presence of one or more unusually large round houses within these sites recalls the building tradition found at high-status ringworks of the Late Bronze Age (Bradley 1993). Even then, these distinctive structures are not confined to defended sites: they are also known from enclosures (eg Davies 1981, fig 14), and they even appear at open settlements (McOmish 1989, 103). Defended sites on the Wessex chalk do possess one novel feature – they are directly associated with a series of timber buildings normally interpreted as storehouses. Such structures have been found in Late Bronze Age open settlements on the chalk and on river gravels, but subsequently they occur in unexpectedly high numbers, although in nothing like the frequency recorded at Middle Iron Age hillforts (Gent 1983). Two possibilities arise: either these locations were used to store food drawn from a range of other settlements, or the first hillforts in Wessex were among the principal locations from which agricultural production was organised.

These questions are important when we consider the close relationship between the hillforts and the subsequent history of the linear ditches system. The distinctive contribution of this present study is the way in which it enables us to relate the development of these boundary earthworks to wider changes in the settlement pattern. The links between these land divisions and the emergence of early hillforts are very close indeed. The defended sites, in our own Study Area and beyond, grew up at major junctions between several different territories. This is especially clear at Sidbury and Quarley hillforts, but the same relationship can be seen elsewhere at sites such as Whitsbury in Hampshire (Bowen 1990, 75) and Buzbury Rings in Dorset (RCHME 1972, 102–4). These, and other similar sites, were placed in prominent locations that were landmarks before they were used as settlement sites. A number were already occupied by round barrows, and their subsequent use as locations for the joining of Late Bronze Age territories further emphasises the significance of such high places. The development of enclosed sites at some of these suggests that their significance persisted even at a time when the Late Bronze Age territorial arrangements were breaking down. Indeed, it seems as if the hillforts and their predecessors preside over much larger areas, formed from the combination of several of the previous territories. We lack structural evidence for an enclosure on Sidbury Hill at this time, but the rebuilding of an earlier boundary on a monumental scale emphasises the importance of the hilltop setting. As we have already mentioned, similarly paired ditches also approach the hillforts of Woolbury and Danebury (Cunliffe 1990, 323–6 and 329; Cunliffe and Poole 1991, 20–22) and, at the latter site, they belong to an early first millennium phase which included a large associated enclosure (ibid, 36). On Sidbury Hill, the double linear earthwork continued to play a significant role in later developments, as shown by the deposit of a human skull placed in the ditch terminal at LDP 100 (Chap 3, Table 22: OxA-3043).

In the same general period that these events were taking place at Sidbury, the Late Bronze Age settlements around the Northern Core Territory were abandoned. This appears to have been part of a wider trend, which also affected the territories radiating from Sidbury Hill to the north and east. The evidence from these areas is less satisfactory than that from the Northern Core Territory, but the pottery assemblages indicate that abandonment followed the same broad chronology. This would be consistent with the late eighth or early seventh centuries BC date suggested for the antler cheek piece recovered from the ditch at LDP 097. The demographic implications of these changes are unclear, but it is at least possible that the establishment of these new centres was accompanied by a movement of population. If this was the case, it might hint at some of the social changes integral with the emergence of hillforts and some of the ditched enclosures. The same may have happened in other areas, where the development of early hillforts seems to take place against a background of population drift towards nuclear sites. Although the territorial arrangements of the earlier period were no longer respected, the boundary system in a modified form still played an important role in the structuring of the landscape. There is evidence from the ditch silts and the environmental data at a number of sites for a greater emphasis on arable cultivation (Chap 6).

Although scattered and often ill-defined, these observations suggest that a major landscape reorganisation was taking place in conjunction with a drastic change in population structure. This carries with it the implication that the allocation of resources was at this time very different than it had been when the Late Bronze Age territories existed. The reasons for this restructuring are difficult to appreciate, but if the early enclosures and those hillforts that replaced them were high-status settlements, land and domesticated resources might increasingly have come under the control of the communities who occupied them.

In such circumstances, we would expect to find territorial boundaries that define much larger areas than was previously the case. It is difficult to identify a coherent system of boundary earthworks in the Upper Study Area that might have defined expanded territories exploited from the hillforts. However, there are signs that parts of the Late Bronze Age ditch system were being recruited to redefine the landscape. In this connection, we can cite the recutting of the Devil's Ditch, probably during the fourth century BC (Chap 3, Table 22: OxA-3046), and renewed activity along the Quarley High Linear on the opposite side of the Bourne Valley.

Although this boundary in its original form predates Quarley Hillfort, there are indications that it may have been partly refurbished at a later date, at least as far as Thruxton Hill (Chap 7). Beyond this stretch, the evidence from LDP 091, on Windmill Hill, indicates that the ditch had not been remodelled at the northern extremity, but its continuing importance was suggested by the insertion of a horse skull into the secondary silts (c 385 cal BC–AD 5, OxA-3047). This ditch faces the Bourne Valley, and it would have been plainly visible from Sidbury Hill – indeed, for all of its course north of the Andover to Amesbury trunk road (A303), it is false crested on the valley side. Taken together, the re-establishment of the Quarley High Linear and the Devil's Ditch boundaries implies that the Bourne Valley was an important topographic element in the new arrangements, but we cannot say exactly how this related to the hillforts in terms of valley resource exploitation.

In addition to the evidence from the ditches, there are other clues in the spacing of hillforts and their topographic setting that imply that larger tracts of land were being exploited. It is surely more than a coincidence that Quarley, Sidbury, Lidbury, and Chisenbury Trendle occupy blocks of land separated by the valleys and coombes associated with the main rivers of the Upper Study Area. If this pattern is extended westwards to include Casterley Camp, we can recognise a spatial arrangement with the hillforts placed at the edges overlooking the major rivers. The pattern is strengthened, if we include the double-ditched enclosure on Coombe Down (Figs 10 and 50), which is now known to date from the Middle Iron Age. This recently excavated site is located to the west of Sidbury Hillfort, on the opposite side of the Nine Mile River drainage.

The form of social organisation within which the hillforts operated is almost impossible to identify at an empirical level, and the range of alternatives is wide. If hillforts developed as high-status settlements, their control over the appropriation of resources might have had a 'feudal' basis (Cunliffe 1990). If they operated at a communal level, as others have argued (Stopford 1987), people may have felt the need to protect their homes and food supply by bringing both together at a single location.

The evidence from the Study Area gives us no indication as to which of these alternatives is the more likely. However, one clue, which suggests a contrasting sequence, may be provided by the recent excavation of Maiden Castle in Dorset. Sharples has argued that this was yet another early hillfort located at the intersection of already established territories (1991a, 258). The east entrance of this enclosure has always seemed anomalous, because it consists of two distinct gateways separated from one another by 40m of rampart. Sharples argues that this unique arrangement was adopted so that the fort provided access to two of the existing land units, separated elsewhere by a boundary ditch (ibid, 58). This implies that the early configuration of territories was still in operation during the use of the early hillfort. This seems to contradict the sequence at Sidbury, where the pre-existing territories appear to have been redundant by the time that the site assumed a central role. However, we should not expect exact parallels. Although broad regional similarities can be recognised, the sequence at any one site will reflect changes taking place at the local level, and it is at this scale that we have been most successful in unravelling the late prehistory of a little known landscape.

Final uses of the boundary system

Three important changes took place during the Middle Iron Age, and each is relevant to our study of prehistoric land divisions. Hillforts changed their character and distribution, becoming more closely integrated than ever in the cycle of agricultural production. The landscape witnessed the establishment of a number of settlement enclosures, and the environmental data from many sources suggest a further expansion of farming (see Entwistle and Bowden 1991 for similar evidence from Cranborne Chase).

In our own Study Area, the environmental evidence reflects these broader trends. The first signs of intensification are scarcely visible in Late Bronze Age/Early Iron Age contexts. By the Middle Iron Age, the evidence is not just confined to the environmental sequences, but also appears in a major structural change in the use of boundary ditches. There are a few stratigraphic signs that might indicate fluctuations in the intensity of cultivation, but overall the impression is one of increasingly organised farming. Field systems were laid out on a more extensive scale than before, and this necessitated the creation of reserved areas of pasture for the control of livestock. Later developments are less clearly perceived, but, by the Roman period, the structure of this landscape was obliterated by a new pattern of landuse centred on a different arrangement of settlements.

The Middle Iron Age saw a change in the character of hillforts. A number of sites went out of use, or continued to be occupied as farming settlements as their defences decayed (Cunliffe 1984a). Other hillforts were rebuilt on a more monumental scale, and in certain cases they now enclosed a considerably larger area. Almost all of these developments can be recognised in our Study Area. Quarley Hillfort apparently went out of use before the Middle Iron Age (Hawkes 1939), but occupation still continued at Lidbury (Cunnington and Cunnington 1917). At Sidbury, the defences were embellished, and a monumental entrance, rather like that at Danebury (Cunliffe 1984b, 25–42), was constructed on the western side during this period. A similar form of entrance is found at Yarnbury Hillfort, where the original earthworks were abandoned in favour of a much larger enclosure (Cunnington 1933). Recent fieldwork at this site has shown that the later enclosure contained a dense distribution of round houses, although many of the surface finds are of Romano-British date (M Corney pers comm).

None of the sites in our Study Area has been excavated on any scale, but work on other Wessex hillforts sheds light on the changing character of these monuments. Although many contain significant numbers of houses, it is not clear whether these existed in greater numbers, or at a greater density, than on other sites of the period. On the other hand, the number and capacity of storage structures found on defended sites is far higher than on other settlements (Gent 1983). This is a trend that may have started in the Early Iron Age, but the large-scale storage of foodstuffs in pits and above-ground buildings is one of the defining characteristics of the so-called 'developed hillforts'.

Although open settlements did exist during the Middle Iron Age, most occupation sites were enclosed (Cunliffe 1984a). With the embellishment of major defended sites, it becomes rather easier to distinguish between hillforts and other enclosed settlements. However, apart from the features mentioned earlier, these sites contain the same range of artefacts, subsistence evidence, and post-built structures as the developed hillforts, and both types of site must have been involved in agricultural production. Detailed statistics are not available, but it seems likely that smaller enclosures increased in frequency during the Iron Age, and, in certain cases, their distribution seems to be closely linked to the position of the major hillforts. Cunliffe has suggested that some of the main defended sites, including Quarley Hillfort, were ringed by a series of equally spaced enclosures, separated from the hillfort earthworks by open areas a kilometre or so across (1984b, fig 10.2).

Not every region shows this distinctive pattern. There are certainly some Middle Iron Age enclosures in the Study Area, but their frequency remains to be established. Still further afield, the Stonehenge Environs Project took place in an area in which Iron Age enclosures – and even Iron Age pottery – were virtually absent (Richards 1990). As we have seen, the same pattern has been identified by field survey around Dorchester. The defences of Maiden Castle were remodelled on a larger scale, while two of the nearby hillforts went out of use. The landscape around the rebuilt monument lacked any settlement sites (Sharples 1991a, 257–63). Geophysical survey of the interior of Maiden Castle shows that its storage capacity increased considerably at this time, suggesting that it might have developed at the expense of its neighbours.

Around Danebury, it appears that enclosed settlements existed in large numbers in the vicinity of the hillfort. This might explain why so few houses have been found on the site, compared with storage structures. Maiden Castle shows a contrasting sequence. We do not know how many houses there were inside the hillfort, but we can be fairly certain that few existed in the surrounding area (Sharples 1991a, 260). This recalls the results of field survey at a number of well-preserved hillforts in Wessex, where surface irregularities suggest a dense distribution of circular buildings (RCHME 1970, 82–3 and 263–5). Unless this arrangement was confined to a very late phase of occupation – and this could only be determined by excavation – it would seem as if they represent a rather different phenomenon: a series of nucleated settlements, dominated less by storage structures than by domestic buildings. Yarnbury, some distance to the west of our own Study Area, is a hillfort of this kind (M Corney pers comm).

Again, it is most unfortunate that we know so little about the internal organisation of the hillforts in our own Study Area, although earthwork survey in the unwooded portion of Sidbury Hillfort does hint at a distribution of round houses similar to that at Yarnbury (D McOmish pers comm). The point is important, as we still do not understand the relationship between these hillforts and their hinterland. It is clear that defended sites in the Military Training Area were complemented by smaller Middle Iron Age enclosures, but their full significance remains to be investigated. We have suggested already that, during the Early Iron Age, the defended sites developed at the expense of other forms of settlement.

We can speak with greater confidence about the linear ditches system during the Middle Iron Age. Certain of the earlier boundaries were recut and new ditches added to create an entirely different layout, defining smaller areas, which no longer contained settlements, but appear to have been created solely to reserve pasture in a more tightly managed arable setting. The origins of these developments are not well dated, but they probably accompanied the development of the hillforts and certainly continued into the Middle Iron Age. The later ditches and, in some cases, the recut forms have a distinctive 'V'-shaped profile and often terminate in what has been described as a 'cleaning slot'. One of the major boundary ditches that had been recut to form a 'V'-shaped ditch had a cattle skull inserted into the primary silts (LDP 090), and similarly placed human and animal skulls were inserted into the terminals of the Sidbury double earthwork, and the ditch on Windmill Hill (LDP 091). In the light of these events, it is worth recalling that the boundaries of Middle Iron Age hillforts were often marked by similar deposits (Wait 1985, chaps 4 and 5; Hill 1989), and that others are found in the filling of corn storage pits (Cunliffe 1984b, 446–57 and 540–3; Wait 1985, chaps 4 and 5; Cunliffe and Poole 1991, 418 and 482). Current work has shown that similar deposits occur in the Study Area. The evolution of 'V'-shaped boundary ditches shows a general conformity to the development of hillfort defences in Wessex, where ditches of this kind are a particular feature of the Middle Iron Age and are often associated with the creation of glacis ramparts (Cunliffe 1978, chap 13). The same is true of recently excavated enclosures in the Military Training Area. Such resemblances should not be exaggerated, but the change in ditch morphology, and perhaps also the inclusion of placed deposits, hints at a common tradition. We have only a limited insight into this possibility. Yet, given the sheer extent of these ditches, and the small scale on which they have been

excavated, structured deposits of this kind may occur much more widely.

The refurbishment of certain of the boundary ditches occurs at several locations, but, in the vicinity of Sidbury Hill and Snail Down, the sequence and patterning are revealed most clearly and appear to have involved the creation of new ditches. In the previous chapter, we discussed such changes and argued that the later ditches had a role in the organisation of pastoral resources. This may not have been so in all cases, for there are examples, such as a stretch of the Devil's Ditch, where the recutting seems to have been connected with the layout of a field system. These observations do suggest, however, that during the period in which developed hillforts were established, selected elements of the earlier boundary system, augmented by fresh ditches, were renewed and integrated into a more intensively worked agricultural landscape.

This is important, for it suggests that one of the most influential interpretations of the linear ditches system is only applicable towards the end of their period of use. Livestock control may have been an incidental function of earlier boundaries, but almost certainly it was not their primary role. What appears to distinguish the later ditches is that they coexisted with evidence for much more intensive farming, and, unlike the earlier forms, they did not define areas of settlement activity in juxtaposition to areas largely devoid of settlement. As far as these later ditches are concerned, we can take the link with hillforts one step further.

The use of ditches to create areas of pasture is not a new idea. It is already foreshadowed in Appelbaum's discussion of the prehistoric landscape on Figheldean Down, where he identified a large enclosure defined by ditches and apparently excluding elements of the surrounding field systems (1954; Fig 10). This he interpreted as an area of pasture used to confine livestock, which at other times of the year would have been turned out to manure the surrounding fields (ibid). Up to this point Appelbaum's hypothesis seems reasonable, but, more interesting than his population and resource statistics is that similar arrangements can be seen at a number of other locations. Yet, in a wider context the Figheldean Down example seems unusual, for areas of reserved pasture seem more typically to occur close to hillforts. The example on Snail Down just below Sidbury Hillfort was discussed in the previous chapter, and mention was also made of the apparently uncultivated area to the north of Quarley Hillfort, but the most striking example is to be found at Yarnbury, just to the west of the Upper Study Area. Here, the hillfort is at the centre of a large area comprising some 120ha and divided from extensive tracts of 'Celtic' fields by ditches (Bowen 1972, plate V; M Corney pers comm; Fig 78).

In each case, the most likely interpretation is that reserved areas of pasture were a necessary development in areas where agricultural resources were under pressure, and a closer management was required. Again, we cannot claim this as an entirely original idea. What is more important is that we can recognise distinctive phases in the use of a system of boundary ditches whose history stretched back over a long period, and that individually these reflect other processes in the development of the prehistoric landscape.

Fig 78   A view of Yarnbury Hillfort and the area enclosed by linear ditches with 'Celtic' fields abutting from the exterior (reproduced by courtesy of the RCHME)

In fact, it is during the Middle Iron Age that the history of linear ditches becomes lost to us. We have already seen that their territorial function may have ceased, to be replaced only in part by new uses. It no longer seems as if these boundaries defined the territories associated with particular communities. It is more likely that those parts of the system that were reused, or augmented, formed just part of an extensively farmed landscape, dominated by the major hillforts. This is not to say that all the inhabitants of the area lived in those hillforts, but the evidence for large-scale food storage at such sites clearly emphasises their close integration into the processes of agricultural production.

With these developments taking place in the Middle Iron Age, our detailed knowledge of the workings of boundary ditches comes to an end. This is partly a result of our inadequate understanding of the Late Iron Age

and the emergence of Romano-British settlement, but it also reflects a real decline in the use of earlier boundaries. This is not to say that notions of territory disappeared, or that ditched boundaries were not created for other purposes. This was undoubtedly the case, but changes in the structure of settlement and landuse into the Roman period resulted in the destruction of a large part of the linear ditches system, which had changed so radically since the Late Bronze Age.

Concluding summary

What are the main conclusions that can be drawn from this study of the linear ditches system?

a)   The first point is perhaps the most important. We

know that the use of these earthworks took place over such a long period of time that they cannot be reduced to just one interpretation. This has been the difficulty of studying their distribution without sufficient evidence of chronology. There is no doubt that some of these earthworks are found with fields, enclosures, and hillforts, but it is no longer acceptable to reconstruct an entire agricultural regime on the basis of these relationships (eg Appelbaum 1954; Palmer 1983). The ditches were already in place before the earliest hillforts were built, and the majority of 'Celtic' field systems belong to a much later part of the sequence. In many cases, their development entailed the destruction of earlier boundaries. For the same reasons, we cannot combine the evidence for these different field monuments to argue for ever increasing population pressure on the landscape, for clearly not all of these elements belong together. It is essential to place these different components of the archaeological record in their correct chronological alignment, and, when we do so, such arguments are significantly weakened. Likewise, it may be unjustifiable to place too much emphasis on agricultural intensification, for our own work suggests that the only convincing evidence for this comes towards the end of a long and complicated sequence. Indeed, one result of our investigations has been to show that arable intensification in fact destroyed much of the linear ditches system.

b)   For rather the same reasons, we can no longer follow the conventional equation between linear ditches and the creation of large areas of grazing land. There is not much evidence to show that the boundary earthworks of the Late Bronze Age cut across existing fields, putting them out of use. The single example (confirmed during the project fieldwork) of a boundary replacing part of an arable field has rather different implications and cannot be regarded as an example of a wider trend involving a greater emphasis on pasture. Moreover, these first boundary earthworks enclosed a pattern of large open settlements, rather than tracts of empty grassland, and there is no indication that such sites had economies that differed radically from their Middle Bronze Age predecessors. It is only in the Early to Middle Iron Age that parts of the boundary system appear to define areas of pasture, but by this time they do so in the midst of an intensively farmed arable landscape. This may be a rather specialised development, as it is perceived most distinctly in the vicinity of some of the hillforts.

c)   Our archaeological sequence also suggests that the relationship between linear ditches and hillforts is less straightforward than had previously been thought. This casts doubt on attempts to combine the territorial pattern defined by the ditches with the hypothesised function of hillforts in order to explain the social organisation of the landscape. Cunliffe has recently taken this route in his interpretation of late prehistoric landholding (1990). He argues that the development of enclosed territories during the Bronze Age reflects wider changes in social organisation. During earlier periods, it is suggested that land was

held in common, whereas the later enclosure of territories is regarded as representing a new concept of land management involving the coercive power of a central authority (ibid). Although attractive, this argument is not based on the boundary system itself, so much as its assumed relationship to the defended sites, which Cunliffe regards as high-status settlements. In specific detail and timing, this argument runs contrary to the evidence for the archaeological sequence in the Upper Study Area. The settlements associated with the establishment of the linear ditches system are open sites, showing no evidence for a hierarchy. Indeed, some large settlements sharing the same material culture attributes remained outside the enclosed territories. The period of radical change between 800 and 550 BC noted by Cunliffe (1990) is marked in the Upper Study Area by a breakdown of the existing territorial arrangements, and it was during this time that new settlements became established, for instance at Chisenbury Trendle and Lidbury. Whatever the character of the social arrangements prior to this, it was only at this time that a distinctive class of settlement emerged. From this stage the use of the Late Bronze Age boundary system implies very different arrangements. Although these are not perceived clearly, they do seem to have involved the organisation of the landscape on a much larger scale, but in favour of single defended sites rather than dispersed open settlements.

d)   One development that has prompted new thinking on the role of Iron Age hillforts has been an increasing concern with ritual and symbols. Although these are difficult to discuss in the context of our own study, both have a place in our interpretation. At one level, we have traced a striking synchronism between aspects of material culture and the changing role of boundary systems. When they were first established, the land boundaries were sited so as to be plainly visible from within the territories. During this period, the pottery repertoires show subtle distinctions at the local level. These observations are absolutely central to an understanding of later transformations, for they imply that people had become accustomed to defining territory in terms of the area that they could view from their own settlements. At this stage, the importance of the local community seems to have been paramount, and there may have been a reflexive relationship between settlement, visibility, and territory.

It seems entirely possible that it was this historical perception of space that contributed ultimately to the disruption of the settlement pattern during the eighth century BC. Open settlements were abandoned in favour of enclosures and hillforts, while pottery styles came to emphasise links across a much larger area. Such changes may have been the outcome of a series of conceptual transformations, perhaps involving an intensification of contacts between communities living at a greater distance. If this was the case, then these altered concerns seem to have been realised through traditional modes of expression. As in the earlier period, it may still have been important to define territory as the landscape visible from the settlement.

But, with a different concept of territory, the sites chosen for occupation were located in positions that gave commanding views into the interiors of several established territories and a wider outlook across the landscape. This can be seen in the construction of the monumental double earthwork on Sidbury Hill, which stresses the significance of this prominent ridge with its conjoining boundaries. Here and at other sites beyond our Study Area, we can recognise changes that appear to transcend the local character of the earliest boundary ditches.

e)   During the Middle Iron Age, there appears to have been an assimilation between hillfort defences and certain elements of the earlier boundary system. The earthworks of the developed hillforts were echoed in the landscape at large, as some of the earlier boundaries were re-established and new additions made. The new ditches had deep 'V'-shaped profiles not unlike those found at the defended sites, while those ditches of the Late Bronze Age layout that were re-excavated took on a similar form. This link seems to have been reinforced by the purposeful deposition of human and animal remains, especially skulls, in the renewed boundary earthworks, echoed by the similar deposits found at hillforts and enclosures. This takes on added significance, when we recall the increasing number of ritual deposits being discovered at these sites (Hill 1989 and in press). In this connection, we should draw attention to the series of shrines found at Danebury (Cunliffe 1984b, 81–7).

f)   Finally, there may be a broad connection between the growing emphasis on land and agricultural production and the provision of special deposits. It is at this level that local developments in Wessex align themselves with broader developments on the Continent. The character of ritual activity appears to have changed in later prehistory. Long-distance exchange networks seem to have faltered in the closing years of the Bronze Age, and we can recognise a growing emphasis on the manipulation of foodstuffs (Barrett 1989a and b). The obsession with genealogy, which seems to have found its expression in the barrow cemeteries of Early Bronze Age Wessex, gave way to an ideology that placed emphasis on the fertility of domesticated resources (ibid; cf Bradley 1990, chap 4). The timing of this change was not the same everywhere, but the general trend seems clear. Ritual came to play a central role in the processes of agricultural production, and, in place of the deposits of exotica, we find human remains, meat joints, and offerings of agricultural tools. The burial of human bodies in corn storage pits sums up the new beliefs most effectively, for here the ideas of fertility and regeneration are directly linked with the treatment of the dead. The placing of skulls in boundary ditches may be an extension of this broad ideological framework, because by this time the ditches were closely involved in the organisation of the agricultural landscape.

Postscript: last reflections on the linear ditches system

There is one point that has been latent in our discussion of the linear ditches system, but which now needs to be emphasised. Virtually all previous hypotheses have sought a single explanation for the origin and function of the linear ditches system; indeed this is implicit in the very names that we have inherited to describe them. These now appear too limited. At a purely empirical level, this is because the system had a lengthy history of creation and modification, but the rejection of earlier hypotheses also demands a new theoretical position.

The interaction between society and the structure of the landscape is central to any discussion of prehistoric land division, but it would be out of place in this present work to indulge in a protracted discussion of these more theoretical issues. However, we must stress that the conclusions reached in previous chapters rule out the possibility of explaining prehistoric territorial boundaries in terms of their utility, especially in the context of changing subsistence practice. If we cannot adequately fulfil the need for a new theoretical stance, we can at least signpost some of the directions that future enquiries might take. Perhaps we have dwelt disproportionately on the later development of the linear ditches system, but this was a course dictated for us by the nature of the evidence. However, it would be unsatisfactory to leave our subject without coming down off the fence to offer something to replace the traditional views that are no longer tenable.

There is certainly a connection between spatial organisation and social organisation, but it is not enough to 'read off' one from the other, since the two elements have a reciprocal relationship. If the organisation of the landscape provides certain clues to the working of prehistoric society, the ways in which that landscape is structured may also play an active role in daily life, by moulding the experience of the people who worked and lived there (Pred 1986). At several points we have referred to the contrast between the use of space within the Late Bronze Age territories and the rather different pattern that may have characterised activities outside them. We made the point that not all of the local Late Bronze Age communities were expressing this opposition in the same manner; there appear to have been rather subtle distinctions. Some communities were defining the extent of their domesticated resources in a formal sense, whereas others appear not to have done so. It was also suggested that the definition of domesticated resources emerged in contradistinction to those resources that were perceived as being natural. The distinction between domesticated and natural resources is of more than passing interest, for it lies at the root of concepts, such as land ownership and community rights.

We have already intimated that the range of activities taking place outside the bounded landscape of the Northern Core Territory may have been of a communal nature, involving more than one settlement. There is some echo of this distinction in the ceramic evidence from nearby sites. The spatial structure imposed by the boundary ditches was preceded by an apparent alignment between some of the settlements, such that those on Dunch Hill and Milston Down came to share a ceramic technology of similar character. This contrasts with the situation in what was to become the Northern Core Territory, and it is this variation that is encapsulated by the local arrangement of linear ditches (Chap 4).

To explain this, we need to recall that the Northern Core Territory, and the sites just outside it, lie alongside an area that seems to have been devoid of settlement during the Late Bronze Age. In other parts of the Study Area, similar strip territories have been recognised (see Chap 7) and, if we discount what are probably later additions, these exist in areas of the landscape that are largely unbounded. The original territorial pattern formalised by the Late Bronze Age linear ditches may have consisted of a series of cohesive blocks separated by tracts of land with little or no settlement. On Brigmerston Down, the process of formalising territories imposed a physical division of space on a settlement pattern that had long been in existence, and it clearly excluded a number of communities close by. There is no sign that this development was connected with the emergence of a pre-eminent settlement, or of a settlement hierarchy.

How then do we explain such an important transformation in the face of so little evidence? One possibility is that the construction of physical boundaries reflects the need felt by some communities to define more closely their domesticated resources. We have already intimated that this is unlikely to have been a response to population pressure. However, it could reflect the growing importance of land and its productivity to communities with a long tradition of sedentism. If this was linked to a kinship structure that tightly bound some groups, but only loosely affiliated others, we might have an explanation for the principles of sharing and exclusion that characterise the ways in which the ceramics were being manipulated (see Chap 4).

Perhaps it is not the individual settlements that should concern us, but their grouping, because at this level of analysis distinctions emerge that seem to reveal variations in the ways in which people were viewing their world. All of the sites around the Northern Core Territory had their origins in the Middle Bronze Age, but it would appear that contrasting historical trajectories emerged in this liminal region, ultimately giving rise to rather different perceptions of the landscape. For instance, the communities occupying settlements such as LDP 112 and LDP 081, which lie in the unbounded area around the Nine Mile River and Bourne Bottom, may well have had a relationship with their environment that differed markedly from those within the Northern Core Territory. This might have been conditioned by the traditional uses of that area, where a range of activities suggesting communal access are evidenced. We are not

suggesting that the subsistence practices were of a different kind than those employed within the Northern Core Territory, but that they may have been structured differently.

The importance of the perception of space in structuring social and productive relations has been recognised by human geographers as a key factor in the constitution of societies. The perception of space (which of course will include the location of settlements and the notion of territory) has its foundations in social practice and labour processes (Soja 1985), and it is these that mediate between ideas of domesticated and natural, or territorial and communal land. The idea that a coercive power was imposing its control over resources through a system of territories gains no support from our evidence; it seems more likely that we are seeing changes that emerge from different attitudes and relations between communities and their resources and, in particular, from different perceptions of domestication.

Our search for the cultural origins of the linear ditches system has encouraged us to hypothesise about events in an area that may have been far from typical, but this is not important. Anomalies are not a threat to archaeological theorising. If we have succeeded in demonstrating that local or contextual variations are a possibility, and that not all superficially similar archaeological phenomena can be reduced to a single explanation, then we will have gone some way towards countering the preoccupation with classification, which so often appears to be regarded as an end in itself. In this respect we find ourselves in agreement with the editors of *The archaeology of context* (Barrett and Kinnes 1988). As individual authors, we have structured our separate contributions, so as to highlight certain contextual themes and, by sustaining these throughout, we have attempted to maintain a balance between the empirical and theoretical parts of this study.

It seems appropriate to conclude this chapter by quoting the first student of linear ditches, Sir Richard Colt Hoare. Although the details of his interpretation differ from our own, the words that he wrote 180 years ago have a familiar ring (Colt Hoare 1812, 18–19):

The history of these numerous banks and ditches which intersect our island in various directions has never been clearly demonstrated; they have generally been called boundary ditches.... The frequent occurrence of these on our downs has opened a wide field for reflection and conjecture; much time was spent in doubt and uncertainty, till at length their connection with British towns became apparent, and ascertained most clearly the original course of their formation and destination.

Appendix 1   Gazetteer of sites

Table 27   Surface collection sites

LDP code	km square	feature	location	description
001	SU 2644	–	Quarley	linear soil mark
002	SU 2644	–	Quarley	linear soil mark
003	SU 2643	–	Quarley	linear soil mark
004	SU 2643	SMR H 28A	Quarley	Quarley Low Linear
005	SU 2544	SMR H 28A	Quarley	Quarley Low Linear
006	SU 2542	SMR H 26A	Quarley	Quarley High Linear
007	SU 2542	–	Quarley	linear soil mark
008	SU 2444	SMR H 20	Thruxton Hill	Quarley High Linear
009	SU 2444	SMR H 20	Thruxton Hill	Quarley High Linear
010	SU 2243	SPTA 1959	Cholderton	The Devil's Ditch
011	SU 2244	SPTA 1959	Cholderton	The Devil's Ditch
012	SU 2243	SPTA 1959	Cholderton	The Devil's Ditch
013	SU 2243	SPTA 1959	Cholderton	The Devil's Ditch
014	SU 1742	SMR 742	Ratfyn Farm	linear soil mark
015	SU 1742	SMR 745	Earl's Farm Down	linear ditch
016	SU 1741	SMR 745	Earl's Farm Down	linear ditch
017	SU 1842	–	Bulford	linear soil mark
018	SU 1841	SMR 778	Earl's Farm Down	linear soil mark
019	SU 1841	SMR 778	Earl's Farm Down	linear soil mark
075	SU 1749	SPTA 1109	Figheldean Down	linear ditch
080	SU 2048	SPTA 1965	Brigmerston Plantation	'Celtic' fields
081	SU 2048	–	Dunch Hill	linear soil mark
093	SU 1842	SMR 745	Beacon Hill	linear ditch
102	SU 2047	SPTA 1976	Brigmerston Down	'Celtic' fields
103	SU 2048	–	Dunch Hill	tree-root disturbances
104	SU 1948	SPTA 1962	Bourne Bottom	'Celtic' fields
105	SU 1847	–	Ablington Down	linear soil mark
106	SU 1848	SPTA 1115	Ablington Furze	'Celtic' fields
111	SU 2048	SPTA 1965	Dunch Hill	lynchets/linear ditch

Table 28   Excavation sites

LDP code	grid reference	feature	location	description
008A	SU 24804421	SMR H 20	Thruxton Hill	ditch section
019A	SU 18434195	SMR 778	Earl's Farm Down	trackway section
020	SU 21375114	SPTA 2232	Sidbury Double Linear	bank section
026	SU 21415106	SPTA 2232	Sidbury Double Linear	bank section
027	SU 21345121	SPTA 2232	Sidbury Double Linear	ditch and bank section
033	SU 21135199	SPTA 2234	Weather Hill	ditch section
039	SU 21305212	SPTA 2238	Weather Hill Firs	bank section
045	SU 21185080	SPTA 2242	Sidbury West Linear	ditch section
052	SU 21104831	SPTA 1959	The Devil's Ditch	ditch section
056	SU 20854820	–	Dunch Hill	hollow-way/ditch section
081A	SU 20464875	–	Dunch Hill	midden/ditch section
082	SU 19625197	SPTA 2310	Coombe Down	hollow-way/lynchet
083	SU 20425184	SPTA 2234	Weather Hill	ditch section
084	SU 20415189	SPTA 2310	Weather Hill	hollow-way/ard marks
085	SU 20425184	SPTA 2242	Haxton Down	pit alignment
086	SU 20425113	SPTA 2312	Haxton Down	hollow-way
087	SU 20444857	–	Dunch Hill	pit section
088	SU 20875081	SPTA 2242	Sidbury West Linear	ditch section
089	SU 20505085	SPTA 2242	Sidbury West Linear	ditch section
090	SU 21564491	SPTA 1959	Pearl Wood	ditch section
091	SU 24575113	SPTA 2247	Windmill Hill	ditch and bank section
092	SU 20474737	SPTA 1971	Brigmerston Down	ditch and bank sections
094	SU 21724599	SPTA 1959	The Devil's Ditch	ditch junction
095	SU 21304392	SPTA 2061	Beacon Hill	ditch section
096	SU 22005059	SPTA 2244	Sidbury East Linear	ditch section
097	SU 22565053	SPTA 2244	Sidbury East Linear	ditch section
098	SU 20584840	SPTA 1971	Dunch Hill	ditch/lynchet section
099	SU 20505085	SPTA 2242	Haxton Down	pit alignment/ditch
100	SU 21505079	SPTA 2232	Sidbury Hill	ditch terminal
101	SU 21485078	SPTA 2232	Sidbury Hill	ditch/terminal

Appendix 2 Pottery methodology and data

Analytical procedure

All prehistoric pottery sherds were sorted into fabric groups with the aid of a binocular microscope set at a magnification of ×30. These descriptive categories refer to the visible inclusions alone and make no reference to the type of clay used in separate wares. No attempt was made to distinguish between nonplastics added deliberately as temper and particles occurring naturally as constituents of the unrefined clay. Each of the fabrics identified either represents a unique combination of inclusion types, or contains the same range of particles, but in varying quantities and/or sizes. A series of charts depicting particle density within a matrix were used (Terry and Chillingar 1955), in an attempt to impose a degree of descriptive uniformity. The sizes of inclusions of less than 1mm were measured microscopically with a graticule. The fabrics of Roman and later pottery were not recorded, since this information would not have contributed towards an interpretation of the linear ditches system.

Apart from the fabric, a number of other details relating to the physical characteristics of each sherd were noted, including size, weight, thickness, surface finish, and the degree of post-depositional abrasion. In addition, every prehistoric sherd with diagnostic features was drawn and verbally described. This information, accompanied by a detailed record of the contextual associations for all pottery regardless of chronology, is available in the archive.

Table 29   The type, quantity, and size range of inclusions, used as criteria to define individual Beaker and Deverel-Rimbury fabrics

fabric	chalk %	chalk size (mm)	flint %	flint size (mm)	iron minerals %	iron minerals size (mm)	grog %	grog size (mm)	ironstone %	ironstone size (mm)	quartz sand %	quartz sand size (mm)	shell %	shell size (mm)
feGS: BKR/1					15	0.03–0.2	20	0.15–3.0			2	0.15–0.3		
feGS: BKR/3	1	0.5–1.0	1	1.0–1.5	7	0.01–0.4	3	0.1–2.0			2	0.1–0.3		
feGS: BKR/4					10	0.03–0.1	2	0.2–0.5			10	0.03–0.3		
feGS: BKR/5	1	1.0–1.5			10	0.03–0.2	7	0.3–2.5			30	0.1–0.7		
feGSsh: BKR/1					10	0.01–1.0	5	0.1–2.0			15	0.03–0.4	2	0.1–3.0
G: BKR/1							15	0.1–3.0						
GIS: EBA/1							25	0.1–2.0	5	0.2–1.0	25	0.1–0.3		
GS: BKR/1			1	0.3–1.0			10	0.1–0.5			20	0.1–0.4		
CFfe: DR/1	2	0.1–0.4	40	0.1–2.0	2	0.1–1.0								
CFS: DR/2	2	0.1–1.0	50	0.1–1.5							5	0.1–0.3		
CFS: DR/3	2	0.1–2.0	30	0.1–4.0							2	0.2–0.5		
F: DR/1			40	0.03–1.5										
F: DR/2			40	0.06–2.5										
Ffe: DR/1			20	0.1–5.0	5	0.1–0.5								
FfeS: DR/8			20	0.1–5.0	20	0.03–0.4					5	0.1–0.4		
FS: DR/3			40	0.1–6.0							5	0.1–0.3		
FS: DR/5			30	0.1–3.0							25	0.1–0.3		
FS: DR/9			40	0.2–4.0							30	0.03–0.7		

Table 30   The type quantity and size range of inclusions used as criteria to define individual Late Bronze Age fabrics

fabric	chalk %	chalk size (mm)	clay pellets %	clay pellets size (mm)	flint %	flint size (mm)	iron minerals %	iron minerals size (mm)	mica %	mica size (mm)	quartz sand %	quartz sand size (mm)	shell %	shell size (mm)	voids %	voids size (mm)
CF: LBA/1	2	0.07–0.7			30	0.07–1.5					1	0.2–0.5				
CFfeS: LBA/1	2	0.06–5.0			7	0.2–4.0	10	0.03–0.15			5	0.1–0.4				
CFfeS: LBA/2	5	0.06–0.5			40	0.15–5.0	30	0.03–0.6			7	0.3–1.0				
CFfeS: LBA/3	3	0.3–2.0			25	0.1–3.0	3	0.03–0.3			3	0.2–0.5				
clSsh:LBA/1			5	0.1–3.0	1	0.5–2.5					25	0.07–0.2	3	0.03–3.0		
FfeM: LBA/1					2	0.15–1.2	7	0.03–0.16	7	up to 0.03						
FfeS: LBA/1	1	1.0–4.0			10	0.1–4.0	10	0.03–0.1			40	0.06–2.5			5	0.2–1.5
FfeS: LBA/2					25	0.2–3.0	15	0.06–0.4			15	0.06–0.4				
FfeS: LBA/3					10	0.1–6.0	5	0.07–1.0			30	0.1–1.0				
FfeS: LBA/4	1	0.1–0.4			2	0.15–1.0	20	0.03–0.7			30	0.03–0.3				
FfeS: LBA/5					2	0.2–5.0	30	0.03–0.6			30	0.1–1.0				
FfeS: LBA/6					7	0.3–5.0	50	0.03–2.0			25	0.03–0.15				
FfeS: LBA/9					5	0.3–5.0	20	0.03–0.2			30	0.03–0.7				
Ffesh: LBA/1					2	0.5–2.0	5	0.03–0.2					20	0.03–4.0		
FS: LBA/1					5	0.07–4.0					50	0.1–0.2				
FS: LBA/2					5	0.2–2.0					40	0.2–0.4				
FS: LBA/4					10	0.2–2.0					15	0.15–0.7				
FS: LBA/6					2	0.5–4.0					40	0.03–1.0				
FSshv: LBA/1					3	0.2–8.0					25	0.06–0.5	3	0.5–4.0	7	0.5–4.0
feSsh: LBA/1					1	0.5–3.5	10	0.03–0.7			20	0.03–0.4	10	0.07–4.0		
sh: LBA/1													30	0.1–2.0		

Table 31 The type, quantity, and size range of inclusions, used as criteria to define individual Iron Age and indeterminate prehistoric fabrics

fabric	chalk		flint		iron minerals		grog		mica		quartz sand	
	%	size (mm)	%	size (mm)	%	size (mm)	%	size (mm)	%	size (mm)	%	size (mm)
CfeGS: IA/1	2	1.0–3.0			20	0.01–1.0	5	0.1–3.0			10	0.03–0.1
CS: IA-RB/1	3	0.3–3.0									50	0.1–0.7
FS: IA/8			5	0.3–0.8							40	0.03–0.7
feGMS: IA/1					3	0.03–3.0	3	0.3–5.0	2	up to 0.3	30	0.03–0.2
feGS: IA/6					20	0.03–1.5	10	0.3–3.5			20	0.03–0.8
feGS: IA/7					10	0.03–0.2	2	0.5–2.0			25	0.2–0.5
feMS: IA/1					20	0.03–0.2			7	0.03–0.3	40	0.03–0.7
feS: IA/1					40	0.03–3.5					20	0.03–0.35
GS: IA/2							15	0.2–3.0			15	0.03–0.4
S: IA/1											40	0.2–0.7
S: IA/2	1	0.3–0.5									25	0.03–0.3
S: IA/4											30	0.2–0.7

fabric	chalk		flint		iron minerals		grog		ironstone		quartz sand		shell	
	%	size (mm)	%	size (mm)	%	size (mm)	%	size (mm)	%	size (mm)	%	size (mm)	%	size (mm)
CFfeS: Indet/4	2	0.3–2.0	2	0.3–2.0	15	0.03–1.0					25	0.03–0.3		
CFS: Indet/1	2	0.7–3.0	15	0.1–4.0							25	0.03–0.3		
CfeIS: Indet/1	3	0.2–1.0			15	0.03–0.2			2	0.5–2.0	40	0.03–0.4		
CfeS: Indet/1	2	0.3–2.0			15	0.03–0.6					20	0.03–0.4		
CGS: Indet/1	3	0.1–3.0					10	0.1–3.0			2	0.03–0.1		
FfeS: Indet/7			15	0.1–2.5	5	0.1–1.0					2	0.2–0.7		
FGS: Indet/1			2	0.5–2.0			15	0.1–2.0			20	0.1–0.3		
FGS: Indet/2			3	1.0–2.0			5	0.1–1.0			10	0.1–1.0		
FGS: Indet/3			10	0.1–4.0			5	0.2–1.5			3	0.2–0.3		
FS: Indet/7			15	0.1–4.0							40	0.03–0.4		
Fsh: Indet/1			15	0.15–2.0									15	0.06–5.0
feG: Indet/1					5	0.01–0.1	7	0.2–2.0						
feGS: Indet/2					30	0.03–0.15	10	0.5–3.0			10	0.07–0.3		
feSsh: Indet/2					7	0.06–0.3					5	0.2–1.0	20	0.03–2.0
feSsh: Indet/3					5	0.03–0.3					30	0.2–1.3	25	0.1–4.0
S: Indet/3														

Table 32 The distribution of Iron Age fabrics within the Study Area

fabric	001	002	008A	018	019	075	082	083	098	100	112
CfeGS: IA/1				+			+				
CS: IA-RB/1				+							
FS: IA/8		+									
feGMS: IA/1			+			+	+				
feGS: IA/6							+				
feGS: IA/7							+				+
feMS: IA/1							+				
feS: IA/1	+						+				
GS: IA/2							+				
S: IA/1	+		+	+	+	+	+	+		+	
S: IA/2		+	+	+			+		+		
S: IA/4			+				+				+

Table 33   The distribution of indeterminate prehistoric fabrics within the Study Area, arranged according to the most likely date for their production and use

fabric	likely date	008	008A	009	017	019	019A	080	081	082	098	100	101	102	103	109	112
CfeIS: Indet/1	EBA																+
CGS: Indet/1	EBA		+			+											
feGS: Indet/2	EBA								+						+		
Fsh: Indet/1	DR or LBA										+				+	+	
feSsh: Indet/2	DR or LBA														+		
feSsh: Indet/3	DR or LBA															+	
CFS: Indet/1	LBA										+				+		
FfeS: Indet/7	LBA			+													
FGS: Indet/1	LBA										+				+		
FGS: Indet/2	LBA				+			+						+			
FGS: Indet/3	LBA					+	+										
FS: Indet/7	LBA										+					+	+
S: Indet/3	ACC (LBA or IA)		+							+		+					
CFfeS: Indet/4	IA			+													
CfeS: Indet/1	IA												+				
feG: Indet/1	IA		+														

Note: The ascription of these wares to specific periods is the result of a comparative exercise, involving the location of parallels for characteristics displayed by each of the indeterminate fabrics within ceramic assemblages of known date.

Table 34   The minimum numbers of prehistoric vessels from excavated and surface collection sites

LDP code	EBA	MBA	LBA	Iron Age	indet
001	–	–	–	2	–
002	–	–	–	2	–
008	–	–	1	–	1
008A	–	–	–	3	2
009	–	–	–	–	1
012	–	–	1	–	–
017	2	4	5	–	1
018	–	–	1	1	–
019	4	2	5	3	2
019A	–	–	–	–	1
075	1	–	–	2	–
080	–	1	8	–	1
081	–	–	14	–	1
081A	–	1	26	–	–
082	1	–	1	10	1
083	–	–	–	1	–
087	1	–	7	–	–
087A	–	–	1	–	–
092	–	4	9	–	–
097	1	1	5	–	–
098	–	2	6	1	4
100	–	–	1	1	1
101	–	–	–	–	1
102	3	4	8	–	1
103	1	1	15	–	4
104	–	–	1	–	–
108	–	1	2	–	–
109	2	5	9	–	5
111	1	–	5	–	–
112	4	5	44	2	2

Appendix 3   Flint data

Table 35   Distribution of percussion angles by assemblage

a) all flake categories combined

percussion angle (degrees)	LDP 104 no	%	LDP 102 no	%	LDP 080 no	%	LDP 081 no	%	LDP 081A no	%
40–44	6	4	–	–	–	–	–	–	1	0.5
45–49	25	16	3	2	2	3	1	4.5	1	0.5
50–54	14	9	13	7	3	5	–	–	12	8
55–59	12	8	36	19	7	12	7	30	56	36
60–64	43	28	56	29	25	42	7	30	54	36
65–69	34	22	63	33	17	29	5	22	20	13
70–74	9	6	18	9	4	7	2	9	4	3
75–79	3	2	1	1	1	2	1	4.5	2	1
80–84	3	2	–	–	–	–	–	–	–	–
85–89	2	1	–	–	–	–	–	–	2	1
90–94	2	1	–	–	–	–	–	–	1	0.5
95–99	1	1	–	–	–	–	–	–	–	–
100–104	–	–	–	–	–	–	–	–	1	0.5
totals	154		190		59		23		154	

b) unretouched flakes only

percussion angle (degrees)	LDP 104 no	%	LDP 102 no	%	LDP 080 no	%	LDP 081 no	%	LDP 081A no	%
40–44	–	–	–	–	–	–	–	–	1	0.5
45–49	3	4	–	–	–	–	1	5	1	0.5
50–54	1	1	7	4	2	4	–	–	5	4
55–59	7	8	34	20	5	11	5	24	48	37
60–64	36	43	53	31	18	40	7	32	48	37
65–69	24	29	58	34	16	36	6	29	19	15
70–74	7	8	17	10	3	7	1	5	4	3
75–79	1	1	1	0.5	1	2	1	5	2	2
80–84	2	2	1	0.5	–	–	–	–	–	–
85–89	2	2	–	–	–	–	–	–	1	0.5
90–94	–	–	–	–	–	–	–	–	–	–
95–99	1	1	–	–	–	–	–	–	–	–
100–104	–	–	–	–	–	–	–	–	1	0.5
105–109	1	1	–	–	–	–	–	–	–	–
totals	85		171		45		21		130	

Table 36   Percentages of percussion angles <60° and >65° by assemblage

site	a) all flake categories combined <60°	>65°	b) unretouched flakes only <60°	>65°
LDP 104	37	35	13	44
LDP 102	28	43	24	45
LDP 080	20	38	15	45
LDP 081	34.5	35.5	29	39
LDP 081A	45	19	42	21

Table 37   Distribution of breadth/length ratios by assemblage

a) all flake categories combined

breadth/length ratio	LDP 104 no	%	LDP 102 no	%	LDP 80 no	%	LDP 081 no	%	LDP 081A no	%
1:5	2	1	8	4	2	3	2	8	1	1
2:5	24	14	42	21	14	20	4	17	32	22
3:5	53	31	64	32	19	28	6	25	39	26
4:5	41	24	45	23	16	23	5	21	31	21
5:5	25	15	25	13	9	13	3	13	22	15
6:5	11	6	6	3	7	10	2	8	11	7
7:5	7	4	6	3	–	–	2	8	10	7
>8:5	8	5	1	1	2	3	–	–	2	1
totals	171		197		69		24		148	

b) unretouched flakes only

breadth/length ratio	LDP 104 no	%	LDP 102 no	%	LDP 80 no	%	LDP 081 no	%	LDP 081A no	%
1:5	1	1	8	5	1	2	2	10	1	1
2:5	14	15	39	23	12	19	3	14	29	22
3:5	33	36	53	31	23	37	4	19	32	24
4:5	21	23	38	22	12	19	5	23	29	22
5:5	10	11	20	12	7	11	3	14	18	14
6:5	6	7	6	4	6	10	2	10	10	8
7:5	3	3	4	2	–	–	2	10	9	7
>8:5	4	4	1	1	1	2	–	–	3	2
totals	92		169		62		21		131	

Table 38   Percentages of breadth/length ratios <3:5 and >5:5 by assemblage

site	a) all flake categories combined <3:5	>5:5	b) unretouched flakes only <3:5	>5:5
LDP 104	46	30	52	25
LDP 102	57	20	59	19
LDP 080	51	26	58	23
LDP 081	50	29	43	34
LDP 081A	49	30	47	31

Table 39   Distribution of flake lengths by assemblage

a) all flake categories combined

length (mm)	LDP 104 no	%	LDP 102 no	%	LDP 080 no	%	LDP 081 no	%	LDP 081A no	%
10–19	–	–	–	–	–	–	1	4.5	3	2
20–29	7	4	10	5	2	3	2	9	22	15
30–39	23	14	36	19	11	19	7	32	44	30
40–49	41	26	46	24	13	22	6	27	40	27
50–59	33	21	42	22	16	27	3	14	16	11
60–69	28	18	35	18	10	17	2	9	12	8
70–79	14	9	12	6	4	7	1	4.5	8	5
80–89	8	5	6	3	1	2	–	–	1	1
90–99	3	2	5	3	2	3	–	–	–	–
>100	2	1	–	–	–	–	–	–	1	1
totals	159		192		59		22		147	

b) unretouched flakes only

length (mm)	LDP 104 no	%	LDP 102 no	%	LDP 080 no	%	LDP 081 no	%	LDP 081A no	%
10–19	–	–	–	–	–	–	–	–	3	2
20–29	5	5	11	7	1	2	2	11	22	17
30–39	14	15	28	17	10	21	6	31	39	31
40–49	21	23	36	22	10	21	5	26	31	25
50–59	21	23	46	28	11	24	3	16	13	10
60–69	19	21	25	15	9	20	2	11	12	10
70–79	8	9	9	5	3	6	1	5	4	3
80–89	1	2	3	2	1	2	–	–	1	1
90–99	–	–	5	3	2	4	–	–	–	–
>100	2	2	1	1	–	–	–	–	1	1
totals	91		164		47		19		126	

Table 40   Distribution of scraper characteristics

	LDP 104	LDP 102	LDP 080	LDP 081	LDP 081A
cortex					
none	4	5	1	2	1
<1/3	1	2	–	1	1
1/3–2/3	1	1	1	–	2
retouch					
regular	3	6	–	2	1
irregular	3	2	2	1	3
hammer					
hard	3	2	2	1	3
soft	3	6	–	2	1
flake type					
preparation flake	1	–	1	–	–
unretouched flake	5	8	1	3	–
number of sides worked					
one	2	2	1	1	2
two	3	3	1	2	1
three	1	3	–	–	1

Table 41   Patination of all struck flint by assemblage

	LDP 104		LDP 102		LDP 080		LDP 081		LDP 081A	
degree of patination	no	%	no	%	no	%	no	%	no	%
none	78	26	11	3	2	2	17	29	50	22
light	133	44	181	51	46	48	28	49	146	64
heavy	91	30	163	46	48	50	13	22	32	14
totals	302		355		96		58		228	

Table 42   Distribution of flake categories by assemblage

	LDP 104		LDP 102		LDP 080		LDP 081		LDP 081A	
flake category	no	%	no	%	no	%	no	%	no	%
shatter fragment	21	9	8	2	2	2	–	–	2	1
preparation flake	50	20	22	7	7	8	2	4	5	2
trimming flake	40	16	19	6	8	10	5	11	22	10
dressing chip	–	–	–	–	–	–	–	–	13	6
other unretouched flakes	134	55	276	85	67	80	41	85	179	81
totals	245		325		84		48		221	

Table 43   Amount of cortex on flakes by assemblage

	LDP 104		LDP 102		LDP 080		LDP 081		LDP 081A	
degree of cortication	no	%	no	%	no	%	no	%	no	%
none	74	30	139	43	32	38	27	56	105	48
<1/3	86	35	127	39	36	43	18	37.5	84	38
1/3–2/3	34	14	33	10	7	8	3	6.5	23	10
>2/3	51	21	26	8	9	11	–	–	9	4
totals	245		325		84		48		221	

Table 44   Distribution of distal termination types by assemblage

distal termination	LDP 104 no	%	LDP 102 no	%	LDP 080 no	%	LDP 081 no	%	LDP 081A no	%
normal	34	15	101	37	18	25	13	40	84	41
hinged	47	21	59	22	10	14	3	9	39	19
cortical	81	37	57	21	22	30	8	24	46	22
faceted	59	27	55	20	23	31	9	27	37	18
totals	221		272		73		33		206	

Table 45   Distribution of distal termination types by flake type and assemblage

a) preparation flakes

distal termination	LDP 104 no	%	LDP 102 no	%	LDP 080 no	%	LDP 081 no	%	LDP 081A no	%
normal	1	2	2	9	–	–	–	–	1	20
hinged	11	20	4	17	–	–	–	–	1	20
cortical	33	60	14	61	3	43	–	–	2	40
faceted	10	18	3	13	4	57	–	–	1	20
totals	55		23		7		–		5	

b) trimming flakes

	LDP 104 no	%	LDP 102 no	%	LDP 080 no	%	LDP 081 no	%	LDP 081A no	%
normal	8	22	8	50	3	33.3	2	50	6	33
hinged	6	16	3	19	1	11.1	1	25	4	22
cortical	12	32	1	6	2	22.2	–	–	3	17
faceted	11	30	4	25	3	33.3	1	25	5	28
totals	37		16		9		4		18	

c) other unretouched flakes

	LDP 104 no	%	LDP 102 no	%	LDP 080 no	%	LDP 081 no	%	LDP 081A no	%
normal	24	19	83	36	15	27	13	45	65	38
hinged	29	23	53	23	10	18	2	6	35	21
cortical	38	30	43	18	16	28	8	28	38	22
faceted	36	28	53	23	15	27	6	21	32	19
totals	127		232		56		29		170	

Table 46   Composition of flint assemblages

category	LDP 104 no	%	LDP 102 no	%	LDP 080 no	%	LDP 081 no	%	LDP 081A no	%
flakes	236	78	296	84	82	85	41	71	209	92
cores	55	19	30	8	12	12	10	17	7	3
retouched pieces	11	3	29	8	2	3	7	12	12	5
totals	302		355		96		58		228	

Table 47   Core data

a) distribution of mean core weights (in grams)

	LDP 104	*LDP 102*	*LDP 080*	*LDP 081*	*LDP 081A*
	154	142	93	73	121

b) distribution of platform cores and
bashed lumps

core category	*no*	*%*	*no*	*%*	*no*	*%*	*no*	*%*	*no*	*%*
platform cores	39	71	25	83	12	100	9	90	6	86
bashed lumps	16	29	5	17	–	–	1	10	1	14
totals	55		30		12		10		7	

c) patination on cores
category

	no	*%*	*no*	*%*	*no*	*%*	*no*	*%*	*no*	*%*
all struck surfaces identical	36	65	26	67	11	92	10	100	7	100
some struck surfaces different	19	35	4	13	1	8	–	–	–	–
totals	55		30		12		10		7	

d) distribution of step/hinge fractures
category

	no	*%*	*no*	*%*	*no*	*%*	*no*	*%*	*no*	*%*
<1/3	26	47	21	70	8	67	9	90	5	71
1/3–2/3	26	47	9	30	4	33	1	10	2	29
>2/3	3	6	–	–	–	–	–	–	–	–
totals	55		30		12		10		7	

e) amount of cortex on cores
degree of cortication

	no	*%*	*no*	*%*	*no*	*%*	*no*	*%*	*no*	*%*
none	6	11	2	7	4	34	6	60	2	29
<1/3	22	40	20	66	6	50	4	40	4	57
1/3–2/3	14	25	6	20	1	8	–	–	1	14
>2/3	13	24	2	7	1	8	–	–	–	–
totals	55		30		12		10		7	

f) rates of platform rejuvenation
category

	no	*%*	*no*	*%*	*no*	*%*	*no*	*%*	*no*	*%*
with rejuvenation	6	14	11	44	7	50	4	50	2	33.3
without rejuvenation	37	86	14	56	7	50	4	50	4	66.6
totals	43		25		14		8		6	

g) proportion of the circumference
of striking platforms worked
category

	no	*%*	*no*	*%*	*no*	*%*	*no*	*%*	*no*	*%*
<1/3	7	17	2	9	–	–	1	17	–	–
1/3–2/3	23	55	6	29	3	30	1	17	2	40
>2/3	12	28	13	62	7	70	4	66	3	60
totals	42		21		10		6		5	

Table 48   Distribution of retouched flakes by assemblage

	LDP 104	LDP 102	LDP 080	LDP 081	LDP 081A
regular tools					
scrapers	4	6	1	1	4
end scrapers	2	1	1	1	–
side scrapers	–	1	–	1	–
borers/awls	–	3	–	1	–
knives	1	1	–	–	–
irregular tools					
notches	–	1	–	1	1
utilised flakes	–	12	–	2	5
irregular tools (composite)					
scraper/notch	1	1	–	1	1
borer/utilised flake	–	2	–	–	–
% of retouched tools*	3	8	3	12	5

*percentage of retouched tools expressed as a proportion of the total number of struck flakes within each assemblage

Appendix 4   Sub-fossil mollusca from excavation sites

Table 49   Species list for LDP 101 (nomenclature follows Kerney 1976)

depth (cm)	20/30	30/45	45/52	53/60	60/70	70/75	75/90	90/95	95/102	102/110	110/125
context	1	3	3	3	4	4	4	5	27	27	34
P. elegans (Müller)	5	4	2	–	1	1	2	6	2	–	2
C. tridentatum (Risso)	–	–	–	–	1	5	20	35	19	16	38
C. lubrica (Müller)	–	–	–	–	2	–	–	7	7	–	8
C. lubricella (Porro)	–	–	2	1	3	1	1	3	1	2	3
Cochlicopa spp.	2	3	3	–	–	–	3	12	1	2	–
V. pygmaea (Draparnaud)	1	12	7	4	7	8	1	4	1	2	–
P. muscorum (Linnaeus)	6	74	64	7	40	42	43	14	9	8	7
V. costata (Müller)	+	+	17	7	14	19	17	9	5	4	2
V. excentrica (Sterki)	3	32	47	13	12	43	39	19	2	3	3
A. aculeata (Müller)	–	–	–	–	–	–	1	18	9	–	–
E. obscura (Müller)	–	–	–	–	–	–	2	2	1	2	–
P. pygmaeum (Draparnaud)	3	1	1	4	3	5	6	7	3	3	7
D. rotundatus (Müller)	–	1	2	1	★	9	11	37	37	14	15
Limacidae	3	–	6	–	6	8	4	2	–	8	1
V. pellucida (Müller)	–	–	4	–	–	1	1	3	2	1	2
V. crystallina (Müller)	–	–	–	–	–	–	6	7	14	9	1
V. contracta (Westerlund)	–	–	–	–	–	–	3	5	11	–	5
N. hammonis (Ström)	–	1	5	–	1	2	2	3	1	2	1
A. pura (Alder)	1	–	–	–	–	6	12	48	30	23	20
A. nitidula (Draparnaud)	–	–	4	2	–	–	6	24	21	7	16
O. cellarius (Müller)	1	1	2	–	1	2	–	9	2	3	2
O. alliarius (Miller)	–	–	–	–	–	–	–	3	4	–	5
C. laminata (Montagu)	–	–	–	–	–	–	1	5	–	–	–
C. bidentata (Ström)	–	–	2	–	–	–	+	6	1	–	–
Clausiliidae	1	1	–	1	1	–	1	–	5	3	1
H. itala (Linnaeus)	5	23	18	7	11	19	64	22	14	5	5
T. striolata (C. Pfeiffer)	–	–	–	–	–	1	–	–	–	–	–
T. hispida (Linnaeus)	4	75	86	10	12	36	11	252	155	61	60
C. nemoralis (Linnaeus)	–	–	1	–	–	–	–	–	–	–	–
Cepaea spp./Arianta	–	3	2	+	2	1	+	3	7	3	4
total shells	35	231	275	57	117	209	257	565	364	181	208
number of taxa	12	13	19	11	16	18	23	27	26	21	22
D2	0.89	0.76	0.81	0.86	0.83	0.86	0.87	0.78	0.79	0.85	0.86
D4	7.91	3.15	4.22	6.12	4.89	6.35	6.59	3.50	3.74	5.46	5.96

+ = present as a non-apical fragment

Table 50　Species list for LDP 027A (nomenclature follows Kerney 1976)

depth (cm)	0/23	23/26	26/33	33/39	39/45	45/50	52/58	58/65	65/69	69/75	75/80	80/85	85/90	90/100
context	1	1	2	3	4	4	4	5	5	6	7	7	7	7
P. elegans (Müller)	1	3	1	4	3	5	7	3	5	2	4	3	2	4
C. tridentatum (Risso)	–	–	–	–	–	–	–	–	–	–	–	–	–	1
C. lubricella (Porro)	–	13	19	14	16	24	31	16	15	28	28	34	47	17
Cochlicopa spp.	2	–	–	–	–	–	–	–	–	–	–	3	–	–
V. pygmaea (Draparnaud)	18	35	42	25	21	27	37	41	15	10	11	10	12	7
P. muscorum (Linnaeus)	38	252	362	345	502	478	485	404	238	206	186	261	223	85
V. costata (Müller)	–	4	22	25	60	59	121	64	85	56	114	152	127	47
V. excentrica (Sterki)	86	138	166	84	145	180	238	374	167	191	114	145	121	43
P. pygmaeum (Draparnaud)	3	6	20	6	12	9	16	19	17	12	19	22	18	11
D. rotundatus (Müller)	–	–	1	–	1	–	–	–	–	–	–	–	–	–
Limacidae	9	5	1	9	8	9	10	7	7	5	6	4	3	3
V. pellucida (Müller)	–	1	–	–	–	–	–	–	1	2	4	2	5	3
V. contracta (Westerlund)	–	–	–	–	–	–	–	–	–	–	1	–	–	1
N. hammonis (Ström)	–	–	–	–	–	1	1	7	2	6	12	18	31	25
A. nitidula (Draparnaud)	–	–	–	–	–	–	–	–	–	1	–	–	–	1
O. cellarius (Müller)	–	–	–	–	–	–	–	–	–	1	–	–	–	–
Zonitidae	–	1	–	–	–	–	–	–	–	–	–	2	–	–
C. acicula (Müller)	–	–	–	–	–	1	–	–	–	–	–	–	–	–
Clausiliidae	–	1	1	1	–	–	1	–	2	–	–	1	1	2
C. intersecta (Poiret)	–	–	–	–	–	–	–	–	–	–	–	1	–	–
C. gigaxii (L. Pfeiffer)	2	3	1	–	–	–	–	–	–	–	–	–	–	–
H. itala (Linnaeus)	9	46	47	41	46	43	55	50	27	63	51	55	57	36
T. hispida (Linnaeus)	12	27	11	13	28	41	47	41	23	34	16	37	13	6
Cepaea spp./Arianta	–	1	+	–	+	1	1	–	+	+	–	1	–	+
total shells	180	536	694	567	842	876	1050	1026	604	617	566	751	660	292
number of taxa	10	15	14	11	12	13	13	11	14	15	13	17	13	17
D2	0.71	0.70	0.66	0.60	0.60	0.65	0.71	0.70	0.74	0.77	0.80	0.79	0.80	0.84
D4	2.41	2.30	1.94	1.48	1.53	1.85	2.50	2.35	2.89	3.31	3.93	3.75	3.97	5.20

+ = present as a non-apical fragment

Table 51 Species list for LDP 027B (nomenclature follows Kerney 1976)

depth (cm)	0/23	23/30	32/38	38/43	43/47	50/55	55/60	60/65	65/70
context	1	9	10	11	11	12	12	12	12
P. elegans (Müller)	+	14	26	93	50	60	54	55	34
C. tridentatum (Risso)	–	1	5	12	53	97	81	105	27
C. lubricella (Porro)	5	18	11	1	–	–	–	–	–
Cochlicopa spp.	–	–	–	2	9	6	4	3	5
V. pygmaea (Draparnaud)	21	9	5	5	2	2	1	–	–
P. muscorum (Linnaeus)	73	138	64	37	12	5	9	8	7
V. costata (Müller)	–	87	56	19	–	2	2	8	4
V. excentrica (Sterki)	95	179	55	23	13	7	3	4	6
A. aculeata (Müller)	–	–	–	–	–	8	5	7	2
E. obscura (Müller)	–	–	–	1	–	–	–	–	1
E. montana (Draparnaud)	–	–	–	1	1	–	2	1	–
P. pygmaeum (Draparnaud)	5	5	4	3	2	4	–	–	–
D. rotundatus (Müller)	–	–	+	10	15	33	14	18	13
Limacidae	11	5	–	3	1	–	–	–	–
V. pellucida (Müller)	2	–	–	–	–	–	–	6	–
Vitrea spp.	–	–	3	1	–	–	–	–	–
V. crystallina (Müller)	–	–	–	–	3	9	1	4	–
V. contracta (Westerlund)	–	–	–	–	2	3	4	–	–
N. hammonis (Ström)	1	8	4	5	4	1	3	3	7
A. pura (Alder)	–	1	–	2	3	16	11	12	3
A. nitidula (Draparnaud)	–	–	1	3	9	3	8	9	–
O. cellarius (Müller)	–	–	–	–	3	9	2	2	7
O. alliarius (Miller)	–	–	–	–	1	3	–	–	2
C. laminata (Montagu)	–	–	3	2	5	–	1	2	2
C. bidentata (Ström)	–	–	5	7	4	8	7	10	6
Clausiliidae	–	4	–	–	–	–	–	2	–
C. intersecta (Poiret)	1	–	–	–	–	–	–	–	–
C. gigaxii (I. Pfeiffer)	3	–	–	–	–	–	–	–	–
H. itala (Linnaeus)	31	83	18	6	1	2	2	5	1
T. striolata (C. Pfeiffer)	–	–	–	–	–	–	–	–	1
T. hispida (Linnaeus)	19	57	7	5	19	13	5	2	6
Cepaea spp./Arianta	3	2	2	6	10	4	4	6	2
total shells	270	611	269	247	222	295	223	272	136
number of taxa	13	15	16	22	23	21	21	21	20
D2	0.78	0.81	0.84	0.81	0.87	0.83	0.80	0.80	0.87
D4	3.47	4.37	5.26	4.35	6.58	4.80	3.91	3.92	6.85

+ = present as a non-apical fragment

Table 52 Species list for LDP 083 (nomenclature follows Kerney 1976)

depth (cm)	0/12	12/20	20/27	27/37	37/48	50/55	55/60	60/67	67/75	75/80	80/85	85/90	90/95	95/100	100/110	110/120	120/140
context	1	1	1	2	2	3	3	3	3	4	5	5	5	5	5	6	6
P. elegans (Müller)	1	3	12	4	3	10	5	3	6	4	9	3	2	1	4	3	+
C. lubrica (Müller)	–	–	–	–	1	1	–	–	–	–	–	–	–	–	–	–	–
C. lubricella (Porro)	–	7	3	1	1	6	6	3	9	9	15	24	36	18	13	–	–
Cochlicopa spp.	–	–	–	–	–	–	–	–	–	–	–	–	–	–	–	1	1
V. pygmaea (Draparnaud)	5	9	10	2	1	14	20	51	55	10	27	12	11	–	1	–	–
P. muscorum (Linnaeus)	15	42	73	78	101	573	686	71	643	575	491	465	467	335	165	55	13
V. costata (Müller)	–	6	24	16	12	60	84	110	414	320	300	503	678	433	129	15	–
V. excentrica (Sterki)	15	14	49	23	15	46	83	185	397	262	243	223	269	248	94	7	2
P. pygmaeum (Draparnaud)	–	–	5	1	–	5	6	18	32	26	37	64	51	31	19	2	–
D. rotundatus (Müller)	–	–	+	–	–	–	–	–	–	–	1	–	–	1	–	–	–
Limacidae	3	3	2	–	–	1	1	–	7	3	2	1	3	4	3	–	–
V. pellucida (Müller)	5	–	–	–	–	–	–	–	–	–	–	5	9	9	7	1	–
N. hammonis (Ström)	–	–	1	–	–	–	–	–	–	–	–	–	–	–	–	–	–
A. pura (Alder)	1	1	–	–	–	1	–	1	–	–	–	–	1	–	–	–	–
O. cellarius (Müller)	–	–	–	–	–	–	–	–	–	–	–	–	1	–	–	–	–
Clausiliidae	1	2	1	2	1	2	2	2	–	3	1	1	1	–	1	1	–
C. intersecta (Poiret)	–	–	1	–	–	–	–	–	–	–	–	–	–	–	–	–	–
C. gigaxii (L. Pfeiffer)	5	4	–	–	–	–	–	–	–	–	–	–	–	–	–	–	–
H. itala (Linnaeus)	–	1	17	6	4	38	42	53	78	51	61	80	107	76	33	11	1
T. hispida (Linnaeus)	17	4	11	3	3	19	95	27	36	9	5	1	–	2	5	–	1
Cepaea spp./Arianta	–	1	+	+	+	–	2	–	2	–	1	1	1	+	+	–	+
total shells	68	97	209	136	142	776	1032	1024	1679	1272	1193	1383	1637	1158	474	96	18
number of taxa	10	13	13	10	10	13	12	11	11	11	13	13	14	11	12	9	5
D2	0.82	0.77	0.79	0.62	0.47	0.44	0.53	0.64	0.73	0.69	0.72	0.72	0.71	0.73	0.76	0.63	0.46
D4	4.58	3.30	3.85	1.66	0.89	0.79	1.15	1.77	2.74	2.20	2.59	2.61	2.50	2.64	3.13	1.67	0.79

+ = present as a non-apical fragment

Table 53   Species list for LDP 097 (nomenclature follows Kerney 1976)

depth (cm)	20/31	31/37	37/43	43/52	52/60	60/70	70/80	80/87	87/97	97/108
context	Ah 3	SH 3	Ah 4	SH 4	5	5	5	5	8	9
P. elegans (Müller)	6	+	5	1	1	+	+	+	5	2
C. lubricella (Porro)	3	1	6	17	29	15	25	31	32	16
Cochlicopa spp.	–	1	–	–	–	–	–	–	–	–
V. pygmaea (Draparnaud)	2	+	7	4	26	35	17	10	11	1
P. muscorum (Linnaeus)	51	25	365	363	464	351	417	302	214	98
V. costata (Müller)	4	1	17	49	149	173	162	185	233	143
V. excentrica (Sterki)	58	20	55	110	195	221	122	132	171	44
P. pygmaeum (Draparnaud)	1	1	–	8	8	3	6	12	16	7
D. rotundatus (Müller)	+	–	+	1	–	–	1	+	–	1
Limacidae	7	2	4	1	2	–	2	3	7	–
V. pellucida (Müller)	–	–	–	–	–	–	1	–	–	–
N. hammonis (Ström)	1	2	–	–	2	–	3	10	20	4
A. pura (Alder)	–	–	–	–	–	1	–	–	–	–
C. bidentata (Ström)	2	–	–	–	–	–	–	–	–	+
Clausiliidae	–	–	1	–	–	–	–	–	–	–
C. gigaxii (I. Pfeiffer)	11	–	6	–	–	–	–	–	–	–
H. itala (Linnaeus)	10	11	10	56	48	37	56	61	81	47
T. hispida (Linnaeus)	2	1	4	23	50	51	8	4	3	+
Cepaea spp./Arianta	+	+	–	+	+	2	+	1	1	+
total shells	158	65	480	633	974	889	820	751	794	363
number of taxa	13	10	11	11	11	10	12	11	12	10
D2	0.75	0.73	0.41	0.62	0.70	0.74	0.67	0.74	0.78	0.74
D4	2.95	2.62	0.68	1.66	2.36	2.81	2.07	2.81	3.57	2.81

+ = present as a non-apical fragment

Table 54   Species list for LDP 092A (nomenclature follows Kerney 1976)

depth (cm)	0/19	19/27	27/32	32/40	40/50	50/60	60/65	66/73	73/80	80/90	90/100	100/120	120/135
context	1	1	1	5	5	5	6	6	8	8	8	9	9
P. elegans (Müller)	3	1	1	+	1	1	2	6	2	2	1	+	1
C. lubricella (Porro)	13	13	10	18	24	22	18	7	4	2	–	–	2
V. pygmaea (Draparnaud)	16	15	21	9	13	10	8	1	2	–	1	2	1
P. muscorum (Linnaeus)	211	519	412	470	627	496	417	93	62	74	49	32	31
V. costata (Müller)	12	43	69	85	90	242	247	106	30	19	17	14	21
V. excentrica (Sterki)	86	69	93	83	101	204	257	72	33	4	3	14	21
E. obscura (Müller)	–	–	1	–	–	–	–	–	–	–	–	–	–
P. pygmaeum (Draparnaud)	5	4	10	8	11	6	6	1	2	–	1	–	1
Limacidae	10	7	4	7	5	6	5	–	–	1	–	–	1
V. pellucida (Müller)	1	2	1	–	–	1	3	9	12	–	–	–	–
V. crystallina (Müller)	–	–	–	–	–	–	–	1	–	–	–	–	–
Clausiliidae	–	1	–	–	–	1	1	1	1	–	–	–	–
C. gigaxii (L. Pfeiffer)	3	–	2	–	–	–	–	–	–	–	–	–	–
C. virgata (Da Costa)	4	1	–	–	–	–	–	–	–	–	–	–	–
H. itala (Linnaeus)	16	37	30	34	36	29	24	19	17	12	27	8	6
T. hispida (Linnaeus)	8	64	48	50	58	446	284	157	119	86	51	26	6
Cepaea spp./Arianta	–	1	–	–	–	+	–	–	–	–	–	+	+
total shells	388	777	702	764	966	1464	1272	473	284	200	150	96	91
number of taxa	13	14	13	9	10	12	12	12	11	8	8	6	10
D2	0.65	0.53	0.62	0.59	0.55	0.74	0.76	0.78	0.75	0.66	0.73	0.77	0.77
D4	1.84	1.14	1.63	1.44	1.24	2.92	3.23	3.45	2.94	1.98	2.72	3.26	3.30

+ = present as a non-apical fragment

Table 55   Species list for LDP 092B (nomenclature follows Kerney 1976)

depth (cm)	33/37	37/42	42/45	45/48	48/52
context	3	3	SH	A/C	A/C
P. elegans (Müller)	+	6	4	14	1
C. lubricella (Porro)	9	17	10	7	2
V. pygmaea (Draparnaud)	12	28	13	4	–
P. muscorum (Linnaeus)	52	200	129	72	26
V. costata (Müller)	101	216	165	105	39
V. excentrica (Sterki)	102	376	88	55	25
P. pygmaeum (Draparnaud)	4	13	3	1	–
Limacidae	2	8	1	3	3
V. pellucida (Müller)	–	1	–	1	2
N. hammonis (Ström)	–	–	–	1	–
A. pura (Alder)	–	1	–	–	–
C. acicula (Müller)	–	1	–	2	–
Clausiliidae	–	1	–	3	–
H. itala (Linnaeus)	21	77	62	37	11
T. hispida (Linnaeus)	2	27	53	68	19
H. lapicida (Linnaeus)	–	1	–	1	–
Cepaea spp./Arianta	–	2	2	3	–
total shells	305	974	530	375	128
number of taxa	9	15	11	16	9
D2	0.74	0.75	0.79	0.82	0.80
D4	2.87	3.02	3.79	4.51	3.92

+ = present as a non-apical fragment

Table 56   Species list for LDP 092C (nomenclature follows Kerney 1976)

depth (cm)	0/11	11/17	17/22	22/27	27/32	32/37	37/45
context	1	2	3(A)	3(A)	4	4	4
P. elegans (Müller)	1	1	8	8	29	49	7
C. tridentatum (Müller)	–	–	–	–	7	16	13
C. lubricella (Porro)	–	–	3	–	1	–	–
Cochlicopa spp.	1	–	–	6	2	1	2
V. pygmaea (Draparnaud)	4	1	3	1	–	+	2
P. muscorum (Linnaeus)	44	6	55	48	22	6	8
V. costata (Müller)	9	5	29	62	17	3	4
V. excentrica (Sterki)	27	6	45	42	12	4	1
A. aculeata (Müller)	–	–	–	–	–	2	–
E. montana (Draparnaud)	–	–	–	1	1	–	–
E. obscura (Müller)	–	–	–	–	1	–	1
P. pygmaeum (Draparnaud)	1	–	–	–	–	–	–
D. rotundatus (Müller)	–	–	–	2	2	22	46
Limacidae	4	1	6	3	9	5	4
V. crystallina (Müller)	–	–	–	–	1	–	–
N. hammonis (Ström)	–	–	–	–	–	–	1
A. pura (Alder)	–	–	–	1	3	1	3
A. nitidula (Draparnaud)	–	–	–	–	–	2	4
O. cellarius (Müller)	–	–	–	–	1	1	1
Clausiliidae	–	2	–	–	9	8	10
C. intersecta (Poiret)	4	–	–	–	–	–	–
C. gigaxii (I. Pfeiffer)	7	–	–	1	–	–	–
C. virgata (Da Costa)	5	–	–	–	–	–	–
H. itala (Linnaeus)	3	4	48	28	4	1	3
T. hispida (Linnaeus)	3	–	26	49	3	10	4
H. lapicida (Linnaeus)	–	–	–	–	1	1	5
Cepaea spp./Arianta	+	5	+	+	3	8	4
total shells	113	31	223	252	128	140	153
number of taxa	13	9	9	13	19	17	19
D2	0.77	0.85	0.82	0.82	0.88	0.82	0.83
D4	3.41	5.60	4.53	4.66	7.08	4.64	4.92

+ = present as a non-apical fragment

Table 57 Species list for LDP 052 (nomenclature follows Kerney 1976)

depth (cm)	130/140	140/150	150/160	160/170
context	5	5	5	5
P. elegans (Müller)	5	5	7	10
C. tridentatum (Müller)	–	–	–	2
C. lubricella (Porro)	1	1	5	2
V. pygmaea (Draparnaud)	1	1	1	2
P. muscorum (Linnaeus)	177	179	154	162
V. costata (Müller)	56	45	73	74
V. excentrica (Sterki)	7	7	12	7
A. aculeata (Müller)	–	–	–	1
P. pygmaeum (Draparnaud)	1	–	–	–
Limacidae	–	–	1	–
V. crystallina (Müller)	–	–	–	1
A. pura (Alder)	–	–	–	1
C. bidentata (Ström)	1	–	–	3
H. itala (Linnaeus)	40	28	47	38
T. hispida (Linnaeus)	–	–	–	8
H. lapicida (Linnaeus)	1	–	–	1
Cepaea spp./Arianta	1	2	+	2
total shells	290	368	300	313
number of taxa	11	8	8	14
D2	0.57	0.51	0.65	0.66
D4	1.32	1.05	1.86	1.93

+ = present as a non-apical fragment

Table 58 Species list for LDP 091 (nomenclature follows Kerney 1976)

depth (cm)	bank sequence					ditch sequence	
	0/14	14/23	23/30	30/35	35/40	115/125	125/135
context	1	4 (bank)	5 (Ah)	5 (SH)	A/C	9	9
P. elegans (Müller)	8	49	11	85	14	7	11
C. tridentatum (Risso)	–	1	4	3	–	6	1
C. lubricella (Porro)	4	4	13	9	1	5	6
V. pygmaea (Draparnaud)	13	8	33	11	3	12	8
P. muscorum (Linnaeus)	102	97	118	59	13	98	124
V. costata (Müller)	2	8	20	19	2	35	33
V. excentrica (Sterki)	77	69	168	111	17	66	44
A. aculeata (Müller)	–	–	–	–	–	1	1
E. obscura (Müller)	1	–	–	–	–	1	1
P. pygmaeum (Draparnaud)	4	–	4	–	–	13	1
D. rotundatus (Müller)	1	29	5	5	4	11	8
Limacidae	–	1	–	–	2	1	–
V. contracta (Westerlund)	2	2	–	–	–	–	1
N. hammonis (Ström)	–	–	1	3	–	–	–
A. pura (Alder)	1	5	4	2	3	6	5
A. nitidula (Draparnaud)	16	13	–	2	–	2	2
O. cellarius (Müller)	–	2	3	–	–	4	1
O. alliarius (Miller)	–	–	–	2	3	1	–
C. laminata (Montagu)	–	2	2	2	5	1	1
C. bidentata (Ström)	1	2	–	7	6	1	1
H. itala (Linnaeus)	13	15	35	23	4	19	15
T. hispida (Linnaeus)	49	8	9	1	2	2	4
H. lapicida (Linnaeus)	1	2	–	–	2	–	–
Cepaea spp./Arianta	2	10	3	5	1	1	4
total shells	297	327	433	349	81	293	272
number of taxa	17	18	16	17	16	21	20

Bibliography

Allen, M J, 1989   Landscape history, in Richards 1989

——, 1992   The environmental evidence, in Bellamy 1992, 41–5 and 55–63

——, Entwistle, R, and Richards, J, 1990   Molluscan studies, in Richards 1990, 253–8

Appelbaum, S, 1954   The agriculture of the British Early Iron Age as exemplified at Figheldean Down, Wiltshire, *Proc Prehist Soc*, **20**, 103–14

Arnold, C, 1972   The excavation of a prehistoric ranch boundary at Quarley Hill, *Proc Hampshire Fld Club Archaeol Soc*, **29**, 37–40

Arnold, D E, 1985   *Ceramic theory and cultural practice*, Cambridge

Ashbee, P, 1966   The Fussell's Lodge long barrow excavation, 1957, *Archaeologia*, **100**, 1–80

Atkinson, R J C, 1957   Worms and weathering, *Antiquity*, **31**, 219–33

Barrett, J C, 1976   Deverel-Rimbury: problems of chronology and interpretation, in *Settlement and economy in the third and second millennia BC* (eds C Burgess and R Miket), BAR, **33**, 289–307, Oxford

——, 1980a   The pottery of the later Bronze Age in lowland England, *Proc Prehist Soc*, **46**, 297–319

——, 1980b   The evolution of later Bronze Age settlement, in *Settlement and society in the British later Bronze Age* (eds J Barrett and R Bradley), BAR, **83**, 77–100, Oxford

——, 1989a   Food, gender and metal: questions of social reproduction, in *The Bronze Age Iron Age transition in Europe* (eds M L S Sørensen and R Thomas), BAR, **S483**, 304–20, Oxford

——, 1989b   Time and tradition: the rituals of everyday life, in *Bronze Age studies* (eds H A Nordström and A Knape), 113–26, Stockholm

——, 1991   Bronze Age pottery and the problem of classification, in *Papers on the prehistoric archaeology of Cranborne Chase* (eds J Barrett, R Bradley, and M Hall), Oxbow Monogr, **11**, 201–30, Oxford

——, and Bradley, R, 1980   Later Bronze Age settlement in south Wessex and Cranborne Chase, in *Settlement and society in the British later Bronze Age* (eds J Barrett and R Bradley), BAR, **83**, 181–208, Oxford

——, Bradley, R, Cleal R, and Pike, H, 1978   Characterization of Deverel-Rimbury pottery from Cranborne Chase, *Proc Prehist Soc*, **44**, 135–42

——, Bradley, R, and Green, M, 1991   *Landscape, monuments and society – the prehistory of Cranborne Chase*, Cambridge

——, and Kinnes, I (eds), 1988   *The archaeology of context in the Neolithic and Bronze Age: recent trends*, Recent Trends Ser, **3**, Sheffield

Bedwin, O, 1983   The development of prehistoric settlement on the West Sussex coastal plain, *Sussex Archaeol Coll*, **121**, 31–44

Bell, M, 1977   Excavations at Bishopstone, *Sussex Archaeol Coll*, **115**

——, 1981   Valley sediments and environmental change, in *The environment of man: the Iron Age to Anglo-Saxon period* (eds M Jones and G W Dimbleby), BAR, **87**, 75–91, Oxford

——, 1983   Valley sediments as evidence of prehistoric land-use on the South Downs, *Proc Prehist Soc*, **49**, 119–50

——, 1987   Recent mollusc studies in the south west, in *Studies in Palaeoeconomy and environment in south west England* (eds N D Balaam, B Levitan, and V Straker) BAR, **181**, 1–8, Oxford

——, 1989   The landsnails, in *Wilsford Shaft: excavations 1960–62* (eds P Ashbee, M Bell, and E Proudfoot), HBMCE Archaeol Rep, **11**, 99–103, London

——, 1990   Sedimentation rates in the primary fills of chalk-cut features, in *Experimentation and reconstruction in environmental archaeology (ed D E Robinson)*, Symposia Ass Envir Archaeol, **9**, 237–48, Oxford

——, and Jones, J, 1990   Land mollusca, in Richards 1990, 154–8

Bellamy, P, 1992   The investigation of the prehistoric landscape between Andover, Hampshire, and Amesbury, Wiltshire, 1984–7, *Proc Hampshire Fld Club Archaeol Soc*, **47**, 5–81

Bohmers, S A, 1956   Statistics and graphs in the study of flint assemblages, part 1, *Palaeohistoria*, **5**, 1–5

Bourdieu, P, 1977   *Outline of a theory of practice*, Cambridge

——, 1979   Symbolic power, *Critique Anthropol*, **13/14**, 77–85

Bowen, H C, 1961   *Ancient fields*, London

——, 1972   Air photography: some implications in the south of England, in *Field survey in British archaeology* (ed E Fowler), 38–49, CBA, London

——, 1975   Air photography and the development of the landscape in central parts of southern England, in *Aerial reconnaissance for archaeology* (ed D R Wilson), CBA Res Rep, **12**, 103–18, London

——, 1978   'Celtic' fields and 'ranch boundaries' in Wessex, in *The effect of man on the landscape: the lowland zone* (eds S Limbrey and J Evans), CBA Res Rep, **21**, 115–23, London

——, 1990   *The archaeology of Bokerley Dyke*, London

Bradley, R, 1971   Stock-raising and the origins of the hillfort on the South Downs, *Antiq J*, **51**, 8–29

——, 1978a   Prehistoric field systems in Britain and north-west Europe: a review of some recent work, *World Archaeol*, **9**, 265–98

——, 1978b   *The prehistoric settlement of Britain*, London

——, 1981   From ritual to romance: ceremonial enclosures and hill-forts, in *Hillfort studies* (ed G Guilbert), 20–27, Leicester

——, 1984   *The social foundations of prehistoric Britain*, London

——, 1986   The Bronze Age in the Oxford area: its local and regional significance, in *The archaeology of the Oxford Region* (eds G Briggs, J Cook, and T Rowley), 38–48, Oxford

——, 1990   *The passage of arms: an archaeological analysis of prehistoric hoards and votive deposits*, Cambridge

——, 1993   Archaeology and the river gravels from the Neolithic to the Early Iron Age, in *The archaeology of the river gravels* (ed M Fulford), Rep Res Comm Soc Antiq, London

——, and Ellison, A, 1975   *Rams Hill: a Bronze Age defended enclosure and its landscape*, BAR, **19**, Oxford

Braithwaite, M, 1982   Decoration as ritual symbol: a theoretical proposal and an ethnographic study in southern Sudan, in *Symbolic and structural archaeology* (ed I Hodder), 80–88, Cambridge

Braun, D P, 1983   Pots as tools, in *Archaeological hammers and theories* (eds J A Moore and S Arthur), 107–34, New York

Britnell, W J, 1976   Antler cheekpieces of the British later Bronze Age, *Antiq J*, **56**, 24–34

Bronitsky, G, and Hamer, R, 1986   Experiments in ceramic technology: the effects of various tempering materials on impact and thermal shock resistance, *American Antiquity*, **51**, 89–101

Brown, A, 1991   Structured deposition and technological change amongst flaked stone artefacts from Cranborne Chase, in *Papers on the prehistoric archaeology of Cranborne Chase* (eds J Barrett, R Bradley, and M Hall), Oxbow Monogr, **11**, 101–33, Oxford

Buckley, V (ed), 1990   *Burnt offerings*, Dublin

Burton, J, 1980   Making sense of waste flakes: new methods for investigating the technology and economics behind chipped stone assemblages, *J Archaeol Sci*, **7**, 131–48

Butler, J J, and Smith, I F, 1956   Razors, urns and the British Middle Bronze Age, *Annu Rep Univ London Inst Archaeol*, **12**, 20–52

Calkin, J B, 1962   The Bournemouth area in the Middle and Late Bronze Age, with the 'Deverel-Rimbury' problem reconsidered, *Archaeol J*, **119**, 1–65

Cameron, R A D, and Morgan-Huws, D I, 1975   Snail faunas in the early stage of a chalk grassland succession, *Biol J Linnean Soc*, **7**, 215–29

Canham, R, and Chippindale, C, 1988   Managing for effective archaeological conservation: the example of the Salisbury Plain Military Training Area, England, *J Fld Archaeol*, **15**, 53–65

Carter, S P, 1990   The stratification and taphonomy of shells in calcareous soils: implications for land snail analysis in archaeology, *J Archaeol Sci*, **17**, 495–507

Case, H J, 1977   The Beaker culture in Britain and Ireland, in *Beakers in Britain and Europe* (ed R Mercer), BAR, **S26**, 71–84, Oxford

Christie, P, 1964   A Bronze Age round barrow on Earls Farm Down, Amesbury, *Wiltshire Archaeol Natur Hist Mag*, **59**, 30–45

——, 1967   A barrow cemetery of the second millennium BC in Wiltshire, England, *Proc Prehist Soc*, **33**, 336–66

Clay, R C C, 1927   Some prehistoric ways, *Antiquity*, **1**, 54–65

Coles, J, and Harding, A, 1979   *The Bronze Age in Europe*, London

Colt Hoare, R, 1812   *The ancient history of south Wiltshire*, London

Conkey, M W, 1989   The use of diversity in stylistic analysis, in *Quantifying diversity in archaeology* (eds R D Leonard and G T Jones), 118–29, Cambridge

——, 1990   Experimenting with style in archaeology: some historical and theoretical issues, in *The uses of style in archaeology* (eds M Conkey and C Hastorf), 5–17, Cambridge

Coombs, D, 1979   The Figheldean Down hoard, Wiltshire, in *Bronze*

Age hoards (eds C Burgess and D Coombs), BAR, **67**, 253–68, Oxford

Crawford, O G S, 1924 *Air survey and archaeology*, Ordnance Survey Professional Pap, 7, Southampton

——, 1953 *Archaeology in the field*, London

——, and Keiller, A, 1928 *Wessex from the air*, Oxford

Cunliffe, B W, 1973 Chalton, Hants: the evolution of a landscape, *Antiq J*, **53**, 173–90

——, 1978 *Iron Age communities in Britain*, 2 edn, London

——, 1984a Iron Age Wessex, continuity and change, in *Aspects of the Iron Age in central southern Britain* (eds B Cunliffe and D Miles), 12–45, Oxford Univ Comm Archaeol, Oxford

——, 1984b *Danebury: an Iron Age hillfort in Hampshire, vol 1 and 2, The excavations 1969–1978*, CBA Res Rep, **52**, London

——, 1984c The Iron Age pottery, in Cunliffe 1984b, 231–331

——, 1990 Before hillforts, *Oxford J Archaeol*, **9**, 323–36

——, and Poole, C, 1991 *Danebury: an Iron Age hillfort in Hampshire, vols 4 and 5*, CBA Res Rep, **73**, London

Cunnington, B H, and Cunnington, M E, 1917 Lidbury Camp, *Wiltshire Archaeol Natur Hist Mag*, **40**, 12–36

Cunnington, M E, 1925 Figsbury Rings: an account of excavations in 1924, *Wiltshire Archaeol Natur Hist Mag*, **43**, 48–58

——, 1930 Romano-British Wiltshire, *Wiltshire Archaeol Natur Hist Mag*, **45**, 166–216

——, 1932 The demolition of Chisenbury Trendle, *Wiltshire Archaeol Natur Hist Mag*, **46**, 1–3

——, 1933 Excavations at Yarnbury Castle Camp, 1932, *Wiltshire Archaeol Natur Hist Mag*, **46**, 198–213

Cunnington, W, 1895 Opening of barrows, &c, near Haxton, *Wiltshire Archaeol Natur Hist Mag*, **28**, 172–3

Curwen, E, and Curwen, E C, 1917 Covered ways in the South Downs, *Sussex Archaeol Coll*, **59**, 35–75

——, 1923 Sussex lynchets and their associated fieldways, *Sussex Archaeol Coll*, **64**, 1–65

Curwen, E C, 1951 Cross-ridge dykes in Sussex, in *Aspects of archaeology* (ed W F Grimes), 93–107, London

Dacre, M, and Ellison, A, 1981 The Bronze Age urn cemetery at Kimpton, Hampshire, *Proc Prehist Soc*, **47**, 147–203

David, N, Sterner, J, and Gavua, K, 1988 Why pots are decorated, *Curr Anthropol*, **29**, 365–89

Davies, S, 1981 Excavations at Old Down Farm, Andover, part 2, *Proc Hampshire Fld Club Archaeol Soc*, **37**, 81–163

Davis, D D, 1985 Hereditary emblems: material culture in the context of social change, *J Anthropol Archaeol*, **4**, 149–76

Deboer, W R, 1990 Interaction, imitation, and communication as expressed in style: the Ucayali experience, in *The uses of style in archaeology* (eds M Conkey and C Hastorf), 82–104, Cambridge

Dent, J, 1982 Cemeteries and settlement patterns on the Yorkshire Wolds, *Proc Prehist Soc*, **48**, 437–57

Dietler, M, and Herbich, I, 1989 Tich Matek: the technology of Luo pottery production and the definition of ceramic style, *World Archaeol*, **21**, 148–64

Ellison, A, 1978 The Bronze Age of Sussex, in *Archaeology in Sussex to AD 1500* (ed P Drewett), CBA Res Rep, **29**, 30–37, London

——, 1980 Settlements and regional exchange: a case study, in *Settlement and society in the British later Bronze Age* (eds J Barrett and R Bradley), BAR, **83**, 127–40, Oxford

——, 1987 The Bronze Age settlement at Thorny Down: pots, postholes and patterning, *Proc Prehist Soc*, **53**, 385–92

——, and Harriss, J, 1972 Settlement and land use in the prehistory and early history of southern England: a study based on locational models, in *Models in archaeology* (ed D Clarke), 911–62, London

——, and Rahtz, P, 1987 Excavations at Whitsbury Castle Ditches, Hampshire, 1960, *Proc Hampshire Fld Club Archaeol Soc*, **43**, 63–81

Entwistle, R, 1989 *Relativism and interpretation in prehistoric archaeology: some thoughts on the formulation of archaeological evidence, with special reference to the use of palaeoenvironmental data*, unpubl PhD thesis, Univ Reading

——, in prep The excavation of a colluvial deposit on the floodplain of the river Avon at Countess Farm, Amesbury, Wiltshire

——, and Bowden, M, 1991 Cranborne Chase: the molluscan evidence, in *Papers on the prehistoric archaeology of Cranborne Chase* (eds J Barrett, R Bradley, and M Hall), Oxbow Monogr, **11**, 20–48, Oxford

Evans, J G, 1972 *Land snails in archaeology*, London

——, 1984 Stonehenge – the environment in the late Neolithic and Early Bronze Age and a Beaker burial, *Wiltshire Archaeol Natur Hist Mag*, **78**, 7–30

——, and Jones, H, 1979 The environment, in Wainwright 1979, 208–13

——, and Vaughan, M P, 1985 An investigation into the environment and archaeology of the Wessex linear ditch system, *Antiq J*, **65**, 11–38

Fasham, P J, 1980 Excavations at Bridget's and Burntwood Farms, Itchen Valley Parish, Hampshire, 1974 MARC sites R5 and R6, *Proc Hampshire Fld Club Archaeol Soc*, **36**, 37–86

——, Farwell, D E, and Whinney, R J B, 1989 *The archaeological site at Easton Lane, Winchester*, Hampshire Fld Club Archaeol Soc Monogr, **6**

Fleming, A, 1987 Coaxial field systems: some questions of time and space, *Antiquity*, **61**, 183–202

——, 1988 *The Dartmoor reaves: investigating prehistoric land divisions*, London

Ford, S, 1982a Linear earthworks on the Berkshire Downs, *Berkshire Archaeol J*, **71**, 1–20

——, 1982b Fieldwork and excavation on the Berkshire Grims Ditch, *Oxoniensia*, **47**, 13–36

——, 1987 Chronological and functional aspects of flint assemblages, in *Lithic analysis and later British prehistory* (eds A Brown and M Edmonds), BAR, **162**, 67–86, Oxford

——, Bowden, M, Mees, G, and Gaffney, V, 1988 The date of the 'Celtic' field systems on the Berkshire Downs, *Britannia*, **19**, 401–14

——, Bradley, R, Hawkes, J, and Fisher, P, 1984 Flint working in the metal age, *Oxford J Archaeol*, **3**, 157–73

Fowler, P J, 1964 Cross ridge dykes on the Ebble-Nadder ridge, *Wiltshire Archaeol Natur Hist Mag*, **59**, 46–57

——, 1983 *The farming of prehistoric Britain*, Cambridge

Gent, H, 1983 Centralised storage in later prehistoric Britain, *Proc Prehist Soc*, **49**, 243–67

Gingell, C, 1980 The Marlborough Downs in the Bronze Age: the first results of current research, in *Settlement and society in the British later Bronze Age* (eds J Barrett and R Bradley), BAR, **83**, 209–22, Oxford

——, 1992 *The Marlborough Downs: a later Bronze Age landscape and its origins*, Wiltshire Archaeol Natur Hist Monogr, **1**, Devizes

——, and Lawson, A, 1984a The Potterne Project: excavation and research at a major settlement of the Late Bronze Age, *Wiltshire Archaeol Natur Hist Mag*, **78**, 31–4

——, and Lawson, A, 1984b Excavations at Potterne, 1984, *Wiltshire Archaeol Natur Hist Mag*, **79**, 101–8

Gordon, D, and Ellis, C, 1985 Species composition parameters and life tables: their application to detect environmental change in fossil land molluscan assemblages, in *Palaeoenvironmental investigations* (eds N R J Fieller, D D Gilbertson, and N G A Ralph), BAR, **S258**, 157–74, Oxford

Grinsell, L V, 1957 Archaeological gazetteer, *Victoria county history of Wiltshire*, **1.1**, 21–279

——, 1958 *The archaeology of Wessex*, London

Guido, M, and Smith, I, 1982 Figsbury Rings: a reconsideration of the inner enclosure, *Wiltshire Archaeol Natur Hist Mag*, **76**, 21–5

Harding, A, and Lee, G, 1987 *Henge monuments and related sites of Great Britain*, BAR, **175**, Oxford

Harding, P, 1990 The comparative analysis of four stratified flint assemblages and a knapping cluster, in Richards 1990, 213–25

——, 1991 *Recent archaeological excavations along the Durrington to Earl's Farm Down water main – Contract B4016*, Archive Report, Trust for Wessex Archaeology, Salisbury

Hawkes, C F C, 1931 Hill forts, *Antiquity*, **5**, 60–111

——, 1939 The excavations at Quarley Hill, 1938, *Proc Hampshire Fld Club Archaeol Soc*, **14.2**, 136–94

Hawley, W, 1910 Notes on barrows in south Wiltshire, *Wiltshire Archaeol Natur Hist Mag*, **36**, 615–28

Hill, J D, 1989 Rethinking the Iron Age, *Scottish Archaeol Rev*, **6**, 16–24

——, in press Denbury and the hillforts of Iron Age Wessex, in *Recent trends in Iron Age archaeology* (eds T Champion and J Collis), Sheffield

Hodder, I, 1977 The distribution of material culture items in the Baringo district, western Kenya, *Man*, **12**, 239–69

——, 1981 Pottery production and use; a theoretical discussion, in *Production and distribution: a ceramic viewpoint* (eds H Howard and

E Morris), BAR, **S120**, 215–20, Oxford
——, 1982 *Symbols in action*, Cambridge
——, 1986 *Reading the past*, Cambridge
——, 1988 Material culture texts and social change, a theoretical discussion and some archaeological examples, *Proc Prehist Soc*, **54**, 67–75
Holleyman, G, and Curwen, E C, 1935 Late Bronze Age lynchet-settlements on Plumpton Plain, Sussex, *Archaeologia*, 42, 53–76
Hurlbert, S H, 1971 The nonconcept of species diversity: a critique and alternative parameters, *Ecology*, **52**, 577–86

Jones, M, 1984 Regional patterns in crop production, in *Aspects of the Iron Age in central southern Britain* (eds B Cunliffe and D Miles), Univ Oxford Comm Archaeol Monogr, **2**

Kerney, M P, 1966 Snails and man in Britain, *J Conchol*, **26**, 3–14
Kerney, M P (ed), 1976 *Atlas of non-marine mollusca of the British Isles*, Conchol Soc, London
Kus, S, 1982 Matters material and ideal, in *Symbolic and structural archaeology* (ed I Hodder), 47–62, Cambridge

Lane Fox, A, 1868 An examination into the character and probable origin of the hillforts of Sussex, *Archaeologia*, **42**, 53–76
Larich, R, 1985 Spears, style and time among Maa-speaking pastoralists, *J Anthropol Archaeol*, **4**, 206–20

McOmish, D, 1989 Non-hillfort settlement and its implications, in *From Cornwall to Caithness: some aspects of British field archaeology* (ed M Bowden, M Mackay, and P Topping), BAR, **209**, 99–110, Oxford
Manby, T G, 1980 Bronze Age settlement in eastern Yorkshire, in *Settlement and society in the British later Bronze Age* (eds J Barrett and R Bradley), BAR, **83**, 307–70, Oxford
Megaw, J V S, 1967 Notes on Iron Age and Neolithic material from Sidbury Camp, *Wiltshire Archaeol Natur Hist Mag*, **62**, 115–7
Mercer, R, 1984 Everley Water Meadow, Iwerne Stepleton, Dorset, *Proc Dorset Natur Hist Archaeol Soc*, **106**, 110–11
Miller, D, 1985 *Artifacts as categories: a study of ceramic variability in central India*, Cambridge
Ministry of Defence, 1973 *Report of the Defence Lands Committee 1971–73*, HMSO, London
Morgan Evans, D, 1992 The paradox of Salisbury Plain, in *All Things Natural: Archaeology and the Green Debate* (eds L Macinnes and C Wickham-Jones), Oxbow Monogr, **21**, 76–80, Oxford
Mortimer, J R, 1905 *Forty years' researches in British and Saxon burial mounds in east Yorkshire*, London

Needham, S, 1981 *The Bulford-Helsbury manufacturing tradition: the production of Stogursey socketed axes during the later Bronze Age in southern Britain*, Brit Mus Occas Pap, **13**

Ohmuma, K, and Bergman, C, 1982 Experimental studies in the determination of flaking mode, *Bull Inst Archaeol Univ London*, **19**, 161–70

Palmer, R, 1983 Analysis of settlement features in the landscape of prehistoric Wessex, in *The impact of aerial reconnaissance on archaeology* (ed G Maxwell), CBA Res Rep, **49**, 41–53, London
——, 1984 *Danebury, an Iron Age hillfort in Hampshire: an aerial photographic interpretation of its environs*, Royal Commission on Historical Monuments (England), Suppl Ser, **6**, London
Passmore, A, 1931 A hoard of bronze implements from Donhead St Mary and a stone mould from Bulford in Farnham Museum, Dorset, *Wiltshire Archaeol Natur Hist Mag*, **45**, 373–6
Piggott, C M, 1942 Five Late Bronze Age enclosures in north Wiltshire, *Proc Prehist Soc*, **8**, 48–61
——, 1950 Late Bronze Age enclosures in Sussex and Wessex, *Proc Prehist Soc*, **16**, 193–5
Piggott, S, 1931 Ladle Hill – an unfinished hillfort, *Antiquity*, **5**, 474–85
——, 1973 The final phase of bronze technology, *Victoria county history of Wiltshire*, **1.2**, 376–407
Pitt Rivers, A L F, 1882 On excavations in the earthwork called Dane's Dyke at Flamborough in 1879; and on the earthworks of the Yorkshire Wolds, *J Anthropol Inst*, **11**, 455–70
——, 1898 *Excavations in Cranborne Chase, Volume IV*, privately printed, London
Powelsland, D, 1986 Excavations at Heslerton, North Yorkshire,

1978–82, *Archaeol J*, **143**, 53–173
——, 1988 Staple Howe in its landscape, in *Archaeology in eastern Yorkshire* (ed T Manby), 1017, Sheffield
Pred, A, 1986 *Place, practice and structure*, Oxford
Property Services Agency, 1986 *Archaeological Working Party Report 1984–1985*, Property Services Agency, South-west Region, Bristol
Pryor, F, 1980 *Excavations at Fengate, Peterborough: the third report*, Royal Ontario Museum, Toronto

Rahtz, P, 1990 Excavations at Great Ditch Banks and Middle Chase Ditch, *Wiltshire Archaeol Natur Hist Mag*, **83**, 1–49
Raymond, F, 1990 The prehistoric pottery, in Richards 1990, 199–207
——, forthcoming in N Thomas forthcoming
Richards, J C, 1984 The development of the Neolithic landscape in the environs of Stonehenge, in *Neolithic studies* (eds R Bradley and J Gardiner), BAR, **133**, 177–88, Oxford
——, 1989 *Excavations at the SPTA FIBUA site, Copehill Down 1987–8*, Trust for Wessex Archaeology, Salisbury
——, 1990 *The Stonehenge environs project*, HBMCE Archaeol Rep, **16**, London
Richardson, K M, 1951 The excavation of Iron Age Villages on Boscombe Down West, *Wiltshire Archaeol Natur Hist Mag*, **54**, 123–68
Ride, D, and James, D, 1989 An account of an excavation at a prehistoric flint mine at Martins Clump, Over Wallop, Hampshire, *Proc Hampshire Fld Club Archaeol Soc*, **45**, 213–19
Riley, H, 1990 The scraper assemblages and petit tranchet derivative arrowheads, in Richards 1990, 225–8
Royal Commission on Historical Monuments (England), 1970 *Dorset III: central*, London
——, 1972 *Dorset IV: north*, London
——, 1979 *Stonehenge and its environs*, Edinburgh
Rye, O S, 1976 Keeping your temper under control: materials and the manufacture of Papuan pottery, *Archaeol Phys Anthropol Oceania*, **11**, 106–37

Salisbury Plain Training Area (SPTA) Archaeological Overlay, Wiltshire Library and Museum Service, Trowbridge
Sharples, N, 1991a *Maiden Castle: excavations and field survey 1985–6*, HBMCE Archaeol Rep, **19**, London
——, 1991b Warfare in the Iron Age of Wessex, *Scottish Archaeol Rev*, **8**, 79–89
Shepard, A O, 1956 *Ceramics for the archaeologist*, Carnegie Institute Washington Publ, **609**
Smith, I F, 1991 Round barrows Wilsford cum Lake G51–G54. Excavations by Ernest Greenfield in 1958, *Wiltshire Archaeol Natur Hist Mag*, **84**, 11–39
Smith, M A, 1959 Some Somerset hoards and their place in the Bronze Age of southern Britain, *Proc Prehist Soc*, **25**, 144–87
Soja, E W, 1985 The spatiality of social life: towards a transformative retheorisation, in *Social relations and spatial structure* (eds D Gregory and J Urry), 90–127, Hong Kong
Spratt, D, 1982a The Cleave Dyke system, *Yorkshire Archaeol J*, **54**, 33–52
——, 1982b *The prehistoric and Roman archaeology of north-east Yorkshire*, BAR, **104**, Oxford
——, 1989 *Linear earthworks of the Tabular Hills, north-east Yorkshire*, Sheffield
Stone, J F S, 1931 Easton Down, Winterslow, S Wilts, flint mine excavation, 1930, *Wiltshire Archaeol Natur Hist Mag*, **44**, 350–65
——, 1932 Saxon interments on Roche Court Down, Winterslow, *Wiltshire Archaeol Natur Hist Mag*, **45**, 583–99
——, 1933a Excavations on Easton Down, Winterslow, 1931–1932, *Wiltshire Archaeol Natur Hist Mag*, **46**, 225–42
——, 1933b A Middle Bronze Age urnfield on Easton Down, Winterdown, *Wiltshire Archaeol Natur Hist Mag*, **46**, 218–24
——, 1934 Three 'Peterborough' dwelling pits and a double-stockaded Early Iron Age ditch at Winterbourne Dauntsey, *Wiltshire Archaeol Natur Hist Mag*, **46**, 445–53
——, 1935 Excavations at Easton Down, Winterslow 1933–1934, *Wiltshire Archaeol Natur Hist Mag*, **47**, 68–80
——, 1936 An enclosure on Boscombe Down East, *Wiltshire Archaeol Natur Hist Mag*, **47**, 466–89
——, 1941 The Deverel Rimbury site on Thorny Down, Winterbourne Gunner, south Wilsthire, *Proc Prehist Soc*, 7, 114–33
Stopford, J, 1987 Danebury: an alternative view, *Scottish Archaeol Rev*, **4**, 70–75

Taylor, C C, 1970　*Dorset*, London

——, 1972　The study of settlement patterns in pre-Saxon Britain, in *Man, settlement and urbanism* (eds P Ucko, R Tringham, and G Dimbleby), 109–13, London

Terry, R D, and Chillingar, G V, 1955　Summary of 'Concerning some additional aids in studying sedimentary formations' by M S Shvetsov, *J Sedimentary Petrol*, **25**, 229–34

Thomas, J, 1991　*Rethinking the Neolithic*, Cambridge

Thomas, K D, 1977　A preliminary report on the mollusca from the lynchet section, in Bell 1977, 258–64

——, 1982　Neolithic enclosures and woodland habitats on the South Downs in Sussex, England, in *Archaeological aspects of woodland ecology* (eds M Bell and S Limbrey), BAR, **S146**, 147–70, Oxford

——, 1985　Land snail analysis in archaeology: theory and practice, in *Palaeoenvironmental investigations* (eds N R J Fieller, D D Gilbertson, and N G A Ralph), BAR, **S258**, 131–48, Oxford

Thomas, N, 1956　Excavation and fieldwork in Wiltshire: 1956, *Wiltshire Archaeol Natur Hist Mag*, **56**, 240–41

——, forthcoming　Snail Down report

——, and Thomas, C, 1956　Excavations at Snail Down, Everleigh: 1953, 1955, an interim report, *Wiltshire Archaeol Natur Hist Mag*, **56**, 127–48

Thorley, A, 1971　Vegetational history in the Vale of the Brooks, in *Guide to Sussex excursions* (ed R B G Williams), 47–50

——, 1981　Pollen analytical evidence relating to the vegetation history of the chalk, *J Biogeography*, **8**, 93–106

Tilley, C, 1982　Social formation, social structures and social change, in *Symbolic and structural archaeology* (ed I Hodder), 26–38, Cambridge

Toms, H, 1917　Record of the Mill Fields valley entrenchment and covered way, Willingdon Hill, *Trans Eastbourne Natur Hist Soc*, (Jan 1917), 45–53

Wainwright, G J, 1979　*Mount Pleasant, Dorset, excavations 1970–71*, Rep Res Comm Soc Antiq London, **37**, London

Wait, G, 1985　*Ritual and religion in Iron Age Britain*, BAR, **149**, Oxford

Waton, P, 1982　Man's impact on the chalkland: some new evidence, in *Aspects of woodland ecology* (eds M Bell and S Limbrey), BAR, **S146**, 75–91, Oxford

Wiessner, P, 1983　Style and social information in Kalahari San projectile points, *American Antiquity*, **48**, 253–76

——, 1985　Style or isochrestic variation? A reply to Sackett, *American Antiquity*, **50**, 160–66

——, 1990　Is there a unity to style, in *The uses of style in archaeology* (eds M Conkey and C Hastorf), 105–12, Cambridge

Wilkinson, J (ed), 1986　*Salisbury Plain Training Area Archaeological Working Party: report 1984–1985*, Property Services Agency, Western Regional Office, Bristol

Williams, G, 1990　Burnt mounds in south-west Wales, in *Burnt offerings* (ed V Buckley), 129–40, Dublin

Williams-Freeman, J P, 1915　*Field archaeology as illustrated by Hampshire*, London

Index

by Lesley and Roy Adkins

Main entries (if relevant) are in **bold**. Figures and tables are referred to by their number, not by their page number. For subheadings, dates are listed in chronological order rather than alphabetical order – for example, Late Bronze Age is listed before Iron Age. In entries with numerous subheadings (such as linear ditches and pottery), the subheadings relating to date are listed first (in chronological order), followed by the remaining subheadings in alphabetical order.

Ablington Down *see* LDP 105
Ablington Furze *see* LDP 106
aerial/air photography/photographs 1, 3, 4, 8, 17, 122, 123, 125, 126, 128, 135, 138, Fig 10
  appearance of linear features 36
  before afforestation 38, 46
  not studied 34
afforestation 23, 25, 38, 46
All Cannings Cross-Meon Hill pottery 89, 135
All Cannings Cross pottery 69, 74, **88–90**, 95, 123, 132, 145, Tables 5, 7, 15, 33; *see also* haematite-coated pottery
Anglo-Saxon pottery Table 1
animal bones Tables 8, 9, 11–14, 18, 20, 21, 46, 50, 53, Table 6
  report in archive 41
  small and fragmentary assemblages 41
  see also bones
antler
  cheek piece (possible) 46, 87, 146, Figs 35, 36, Table 11
  pick 46, 120, Table 9
arable cultivation *see* cultivation
archive 26, 29, 41
ard marks
  Dunch Hill 50
  Weather Hill 49, Figs 40, 41
augering/auger surveys 25, 26, **34–9**, 138
axes (flint) 31, 56, 57

banjo enclosures (associated with linear ditches) 13
banks (of linear ditches) 38, 40, 56, 74, 112–15, 116, 119, 123, 126, Figs 68, 69
barrow cemeteries 4, 21, 138, 151
  damage 23
  excavation 21
  linear ditches aligned with 141
  Snail Down 23, 133
barrows *see* round barrows
Beacon Hill
  buried soil 123
  charcoal 123
  excavation 56, Fig 49
  fields/field system 54, 123, Fig 72
  linear ditch/features 56, 123, Figs 14, 49
  pottery 54, 123
  surface collection Fig 13
  see also LDP 093, 095
Beaker pottery 20, **71**, 72, 74, 86, 91, 94, 98, Tables 10, 23
  Dunch Hill 53
  fabrics Table 29
  North Kite 12
Berkshire Downs
  Deverel-Rimbury pottery (rare) 15
  field systems 126

Late Bronze Age settlement 4
linear earthworks/ditches 8, 14–15, 27, 126, 139, 145, Fig 6
Middle Bronze Age material (scarce) 139
survey 141
bones 39
  assemblages (poor quality) 100
  Brigmerston Down 55, 115
  Dunch Hill midden 128
  Haxton Down 49
  for radiocarbon dating 41, 46, 49, 50, 55, 60, 67, 68, 115, 120, 122, 130, Table 22
  Windmill Hill 57
  see also animal bones
Boscombe Down East enclosure
  described as pastoral enclosure 8
  cut by linear ditch 10, 21
  Deverel-Rimbury 15, 21
  excavation by Pitt Rivers 8
  joined to linear earthwork 8
  Middle Bronze Age 10
  linear ditch dating 15
  pottery (Deverel-Rimbury) 8, 21
Boscombe Down West (Iron Age enclosure/settlement) 21, 135
boundaries *see* linear ditches
Bourne Bottom
  'Celtic' fields Table 27
  flint procurement site 131
  see also LDP 104
Bourne Valley (flint procurement sites) 31
Bowen, Collin 12
Brigmerston Down
  bone 55, 115
  buried soils 53, 55, 112–15, 119
  burnt flint 31, 119, Fig 18, Table 3
  carbonised cereals 102, 119
  enclosures 33, Figs 21, 76
    fieldwalking by Salisbury Plain Conservation Group 33
  environmental samples 55
  excavations 53–5, Fig 21
  flint assemblage 91, 92–8
  flint (worked) 53, Table 3
  linear ditches 53–5, 112–16, 119
    double-banked Fig 47
  linear features Fig 14
  molluscan sequence 112–16
  postholes 53, 119, Fig 47
  pottery 33, 53–5
    Deverel-Rimbury 53–5
    Middle Bronze Age Fig 21
    Late Bronze Age 31, 53–5, Fig 21
  radiocarbon dating 55, 115
  round barrow Fig 76
  settlements 50, 91, 127, 132, 139
    abandonment 123, 135
  surface collection 130, Figs 15, 21
  tree cast (fossil) 112
  see also LDP 092, 102
Brigmerston Plantation 33, 126, 134
  see also LDP 080
Bronze Age *see* Deverel-Rimbury, Early Bronze Age, Middle Bronze Age, Late Bronze Age
bronzework (Late Bronze Age) 21
bronzeworking 142
Bulford *see* LDP 017
buried soils 41, 58, 60, 67, 87, 123, 126, 128
  Beacon Hill 123
  Brigmerston Down 53, 55, 112–15, 119
  carbonised cereals Table 26
  Devil's Ditch 53

environmental samples 102
flint (worked) 56
molluscan analysis 127
radiocarbon dating 122
Sidbury Double Linear Ditch 41, 42, 46, 105, **106**, Fig 29
Sidbury East Linear Ditch 46, 112, Fig 35
Windmill Hill 56, 116–19, Fig 35
burnt feature (Dunch Hill) 53
burnt flint 29, **31**, 50, 127, 128, **130–31**, Fig 18, Table 3
  associated with Late Bronze Age Plain Ware pottery 31
  from Brigmerston Down 31, 119, Fig 18, Table 3
  from burnt mounds 31
  distribution Fig 17
  from Dunch Hill 31, 50, 53, 128, Fig 18, Table 3
  forming an enclosure 130
  guide to prehistoric/Romano-British activity 31
  by Nine Mile River 142
  in pits 130–31
  from ploughed-out settlements 33
burnt mounds 130–31
  Countess Farm 142
  nearby bronzeworking 142
  source of burnt flint 31
  South Lodge Camp 10
Buzbury Rings, Dorset (hillfort) 146

carbonised cereals 102, 119, 120, 127, Table 26
Casterley Camp (hillfort) 146
cattle skulls
  Devil's Ditch 53
  linear ditches 148
  for radiocarbon dating 46, 53, 60, 68, 134
  Sidbury Double Linear Ditch 46, 60–67
  Sidbury Hill 134
'Celtic' fields/field systems 4
  absent from enclosures 135
  adoption 16
  associated with Middle Bronze Age settlements 138
  on Beacon Hill Fig 72
  boundaries formed by linear ditches 4
  compared with coaxial field systems 12
  cut/crossed by linear ditches/earthworks 4, 12, 137–8
  on Earl's Farm Down Figs 22, 24
  later than linear ditches 138
  relationship to linear ditches 125, 137
  Romano-British 126
  on Snail Down Fig 33
  on Sussex Downs 8
  see also fields/field systems
cemeteries (Middle Bronze Age) 138
  see also barrow cemeteries
cereals *see* carbonised cereals
Chalton, Hampshire (Late Bronze Age settlement) 141
charcoal 130
  Beacon Hill 123
  Dunch Hill 53
  identification 119
  for radiocarbon dating 60, 119, 134, Table 22
  Sidbury Double Linear Ditch 42, 46, 103, 119
  Sidbury Hill 102, 119
cheek piece (antler) 46, 87, 146, Figs 35, 36, Table 11

Chiselbury hillfort (abuts cross-ridge dyke) 13
Chisenbury Trendle 21, 150
  hillfort 146
  levelled by RAF 21
  pottery (All Cannings Cross/Early Iron Age) 21, 89, 145
  settlement (All Cannings Cross/pre-hillfort) 89
Cholderton
  flint procurement area 29, 31
  see also Devil's Ditch
clearance (for cultivation) 55, 115
coaxial field systems (on Dartmoor) 12
Colt Hoare, Sir Richard 4, 6, 8, 152
contour survey (of linear ditch) Fig 48
Coombe Down enclosure/settlement (Middle Iron Age) 21, 68, 146, Fig 50
  see also LDP 082
Copehill Down
  linear ditch 102
  Neolithic pit
    environmental evidence 102
    molluscan fauna 106
cores (flint) 29, 91–2, 95, 97–8 Figs 59, 60, Tables 46, 47
Countess Farm (burnt mound) 142
covered ways 8, 9
Cranborne Chase
  earthworks 8
  enclosures, Deverel-Rimbury 139
  field systems 4, 138
  fieldwork 138
  flintwork 92
  lack of Late Bronze Age activity 138
  linear ditches absent 6
  Middle Bronze Age activity 4
  pottery (Deverel-Rimbury, neutron activation analysis) 72, 139
  Project 6, 17
  radiocarbon dates 10
  settlement, Deverel-Rimbury 139
Crawford, O G S 1, 4, 8, 12, 14, 18
cremation cemetery (Kimpton, Middle Bronze Age) 21
cross-ridge dykes 4, 8, 9, 13
crouched inhumation (on Dunch Hill) 128, Fig 46
cultivation
  Middle Bronze Age 126, 139
  Late Bronze Age 139
  Iron Age 105, 108, 116, 120, 121, 129
  Romano-British 36, 105, 108, 111, 112, 116, 120, 121, 130
Curwen, E C 9

damage (to sites) 1, 23, 24, 39, Figs 11, 12
  see also destruction
Damerham Knoll (hillfort) 13
Danebury Environs Project 18
Danebury hillfort
  approached by paired ditches 146
  excavations 11–12, 134
  pre-hillfort enclosure 143
Dartmoor
  coaxial field systems 12
  field project 1
  reaves 6, 12, 14
dating of
  field systems 4, 129–30
  linear ditches 4, 10, 13, 15, 58, 77, 122, 137–49
  sites 58–67
decoration (on pottery) see style
destruction (of sites) 8, 17, 23, 24, 27, 101, 126, 138
  on Marlborough Downs 1
  Romano-British 121, 149

see also damage
Deverel-Rimbury
  enclosures 139
    Boscombe Down East 15, 21
    Marlborough Downs 127
    Martin Down 6–8
    South Downs 127
  field systems 16
  pottery 29, 69, 71–4, 86, 88, 98, 120, 127, 129, 130, 139, Figs 51, 52, Tables 1, 2, 4, 5, 10, 17, 19, 23, 33
    Boscombe Down East 8, 21
    Brigmerston Down 53–5
    considered as Late Bronze Age 10
    Cranborne Chase (neutron activation analysis) 72, 139
    Dunch Hill 55, 98
    fabrics Table 29
    Martin Down 10
    rare on Berkshire Downs 15
    Snail Down 133
  settlements 16, 139
Devil's Ditch 123, 125, 133, Figs 8, 14
  abutted by lynchets 53, 125
  buried soil 53
  cattle skull 53
  as county boundary 25, 125
  cut through fields 123
  earlier/later than fields 125
  environmental evidence/samples 53, 102, 125
  excavation 53, 126
  flint (worked) 53
  molluscan sequence 116
  overlain by lynchet 53
  pottery (Romano-British) 53
  radiocarbon dating 53
  recutting/remodelling 53, 124, 125, 135, 146, 148
  relationship to Celtic fields 125
  survival 25, 125
  see also LDP 010–013, 052, 094
distribution of
  burnt flint Fig 17
  'Celtic' fields (on Beacon Hill) Fig 72
  linear ditches 4, Fig 1
  metalwork (Late Bronze Age) 138
  pottery 27
    fabrics 72, Table 23
    Middle Bronze Age Fig 46
    Late Bronze Age 132, Fig 46
    Iron Age Table 32
  round barrows 122, 141
  settlements
    Middle Bronze Age Fig 71
    Late Bronze Age Fig 71
  surface collection sites 27
ditches see linear ditches
Dorchester, Dorset (environmental evidence) 101
double-banked linear ditches 53, 122, 126, Fig 47
double banks (of linear ditches) 25, 53, 124–5
double-ditched enclosures (Middle Iron Age) 146
double linear ditches/earthworks 87, 133, 134, 143, 146
downland (ancient), in Military Training Area 23, 24, 101
drift geology see geology
Dunch Hill
  animal bones 50, 53
  ard marks 50
  burnt feature 53
  burnt flint 31, 50, 53, 128, Fig 18, Table 3
  charcoal 53

crouched inhumation 128, Fig 46
  field system 50
  flint (worked) 50, Table 3
  flint assemblage 91, 92–9
  hollow-way (alongside linear ditch) 50, 128
  linear ditch 55, 128
    contour survey Fig 48
    overlain by lynchet 125
  linear features Fig 14
  lynchets 55, 124–5, 128, Fig 46
  midden 31, 49–50, 77, 80, 87, 91, 95, 123, 128, Figs 45, 73
  pottery 77, 141
    Beaker 53
    Early Bronze Age 71
    Deverel-Rimbury 55, 98
    Middle Bronze Age 94, Fig 46
    Late Bronze Age 31, 77–89, Fig 46, Table 24
      Plain Ware 50, 53, 55, 72, 128
    Early All Cannings Cross 50, 77, 88, 123
    All Cannings Cross 74, 95
    Iron Age 55
    distribution Fig 46
  radiocarbon dating 50, 80, 88
  sarsen pebbles 131
  settlements 33, 49–50, 53, 72, 74, 86, 91–8, 127, 128, 131, 134
    abandonment 123, 135
    Middle Bronze Age 129, Fig 51
  surface collection 49–50, 53, Fig 15
  tree-hole/hollow survey 33, 94, Fig 46
  see also 056, 081, 081A, 087, 098, 103, 111
Dunch Hill Plantation 122, 126, 128
dyke systems 14, 16

Earl's Farm Down
  augering 36
  Celtic fields Figs 22, 24
  excavation 36, 122
  geophysical survey 36
  linear ditches/features 36, 126, Figs 14, 22, 24
  pottery 27, 135
  round barrows 20
  settlements 77
  surface collection 135
  trackways 36, Fig 24
  see also LDP 015, 016, 018, 019, 019A
Early All Cannings Cross pottery 46, 50, 77–80, 88–9, 122, 132, 135, 142–3, Fig 58, Tables 2, 5
Early Bronze Age
  barrow cemeteries 138, 151
  environmental evidence 101
  flat cemetery (Easton Down) 21
  pottery 29, 71, 127, Tables 1, 2, 4, 5, 33, 34
  see also round barrows
Early Iron Age
  enclosures 145
  pottery 21, 89
  settlements 138
Early Medieval pottery Table 1
earthworks see covered ways, cross-ridge dykes, field systems, linear ditches, ranch boundaries, spur dykes
Easton Down
  Early Bronze Age flat cemetery 21
  flint mines 20
  linear ditch 126
Easton Lane, Winchester
  excavation 10
  land divisions Fig 4
  linear ditches 15

settlements (enclosed and open) 141
enclosures
  Middle Bronze Age 130
    Boscombe Down East 10
    Plumpton Plain, Sussex 139–41
    replaced by open settlements 139–41
    Thorny Down 21
  Deverel-Rimbury 127, 139
  Early Iron Age 145
  Middle Iron Age 21, 146, 147, 148
  Boscombe Down East 8, 10, 21
  Boscombe Down West (Iron Age) 21
  Brigmerston Down 33, Figs 21, **76**
  Brigmerston Plantation 33
  burnt flint (formed by) 130
  Celtic fields absent 135
  Coombe Down (Middle Iron Age) 21,
    Fig 50
  on Figheldean Down 120–21, 142
  Lidbury 89, 135
    abutted by earthwork 143
  linear ditches (relationship with) 9, 12–13
  linear earthworks/ditches (joined to) 8
  on Milston Down 72
  pre-hillfort (joined to linear earthworks)
    143
  replaced by hillforts 146
  on Snail Down 67, 88, Figs 10, 33
  Yarnbury 145
  see also hillforts
environmental
  analysis 101–21, Figs 63–70, Tables 25,
    26
  columns
    linear ditches Fig 35
    Sidbury Double Linear Ditch 46, Figs
      28, 29, 31
    Weather Hill Fig 37
  data/evidence 18, 68, 100, 139, 142,
    146, 147, Fig **70**
    Avebury 101
    Copehill Down (Neolithic pit) 102
    Devil's Ditch 125
    Dorchester, Dorset 101
    Stonehenge environs 101, 102
  samples/sampling 40
    Brigmerston Down 55
    buried soils 102
    Devil's Ditch 53, 102
    Sidbury Double Linear Ditch 42, 46
    Sidbury East Linear Ditch 46
    Weather Hill 49
    Windmill Hill 57
  sequences
    Sidbury Hill 120
    Windmill Hill 120
Everleigh (possible henge) 20
excavation programme 3, 39–41
excavation sites 41–57
  in Upper Study Area Fig 14
  in Study Area (earlier) Fig 8
excavations of
  barrow cemeteries 21
  Beacon Hill 56, Fig 49
  Boscombe Down East enclosure 8
  Brigmerston Down 53–5, Fig 21
  Danebury hillfort 11–12, 134
  Devil's Ditch 53, 126
  Dunch Hill 55
  Earl's Farm Down 36, 122
  Easton Lane, Winchester 10
  Haxton Down 49, Figs 42–44
  hollow-ways 49
  Lain's Farm 36
  Lidbury 143
  linear ditches 6–8, **40–57**, 90, 102, 122,
    126, 133, 134, Figs 23, 26, 35, 44
  lynchets 68

Maiden Castle, Dorset 147
pit alignments 49, Fig 44
Quarley High Linear 134
Quarley Hill 8, 11, 12, 16, 143–4
round barrows 21, 42
St Catherine's Hill 8
Sidbury Double Linear Ditch 132, Figs
  27–31
Sidbury East Linear Ditch **46**, 133, Fig
  35
Sidbury Hill Fig 26
Sidbury West Linear Ditch 49, 133, Fig
  44
Snail Down 42, 46, 49, 67, 132, 133,
  Figs **32, 33**
South Lodge Camp 9–10
Thwing 10
Weather Hill **49**, 67, Fig 37
Windmill Hill 56–7, 134

fabrics (of pottery) 71–90, Tables 24,
  29–33
Fen Edge
  land divisions 10
  linear ditches Fig 1
Fengate (land divisions) Fig 4
fields/field systems
  Bronze Age 3–4
  Middle Bronze Age 125–6, 138
  Deverel-Rimbury 16
  Late Bronze Age 125–6
  Iron Age 34, 122, 128, 138
  Middle Iron Age 147
  Romano-British 34, 50, 128
  on Beacon Hill 54, 123, Fig 72
  on Berkshire Downs 126
  on Cranborne Chase 4, 138, 139
  damage 24
  dating 4, 129–30
  destruction 23, 24
  on Dunch Hill 50
  on Dunch Hill Plantation 122
  linear ditches
    cut/crossed by 8, 10, 16, 123, 150
    later than 36, 123
    relationship with 12
  lynchets (abut/overlay Devil's Ditch) 53
  management 1
  project 1
  on Tidworth Golf Course 122
  on Weather Hill 49, 108
  of Yorkshire Wolds (not surviving) 12
  see also 'Celtic' fields
field methodology 26–68
  see also excavation
fieldwalking
  grid for surface collection 27, Fig 13
  undertaken by Salisbury Plain
    Conservation Group 33
  see also surface collection
Figheldean Down
  augering of linear features 34–6
  enclosure 142
    pastoral 120–21
  hoard (Late Bronze Age bronze axes) 21,
    142
  linear ditches/features 36, Fig 14, Table
    27
  trackways 36
  see also LDP 075
Figsbury Rings hillfort 20, 21
  Late Bronze Age sword 21
  possible henge below 20
flat cemetery (Early Bronze Age, Easton
  Down) 21
flint
  assemblages 29, 31, 91–100, Figs 59–62,
    Tables 35–48

axes 31, 56, 57
cores 29, 91–2, 95, **97–8**, Figs **59, 60**,
  Tables 46, **47**
mines 20
procurement sites 29–31, 91, 97, 98,
  99–100, 131, 142, Fig 16
scatter 31
scrapers 95, 98, Fig **61**, Tables **40**, 48
struck 29, 31, 127, **128**
  from midden on Dunch Hill 128
worked 29, 39, 42, 49, 50, 53, 56, 92,
  93, 94, 129, Table 3
  associated with Late Bronze Age Plain
    Ware pottery 31
  surface collection 138
see also burnt flint
flintwork 92, 142
fossil tree hollows see tree hollows (fossil)

geology 119
  of Study Area 20, 34
  of Upper Study Area Fig 16
geophysical surveys/work 25, 26, **34–6**,
  128, 138
  at Maiden Castle, Dorset 147
  at times of little value 46
grassland (ancient), of Military Estate of
  Salisbury Plain East 20, Fig 9
  see also downland
Grooved Ware 20
Gussage Cow Down (Late Iron Age site)
  13

haematite-coated pottery 87, 88, 89, 90,
  134, 135, 145, Table 7
Hawkes, Christopher 4, 8, 17, 18, 20
  work at Quarley Hill 10, 12, 16, 143–4,
    Fig 3
Hawley, Colonel 21, Fig 76
Haxton Down
  bones 49
  excavation 49, Figs 42–44
  flint (worked) 49
  linear ditch/features 49, Fig 14
  lynchet Fig 44
  pit alignments 49, 60, 133, Figs 42–44
  postholes 49, Fig 44
  pottery (Romano-British) 49
  radiocarbon dating 49
  tree casts/hollow (fossil) 49, Fig 42
  see also LDP 085, 086, 099
henges (possible sites) 20
hillforts 121, 134, **145–9**, **150–1**
  Buzbury Rings, Dorset 146
  Casterley Camp 146
  Chiselbury 13
  Chisenbury Trendle 89, 145, 146
  Damerham Knoll 13
  Danebury 11–12, 134, 146
  dating 13
  development 16, 143, **144–6**
  Figsbury Rings 20, 21
  houses 147–8
  at junctions of territories 146
  Ladle Hill, Hampshire 13, 143, Fig 77
  Lidbury 21, 143, 146, 147
  Liddington Castle 13, 143
  linear ditches
    associated with 9
    later than 150
    location influenced by 8, 13
    located at meeting points 13
    overlay 13
    relationship with 12–13, 145–9, 150
  linked to smaller enclosures 147
  Middle Iron Age change 147
  Quarley Hill 18, 20, 21, **143–4**, 146, 147,
    Figs 8–10

replaced enclosures 146
Sidbury Hill 18, 20, 23, 38–9, 42, 46,
    87, 89, 90, 103, 133, 143, **144**, 146,
    Figs 8–10, 12, 25, 26
  spacing 146–7
  storage structures 147–8
  in Study Area Fig 8
  Uffington Castle 13, 14, 143
  Whitsbury, Hampshire 146
  Woolbury, Hampshire 13, 143, 146
  Yarnbury Fig 78
  Yorkshire Wolds (virtually absent) 16
hoards (Late Bronze Age axes)
  Figheldean Down 21, 142
  Nine Mile River 131
hollow-ways 33, Fig 73
  alongside linear ditches 128
  distinguishing between linear ditches 38
  on Dunch Hill 50, 128
  interpretation of some linear
      ditches/feature 34, 36
  seen from the air 36
  on Weather Hill 49, Fig 40
  see also trackways
horse skulls
  radiocarbon dating 60, 68, 134
  Windmill Hill 57, 134, 146, Fig 35
houses (within hillforts) 147–8
human bones
  Sidbury Double Linear Ditch 42
  Sidbury Hill 134
  tree hollows 128
human burials 134
human skulls 67
  radiocarbon dating 42, 46, 68, 134
  Sidbury Double Linear Ditch 42, 60
  Sidbury Hill 134, 146

inhumation (crouched, from Dunch Hill)
    128
Iron Age
  cultivation 105, 108, 116, 120, 121, 129
  ditches 135, Fig 39
  enclosed site (Chisenbury Trendle) 21
  enclosures 21, 108
  fields/field systems 34, 122, 128, 138
  linear ditches
    additions 111
    development 137
    modifications 67
    recuts 111
  pottery 29, 74, 88, 123, 127, Tables 1, 2,
      4, 5, 7, 19, 33, 34
    distribution Table 32
    Dunch Hill 55
    fabrics Tables 31, 32
    paucity 90
    Quarley High Linear 134
    Weather Hill 67
  settlements 36, 70
    Boscombe Down West 135
    Old Down Farm 21
  stock enclosures 108
  see also Early Iron Age, hillforts, Middle
      Iron Age

Kimpton (cremation cemetery/urnfield)
    18, 21

Ladle Hill, Hampshire, hillfort 143, Fig 77
  overlay linear ditches 13
  pre-hillfort ditch (associated with linear
      ditch) 143
Lain's Farm 36
Late Bronze Age
  bronzework 21
  crouched inhumation (Dunch Hill) 128
  cultivation 139

fields 125–6
  hoard (Figheldean Down) 21
  lacuna 21
  metalwork (distribution) 138
  metalworking 131
  Plain Ware pottery 46, 50, 58, **69–70**,
      73–4, 75, **77–89**, 92, 94, 120, 122,
      127, 132, 139, Figs **51**, **53–57**, Tables
      1, 2, 4, 5, 7, 10, 15, 17, 19
    from Brigmerston Down 53–5
    burnt flint (associated with) 31
    distribution 132
    from Dunch Hill 53, 55, 72, 128
    from Earl's Farm Down 135
    from lynchets 133
    from Milston Down 72
    from Northern Core Territory 91
    settlements (associated with) 127
    from Sidbury East Linear Ditch 133
    from Sidbury Hill 134, 135
    from Snail Down 133
    style 80–86
    worked flint (associated with) 31
  pottery 29, 46, 58, **74–80**, 130, Figs 17,
      21, Tables 33, 34
    from Brigmerston Down 31
    distribution Fig 46
    from Dunch Hill 31, 77–89, Fig 46,
        Table 24
    fabrics Tables 24, 29
    from Milston Down 33, 77–89, Table
        24
    from Northern Core Territory 77–80,
        85–8
  settlements (open) 41, 53, 58, 71, 87,
      127–35, **138–43**
    abandoned 135, 145, 146
    Berkshire Downs 4
    Brigmerston Down 50
    at Chalton, Hampshire 141
    distribution Fig 71
    on Dunch Hill 33, 49–50, 131
    lack of evidence 138
    on Milston Down 131
    at Potterne 138
  sword (from Figsbury Rings) 21
  see also flint assemblages, linear ditches,
      middens
Late Iron Age
  Gussage Cow Down site 13
  pottery 90
LDP 001 90, Tables 1, 27, 32, 34
  see also Quarley Hill
LDP 002 Tables 1, 27, 32, 34
  see also Quarley Hill
LDP 003 Tables 1, 27
  see also Quarley Hill
LDP 004 Tables 1, 27
  see also Quarley Hill
LDP 005 Table 27
LDP 006 Table 27
LDP 007 Table 27
LDP 008 29, 77, Fig 16, Tables 1, 24, 27,
    33, 34
  see also Quarley High Linear, Thruxton
      Hill
LDP 008A 90, 134, Tables 5, 32–34
  see also Quarley High Linear, Thruxton
      Hill
LDP 009 Tables 1, 27, 33, 34
  see also Quarley High Linear, Thruxton
      Hill
LDP 010 123, Tables 1, 27
  see also Devil's Ditch
LDP 011 123, Tables 1, 27
  see also Devil's Ditch
LDP 012 29, 77, 123, Fig 16, Tables 1,
    27, 34

see also Devil's Ditch
LDP 013 123, 126, Table 27
  see also Devil's Ditch
LDP 014 Table 27
LDP 015 Tables 1, 27
  see also Earl's Farm Down
LDP 016 Tables 1, 27
  see also Earl's Farm Down
LDP 017 70, 77, Tables 1, 23, 24, 27, 33,
    34
LDP 018 70, 77, Tables 1, 24, 27, 32, 34
  see also Earl's Farm Down
LDP 019 27, 70, 90, Tables 1, 23, 24, 27,
    32–34
  see also Earl's Farm Down
LDP 019A 36, Fig 22, Tables 5, 27, 33, 34
  see also Earl's Farm Down
LDP 019B Fig 22
LDP 020 41, 103, 120, 133, Figs 26–28,
    Table 28
  see also Sidbury Double Linear Ditch
LDP 020A 41, 103, 105, Fig 28, Table 25
LDP 020B 102
LDP 026 41, 105, Table 28
  see also Sidbury Double Linear Ditch
LDP 027 42, 102, **105–8**, 111, 115, 116,
    120, 133, 135, Figs 29, **64**, 29, Tables
    6, 28
  see also Sidbury Double Linear Ditch
LDP 027A 102, 105, **106–8**, 111, 112,
    115, 116, Figs **64**, 70, Tables 5, 50
LDP 027B 105, **106**, Figs **64**, 70, Table 51
LDP 033 111, Table 28
  see also Weather Hill
LDP 039 Table 28
LDP 045 Table 28
  see also Sidbury West Linear Ditch
LDP 052 53, 68, 102, **116**, 123, 125, 126,
    Figs 43, **69**, 70, Tables 28, 57
  see also Devil's Ditch
LDP 056 129, Fig **74**, Table 28
  see also Dunch Hill
LDP 075 Tables 2, 23, 32, 34
  see also Figheldean Down
LDP 080 31, 70, 74, 77, 86, 87, 88, 91,
    92, 94, 95, 96, 97, 98, 128, 132, 141,
    Figs 15, 17, 18, 21, 51, 52, 58, 60,
    Tables 2–4, 23, 24, 33–48
  see also Brigmerston Plantation
LDP 081 31, 53, 70, 77, 91, 92, 93, 94,
    95, 96, 97, 98, 128, 132, 139, 152,
    Figs 15, 18, 46, 56, 61, **73**, Tables 2, 4,
    24, 33–48
  see also Dunch Hill
LDP 081A 31, 41, 49–50, 53, 60, 70, 74,
    77, 86, 87, 88, 91, 92, 93, 94, 95, 96,
    97, 98, 120, 123, 128, 129, 132, 141,
    142, Figs 18, 45, 46, 56–58, 61, 73,
    Tables 3, 5, 16, 22–24, 28, 34–50
  see also Dunch Hill
LDP 082 68, 77, 89, 121, 129, 133, Figs
    50, **75**, Tables 5, 23, 24, 28, 32–34
  see also Coombe Down
LDP 083 49, 60, 67, 90, 102, **108–12**,
    115, 116, 127, 135, Figs 37, 38, **65**, **66**,
    70, Tables 5, 12, 22, 28, 32, 34, 52
  see also Weather Hill
LDP 084 49, 129, Figs 40, 41, Tables 5, 28
  see also Weather Hill
LDP 085 49, Figs 42, 43, Tables 13, 28
  see also Haxton Down
LDP 086 Table 28
  see also Haxton Down
LDP 087 53, 70, 71, 77, 86, 130, Figs 46,
    56, Tables 5, 23, 24, 28, 34
  see also Dunch Hill
LDP 087A 53, 70, 77, Tables 5, 24, 34
LDP 087B 53

LDP 088 Table 28
  see also Sidbury West Linear Ditch
LDP 089 49, Table 28
  see also Sidbury West Linear Ditch
LDP 090 53, 60, 68, 123, 125, 134, 148,
  Fig 34, Tables 5, 22, 28
LDP 091 31, 56–7, 60, 68, 102, **116–19**,
  120, 134, 146, 148, Fig 35, **69**, 70,
  Tables 22, 28, 58
  see also Windmill Hill
LDP 092 53, 55, 58, 60, 67, 69, 70, 74,
  77, 86, 87, 101, 102, **112–16**, **119**, 120,
  121, 122, 126, 127, 132, 139, Figs 21,
  47, 52, 55, **68**, Tables 5, 17, 18, 22–24,
  28, 34
  see also Brigmerston Down
LDP 092A **115–16**, Fig 70, Table 54
LDP 092B 102, 116, 120, Fig 70, Table 26
LDP 092C 102, 112–15, 116, Fig 70,
  Table 56
LDP 093 Fig 13; see also Beacon Hill
LDP 094 Table 28
  see also Devil's Ditch
LDP 095 56, 123, Figs 49, 72, Tables 5,
  21, 28
  see also Beacon Hill
LDP 096 46, 68, 133, Fig 34, Table 28
  see also Sidbury East Linear Ditch
LDP 097 58, 68, 69, 70, 71, 74, 77, 87,
  102, 108, **112**, 120, 121, 133, 146, Figs
  35, 36, 67, 70, Tables 10, 11, 28, 34
  see also Sidbury East Linear Ditch
LDP 098 55, 58, 70, 74, 77, 87, 90, 122,
  123, 126, 127, 128, 132, Figs 21, 46,
  48, 52, 55, Tables 5, 19, 20, 23, 24,
  28, 32–34
  see also Dunch Hill
LDP 099 49, 60, 133, Fig 44, Tables 5,
  14, 22, 28
  see also Haxton Down
LDP 100 42, 46, 60, 67, 68, 77, 87, 89,
  102, 116, **119**, 133, 134, 146, Figs 26,
  30, Tables 5, 7, 8, 22, 24, 28, 32–34
  see also Sidbury Hill
LDP 101 38, 46, 60, 68, 102, 103, 105,
  116, **119**, 120, 121, 132, 133, 134,
  143, 144, Figs 26, 31, 63, 70, Tables 5,
  9, 22, 28, 33, 34, 49
  see also Sidbury Hill
LDP 101 Tables 33, 34
LDP 102 31, 70, 71, 72, 77, 86, 87, 91,
  92, 93, 94, 95, 96, 97, 98, 126, 127,
  130, 132, 139, Figs 15, 17, 18,
  21, 51, 52, 55, 60–62, 76, Tables 2, 3,
  23, 24, 27, 33–48
  see also Brigmerston Down
LDP 103 33, 53, 70, 71, 72, 77, 86, 94,
  98, 128, 139, Figs 46, 51, 52, 55, 56,
  Tables 2, 23, 24, 27, 33, 34
  see also Dunch Hill
LDP 104 31, 70, 77, 91, 92, 94, 95, 96,
  97, 98, 99, 131, 142, Figs 15, 16, 18,
  59, 61, 62, Tables 2, 3, 24, 27, 34–48
  see also Bourne Bottom
LDP 105 142, Fig 15, Table 27
LDP 106 142, Fig 15, Table 27
LDP 107 128
LDP 108 33, 70, 72, 77, 130, 139, Figs
  21, 76, Tables 2, 23, 24, 34
LDP 109 33, 69, 70, 72, 73, 74, 77, 87,
  98, 126, 127, 130, 139, Figs 21, 51,
  52, 55, 76, Tables 2, 23, 24, 33, 34
LDP 110 129, 130–31
LDP 111 70, 71, 86, 94, 98, Figs 15, 46,
  55, Tables 2, 23, 24, 27, 34
  see also Dunch Hill
LDP 112 33, 70, 71, 72, 74, 77, 88, 98,
  127, 132, 139, 142, 152, Figs 19, 20,

51–55, 58, Tables 2, 4, 23, 24, 32–34
Lewes, Sussex (pollen diagrams) 101
Lidbury
  enclosures 89, 135
    abutted by earthwork 143
  excavations 143
  hillfort 21, 143, 146, 147
    linked to boundary ditch 143
  pottery 89, 135
  settlement (All Cannings Cross) 89–90
Liddington Castle hillfort 13
  associated with linear ditch 143
  Early All Cannings Cross pottery 143
linear ditches
  Middle Bronze Age origin (no evidence)
    74, 137
  Late Bronze Age
    construction 58, 69, 101
    Plain Ware within silts 87–8
  Iron Age
    additions 111
    development 137
    modifications 67
    potttery 90
    recuts 111
  Middle Iron Age recutting/building 148
  Romano-British,
    not functioning 70
    pottery 68, 136
  banjo enclosures (associated with) 13
  banks 38, 40, 56, 74, 112–15, 116, 119,
    123, 126, Figs 68, 69
  barriers (not designed as) 87
  barrows/barrow cemeteries (aligned on)
    141
  on Beacon Hill 56, 123, Fig 49
  on Berkshire Downs 27, 126, 139, 145
  at Boscombe Down East 15
  boundaries of 'Celtic' fields 4
  on Brigmerston Down 53–5, 112–16,
    119, Fig 47
  on Brigmerston Plantation 126
  buried soil Fig 35
  cattle skull 148
  'Celtic' fields
    earlier than 138
    relationship with 125, 137
  confirmed by auger survey Fig 23
  confirmed by excavation Fig 23
  construction 75
  contour survey Fig 48
  on Copehill Down 102
  cut across/crossing
    Boscombe Down East enclosure 21
    'Celtic' fields 4, 137–8
    fields/field systems 8, 10, 16, 123, 150
    settlements 127
  dating 4, 10, 13, 15, 58, 77, 122, **137–49**
  destruction/damage 17, 24, 39, 126
    Romano-British 41
  distinguishing between hollow-ways 36,
    38
  distribution 4, Fig 1
  double 87, 133, 134
  double-banked 53, 122, 126, Fig 47
  double banks 25, 53, 124–5
  on Dunch Hill 55, 125, 128, Fig 48
  on Dunch Hill Plantation 126
  on Earl's Farm Down 36, 126, Fig 24
  on Easton Down 126
  at Easton Lane, Winchester 15
  enclose Northern Core Territory 122
  enclose Southern Core Territory 122
  enclosures
    joined to 8
    relationship with with 9, 12–13
  environmental columns Fig 35
  environmental setting 101–21, Figs

63–70, Tables 25, 26
  excavations 6–8, **40–57**, 90, 102, 122,
    126, 133, 134, Figs 23, 26, 35, 44
    by Pitt Rivers 6–8
  in Fen Edge Fig 1
  field systems
    earlier than 36, 123
    relationship with 12
  on Figheldean Down 36
  on Haxton Down 49
  hillforts
    earlier than 150
    at meeting points of ditches 13
    overlain by 78, 13, 133
    position influenced 8, 13
    relationship with 9, 12–13, 145–9, 150
  human skulls 146
  intersecting on Quarley Hill 132–3
  intersecting on Sidbury Hill 132–3
  lynchets (overlain by) 74, 105, 125, 127,
    128
  management 17
  on Marlborough Downs 145
  on Martin Down 10
  on Milston Down 126
  morphology 67–8
  in Northern Core Territory 58, 69, 77,
    100, **126–8**
  postholes alongside (not proven) 126–7
  preservation 39
  on Quarley Hill 102, 133, **134–5**, Fig 3
  as ranch boundaries 8–9, 16, 137
  recutting/remodelling 123–4, 125, 133,
    134–5, 143, 144
    Iron Age 67–8
  re-established 151
  restructuring 134
  roads (interpretation) 6, 8
  round barrows (position influenced by)
    138, 146
  settlements (relationship with) Fig 71
  on Sidbury Hill 38–9, 58, **132–4**, 143,
    Figs 14, 25, 26
  silting 41
  on Snail Down 21, 46, 49, 67, 123–4,
    132, 133, Figs 14, **32**, **33**, **39**
  as soil marks 25
  on South Downs Fig 1
  in Southern Core Territory 58, **123–6**,
    Fig **72**
  in Stonehenge area 141
  system of boundaries 8
  of Tabular Hills 4, Figs 1, 5
  topography (relationship with) 36, 138,
    141
  trackways (later) alongside 36, 38
  on Weather Hill 49, 108–12, Fig 37
  on Windmill Hill **56–7**, **116–19**, 134, 146
  at Winterbourne Dauntsey 126–7
  of Yorkshire Wolds 4, 10, 16, Figs 1, 2
  see also Devil's Ditch, linear earthworks,
    linear features, Sidbury Double
    Linear Ditch, Sidbury East Linear
    Ditch, Sidbury West Linear Ditch
linear earthworks
  of Berkshire Downs 8, 14–15, Fig 6
  'Celtic' fields cut by 12
  damage/destruction 1, 8, 23
  hillforts located at meeting point 13
  joined to pre-hillfort enclosures 143
  on South Downs 8
  still used as boundaries 1
  see also linear ditches, linear features
linear features 36, Figs 14, 22
  appearance on aerial photographs 36
  some known to be hollow-ways 34
  some proved to be Roman or later
    trackways 138

see also hollow-ways, linear ditches, linear earthworks
linear territories (in Northern Core Territory) 72
long barrows (earlier Neolithic) 20
lynchets (of field systems) 4, Figs 74, 75
  abut Devil's Ditch 53, 125
  on Dunch Hill 55, 124–5, 128, Fig 46
  on Dunch Hill Plantation 128
  excavation 68
  on Haxton Down Fig 44
  overlying
    Devil's Ditch 53
    linear ditches 74, 105, 125, 127, 128
    Sidbury Double Linear Ditch 46
    Sidbury East Linear Ditch 112
  pottery 87, 89, 90
    Late Bronze Age Plain Ware 133
    Iron Age 68
    Romano-British 53, 68
  Romano-British 112
  at Sidbury Double Linear Ditch 105, 108
  on Weather Hill 108
  on Windmill Hill 57

Maiden Castle, Dorset 147
management of sites 1, 17
manuring (origin of prehistoric pottery) 31–3
Marlborough Downs
  enclosures 127, 141
  linear ditches 145
  Middle Bronze Age activity 4
  pottery 69
  sites destroyed by ploughing 1
Martin Down
  described as pastoral enclosure 8
  Deverel-Rimbury enclosure 6–8
  linear ditch cuts field system 10
  pottery (Deverel-Rimbury) 10
Martin's Clump flint mines (earlier Neolithic) 20
medieval
  land division 14
  landuse 13
metalwork (Late Bronze Age) 138
metalworking (Late Bronze Age) 131
midden (Dunch Hill, Late Bronze Age) 31, 49–50, 77, 80, 87, 91, 95, 123, 128, Figs 45, 73
  animal bones 50
  burnt flint 50
  flint assemblage 98
  flint scrapers 95
  pottery
    Late Bronze Age 60, 128
    Early All Cannings Cross 123
  radiocarbon dating 88, 123
  worked flint 50, 92, 93, 94
midden (East Chisenbury) 135
midden (Quarley Hill) 8
Middle Bronze Age
  activity 4
  cemeteries 138
  cremation cemetery (Kimpton) 21
  cultivation 126, 139
  enclosures 10, 21, 130
    replaced by open settlements 139–41
  fields/field systems
    at Cranborne Chase 138
    Southern Core Territory 125–6
  linear ditches (no evidence for construction) 74, 137
  pottery 33, 46, 58, 69, 72–4, 94, 130, Figs 17, 21, 46, Table 34
  secondary burials in barrows 21
  settlements 6, 127–30, 133, 138–42
    associated with Celtic fields 138

distribution Fig 71
  on Dunch Hill 77, 129, Fig 51
  on Milston Down 77
  in Northern Core Territory 77, Fig 51
Middle Iron Age
  Devil's Ditch remodelled 124
  enclosures 21, 146, 147, 148
  field systems 147
  hillforts (change) 147
  linear ditches (recutting/building) 148
  occupation 147–8
  open settlements 147
  pottery 67, 90
Military Estate of Salisbury Plain East, ancient grassland/pasture 20, 26, Fig 9
Military Training Area
  ancient downland 23, 24
  area covered 1
  damage/destruction (of sites) 23–4, Figs 11, 12
  excavation programme 39
  preservation of linear ditches 39
  surface collection 138, Table 2
    limited in old grassland 25
  survival of earthworks 23
Milston Down
  enclosure 72
  fieldwalking by Salisbury Plain Conservation Group 33
  linear ditch/features 126, Fig 14
  pottery 141
    Early Bronze Age 71
    Middle Bronze Age 33
    Late Bronze Age 33, 72, 77–89, Table 24
    All Cannings Cross 74
  round barrows Fig 20
  settlements 72, 74, 86, 127, 131
  surface collection 130, Figs 19, 20
molluscan
  diagrams Figs 63–69
  evidence 18, 101, 102–19, 120, 127, 135, Tables 25, 49–58
  fauna 106, Fig 29
Mortimer, J R 6, 13, 14
mould (for casting axes, from Nine Mile River) 131, 142

Neolithic
  flint mines 20
  Grooved Ware 20
  long barrows 20
  Peterborough Ware 20
  pits 102, 106
neutron activation analysis (of pottery from Cranborne Chase) 72, 139
Nine Mile River 18, 21, 72, 100, 120, 126, 130, 133, 142, Figs 8, 14
  burnt flint 142
  burnt mound 130–31
  hoard of axes 131
  mould (for axes) 131, 142
Northern Core Territory 21, 53, 132–3, 139, 142, Fig 10
  flint assemblage 92–5, 98
  linear ditches 58, 69, 77, 100, 126–8
    alignment 141
    enclosed by 122
  linear territories 72
  pottery
    Early Bronze Age 71
    Late Bronze Age 77–80, 85–8, 91
    All Cannings Cross 74
  settlements 72, 91–4, 135, 141
    Middle Bronze Age Fig 51
  surface collection 29
North Kite 15
  ditch sequences 42

overlying linear earthwork 12
  pottery (Beaker) 12

Old Down Farm (Iron Age settlement) 21
Old Marlborough Coach Road 33, 49, 108, Fig 43
open settlements *see* settlements

pastoral enclosures 8, 120–21
pasture (ancient), Military Estate of Salisbury Plain East 26
Peterborough Ware 20
pick (antler) 46, 120, Table 9
pit alignments (on Haxton Down) 49, 60, 133, Figs 42–44
pits 60, 102, 106, 133
Pitt Rivers, General 4, 6, 8, 9
Plain Ware *see* Late Bronze Age
Plumpton Plain, Sussex (Middle Bronze Age enclosures) 139–41
pollen analysts 6
pollen diagrams 101, 102
population (change in structure) 146
postholes 129
  alongside ditches (not proven) 126
  on Brigmerston Down 53, 119, Fig 47
  on Haxton Down 49, Fig 44
  on Weather Hill 49, Fig 40
post-medieval pottery Table 5
  from Beacon Hill 54, 123
Potterne (Late Bronze Age settlement) 138
pottery 39, 40, 41, 50, 69–90, Tables 10, 15
  Beaker 12, 20, 53, 71, 72, 74, 86, 91, 94, 98, Tables 10, 23, 29
  Early Bronze Age 29, 71, 127, Tables 1, 2, 4, 5, 33, 34
  Middle Bronze Age 33, 46, 58, 69, 72–4, 94, 130, Fig 21, Table 34
    distribution Fig 46
  Deverel-Rimbury 8, 10, 15, 21, 29, 53–5, 69, 71–4, 86, 88, 98, 120, 127, 129, 130, 133, 139, Figs 51, 52, Tables 1, 2, 4, 5, 10, 17, 19, 23, 29, 33
  Late Bronze Age 29, 31, 33, 46, 50, 58, 60, 74–80, 130, Fig 21, Tables 1, 2, 33, 34
    distribution Fig 46
    fabrics Table 24
    Plain Ware 46, 50, 53–5, 58, 69–70, 73–4, 75, 77–89, 91, 92, 94, 120, 122, 127, 128, 132, 133, 134, 135, 139, Figs 51, 53–57, Tables 1, 2, 4, 5, 7, 10, 15, 17, 19
    style 80–86
  Early All Cannings Cross 46, 50, 77–80, 88–9, 122, 132, 135, 142–3, Fig 58, Tables 2, 5
  All Cannings Cross 69, 74, 88–90, 95, 123, 132, 145, Tables 5, 7, 15, 33
  All Cannings Cross-Meon Hill 89, 135
  Iron Age 29, 55, 67, 68, 74, 88, 90, 123, 127, 134, Tables 1, 2, 4, 5, 7, 19, 31, 32, 33, 34
  Early Iron Age 21, 89
  Middle Iron Age 67, 90
  Late Iron Age 90
  Romano-British 27, 29, 33, 42, 46, 49, 53, 54, 68, 90, 121, 123, 134, 136, Tables 1, 2, 4, 5
  Anglo-Saxon Table 1
  Early Medieval Table 1
  post-medieval 54, 123, Table 5
  before linear ditch construction 71–5, Figs 51, 52, Table 23
  from Brigmerston 141
  from Brigmerston Down 53–5

dating 58, 60
destruction by cultivation 138
distribution 27, Fig 46
from Dunch Hill 141
fabrics 70, 71–90, Tables 29–33
    distribution 72, Table 23
haematite-coated 87, 88, 89, 90, 134,
    135, 145, Table 7
from lynchets 87, 90
from Marlborough Downs 69
methodology 70, 154–6
from Milston Down 141
neutron activation analysis 72
from Sidbury Double Linear Ditch 42, 46
from Sidbury East Linear Ditch 46
styles 89–90
surface collection 138
survival 27
procurement sites *see* flint

Quarley High Linear Fig 3
excavation 134
pottery 134
refurbishment 146
see also LDP 006, 008, 009
Quarley Hill
excavations 8, 11, 12, 16, 143–4
hillfort 18, 20, 21, **143–4**, 146, Figs 8–10
    disused before Middle Iron Age 147
    later than Quarley High Linear 146
    overlay linear ditches 8, 13
    work by Hawkes 10, 12, 143–4, Fig 3
linear ditches 102, 133, **134–5**, Fig 3
    intersect 132–3
midden 8
see also LDP 001–007
Quarley Low Linear *see* LDP 004

radiocarbon dating 10, 18, 20, 42, 46, 49,
    50, 53, 55, 57, **58–67**, 68, 69, 115, 119,
    120, 122, 123, 129, 130, 133, 134,
    144, Table 22
ranch boundaries 4, 6, 8–9, 16, 137
Ratfyn Farm *see* LDP 014
reaves (of Dartmoor) 6, 12, 14
resistivity surveys *see* geophysical surveys
roads (interpretation of linear ditches) 6, 8
Romano-British
'Celtic' fields 126
cultivation 36, 105, 108, 111, 112, 116,
    120, 121, 130
fields/field systems 34, 50, 128
linear ditches
    degraded by farming 40
    destroyed 121, 149
    not functioning 70
lynchets 112
ploughing 40
pottery 27, 29, 42, 46, 49, 90, 121, 123,
    Tables 1, 2, 4, 5
    Beacon Hill 54, 123
    Devil's Ditch 53
    Earl's Farm Down 27
    linear ditches 68, 136
    lynchets 53, 68
    Quarley High Linear 134
    Salisbury Plain Conservation Group
        fieldwalking 33
settlements 36, 70, 136, 149
round barrows 102, 122, 131
associated with boundary ditches Fig 23
on Brigmerston Down Fig 76
distribution 122, 141
on Earl's Farm Down 20
excavation 21, 42
influence over linear ditches 138, 141,
    146
on Milston Down Fig 20

secondary cremations 127
on Snail Down 42
in Study Area 21

St Catherine's Hill (excavation) 8
Salisbury Plain Conservation Group
    (fieldwalking/surface collection) 33, Fig
    20
sarsen pebbles (from Dunch Hill) 131
scrapers (flint) 95, 98, Fig **61**, Tables **40**,
    48
secondary burials 21, 127, 134
set aside (surface collection difficult) 25,
    123
settlements 72
Deverel-Rimbury 16, 139
Middle Bronze Age 6, **127–30**, 129, 133,
    138–42, Fig 51
    distribution Fig 71
Late Bronze Age 41, 49–50, 53, 58, 69,
    71, 87, **127–35**, **138–43**, Fig 51
    abandoned 135, 145, 146
    distribution Fig 71
    lack of evidence 138
All Cannings Cross 89
Iron Age 36, 70, 135
Early Iron Age 138
Middle Iron Age 147
Romano-British 36, 70, 136, 149
abandoned 122, 123, 135, 143, 145,
    146, 150
at Boscombe Down West 135
on Brigmerston Down 50, 91, 123, 127,
    132, 135, 139
on Brigmerston Plantation 134
at Chalton, Hampshire 141
at Chisenbury Trendle 89
on Coombe Down 68
on Cranborne Chase 139
dislocation 88
on Dunch Hill 33, 49–50, 53, 72, 74, 86,
    91–8, 123, 127, 128, 129, 131, 134,
    135, Fig 51
on Earl's Farm Down 77
at Easton Lane, Winchester 141
at Lidbury 89–90
linear ditches (cut by) 127
on Milston Down 72, 74, 86, 127, 131
    All Cannings Cross pottery 74
in Northern Core Territory 91–4, 135,
    141, Fig 51
    All Cannings Cross pottery 74
shift of focus 89
on Sidbury Hill (pre-hillfort) 89
on Upavon Aerodrome 89
Shipton Plantation, flint procurement site
    31, Fig 16
Sidbury Double Linear Ditch **41–6**, 49,
    108–11, 132, 135, Fig 25
abutted by Iron Age enclosures 108
abutted by Weather Hill linear ditch 67
animal bones 46
antler pick 46
buried soils 41, 42, 46, 105, **106**, Fig 29
cattle skull 46, 60–67
charcoal 42, 46, 103, 119
environmental column/samples 42, 46,
    Figs 28, 29, 31
excavations 132, Figs 27–31
flint (worked) 42
human bones 42
human skull 42, 60
lynchets 105, 108
    overlain by 46, 105
molluscan sequences/fauna 103–8, Fig 29
pottery 42, 46
radiocarbon dating 42, 46, 60
replaced a previous boundary 120

tree cast/hollow (fossil) 106, Fig 29
see also LDP 020, 026, 027
Sidbury East Linear Ditch 38–9, 134
antler cheek piece 46, Figs 35, 36
bones 46
buried soils 46, 112, Fig 35
environmental columns/samples 46, Fig
    35
excavations **46**, 133, Fig 35
lynchet, overlain by 112
molluscan sequence 112
pottery 46
    Middle Bronze Age 46
    Late Bronze Age 46, 133
radiocarbon dating 46
recutting 143
see also LDP 096, 097
Sidbury Hill
cattle skull 134
charcoal 102, 119
double linear earthwork 146
environmental sequences 120
flint assemblage 31
flint procurement site 31
haematite-coated pottery 145
hillfort 18, 20, 23, 38–9, 42, 46, 87, 89,
    90, 103, 143, 144, 146, Figs 8–10,
    12, 25, 26
    association with linear ditches 144
    damage 23, Fig 12
human bones 134
human skull 134, 146
linear ditches/features 38–9, 58, **132–4**,
    143, Figs 14, 25, 26
    excavations Fig 26
    intersection 132–3
    overlain by hillfort 133
molluscan fauna 119
pottery
    Late Bronze Age Plain Ware 134, 135
    haematite-coated 134, 135
pre-hillfort enclosure (possible) 146
pre-hillfort settlement/occupation 87, 89,
    133, 134, 145
radiocarbon dating 134, 144
see also LDP 100, 101
Sidbury West Linear Ditch 38, Fig 12
cut by pit 60
excavation 49, 133, Fig **44**
radiocarbon dating 60
see also LDP 045, 088, 089
skulls
cattle 46, 53, 60–67, 68, 134, 148
in ditches 58, 151
horse 57, 60, 68, 134, 146, Fig 35
human 42, 60, 67, 68, 134, 146
Snail Down
barrow cemetery 23, 133
'Celtic' fields Fig 33
ditches
    Iron Age 135, Fig 39
    Middle Iron Age 67
enclosures 67, 88, Figs 10, 33
excavations 42, 46, 49, 67, 132, 133,
    Figs **32**, 33
linear ditches/features 21, 46, 49, 67,
    123–4, 132, 133, Figs 14, **32**, **33**, **39**
pastoral enclosure 108, 120–21
pottery
    Deverel-Rimbury 133
    Late Bronze Age Plain Ware 133
    Middle Iron Age 67
round barrows (excavation) 42
trackways Fig 33
snails 40, 41
diagrams 102
species Table 25
see also molluscan

Snelsmore Bog, Berkshire Downs (pollen diagram) 101
South Downs
  enclosures (Deverel-Rimbury) 127
  linear ditches/earthworks 8, Fig 1
  Middle Bronze Age activity 4
Southern Core Territory 21, Fig 10
  enclosed by linear ditches 122
  fields 125–6
  linear ditches 58, 123–6, Fig 72
South Lodge Camp 9–10
Spratt, Don 13–14, 16
spur dykes 4, 8
  as territorial boundaries 9
stock enclosures (Iron Age) 108
Stonehenge environs
  environmental evidence 101, 102
  Iron Age enclosures scarce 147
  Iron Age pottery scarce 147
  linear ditches 141
  surveys 12
Stonehenge Environs Project 29, 141, 147
  landscape study 21–3
  Late Bronze Age open settlements identified 145
  surface collection methodology 27
Stone, J F S 4, 8, 18, 126, 127, 139
storage structures (in hillforts) 145, 147–8
Study Area
  choice 3, 17–18, 20
  earlier excavations Fig 8
  geology 20
  location 18–21, Fig 7
  see also Earl's Farm Down, Upper Study Area, and individual sites
style (on pottery) 80–86, 89–90
surface collection
  on Beacon Hill Fig 13
  on Brigmerston Down 130, Figs 15, 21
  burnt flint 29, 31, 50, Fig 18, Table 3
    distribution Fig 17
  on Dunch Hill 49–50, 53, Fig 15
  on Earl's Farm Down 135
  flint assemblages 91
  flint (worked) 29, 50, 93, 94, 129, 138, Figs 59–62, Table 3
  methodology 26, 27, Fig 13
    in Stonehenge Environs Project 27
  in Military Training Area 138, Table 2
  on Milston Down 130, Figs 19, 20
  in Northern Core Territory 29
  pottery 27, 29, 31, 49–50, 70, 138, Tables 1, 2, 4
    distribution Figs 17, 21
  in set aside 25, 123
  sites 23, 26, 27, 125–6, 130, 142, Figs 13, 15, 17, 19, 21, Table 3
    in Upper Study Area Fig 14

strategy 33
survival of
  Devil's Ditch 25
  downland (ancient) 101
  earthworks 23, 25
  evidence (in Upper Study Area) 21–5
  pottery 27
Sussex Downs ('Celtic' field systems) 8

Tabular Hills
  dyke system 16
  linear ditches 4, Figs 1, 5
  territorial organisation 14, Fig 5
territorial boundaries see linear ditches
Thorny Down (Middle Bronze Age enclosure) 21
Thruxton Hill, flint procurement site 29–31, Fig 16
Thwing 6
  at meeting point of dykes 13
  excavations 10
Tidworth Golf Course, field system 122
Toms, Herbert 4, 8
topography
  linear ditches (relationship with) 36, 138, 141
  of Upper Study Area Fig 23
trackways 129
  alongside linear ditches 36, 38
  Earl's Farm Down 36, Fig 24
  Figheldean Down 36
  Snail Down Fig 33
  some linear features proved as such 138
  see also hollow-ways
Training Area see Military Training Area
tree casts/hollows (fossil) 101
  Brigmerston Down 112
  Dunch Hill Plantation 128
  Haxton Down 49, Fig 42
  Sidbury Double Linear Ditch 106, Fig 29
tree-hole/hollow survey, Dunch Hill 33, 94, Fig 46
tree hollows in Dunch Hill Plantation 128
trees uprooted in 1989/90 winter, survey 33

Uffington Castle, hillfort 13, 14
  associated with linear ditch 143
unenclosed settlements see settlements
Upavon Aerodrome
  pottery (Early All Cannings Cross) 89, 135
  settlement (All Cannings Cross) 89
Upper Study Area
  air photographic evidence Fig 10
  survival of evidence 21–5
  topography Fig 23
urnfields see Kimpton

Vespasian's Camp (pottery) 145

Weather Hill
  ard marks 49, Figs 40, 41
  bone 49
  ditches, Iron Age 135
  environmental column/samples 49, Fig 37
  excavation 49, 67, Fig 37
  field system 49, 108
  hollow-way 49, Fig 40
  linear ditch
    abuts Sidbury Double Linear Ditch 67
    dating 67
    excavation 49, Fig 37
    molluscan sequence 108–12
  linear features Fig 14
  lynchets 108
  postholes 49, Fig 40
  pottery 49, 67
  radiocarbon dating 49, 67
  see also LDP 033, 083, 084
Whitsbury, Hampshire (hillfort) 146
Williams-Freeman, J P 4, 12
Windmill Hill
  bone 57
  buried soil 56, 116–19, Fig 35
  environmental samples/sequences 57, 120
  excavation 56–7, 134
  horse skull 57, 134, 146, Fig 35
  linear ditch 116–19, 134, 146
    buried soil Fig 35
    environmental column Fig 35
    excavation 56–7, Fig 35
  linear features Fig 14
  lynchet 57
  radiocarbon dating 57
  secondary burials 134
  see also LDP 091
Winterbourne Dauntsey (excavation of postholes/ditch) 126–7
woodland clearance 101
Woolbury, Hampshire, hillfort 13
  approached by paired ditches 146
  associated with double linear earthwork 143
worked flint see flint

Yarnbury
  enclosures 145
  hillfort Fig 78
Yorkshire Wolds
  dyke system 14
  field systems (not surviving) 12
  hillforts virtually absent 16
  linear ditches 4, 10, 16, Figs 1, 2
  territories Fig 2